if i knew, don't you think i'd tell you?

Also by the author

Jann Arden Management
Box 23125, Connaught P.O., Calgary, AB T2S 3B1
Manager: Nikki Shibou

www.jannarden.com • email: jannsfanns@jannarden.com

if i knew, don't you think i'd tell you?

jann arden

INSOMNIAC PRESS

Interior illustrations by Jann Arden
Edited by Mike O'Connor and Tim Strain
Copy edited by Lorissa Sengara
Designed by Mike O'Connor

National Library of Canada Cataloguing in Publication Data

Arden, Jann
        if i knew, don't you think i'd tell you? / Jann Arden.

ISBN 1-894663-36-5

1. Arden, Jann. 2. Singers--Canada--Biography. I. Title.

ML420.A676A3 2002   782.42164'092   C2002-903817-0

The publisher gratefully acknowledges the support of the Canada Council, the Ontario Arts Council and the Department of Canadian Heritage through the Book Publishing Industry Development Program.

Printed and bound in Canada

Insomniac Press
192 Spadina Avenue, Suite 403
Toronto, Ontario, Canada, M5T 2C2
www.insomniacpress.com

THE CANADA COUNCIL | LE CONSEIL DES ARTS
FOR THE ARTS | DU CANADA
SINCE 1957 | DEPUIS 1957

ONTARIO ARTS COUNCIL
CONSEIL DES ARTS DE L'ONTARIO

to my gram
Clara Grace Johnson

INTRODUCTION

There are sixty or so little books, of various sizes and colours, filled with the sordid tales of my life. They rest soundly and peacefully in an old trunk in my basement. I have been writing "journals" for over 25 years. My mother has been instructed to burn them upon my unlikely demise, "I am not burning your diaries", she says with much conviction, "so there".

There are books with locks and long lost keys, ones made from fine Chinese paper, old school binders, black leather, red vinyl, plastic with some kind of liquid swishing around in the cover, ones with puppies adorning the front and kittens gracing the back. There is every imaginable shape and colour. I counted them. There are over sixty. That's two a year since I began my journey into jotting it all down. Reading them I have to say, can be more painful than a bad break-up. I do laugh, I do want to cry, but mostly, I try to remember who that person was scribbling things down well into the dark prairie nights. You re-live yourself growing up. It is quite damningly and alarmingly clear. The secret codes that I will never ever figure out. (Perhaps I should send them into some F.B.I. code-breakers). Initials that were obviously someone I couldn't possibly give away at some time, I just don't remember. You'd think a person would remember something as important as "I saw JDC's thing today at lunch". I have no idea who that could be. Time I think, to go through my yearbooks and do some Private Investigative work.

Journals are interesting pieces of time. Not only are they a mental recollection of a time gone by, but a very physical one, especially when they are hand written, which mine were. I can see myself literally growing up by how I signed my name at the end of every entry. If I were to make one of those "flash" books that you flip through with your thumb of all my signatures, it would be a glimpse at time itself. I should make one of those some rainy day; I really should.

In the last few years, my diaries, my journals, have leapt off of their bits of paper and into cyberspace. When we started my website, jannarden.com, I wanted it to be some-what interactive. I wanted there to be a reason for people to log on everyday. Something that made them want to know what was going on in my world. I thought to myself, "my journal...that's it!" I wasn't the least bit wary about doing it either. I don't have secret codes anymore; I don't bother with them. I figure there are not many things that I get up to that I couldn't write down. I don't need to censor myself at this point in my life or my career. I just write like no one is reading. I sing like no one is listening. I have found that to be the most gracious way of being accurate about any-thing I do. I have to be honest with someone; it might as well be me.

This book, if it is indeed a book, has been a wonderful experience for me to be involved in for me to "write". I found myself constantly thinking out loud, "did I say that?" I found myself nodding my head in agreement most of the time. I didn't cringe quite as often as I did in say, grade 8. Reading through the last two years has been utterly bittersweet. My Grandmother's long illness and subsequent death was hard the first time, never mind the second time. It was good to remember her in such detail no matter what sadness slipped back into my heart and head. There were the days I wrote about being here at my house, as boring as it sometimes is, that made me smile and wish for winter in the midst of summer's heat, or as the snow came down in sheets, pray for summer to come once again. The endless tales of my glorious three cats. God help me. I have too many cats and too many plants. I am my mother...

I think so much of our lives is about remembering. And that is what this little endeavour is. It's about remembering how far I've come, and how far I have slipped back. This is about being able to fail and get up and fail and get up, and hopefully in all of that, show you that it's perfectly fine to be perfectly un-fine whenever you need to be. This is my snapshot of the world. I don't think writing my diaries has been much of a departure from writing my music. It's about capturing bits of time, and remembering them for a minute or two; until you want to remember them or look at them or

listen to them again - which is why pages have been left open for you to record your thoughts here also. That's all this is...
It was raining all night here last night.
One of my cats wandered home at 6am this morning.
My house guest wanted to let him in quietly, but ended up setting off the alarm and scaring the hell out me.
I thought the end was near once again.
Just another day here on the prairies.

I'll have to write that down somewhere...

Day 2
04-April-2000 04:02 pm

I've got the fake fireplace on. The cats are chasing around a tampon (yes, a tampon)! It is their favourite toy. I have no idea where they got it from. It's a new one, if that is what you were thinking.

God knows where we'd be without that little invention. My gram says they used to have to use old rags, and wash them out all the time. Jesus. My poor gram. She is in a nursing home here in Calgary.

Have a good day. Eat some vegetables. Talk one of your friends into buying my record. Please.

Day 3
05-April-2000 12:56 am

I live in the foothills of the Rockies, so it is a fantastic view in any direction I choose. There are even bear warnings out here. I have to get up at 7:30 am to put the garbage cans out. You can't put them out the night before because of the bears. Lord.

    I have yet to see one, and I am hoping that I won't. I wonder if my Tae-Bo will have any effect on the wildlife out here as far as protecting myself goes.

Take time to think about who you want to be.
Listen to a friend.
Say your prayers.

Day 4—Part I
06-April-2000 02:09 pm

When I first moved here, I watched the kids next door skate. It was like being in a Hallmark card. I felt old. I felt like getting to this moment was just suddenly upon me. There were no years leading me up to a point. Just this immediate bang.

It's funny how life passes. How it forces you to survive all things. It forces you to decide, even when you don't want to. Life makes you live.

I don't think I have ever wanted to give up. Even when I have failed at everything (or so it seemed) I would rather have faith in myself than confidence any day of the week. Faith has never yet failed me. Confidence has.

Day 4—Part II
06-April-2000 02:09 pm

Try to be good to other people, and I am telling you, it takes a lot of effort most days. People are struggling. Know that. Be good to them.

You won't believe what starts happening to your own life. It opens up into this light. Things start going on around you that seemed impossible. Good things.

Also know that sometimes, good things...seem like bad things. You won't know that until much later. Bear with it. Life is unfolding.

Day 8—Part I
09-April-2000 05:18 pm

The geese woke me this morning. Honking like a flock of taxis. They (the "goosies"), walk around on the ice like curlers. I picture them with their little hats and shoes and brooms, calling for the next rock.

Day 8—Part II
09-April-2000 05:18 pm

I am in an industry where people look at me and expect me to be a certain way. To look a certain way, to be thin and pretty and tall and perfect. And you know what? I am all those things. You have to look very carefully, with a true heart, and you'll see me.

That's the only way to look at anyone.

Day 9—Sorry, language in this one may not be suitable for all ages!

11-April-2000 02:56 pm

The power went out here last night. Shit. I was fucking scared. I mean it was BLACK. I thought someone was finally coming to get me, or that the cats had finally had it with the dry food, and were on a mission to kill me and hide me in the litter, only to be found by my Hungarian housekeeper next Monday when she comes to clean. (I do clean my own litter, but if I was dead I couldn't do it now could I?)

Going to buy more books. Must stop. Reading is ruining my social life.

Must go see gram today sometime. Mom and I gave her a bath the other night, she said we were trying to kill her. I remember my mom giving me baths, and I recall her trying to kill me too!!!!

sorry so late!

13-April-2000 02:21 am

Here comes the wind. It is blowing the trees around like blades of grass. Lord. If you don't hear from me tomorrow, send someone to check if the house is still here, will ya?

Another day, another snowflake

14-April-2000 04:51 pm

The cat (sweet pea) is licking my hand as I write this (backwards tongue; I need to buy a cat that speaks English). She cannot stand it if I am not paying enough attention to her. What a little rat.

I painted all day yesterday. Finished 2 of them. I am on a streak. My mom asked me if they were the same old "nude people" that I do, or were they "flowers"?

She always wants me to paint hair on them. I guess she's on to me. I am no Joni Mitchell.

feet on ground...
15-April-2000 08:06 pm

I just spent 4 hours on a plane. It was so turbulent. I get nervous. After all these years of flying. I still panic. I still wonder if I'll ever see my friends and family again. Flying makes one very dramatic. I write speeches in my head; I save the world. I change humanity. All up there at 37,000 feet. I think differently. My perspective is altered.

You have to give up your power. You have to give up control. You have to trust someone else with your life. It is the one thing we cannot seem to do in relationships. Give ourselves up to them; our others, our partners, our mates, our companions. Our husbands and our wives. We have to have control and power and status.

In a plane you have nothing. You have a crappy set of headphones and a bad movie. Everyone is suddenly very equal. You are not an individual. You are part of a crowd— all headed the same way. Flying teaches you something about money. How unimportant it is. It means nothing. It cannot save you in first class when things go terribly wrong. Money. How everyone prays when there is the first sign of trouble up there.

"I'll never do this again or that again!"

All the promises that are made.

Flying is so interesting. I learn so much about myself. I

try and bring my flying philosophy to the ground with me when I land. To remember how great my life is. How happy I am just to be. And how much I love, and am loved.

ja

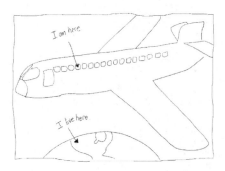

Star searching

17-April-2000 01:56 pm

Whenever I have an idea, I have to stop and consider its source. I find it amazing that things pop into my head. All my songs have this eerie quality, because of the fact that I have no clue as to their origin. It is odd. The whole process is odd. I lay in bed and wonder why the hell I thought a particular thing? A particular group of words...What they mean? What do they really mean? I don't know what my songs "mean." Do they mean one thing? Or do they mean nothing? Or everything?

I feel so lucky to be here. On the earth. With this body. With my family and my friends. It is so exciting to wonder where we are all headed. Really headed...someday.

Christmas??

18-April-2000 01:47 pm

My dad always said that the further you go in, the farther you can go out. It is extremely difficult to look into yourself and see all the cracks. But in the immortal words of Leonard Cohen, "That's how the light gets in." I love that idea.

I am not my body...

19-April-2000 09:47 pm

The body sees an end to itself,
where the soul does not.
My soul has confidence,
whereas my body has no esteem.
We are part light and part mass.
We are skin and bone and shards of white.

Peace of it all...

21-April-2000 03:41 pm

Who really, honestly knows what is out there? I know that there is a God. An infinite goodness that directs my life. I feel it. I hold it in my heart I never feel alone. I have a sense of direction under my feet. I have a feeling of calm like a piece of light in my heart. Myself. A piece of it all. I am, as you are, a piece of something so bright and so beautiful, that we are often blinded by it and to it. We are so caught up with being a physical entity, so caught up with the instant gratification of making ourselves feel like we don't have bodies, that we neglect our spirits. We shove them away where they barely whisper directions to us any more. If we could only learn to listen to our hearts again. It starts with a thought. Just a thought. You can do anything. Trust me. I fail and get up again. In a sense, failure has fuelled my imagination, and let me live a freer, happier life.

Easter thoughts...I think??

23-April-2000 08:00 pm

It's Easter for the Christian world. If Jesus pops out it'll be spring in 6 weeks or something like that...
    Kidding. I'm kidding.

political THOUGHTS....

24-April-2000 12:02 am

Life is unfolding as it should.

The Visit

26-April-2000 08:50 pm

I love my mom. I love my dad.
They have taught me many things...
Strive to be fair and without prejudice.
Strive to be kind and generous.
Strive to be a good listener.
Strive to change the world.
Strive for mercy and forgiveness.
Strive for excellence.

I feel lucky.
I feel good.
I am watching my life unfolding like a dream unfolds.
It's really something.

The world is still a beautiful place.

watch your step!
27-April-2000 01:31 pm

It is hard to believe that men still feel the need to go to war. Let's get our guns and go and shoot at people. Let's shoot at them because they don't think like we think, they don't look like we look, they don't have the same God as we do. Let's kill them and take their land and rape their daughters and steal their cattle and slaughter their mothers. In the name of our God almighty, we'll win. We will be victorious!

It seems very few of us get war. We all cry out in protest, yet the fighting goes on, without any sign of letting up. Our leaders fail us. They lead us into battle to secure their place in history. Like building a pyramid for themselves...killing to be remembered.

I don't know about you, but I am haunted by the Holocaust. I think about it every day. My parents have pointed out on several occasions that many peoples have been wiped out the same way. They have been beaten into submission by the long arm of intolerance. The Romanians struggled, the Chileans perished under the dictatorship of Pinochet...The hundreds of tribes of Africa that are forever locked in some strange idea of ethnic cleansing...Eritrea, Ethiopia, the war in Serbia, neighbours killing neighbours that they have lived beside for 40ty years. Because they are afraid of what will happen to them if they don't do what they are told by their leaders. Leaders???? What shame. On and on. The faces on the TV, yearning for peace. Pleading with us to understand what is happening to them.

Politics.

If only we truly realized the wonderful freedom we have here in Canada. The bliss of peace. If we could live a day in the life of someone, some innocent one, who lives in peril and fear because of war. Utter torment. So terrible. You have no idea. War. Hopelessness. No one wins. There is no winner. Everyone loses. Everyone. It comes down to people wanting more than they already have. It comes down to people wanting others to be how they are. Sameness.

It is about sameness. Why are we so threatened by our differences? I have no clue. I thrive on difference. I cherish the newness of every single person I meet. What they bring to my life. How they make me better and richer and deeper. Imagine killing someone.

How?

And I don't mean in self-defense either. Just randomly. Because of something you can't even see. Just because they live on the other side of the road.

I will never understand it.

I don't want to.

I will oppose it all my life.

Ghandi was on to something.

Peacefulness.
Live and let live.
Who the hell do we think we are?
Please be fair to each other.
Please.

ja

May 2

03-May-2000 11:32 am

I had a long walk with my mom today. I don't know how I got so lucky to have her in my life. How she turned out to be MY mom.

I followed mom into town to help feed gram at the nursing home. Gram is failing so badly. She moans and cries and is generally very confused and scared. It must be so hard. It is heartbreaking and enlightening all at once. She told me she loved me today, and I told her that I loved her.

She was such a fun gran. She was perfect in every way. My gramma, Clara Johnson, was one of 17 children. I love my gram.

Today is forever. Breathe.

another human being…

04-May-2000 07:47 pm

I feel quiet today.

I drove to Edmonton yesterday to see my friend Kerry give a presentation about her society: the East Africa Maternal/Newborn Aid Society. She has changed the hearts and minds of so many people. She talks openly about female genital mutilation—or FGM. And she talks endlessly about the premature babies that are born because of it. The girls starve themselves the last month of their pregnancy, because it is so difficult to give birth because of the genital defect. The little girls' vaginas are "cut off and sewn up"…horror…leaving this grotesque thing between their legs…it is so horrible. Unrecognizable. Unreal what they do to women. It's cultural, but still, completely unnecessary. It is a strange world. You have no idea what they do to these poor young children. That's what they are too. Children. For the most part the mothers perform the "surgeries" in horrible conditions. Unsanitary and filthy conditions. Infection is lethal, and deadly, and always a threat—no matter. They use a piece of glass or an old razor to cut off the clitoris; that is the "smaller" procedure. The more aggressive operations, if you could call them that, cut OFF everything, leaving a tiny hole for urine and menstrual blood. 95% of East African women—little girls—are circumcised. No pain killer in the world can fix that.

It could be you. It could be your daughter. Your mother. Labour lasts 5 days, and babies are often born dead. They cannot get out of the hole that is left. Some had been dead probably after 2 days. Still they push and push. So afraid. So much pain. Bladders are ruptured, as are the rectums, if they even survive the birth of their dead baby

I was so affected by this presentation. I went to Africa with Kerry. She is an angel among us. It changed my life, that trip. It really was profound.

I don't know what else to say. I feel so bad, but very hopeful that tomorrow...never comes.

ja

It's a dog's life!

07-May-2000 06:46 pm

Why can't people be more like dogs? A dog is always so happy to see you, no matter how long it's been—since he saw you. A dog thinks you're perfect just the way you are, that you look so good in every colour. A dog likes your breath in the morning. A dog will wait until you've eaten, so he can eat...I'll wait, he thinks to himself...she's busy. A dog would die to save you, never thinking about himself. A dog will run as long as you do, he never says, wait up! A dog never says, we never do what I want to do or I have already seen that movie or I don't want to go there or we never do anything with MY friends. A dog will lick your tears away. A dog doesn't care if you're a drunk or you've lost your job or if you're divorced. A dog would never judge you. A dog doesn't care how popular you are at school or if you have no legs or can't see or hear or talk.

I've been dating the wrong species.

when you lose, don't lose the lesson!

09-May-2000 09:59 am

My cats have flipped their wigs.

I didn't understand why I got myself into the situations that I did. Why sex was so important to my self-esteem. That I needed men to want me, to desire me like a movie scene. It fills my head with blood now to think about all the times all the faceless heads and the small towns and the bars and the starless nights. I did bad things (according to me), but I know that I am better off for them.

Don't get me wrong. I don't regret any part of my life. I rarely go back to those old times. I hear them in my head though, whispering to me...warning me. I know my life will be based on memories. What I choose to be will be based on what I do with those memories. Even the bad ones shine somehow. The lessons still unravel even today. And it's always a different lesson, from the very same memory. Every time I think of one of those days or nights or moments... the lesson is so different.

feet on ground, heart in hand...—Part 1

09-May-2000 01:58 pm

I love my parents. What I am is because of what they taught me. I am such a balance between the two of them. I have never seen people work harder at everything than my parents. I never want them to die. And I know that they won't. Neither of them is scared of dying. They've talked about it since we were kids.

"Well, we all have to go." or "There's not a single thing to be afraid of, I'll see my mom and dad" or "I don't care what you do with me, I just want you to have a nice lunch afterwards."

Absolutely hilarious.

My dad at one point was going to build them a casket. He said it would be cheaper than buying one. We told him that we would more likely rent one... That put an end to that project.

feet on ground, heart in hand...—Part 2

09-May-2000 01:58 pm

Singing? It has nothing to do with who and what I am. It is only a voice in amongst 6 billion. I am just trying to find my way. You are listening to me, but I am listening to you too.

Wrong place, wrong time

10-May-2000 07:07 pm

They found a woman's body under a car today. It is horrible being on either side of that death. Whether you are the family of the victim, or the family of the accused. It is a nightmare. We all die a little bit. I know.

Where are the life preservers?

12-May-2000 03:49 pm

Shrodie just brought me a mouse. He does every day. He just roars and drops this fake mouse at my feet. Thank you, I always say, and he goes off to fight another war.

I need one more coffee.

sorry so late...

14-May-2000 03:23 am

I bought enough cat food for a year at Costco. Enough deodorant to dry up Lake Erie, and enough feminine protection to take me well into the next century.

Went and saw gram with mom after we shopped. She was sleeping pretty soundly. We didn't stay long. Return to sender...that's what it seems like. Back to the beginning

Poppies, sports and crib...they all smell the same to me.

17-May-2000 11:49 am

Someone was playing electric guitar at 8:15 am. I think I am going to find them and offer a free lesson.

I bought seeds today, you know, the planting kind. My friend tells me that I bought opium something or other. Can they sell that? Poppies????

Apparently, if you go out in the morning, and scrape the sides, it crystallizes, and people would smoke that? How fucking desperate do you have to be to raid the flower pots? I bet people have tried to smoke everything in the garden. Potato anyone? Cabbage?

If you can't smoke it, you can ferment it and drink it.

Ahhhh, nature.

I don't really care for sports. Too many smells. I mean I like sports, and I like smells just not together.

Go home gram...

18-May-2000 11:05 pm

What do you say to a mother losing her mother?

Gram has not taken food or water for a week. She is "mouth breathing." They say that is one of the things that happens on the way to "shutting down" one's body.

Gram made the best roast beef, and gravy that you could lie down in and the best cream puffs...I mean the real cream puffs—real cream, and puffy, big. We could hardly wait to pop the whole things into our drooling heads.

She always had ice-cold milk in the fridge. It was always better than what we had at home.

We'd stuff ourselves with cream puffs and drink ice-cold milk until we couldn't any more. Gram never said, now that's enough. Never. Gram would throw her head back when she laughed. Big, hearty, glad laughter that made you laugh even if you didn't get the joke. I remember how she wrapped her Christmas presents for us. Just like they did it at the mall. We marvelled at the precision. Her handwriting was perfect, with curls in all the right spots. The "R's" and the "S's" were spectacular. Crying is all you can do sometimes.

My gram will be 88 years old on the 27th of this month.

Go home gram.

jann

Goodbye gram

23-May-2000 12:26 am

Gram, you are the sea and the air.
The trees and the breath in my lungs.
You breathe out, and I, in.
You are the yellow moon we saw last night,
that took our hearts by surprise.
It was so big and bright and low to the ground.
It dipped down to pick you up and carry you away.
You are me, and mom and all of us left behind.
I can hear you. I swear I can.
Goodbye for now.

Love your only granddaughter,
jann

Countdown to tour!!

23-May-2000 01:18 pm

Shrodie...get off the keyboard. Thank you. My cats always know when I am going away. They HATE the black suitcase. They all get INTO the black suitcase, in faint hopes of coming along just this one time. Endless, mindless entertainment happening here.

I find myself thinking about the last time I will tour... when will it be? I hope to God that I am not reading teleprompters to remember the words for I would die for you, after all, most of them are Ya Ya Ya.

When I do forget a word or two—I just replace it with the word sandwich.

Pulled a long hair out of one of my cat's asses today. What the hell? Glad it wasn't my ass.

This 'dying' business

08-June-2000 12:29 am

It is a hard task, this dying business.

My Great-aunt Ern got cancer at eighty years old. You'd think one would be safely and soundly out of harm's way. Not so.

She got some kind of cancer that ran through her like a train. She did chemo, and lost her hair, and carried on like that was what you were supposed to do. She drank copious amounts of any wine she could muster up, and got through it.

I remember a conversation we had at a family reunion. (Ern was gram's older sister.) She said, after throwing her wig into a blazing campfire, that it was not easy to die. She said that she was ready two weeks before, but it is just not that easy to die. I will never forget that.

It is not easy to die. Not easy for the "spirit" to separate itself from the "ego." It must tear and pull and be a ferocious battle of wits for them to do so.

My gram lay dying for almost 13 days. She had no food or water. She lost almost half of her body weight. She would not die. She wasn't ready to go.

Who knows what the spirit and ego must decide in order for that to happen. And then in what seems to be a fleeting second, off they go, with grace and speed and most of all, peace.

Those who witness death talk about the peace. The "letting go." The release of a thousand heartbreaks all in that moment. One of life's little miracles.

It is not easy to die. It was never meant to be. I wonder if we are learning anything from all of this living and dying?

I must be tired. I must still be here.

j

Four hours to count sheep

09-June-2000 12:37 am

I did not sleep. Sleep is a funny thing. Fickle and elusive. When you really want it, it runs from you, hides under the sheets, and shadows. You wait for it to come to you like a lover (you know how they can be).

After all that my parents have been through they are my heroes. Everything that I am is because of their unconditional love for me. It makes me stand up every day and face the music as it were. I love them so much.

I am so remorseful about the stupid things that I did growing up. And I am still growing up. I will always be growing up.

Oh no, not the bug again?!

11-June-2000 12:53 am

I keep thinking to myself, who I would ever drive 10 hours to see??? Not a single person crossed my mind, but then there it was—Karen Carpenter. I would drive forever to see her for a moment. Just a wee moment.

Next time.

The Show Must Go On

13-June-2000 12:34 am

It was a long, hard day yesterday. My little bug turned into a viscous monster. I was so sick. Never mind A show...but TWO shows? I swear I left my body. I was a body of water, floating over myself into nothing.

I finished the second performance, took my clothes off, stood in the shower and cried like I haven't since forever. There I was, like a hockey player, having a shower with the nozzle from hell. I think it was a fire hose actually. No fireman however...alas. I used some kind of soap that I happened to use in my you know what, and it was like Vick's Vapo rub for at least 20ty minutes. Very interesting indeed. I cried right through that as well. I could have cared less if I was burning the whole works off. I didn't, thank God. I was thinking of using it again some time this year.

It was 5:30 in the morning when we rolled in. I lugged my suitcase upstairs, pulled the curtains shut—no cracks can be left unchecked...no light can get in (that is of paramount importance).

I can stand almost anything, but not the rays of light that burn through hotel curtains. I will use any means possible to do the job. Shoes, chairs, lamps...bellman.

The Point

18-June-2000 07:00 pm

I am tired today. The cold hangs on. I am the phlegm queen.
I hork it up every few seconds, roll it around in my cranium,
and spit it as far as I can...though sometimes you can't spit.

You roll it around long enough to disgust yourself, and
swallow it back down, so as not to offend anyone within
earshot or eyeshot. The taste of sodium is prevalent. Like
the Pacific Ocean. Like the Dead Sea. Salt. And more salt.

Had the best Vietnamese food yesterday. I was in heaven. A good meal is worth every minute of the 3 hour walk to
find that damn restaurant. We took a cab back to the hotel.
The driver was interesting. He looked 89 years old. I was
concerned on a few of the corners we took. He was all sinew
and gristle. I want to be like him when I get there. Eighty-
nine. Terrorizing tourists in a yellow cab. Careening around
every corner in town. Smoking drum, and having black coffee all day long. Hurray.

The Chip Gods???

19-June-2000 06:28 pm

I am starving. Need to eat some livestock. I like meat. What can I tell you? I wish that I did not, but I do. They say that beef is not safe. Pork is not safe. Chicken is not safe. Yeah, from me. Not fucking safe from me!!

They say that they will someday breed "boneless" chickens. They'll just flop around like worms in the rain. Ehhhhh Gads. Good eatin'!!!

What is next? Skinless?

You're Right!

I saw an old friend from college. She was the first girl Patrick ever saw naked (my brother Pat). He loved that, I'm sure. She didn't know it at the time. Just as well. She lives in L.A. and just happened to be in town. It was so odd seeing her. We see each other every few years. She has had an amazing life. She makes the most gorgeous jewellery I have ever seen. I bought a bunch, and plan on wearing it everywhere.

She has a new baby. He is so adorable. He is a big boy. Smiles like he knows the secret of life. Little rat, I'm sure he does know; they do at that age. They just can't speak English, and by the time they can, they've all but forgotten what the secrets were.

God is ingenious.

Glad to be home.

01-July-2000 11:34 am

I have been sleeping for almost 12 hours. A sleep so full of bits and pieces of dreams and pictures and fragments of moments unrelated to each other in any way that I am soaked to the bone with the effort of trying to awake from it all. I feel as though I have been running like mad from my own life. I don't know how else to put it. I think though, that it was a good dream. One that spoke of completion and absolution. That I could run, and not have to turn back, look back, go back. It is grey and dark and peaceful. The geese aren't even out. They are dreaming their own dreams (probably involve shit of some kind...)

We are all getting ready for the memorial for gram. When I talk to mom and dad, I somehow manage to see home. I hear every word. Thank God for that. I am supposed to help mom pick music. She wants some hymns. I don't know a one, with the exception of Amazing Grace. That is quite sad (not the song, but the fact that I don't know any other hymns) You are eternity walking about like a house on fire. You are everything. And everything is you. My gram showed me that every moment of every day of her life. A big pure blazing heart. God. My gram was all of it.

Sometimes it's best to walk with your hands in your pockets

03-July-2000 12:06 am

My high school reunion was...a virtual time machine. I walked back into 1977. I walked back into a room full of nervous, intimidated people. Some visibly drunk by 6:30 in the evening. Some tired and hopeless and sick of life at the age of 38. Some married for 18 years with 3 kids and some not. Some changed, and some unchanged. Some beyond recognition, and some still, seemingly, in the very same clothes they graduated in. Same glasses. Same can of beer in their hand. Weary teeth and thinning hair and blowing smoke into the air like they were expelling horrid memories as fast and as hard as they could.

And then there were some still as full of glee and as joyous as they always were, kind-hearted and giving. Traits that do not tarnish with any amount of time passing. They greeted you with sparkling eyes and open arms, asking how you were and meaning it.

The mean ones were still mean (one in particular), still smouldering with jealousy and resentment. Still judging us all with their eerie, misguided sense of justice and false righteousness. Throwing glances like knives. Throwing around hurtful words like they were salting wounds. Seething with unhappiness. Blistered and cracked like dry forgotten earth. Time will not change them. Their character will indeed become their fate. There is no peace for the unkind. They wallow in heaviness like a pig in mud. Their bliss is their ignorance. The world has its own system of reward and punishment. They will find that out by tiny inches as life goes by. Slowly. Painstakingly. They will remain as they are. Hardened. Ridged. Lost. Looking at the rest of us like we have somehow missed the boat. Missed the point. Looking at us pathetic few who should change our ways, become more like them. Perfect and successful in every way. Casting stones quicker than you can fry an egg. Judging us.

It's hard to get your head around. How people can have their heads so far up their asses is beyond me. I enjoyed it nonetheless. Seeing everyone. Looking back, seeing the days so clearly. The seconds. The minutes. The hours. The weeks. The months. The years. Not that I have tried to forget the person I was in high school. Not that I ever abandoned her. But it seems so long ago that I forgot how much I had chosen to leave behind me. How much of me couldn't come with me on the trip I was about to take. The bell rang, and I started running like mad. I ran out of my parents' driveway, out into the fog and mystery, and out of the innocence of childhood.

Maybe that's why everybody is nervous going back there. It takes years to undo what has been done growing up. The ones who were picked on and buggered. The ones who were laughed at and ostracized for wearing the wrong shirt. The wrong haircut. Soaked armpits. Not athletic enough. For picking their nose and eating it, watched unknowingly. For being fat and ugly and unwanted. That's who we were. All of us. Not just some. All.

There were fewer than 60 of us all told. We knew each other so well. Or so we thought. What can you possibly know about anybody at 18? You barely know yourself. I still don't know myself. It is my lot not to. That is the human path. To find out.

The people that I have kept up with are in my life for a reason. For they are gallant and honest and good people. I am so lucky to have them.

Those without sin, cast the first stone.

I am keeping my hands in my pockets.

jann

If pigs start to fly...I'm moving.

04-July-2000 05:21 pm

The house is moving beneath me. Roaring, horrible thunder and scorching flashes of white lightning. Yikes.

I shut the windows and immediately hung the phone up. If I see a pod of killer whales, I'm moving. So much rain. So many endless waves of it. God is crying. Bawling. Weeping. The world is wet with it. The steam is rising now. It's floating just above the water. Avalon. If Merlin suddenly appears, I'm moving.

My past is present today. I like to hold it there in front of me, so I can revel in the hurt. I don't have a clue as to why. It does feel good, and then it just feels tiring. You start feeling the weight of your stupidity. Like running against the wind. Like running underwater. Like running into a frozen pole, and sticking your tongue to it just for good measure. It's not always there...just once in a while.

The truth is marching on

09-July-2000 05:43 pm

My gram's memorial was yesterday. It was a sunny day. Not one cloud, although they too would have been welcome.

I feel at times that I need to make myself a suit of iron, but then I realize that my actions will drown the words, as they always do, and it will be my deeds that define my character in the end.

My gram taught me that. She lived love. She spoke love. She breathed love. That is what she was.

Ahhhh Summer

13-July-2000 10:35 am

It is late afternoon. It has been a perfect day, although I know there surely is a war raging somewhere.

Had the boat out. Went for a paddle to the public beach. Kids mucking about in the sand like crabs. Building castles, and destroying them with great glee. I remember doing it myself. It was fun seeing them destroyed. Ruined. Wrecked. Divine oblivion. Nobody got hurt. Nothing had to die. It was all a game.

Summer had stuck us down with her warmth and carelessness. Summer will never be as good as it was when you were a kid... Popsicles never taste that sweet and cold again. Freezing your lips and your tongue and your eyes...blood-red dye for days. Salt-and-vinegar chips with grape pop and ice cubes that melt too quickly. Fried fish and feet dangling off the wharf into the blue. The smell of gasoline, and rainbows on the water.

Spinning the bottle. Beer. My mother drank rum and coke. She still does. Just one. I loved to drink her drinks. She'd say, that's enough jann. Hot dogs were heavenly. Hamburgers were for the boys. Soft ice cream cones so white and cool; they made you feel like you could never possibly die.

Tree forts that went straight up into the clouds and cow

patties, steaming in the heat, fresh out the patty makers. We would chuck them at each other, covered in shit and laughing all the while.

The blurred waves you see on tar country roads. Your shoes would stick. We could draw our names in them, and watch the cars from the ditch roll over every letter.

Campfires and marshmallows and chocolate-covered graham wafers wrapped in foil.

Seeing a penis for the first time. Letting them look at me, pants down and waiting for the remarks of OH Gross!! And OH MY God!!

Kissing them for bubble gum and thinking how bored I was. They weren't. It was all we did the summer I was 12. Boys boys boys... We kissed and looked at each other like we were the dirtiest things alive. We were so quiet the next day at school. Like it never really happened at all. I was fine with that. I wondered what the big deal was with my vagina anyway. Silly boys.

It was grand and glorious. The summers. Like today.

I am alone and sitting here thinking of them. Thinking of the kisses with my lips tightly shut to block those daring little tongues from getting in. And I am spinning the memories around in my head. They are so vivid and tender. Growing up... I still am.

j

The Drive-In

17-July-2000 11:40 am

I used to date a boy in high school that had a car. He would pick me up and take me to the 17th Avenue Drive-in, which incidentally is no longer there. Shitty. We never watched the movies. We never kissed either, we talked until we couldn't talk any more. Sometimes he would let me bring 3 of my friends. He was such a sweet, passive boy. I wonder where he is...

We wandered the snack bar...ate the biggest pickles that I have ever seen. They were in a jar that looked as though it was part of a biology experiment. They came attached to a wooden stick. They had every food group in a jar filled with some kind of brine.

They sold hot dogs that were always absorbed into the bun. Hard to put mustard on. Hard to wedge open. The bun and wiener were fused together in foil with a picture of a hot dog printed on it.
Redundant?

I never had sex at a drive-in. I wanted to. I was afraid of being naked with myself, never mind anyone else. I remember this guy that wanted me to give him a hand job. I didn't have a clue how to do it successfully, so I said to him, "I can't because I don't know how." He looked at me like what's to know? He proceeded to show me, and I remember laughing out loud at how funny it looked. Sex is as funny as hell when you're 14 years old. (Well for me it was.) I laughed and laughed.

He never took me out again.

A Walk in the Cemetery

24-July-2000 04:11 pm

I have spent the week doing as little as possible. Although for me, that is really not the case at all. I walked through a wonderful old cemetery the other day. I looked carefully at the headstones, and took a moment or two to ponder how they may have left here. What their family life was like. What they did. I took time to brush off some of the plates that the moss had grown over. Names were plain and simply worn away with the passing of time. I barely made out the words "Edward...1864..." I couldn't read the last name at all. I wondered who he was.

Some people may find it a wee tad creepy to wander through the tombstones; I did not. It was so serene. I felt as though I was walking with beings that knew everything. That all the questions had been asked, and that they were so at peace with the vastness of space and time. Not struggling. Not looking in a mirror and questioning if they were pretty enough. That their breasts were the right size. Not wishing for longer legs or a smaller nose or a better-looking vagina...Yes!! Now finally they can fix the unsightly ones!!! What in the hell is that about? What are we thinking??

The Lost and Found

01-August-2000 02:47 pm

Sadly, the boys that I ran with shot everything, and snared everything and squashed everything that took in a breath.

You have no reverence for life when you are 10. You think that you will live forever. Quite suddenly you realize that you definitely will not. Some distant someone that you knew, or your family knew, up and dies, and life suddenly changes its pleasant face.

I remember when the boy down the street died of an asthma attack. He was 10 years old. Died right in the playground. Right there helplessly in front of everybody. We were all so upset. I had months of sweaty dreams, wondering when my ticket would come up.

I was next, it was only a matter of time... every breath was laboured. I felt the air go in and out of my lungs for the first time in my little life. I changed the way I thought about myself. I stopped being innocent. I knew better... I felt mortal. I felt human. I felt time go by.

Isn't "Good Liar" an Oxymoron??

02-August-2000 03:52 pm

I am the worst liar in the history of the world. I couldn't lie my way out of a paper bag. My head goes red, and I get a Slavic accent. That's how bad I am.

the future is NOW

06-August-2000 01:43 pm

I am Martha Stewart, only shorter and poorer.

Don't try...just do

06-August-2000 08:27 pm

You are not broken. You are not broken. You are not broken.

Clouded Perceptions

08-August-2000 11:36 am

To look down at a cloud. What would early man have thought of soaring through the air? You glance around the cabin of a plane, and see everyone reading, or fidgeting, or talking or sleeping. Not a soul looks out the window. In fact, people shut them so they can see the movie better. It struck me today as completely insulting. To not look out and see the sky above you and beneath you. A marvel of man and science and God.

The Wright brothers would have screamed all the way to Maui. They knew of the intricate beauty of flight. The desire to be up there with the sky around you. Cutting the clouds with a wing tip. The view of time from the comfort of a chair. We are blind to it. Deaf to it. Fearful of it. Funny how we find it so tragic when a plane crashes. We are ooh-ing and aaah-ing and saying, "how terrible, and oh my God!" Try hunger for a lifetime.

40,000 children died of hunger. Today.
10,000 children are sold for sex. Today.
Thousands of graves are being uncovered in Bosnia...
Full of women and children. Today.

A plane crash??? We think that is the world's greatest

tragedy. It isn't. It is one of the many perils of capitalism and modernism and the race to get there faster and more comfortably. It is one of those things. A tragedy? No.

You can break your neck on a walk around the block. At least you have food in your gut. At least you are not being thrown out of your house in the middle of the night, lined up, and shot because you're the wrong colour. Imagine.

You are free to die at your own leisure. Half of the world is not. More than half in fact. They die at the hands of something ugly and beyond their control. It is called hatred. It is called poverty. A plane crash? No. That's just bad luck.

Every child that I spoke to in Africa wanted one thing, and one thing only: the chance to go to school. Not food, even though they were starving. Not thinner thighs. Not new shoes. Not a trip to Disneyland. School. Not a birthday party. Not a new haircut. Not clothes or bikes or dolls. Not candy or the Spice Girls or the whatever boys... School.

That there are no schools is a tragedy. No food is a tragedy. A plane crash? That's just a good 60-second sound bite for the networks.

We have forgotten each other.

We have forgotten ourselves.

ja

Where Are You Now?

09-August-2000 02:19 pm

I am thinking of you. Up there.
How I love you. I miss you.
What is living without yearning for something?
And the thing is, we really don't know what it is that we
yearn for.
You cannot quite put your finger on it.
But it's burning slowly in your body,
never clear enough or strong enough
to burst into flame.
So you yearn.
That's what we do.
We want.

Where are you now?

...and the ground opens up, and takes back her children,
plants them like seeds,
and waits for spring to come again...

I can see you standing on a road somewhere.
Hair blowing, dress blowing.
Eyes focused and bright.
Your beautiful hands holding a suitcase.

Good shoes. Comfortable shoes.

That sweater over your arm, just in case...

Looking off over the fields of wheat and mustard, and walking away.

You look back and tell us all to stay.

Then you smile,

and turn,

and disappear into the sun.

I swear, I saw you wave just now...

jann

Don't Forget Your Shoes

11-August-2000 10:44 am

The ocean is magnificent. You can sit and watch it for hours and hours. It is balance. It is perfection in motion. The sound moves your body ever so slightly, side to side, back and forth, in and out. You stand there, and suddenly realize that you are a part of it. And you cannot believe how big you are all of a sudden. I always want to jump in. Clothes and all. I want to leap in, and never stop swimming for home. So thirsty.

I have had dreams where I am drinking water, and I can never quench my thirst. I just keep drinking, and drinking...until finally, I wake up and pee. I have that dream a lot. Maybe it means I am an idiot for writing the dream down in this journal. Sure, that's it.

The Smell of Fall—Part I

18-August-2000 01:28 pm

I am home for a week. The cats are bringing me mice. They found the ones that I had hidden away—successfully—all these months.

You'd think that they had found a case of cold beer. You'd think that they had found the Holy Grail. You'd think that they had found the fountain of youth. What they had found was merely a few bits of hair glued to a ball. (I never was too excited about a few bits of hair glued to a ball)... Everybody's different.

Anyway, they (the mice) all end up on my bed at some point during the night. I hear these faint little roars at about 4 am, and behold, the KILL!!

I say thank you and fall back asleep. It's the least I can do, seeing that they spend most of their time hunting for me.

Mice are not too bad, tossed in with a bit of blue cheese and romaine (they have to be quite dead or they eat the cheese).

The Smell of Fall—Part II

18-August-2000 01:28 pm

I feel fall.
It is on the verge.
In the wings.
On deck.
You can smell it.
The dirt and the seeds and the dying leaves.
The water is darker and deeper somehow.
The "hood" is slowing down.
The kids aren't as noisy at 7 in the morning.
Not as many BBQs fired up at 8 o'clock at night.
School is going back!
Thank God!—the mothers say.

Apples are rotting on the ground,
and the sun is diving into the western hills as fast as it can.
The pumpkins are getting fat and orange.
Wee ones are already counting the days to Halloween.
Thinking about their costumes
and the candy
and the ghouls and the ghosts
and the parties
and the full moon and the shadows in the doorways.

You start wearing sweaters in the cool of the evenings.
You start looking for that "other" glove just in case...
It's a good time to start playing bugger rummy again,
and drink hot chocolate out on the deck. (Under the green
umbrella no less.)
You listen to Floyd Kramer at night,
and Carly Simon in the afternoons.
This is my favourite time of year.
I like people more for some reason.
I can take them in larger doses.
I am more forgiving.
I am more hopeful.
The colours are my colours.
Red and rust and yellow and orange and pinks and pearls and
violet and peach and pepper.
I can see my breath even now.
Here in the kitchen, with coffee
and this crazy machine that I cannot seem to work for the
life of me.

jann

Face Value

19-August-2000 04:13 pm

A bike rolls down the path. Hair blows back, eyes water with pure youthful glee. A hundred clouds spatter the sky. They'll meet later, and make it rain, I am sure. There are a dozen yellow leaves apologizing for turning too soon. Sorry sorry sorry.

I love watching the sprinklers, the grass—as if it's (the grass) going to do something. Moments of such peacefulness. You believe for a moment in everything good.

Love and Hate and Life

21-August-2000 12:37 am

How is it that we can hate who we once loved. Love and hate? Are they so close that they are part of each other? I fear they are.

Lovers kill each other all the time. They kill them slowly with words, or expedite the task swiftly with a frying pan. We give ourselves away—"in love." We become someone new somehow. We lose ourselves.

When love is good, when love is safe and sound, you will find yourself. You will know how much more you can be. You will realize that you can take on the world, and lose without regret. You will want to try everything. You will want to work on your life, and make it better. You will have someone telling you that you can. When love is good, you don't fear mistakes. When love is good, you find a place for your jealousy. Jealousy can be sweet and kind and endearing when used in small doses.

You think that love will never find you again.

It will.

It does.

So Far From Home

26-August-2000 01:54 pm

Home. That place that burns in our memories, like a memory is supposed to; a tire swinging from a tree, an old dog, a sandwich on a plate, picking burrs from your good school pants, fresh air, a quarter in your pocket, the wind catching your breath and carrying it away with all your troubles. Home.

I pull into the driveway and I am 10 years old. I go straight to the fridge and open it up and eat whatever is sitting there from the night before. I call their names, and I hear them answer from up the stairs, "We're up here!"

And I am home and safe and sound and I am nobody at all, except for theirs...I belong to them.

They are talking about moving for the first time in 32 years. Even if they do, no matter who lives there, even if they tear it down and build over top of all of our dead dogs buried out back, even if they erase all that time with skyscraper's and a hundred parking lots, even if they burn every tree and scorch the sky with brick and concrete and a thousand bits of glass, even if they take a big machine and push every piece of dirt into tomorrow... that house will be home for me until the day I die.

Southern Thunder

28-August-2000 06:18 pm

My God the rain...
It looks like a Monet painting out my window
blurred and undefined.
Kind of like a mistake.

To Know or Not to Know

30-August-2000 03:42 pm

I am listening to Jeff Buckley. There is an eerie quality to his voice that speaks of time and loss and forever with the intake of a single breath. The fact that he died in such a bizarre fashion adds to the void that is his sound, and his sound alone. The deep "kiss me please kiss me, kiss me out of desire" you believe him with all that you are.

That is what makes music important and healing.

Miss Quotes

31-August-2000 03:57 pm

I marvel at words. I savour them like a rare steak and a fine red wine. Words are what my world relies on. Words are what I sell at the end of the day. As much as a word cannot be for sale, we buy them every day. We buy them like we buy food. We use them like we do gasoline. We hang them on our walls, we send them to our friends and our enemies. We need words to live. We need words to tell ourselves that we are here at all.

Sex is Not a Sport

01-September-2000 05:23 pm

What is it about sex that makes us all crazy? Humans model their entire lives around it. They sell things with it. They get ahead in the game with it (no pun intended).

Love is the unknowing of everything. The grace of peace. The ease of friendship.

Sex, on the other hand, is pounded into us, as some sort of sport that we have to be good at. I don't know about you, but when you dearly and truly love another human being, you fall apart when they smile at you, never mind touch you.

Sex is not a sport. It is a language.

Choose your words well.

It Finally Stopped

05-September-2000 11:08 am

It rained all day today. God's tears. The tears of saints and the long gone. It rained with heaves and sighs. You could hear the sky break above you like an egg. I don't know how much I liked it. I felt damp and cold all day. I felt like I had to lie down and sleep it off. Like I was drunk with all the water falling. It was too much.

It rained forever. I listened to it as I lay in bed last night. I kept wondering when it would end. I finally got up and shut the window. The dripping was maddening. I found nothing soothing about any of it. Just rain and more rain. The cats listened intently, like something was about to happen. Their little ears never stopped twitching with anticipation. Nothing would happen to end their curiosity. Just more rain.

We were all exhausted when the sun finally showed up this morning. Trees were drowning by 4 am. Swept away into the lake by 5, and we finally floated off, onto the highway, by 6:34. The cops pulled us over and said, hey, this is no place for a house full of cats and a lounge singer. We were ticketed for having illegal tinted windows.

I am glad that it's stopped. It is so quiet. You don't know quiet like this too often. You don't realize how noisy it is until you HEAR the silence of the rain stopping. When the last drip falls from the petal of a geranium, and then nothing.

And the smell! It's like falling in love. That fresh beautiful scent that infiltrates your body with such stealth. You feel as though you were just born. Everything new and alive. Clean. So very clean.

jann

I do strange things with my time
09-September-2000 11:37 pm

Joke—Drunk woman at bar: "Hey bartender, I've got terrible heartburn."

Bartender: "No you don't, your tit's in the ashtray..."

The world is falling apart

11-September-2000 11:46 am

A woman went to get some sugar cane to make a meal for her family—somewhere in the jungles of South America. When she returned, she made a grisly discovery. Her entire family had been butchered by a group of guerrilla soldiers, who felt the need to "penalize" the whole village for giving food to the "other side"...Her husband, two sons, and daughter had been shot point blank in the head. Her daughter lay clinging to life, after having a bullet ricochet off her skull and wedge itself up into her cranium, bleeding profusely. She rolled her daughter onto a piece of canvas and started to pull her out of the village. She pulled her for fifty miles, managing finally to reach a refugee camp, only to have her beloved little girl pass away hours later. A weeklong pull up the side of a rugged mountain, only to lose her only living family member.

I got up and phoned room service for more cream.

She then had to dig a hole for her dead child, far outside of the camp so as to not add to the disease and rancid smell that already beleaguered the massive camp. She had no shovel or hoe or rake or any help. She dug with a kitchen spoon that she borrowed, until the hole was deep enough to bury her 110-lb. girl. It took her 4 days. No marker. No stone. No sign of who lay there in that shallow grave.

I sent some clothes out to be washed and folded and wrapped in paper for prompt delivery tomorrow before my meeting. I need those clothes. I have to have those black pants.

She stood in the 120-degree heat waiting for a half cup of rice that she would end up carrying in her bare hands, as she had no bowl or cup of any kind. She knelt down on a piece of corrugated, worn-out box, and delicately ate her ration of rice. Like a lady. With dignity. And she cried in utter silence. Not praying for anything at all. Blank.

I am pissed off because my fucking cell-phone charger is screwed up again. I had it plugged in all day, and nothing. It is dead. Christ. What a piece of shit this thing is. 45 bucks to replace it. I just bought the goddamn thing.

She has the rags on her back. She has nothing but dirt to lay her head on tonight. No one is left, save her. She has no wood. No fire to warm her. No one to hold her and console her grieving heart. There are gunshots off in the misty blackened hills. Her tears fall onto the hard ground.

I hope they plant the trees in my back yard...God it's been two weeks and I have NO TREES! I want privacy next summer. The 18-foot spruce are only about $1000??? Hhmmmm, I wonder if I should order some 8-foot and some 10-foot as well????? I'll phone in the morning...what is with this air conditioning...does it have anything but FREEZING!!!!

She throws up in the night from crying so much. From being so sad. From the loss that she is now so clearly reliving over and over again. A man yells at her over the stink she's made with her vomit. "Move!" he says harshly. "Move over there!" he yells. A rat is eating what she threw up with great glee. She cannot find the strength to wave it away.

I love the pillows here...they are the kind you can hug. All feathers and that wonderful fresh smell.

She lay in the dark. Shooting in the hills drowns her moaning.

I am so ashamed of my life and myself. I don't understand anything, or anyone. I don't want to be a person today.

The terrible things she endures are my shame.

jann

Holes are Part of the Whole

13-September-2000 08:22 pm

I have been thinking about forgiveness today. I don't know if it is possible, for me at least, to forgive everybody for everything they've done. Some things you just never get over. Some things you hang on to just to remind yourself that you are human and fallible and a badass motherfucker that shouldn't be screwed with. I am sure that I have done unforgivable things to other people. I can think of a dozen of those things, just sitting here. It's not that hard. I am an asshole. But at least knowing that I am one gives me hope of not being one.

Forgiveness has its own due time. Its own arrival date. Just when you think you cannot forgive a deed, you suddenly find yourself free of "its" pain. That's when you know that the forgiveness you sought has taken hold of your heart. Until then, it is just a word.

And no, you won't always find that peace. Many of us will live with large holes throughout our bodies, all our lives. Hey, certain cheeses have holes, they are supposed to.

Maybe people are too.

Will They Remember Us All?

14-September-2000 08:12 pm

I was walking home from a movie last night, walking past the homeless people, and the piles of garbage, and the piss in the doorways, and the hot-dog vendors, and the cars racing by, yelling something insulting...(I couldn't quite make it out.) I walked past the bits of paper clinging to a fence, the prostitutes, the runaways. It never ends. 24 hours a day, it goes and goes and goes. The living and the dying all wrapped up into a moment that is unending. Here and gone with very little notice from anyone. How can the world possibly remember us all?? What can we leave behind? How can we mark the earth with ourselves, to not be forgotten.

As much as we try we cannot.

Man's best friend???

16-September-2000 05:55 pm

The clouds were dripping from the sky on our journey today.
Fifty feet in the air, and hanging like they had to pee for
hours. They were moving the opposite way we were driving,
they looked as though they were moving a thousand miles an
hour. Incredible.

The sun came through the tiniest of cracks, burning into
my arm, my bones, my clothes. It felt so good. So very good
to feel the sun and watch those clouds glide like an ice cube
on a glass table. Effortless and graceful.

In all of this peacefulness though came the jolt that is
reality. Backed-up traffic and sirens and fluorescent cones
and flares and that eerie silence that comes with the mind
wondering what could have happened? A van had veered off
the highway into a ditch, and caught fire and burned the pas-
sengers to a crisp. Just like that. Over. Finished. Gone.
Period.

A man was walking down Church street today, yelling at
the top of his lungs, and jerking at the collar of his pet. His
loyal friend, his dog. It was pathetic, and I swear to God, I
wanted to cry and then I wanted to jump out of the vehicle,
and fucking kill him. I felt so bad for that poor dog, who I
swear to you was not doing a thing but walking beside him
that poor dog who is stuck with that piece of shit.

The world is crazy. You see the good, but it is harder and harder to hang on to it. It is somehow diminished by the hardships of others. Other beings, other countries, other wars. Them. I don't know what to do half the time. The other half of the time, I am truly filled with glory and triumph. I am being who I want to be. I am being.

That is the beginning I seek every day. The being.

jann

Never Gone

18-September-2000 02:05 pm

A single leaf is clinging to a branch outside the window. A single, bright red-and-yellow leaf hangs on for dear life. Fall has slipped through the arms of summer, and is stealing the breath from her lungs.

Fall has slipped in through the back door, and into the school books and the new little clothes all lined up for the day. The sweaters and the high socks and the T-shirts and the brand new white runners. Slipped in to cut the days shorter, and make the nights longer and darker and colder.

Fall has wept his icy tears and scorched the geraniums with frost. All blackened now, and bowing their heads. Fall is laughing and bending over at its waist with happiness. Summer is gone and nearly forgotten by all who enjoyed her warmth. Fall and his brother winter will steal every bit of green and bury it with the flowers and the freckles somewhere out beneath the ice of the lake.

The evergreens seem undaunted by it all. They stand guard over the house, the birds and the cats and me. They stand defiantly, saying that they are oblivious to the comings and goings of any of the seasons. Lucky bunch of trees. They spend their days and their evenings catching snow, and seeing who can hold the most. It is a game they play right up until the first day of spring, when it just gets too hard to do any more.

A leaf hangs like a tear out there on my tree. It looks through the window with an eerie sadness that seems to say,

"I will be back before you know it.
I am never gone.
I am sleeping the cold away.
I am alive and unchanged.
I am forever and a day.

Just like you..."

jann

Long Live Huckleberry Finn

19-September-2000 03:31 pm

The leaf is gone. I looked for it when I sat down, and it was gone. On the ground somewhere turning into something else again.

Don't you love how the moon looks when it's bright and big and lighting the road you're on? I remember being a kid, and riding my blue one-speed bike home from Leonard's place, and how bright it was. It seemed like daylight. I was hardly ever scared if the moon was lighting my way.

I just had to remember to keep my mouth shut (not an easy task I might add), so the bugs wouldn't end up in my teeth and lungs. God, I hated that feeling. I almost crashed a hundred times over those bugs. Just the thought made me wobble. I pedalled as fast as my legs could go down this huge hill, so that I could somehow manage to get up the even bigger hill on the other side. I always found myself going through fiercely cold patches and then the warm ones, you'd pray for the warm ones, but the warm ones almost always had a swarm of mosquitoes idly waiting for me to come home. Buggers.

I don't remember even breathing when I rode home. It seems as though I took a breath at the top of the hill, and then held it until I was in the back door of the house. I ran straight for the fridge, had a glass of milk and some celery and joined everyone already watching TV. I watched Star Trek, and that was it. I was in love with William Shatner. I used to get butterflies watching him, long before I even knew what butterflies were. I know now. I still love him. I can't see a salt-and-vinegar chip without thinking of William Shatner...long story.

The leaf is gone.

I have my gram's pyjamas on a rocking chair in my room. Her little name embroidered on them. I hope I live that long. She was never sick really. Just her mind went. Where it went is anybody's guess. God she was fun. I miss her every day. I miss Leonard and Dale too. I miss those times. I had a perfect childhood. I was Huckleberry Finn, and the world was good, and nothing bad ever happened to anyone. I believed in God, and I knew that mom and dad would never ever die.

I still believe that.

jann

Have you hugged your fish today?

20-September-2000 04:42 pm

It's cold today. It looks cold. The geraniums look cold. The grass looks miserable. The clouds look confused. I feel sorry for the fish out there hovering at the bottom of this dark, pathetic excuse for a lake. They say fish are happy for the most part. They like "bumping" into each other, apparently it feels really good to them. Who knew???

Next time I go swimming in there, I'll try and grope one or two of them fishies. Certainly could not hurt to have a friend in low places. They may end up saving my life one dreary day, when I go ass over tea kettle into the abyss.

I don't like fish. I don't like to eat them or feel them or look at them. It's not personal. In fact, I have no doubt that they feel the exact same way about me.

Never get involved with a fish on any level.

The Business of Music

21-September-2000 01:31 pm

I never set out to be anything at all. I just set out.

No More Prairie Lobsters

23-September-2000 06:17 pm

There is nothing sadder than running out of gas in the middle of nowhere, and all the while knowing you would. You watch the little red arm for miles and miles and miles. You watch it slip past the "E" in empty, into the red—the red arm signalling the end of the end of the road. I have done it so many times. If you don't watch the needle, you will run out faster. It is a proven fact. The radio takes up precious fuel as well. And talking will surely add to the confusion. The heater most certainly cannot be on. The fan, well, would mean a quicker death for sure. You must roll onward in utter silence, and watch the time fade into the horizon...along with the fading hopes of reaching your destination.

You could compare that experience to so many things in life. It is a perfect metaphor for living. Knowing that time is slipping past the "E," and you cannot fill up even if you do find a station. Ironic.

We are apparently running out of lobsters here as well. (Not on the prairies, as we ate all of ours here long ago. Not a single one remains hidden in these barren fields of wheat. Not one.)

Floundering

25-September-2000 11:41 am

It is the hardest thing, the being here. I find being on the earth rather odd. Being alive. This whole concept, well, weird. I mean, take hatred for example, the idea of hating someone for no reason. When you think about what hatred is, and why we hate...I don't know about you, but my head fills with blood, and my heart empties of it. Shame pure and simple. We hate each other I am someone's enemy. It seems that it is us hating ourselves; hating things in ourselves that we project onto and into others. Things we cannot stand to know, and cannot accept in ourselves.

It's an old idea. An idea that once somehow embraced survival. Tribe against tribe. Survival. The food supply. Having enough to feed your own clan, and doing away with everyone else that threatened that. It seems the world has changed, but human beings haven't. We stayed the same. We adjusted to the environment, but not in how we see and treat each other. "They" are still a threat to our getting "ahead." We are still the tribe. Still the group. Us against them. White and black. Muslim and Christian. Who in the hell do we think we are?

If you were dangling from a bit of rock, a thousand feet in the air, and a hand came down to help you, would the colour matter?

People are good, or we would not exist here. Life would end in a blaze. Goodness does prevail. And I know how hard it is to be good to someone who is not good to you. That is where honour and dignity lie. Smile in the face of it. Extend your hand. Fear not the wicked. They are fragments of ourselves forgotten. Remind them.

j

Not Just Any Olive
29-September-2000 03:46 pm

It is raining here.
It is raining cats and dogs and Buicks.
I love it. Grey and cloudy and bleak.
Like a good movie.
Like a song.
A really great bowl of Kalamata olives.
Yeah, that's it.
Olives. Like Olives.

It's hard to stay grounded when your feet don't touch
05-October-2000 02:49 pm

I don't know if there is anything more beautiful or more horrible than someone crying. That weeping that starts in
another world, one far away from here. The muffled whimpering that only a mother can hear. I hate to see it, and yet
I am compelled by it. I want to watch the teary goodbyes at
the airport. The relieved hellos. I like to go to the airport
just to see people missing each other. I spend so much time
in them. I am in airports three or four times a week it seems.
I never thought much about it until I started noticing the
people around me. Hearts on sleeves, roaming the gates,
looking for their plane. Some wanting to go somewhere, and
some not. The businessmen and their phones and papers
and loud voices, wanting the line to move along more quickly.

My feet don't touch the ground when I travel business
class.

Did You Hear That...

11-October-2000 01:14 pm

Rumours are naughty little things. Their origins mysterious; their intent unknown. The classic story of the Big One that got away. It (the fish) just seems to get bigger and bigger as time wears on.

Rumours can be interesting, devastating, hurtful, humorous. Rumours can be fascinating. How do they start? Who starts them? Well, we do of course!

Every time we repeat a story that we heard from someone who heard it from somewhere that knew the person who saw it happen to the guy who was in jail who had the tumour on his leg from being held hostage by the nun from Italy who fought off a black panther while driving the cocaine to that girl who was a hooker for a while after she got back from meeting the Backstreet Boys who impregnated her mother when they went for milk...

Wow...that was a long one. I think you get the point.

I wonder what the point of a story is. Especially a hurtful story. Why do people pass on useless information on such a massive comprehensive scale. It's like we're working off a grid, who will cover what territories, what streets, what houses...

Quite remarkable.

I think there is truth in all these things. How do you ever separate the shit from the shinola?

Number 1: Know your source.

Number 2: Never add on to a story without being positive that it will not be traced back to you.

Number 3: Always lie about who told you.

Number 4: Wait a few months before passing the story along.

Watch them squirm. I like a good rumour actually. I often find myself in the middle of them. I heard recently that I was a "sugar momma" who had a yacht...I love that one, I feel really famous (and I never feel famous). That some sweet soul took the time to make that up warms my heart.

I heard that I had killed myself a few years ago....I may have, so I can neither confirm nor deny this rumour.

I heard that I was married with kids, and that I was abandoned by my husband because he was in love with another man...now I finally know the truth.

We are all victim to the rumour mill. Imagine how great our lives are because of them. The countless people we sleep with, the parties, the men, the women, the drugs. Wow!!

I was once told that I set a house on fire (it was a garage for crying out loud).

I was once told that I did a gig at this place that was fantastic, and that I played Insensitive 5 times in a row for the encore (never heard of it in my life).

I heard that I have had affairs with all my band members, including the bus driver, and he thought I was terrible in bed (well no kidding, because we were doing it on the hood of a car—dumb ass).

I need to go and nuke my decaf. (Now some of you may think that I said my "cat"...that I was going to nuke my...you know what I mean.)

Now get out there and make something up about me will ya?

ja

Cyber Trees

17-October-2000 12:29 am

The written word. Truly the most remarkable human invention ever. I breathe and live words. They are the most important things we have. The book. The book...think about a book. What a perfect invention. The best and most important ever.

It's been awhile...—Part 1

21-October-2000 04:16 pm

Being a person is like being an old paper bag.
You can never get the wrinkles out once they're in.
You can't make it hold a lot of water.
You can't make it carry too much.

Just like us.

It's been awhile...—Part 2

21-October-2000 04:16 pm

Sometimes that's all you get in life. The inside of your own
ass.

the clocks tick on...

There are 6 billion people in the world. I know but a few hundred of them. I would say that I know 6 of those people really well. I would say that I know 4 of those people really, really well, and I would be stretching it to say that I know one of those people better than they knew themselves. But then again, I hardly know myself. I don't know anyone famous. I don't hang out with anyone famous.

I live in Alberta for God's sake.

And the beat goes on…

24-October-2000 12:43 am

Change is in the air. I can feel it. I can feel it looming and circling. I can hear its plodding footsteps across my heart late at
night. Resisting is only prolonging the worry and the frustration of being where you are. The universe is funny that way. It
will pick you up no matter what your wishes are. It will pick you
up and drop you off at a stop, nowhere even on your regular
route. It is a bugger that way. Why do we not heed the signs?
Why do we run from change rather than embrace it? Why do
we do the things we do? I like change well enough. I like new
things; new faces, new places. But on the other hand, I really do
not like to travel. Could I have picked a more stationary job? I
doubt it. The universe is funny that way. Last week I was in two
different hotels. It is usually a lot more. It's hard sleeping in so
many beds (said the nun to the preacher). But how grateful I am
to have a bed at all.

The thing about hotels is this: I am always wandering
around in the dead of night looking for the toilet. Backing
into closets and hallways and chairs. Where is the bloody
toilet? That is always a challenge. Where is the toilet? How
far back is the toilet paper? Is it underneath the counter by
the sink? Is it on the opposite wall? Is it in another room?

no beginning, no ending...

25-October-2000 06:17 pm

Death can either take you quietly or, as in most cases, take you kicking and screaming. Death can be discreet or obvious, depending on one's needs. Death can be a fear or a desire, a friend or foe. Death is the common denominator. Death—the great plain on which equality is measured and dished out. When? Where? How? Who? Why? What are we? Are we balls of light? Are we bags of bones? Are we spirit? Are we a billion trillion cells floating without meaning in even more nothingness than even imagined? Or are we everything. Are we all of it? Are we it? Death more often than not brings mercy. Death the cure, not the demon stealing life, but rather offering life anew. Death brings change. Near-death, even more change. Why do we take our lives to the brink of disaster in order to be able to see it for what it really is? Precious. Perfect. Glorious. Divine. It is the shit that has made my life liveable. The horrible mistakes that make me able to tolerate being here at all. No other teacher is quite as effective as loss, failure, death.

wise words...

27-October-2000 04:06 pm

I have fucked up a lot. In fact, here I go to probably fuck up
some more.

quiet Saturday...

28-October-2000 04:06 pm

I don't know quite what to write.

Baseball Season

05-November-2000 03:18 pm

At least my tits are real.

Kindness and Mercy

11-November-2000 01:48 pm

I don't know. And I don't know if I want to know. They say that ignorance is bliss. It probably is. I doubt the things we do know are really of any value anyway. The Dow. The NASDAQ. The price of toilet paper. What season you are. Hey, I can wear that, because I'm a winter. What time the bus comes. The rise and fall of your mutual funds. What somebody said about somebody you know. What's cool. What's now. What's hip. The things we know.

What do we know that's really quite important? Not much. We think the things we know are important, but they're not. We need to know what kindness is. We need to understand what mercy is. We need to know and understand and believe in God. All of the gods. Everybody's God. Not just our own.

Understand what it is to have faith in something we do not see any more. That we do not recognize, because our lives are too busy to take in the miracles all about us. If you really watched, if you really saw, you would take in the longest deepest breaths, and be in awe of your own life. Life itself. You would be fearless.

We just don't accept anything that we don't understand, or that we do not see in front of us at any given moment. If we cannot touch it, it cannot be "real." I like the not knowing. It seems to suddenly create endless possibilities for change. I don't know what my next word will be.

Whether that's important or not is anybody's guess.

jann

Taking Stock

12-November-2000 03:46 pm

Being who you are is quite simply that. God's own design.
He made us as we are meant to be. Who we are.
But you CAN choose to be a prick.

Random Thoughts

16-November-2000 12:25 am

If a guy can shoot John Lennon, then anything can happen.
If a bunch of guys can string up Jesus, then anything can happen, and anything did. If an African-American can get
dragged behind a truck for miles and miles, until he falls
apart, then anything can happen. We all fall apart right along
with him. Because we're him, and he's us. And we are the
same after all.

The Peace of Sleep

19-November-2000 02:22 pm

Sleeping. What a weird thing it is. To have to shut down one's own body in order to keep going ahead. To completely leave yourself wide open to danger and bodily harm. To close your eyes, and go to a whole other realm of being. Another dimension. And it is another dimension. We dream. We ponder and wonder and figure. We become bits of vapour. We are briefly—oh so briefly—ourselves. Bright and bold and bigger than ever. We sleep to gather up the little truths that evade us through the day. The ones we don't see. We sleep to renew, and relive and revive.

It is so nice to sleep with someone you love and trust. You surrender yourself to them. You lie there and know that you are safe and well, and that nothing could ever happen to you, and even if it did, it wouldn't matter. Companionship. Comfort. Reliability. The hand that brushes your thigh, and a foot that grazes your leg. You never want to wake up.

I am sleeping well these days. I am home. The place I miss, the person I miss, is right here waiting for me every time.

I Love Music

27-November-2000 12:29 am

I just got back from seeing Tina Turner, she looks simply wonderful. I spent most of my time looking around at everybody else. I looked at how people watched her and each other. The lit-up faces, singing at the top of their lungs. The lighters waving in the balconies, glittering like stars. The flashes of cameras and the roar of bodies, making those haunting sounds, the ones without words.

Concerts are interesting things. Having been on either side of them, it never ceases to amaze me the power of music. The way it can shape so many of us into different beings for a moment or two. The way it joins the un-joinable. Gives us a commonness that is unmistakable. We are joined by vibration and movement and sound. We are joined by this blissful, rich spirituality that sweeps us up and away from everyday life.

I loved the feeling of weightlessness. So many voices. So many hearts pounding.

"Great"-Aunt Sue

29-November-2000 01:04 pm

My Great-aunt Sue died today. I believe she was 93 years old. She was such a fun girl. My Uncle Reg and my Aunt Sue owned a confectionery...remember that word? She would give Pat, Duray and I each a paper bag to fill up with candy. It was like making a wish that came true. Filling that bag as full as I possibly could. Racing down every aisle, making sure not a single treat was missed. Licorice and wax lips and those tubes of wax you'd drink and then chew up like gum. Mojos and sponge toffee and banana chews and chicken bones and dubble bubble and bar sixes...(what became of them??), charleston chews and kit kats and peppermints and raspberry gummies. So much candy. We had the jitters all the way home.

She was one of the older children in my Gram's family. In fact, when her mother died at 42 years old after giving birth to her 17th child, Gordon...Aunt Sue took over things. The younger kids, including my Gram, called her "Mother." Heartbreaking to lose a mother so young. Not fair at all. I can't imagine. Don't want to either.

When Aunt Sue was 90ty, mom and I took her and gram (who was 84 at the time) to a bar. We bought them a beer and watched them talk about nothing and everything. Neither of them could hear what the other said, but that didn't seem to deter them much. It was so adorable. I played VLTs and drank Diet Pepsi. Won 25 dollars and bought the round with it. I will never forget how mom and I laughed at that day. We said, "Well, that'll be us soon"...not soon enough for me some days...

Sue and gram are together again. They await only 3 more, and then it will be done. They came and went with little fanfare, little glory was theirs. They simply were. 17 children. They shared one pair of skates among them. I have seen where the old lake was, and my hair stood on end. I pictured them out there, breathless and motherless, somehow managing to smile, and get on with it.

Crush, Crushing, Crushed

15-December-2000 01:38 pm

What is a crush? Why do we have them? What gives you that upside down feeling in your legs and thighs and parts unknown to you 'til you feel them for the first time?

Infatuation. It's quite simply the most interesting thing to me. Eyes that melt you like the sun melts asphalt. You think of nothing else but "them." The one, and only one, person that captivates your every desire. The secret wishes you make in the middle of the night. You pull your legs up around you—and you feel like air is all that your body is made up of.

The crush of your body folding in on itself like a big old book. The welling of juices. Watering eyes. Throbbing parts that make you blush so brightly it lights up the room.

Wanting. Hoping. Pleading with the gods to help you attain the unattainable.

Why do we like some and not others? Does not every soul have the potential to be a lover? Is there not something about every being that could capture your heart? No, there is not. It is only a wee few who can do that. That is why love seems so elusive. First, you have to find someone to love. Loving is not the obstacle, finding someone TO love is. It is our purpose in life, to be in constant pursuit of a partner. We do not want to be alone.

I like being alone. It just seems that I seldom am. So I try to be alone in my head. I simply want to pursue the joy of simple thinking. Travelling in my mind to every possible corner there is to travel.

The crush. How I love that feeling of drunken disarray in my heart. No control. NONE. I just go where every beat takes me. I do not hesitate to drink it all in like cold beer on a blistering hot day.

jann

Dear Dave,

18-December-2000 01:04 pm

I dreamt about David Hart last night. He was a keyboard player that I worked with over 12 years ago. I have a difficult time thinking about him, or thinking about that time in my life at all.

He was an interesting man. As I recall, he was almost 20ty years older than me, something like that anyway. I had met him while working in a country show band with a guy named Larry Michaels...where the hell is he now? (Not David, Larry.) I remember Larry's brother looking like a 500-lb. Elvis. It was a very weird set-up.

Anyway, David and I met and went off on our own to do this kind of odd lounge act called Hart and Soul. We played nothing but ballads. I drank Grand Marnier, and sang like I didn't need the money, er...wait a minute, we didn't make any money. We had the most bizarre following imaginable. Every walk of life sat before us and drank their troubles away. (Or drank and made trouble.) Either/or, it made for a very diverse, sorrow-filled night.

I don't think I was ever able to get through it, a single night that is, without drinking. I have so many regrets about that time, but David was not one of them. He taught me so much about music. About the blues and about life. He was always very good to me. I slept many a night on his floor after we rehearsed—somewhere way up in N.E. Calgary. I would take the LRT, or drive my piece-of-shit Maverick up there. It is such a blur to me now. Maybe purposely, but blur it is nonetheless.

I sang Olivia Newton-John songs and Karen Carpenter, and Tom Waits for God's sake. I mean depressing with a capital D double S. The mood was still and drunk and dark. People were so quiet. I could hear myself breathe in to sing the next note. I sang Send in the Clowns and The Way We Were, and Don't Cry Out Loud...I can just see me there right now—the Buffalo Paddock Lounge in Banff. In fact, I ran into a guy that used to run the Paddock not three months ago, and he remarked quite matter-of-factly that David and I drank more than anybody else he ever had play in there. Kind of makes you want to bury yourself some-where out in the back forty. Been there, drank that, so they say.

I can choose to regret or incorporate. I blend all the memories like a load of laundry, and wash away madly, always hoping for some answers and some comfort at the end of the day. Sometimes I get them, sometimes I don't. Either way, I own them all. They, the memories, are my life. They are the fabric of who I am and who I will be. No escape. I take them with me into every dream and every inch of daylight. Like I took David last night.

In the dream, I had met his ex-wife, and she was showing

me slides of him on her family-room wall. I was crying, weeping really, about how he looked. So tired and thin and worn out by life. I don't know what happened to David Hart. I heard that he was in Florida at one point. His son, Spad, used to come to my shows once in a while in London, Ontario. I wonder where HE is?

Then I heard that he was in a band that did nothing but jann arden covers...I don't know where he is or whatever became of him. I wish I did. I would so like to talk to him someday, just to see how he is. To thank him for all the lessons I probably learned at his expense. I know that he was heartbroken when I met my then manager Neil and left to pursue a recording deal. I remember David saying that he was too old and ugly. That they wouldn't want him, just me. It makes me feel so sad now. I used to beg him to wear his teeth when we did our gigs...he was funny that way.

Honestly, David had a warmth in his body, and in his soul, that only comes from sorrow and defeat. He had a painful beauty that seeped out of every pore. He was a great musician and a great cook. He always shared his cigarettes with me, even if he was down to his last one, you know how that can be...

Dave, wherever you are, I hope you are happy and healthy and playing piano like you don't need the money. I remember you so clearly. I remember you like I can remember me then. You, are a painting in my heart.

love jann

I Need a Pattern

20-December-2000 08:26 pm

I just shovelled the driveway. Holy good God almighty, that was not easy. I am soaked to the bone. I think I need to devise a system. I was watching the other guys doing it, and they seem to have some sort of pattern that they follow. I need one of those. I suppose it's like mowing the lawn. You know how guys mow the lawn into nice golf-course-type patterns? I sort of start in the middle and go everywhere there is snow. I suck. I need a blower maybe...yeah, that's what I need.

Shrodie is a nut ball today. He has finally lost his marbles. His noodle. His beans. He's leaping across chairs and tables and Christmas trees. (The cats knocked it down once already.) They are eating the spruce needles off the floor. Is that bad? Sweet pea has eaten off several of the bows I had so carefully made, and maybe baby has disappeared into thin air. I have to go and open cupboards and drawers to try and locate the little rat. She is here somewhere. The dryer???? Kidding of course.

It was so cold last week, I froze my cans off. I went to Eaton's and bought a big white puffy coat. Very cozy and yet unattractive. You can't have it both ways in this country. It has a hood that is so large, I may be able to carry my groceries in it. The sleeves are so long that shoplifting should not pose any problems. Kidding again.

A Peaceful World

25-December-2000 03:27 pm

So, it's Christmas is it? For so many of us, it wouldn't matter
what it was called, or what it turned into, because this is a
day that is about love. It is about family. The family you were
born into, or the one that found you, or the one you created
for yourself. It is about compassion and being together. To
enjoy good food and stories and laughs and memories. It is
about being grateful, if only for a few hours.

Christmas is a wonderful invention really. It makes us
drive home to see the folks...hummin' and hawin' all the way.
Families are funny things...but that's a whole other entry. It
makes us sit down and have a meal with the people that we
take for granted the most. It makes us sit down to talk and
remember and recall and relive.

It forces us to play cards and watch old movies. To not
think of what you need to buy for the office or how many
shares you need to trade in the morning. Yes, as corny as all
of it seems. The stupid marketing that swirls around us
starting in August for crying out loud. As goofy and silly and
plastic as it can get, it's so wonderful still. Just to see my
mom and dad and my brother and sister-in-law, and the kids
and my friends and my foes... Just to sit there, doused in candles and potatoes and gravy, and hear them talk and laugh
out loud.

Just Feeling Good

27-December-2000 11:35 am

I wish they had Jolly Jumpers for big people.

The Matter of Life and Death

28-December-2000 04:25 pm

Everything is white. Vivid and totally clear. Every branch heavily laden with clumps of snow. They can hardly hold themselves up. It is painfully beautiful to look at. The weight of the world hanging from a branch.

There is so much beauty in pain. Sorrow and defeat have their own majestic pose. They are steadfast and solitary till the end. Anyone who has witnessed someone dying knows what I mean. The final breath that seeps out of a person's lungs like a sigh. It is a beautiful relief for them and for you. I think about dying a lot. Perhaps too much. But I truly feel it makes me appreciate life all the more.

The Lost and Found

04-January-2001 12:47 am

The cat, shrodie, is sitting here watching me type this. He is going for a haircut tomorrow. I call it the "Lion King." He hates it. He feels self-conscious, if that's possible for a cat. Hisses at me for days. Won't eat. Won't sleep. He just tries to be as miserable as possible. Can't say I blame him. It's like having a seven-year perm. I remember mom giving me one of those. I could smell the scalp melting off of my head. What a stench!

The BBC news is on the telly. Love the BBC news. There is something a little campy about the Brits. They have this way of making everything look hysterical. Bombings don't really look all that bad. Maybe it's the accent? The newscasters seem to be endlessly entertained with themselves. I can't really put my finger on it. It's just really fun to watch.

Beauty is in the Heart

05-January-2001 06:26 pm

It's hard to know who you are. It's hard to know what being yourself is. We all spend so much time trying to be what we think other people want us to be that we lose sight of everything important about ourselves. It is SO easy to do.

We take pieces from other people that we like, that we think we need, and we add them onto ourselves. They don't really fit all that well, but we glue them on anyway. Slowly we cover ourselves up, without even realizing what we've done. You look in the mirror one day, and wonder what face is looking back out at you. I have done that very thing more than one time in my life.

Beauty is in the heart. It is in a salty wet tear. It is in weeping and laughing and failure. Beauty is in comfort and knowing. It is in knowing that you are fine and well and perfect. Beauty is not made, it is born from acceptance of self. It is in you. Complete. Beauty is ugliness, and ugliness is truly amazing and heavenly. Confused?

You're on the right track.

The Sun Will Come Out Tomorrow

08-January-2001 11:55 pm

I feel heavy and lonely and far away from any divine purpose. Life is like that. Some days are diamonds, and some days are stones. Either way, you have to drag yourself through them, and wait for the sun to come up the next day.

A Girl

09-January-2001 04:46 pm

There is a girl on a dock holding a fishing rod with a tiny fish dangling from its line. So many years ago. There is a girl without a line on her face, squinting into the sun with a hand on her brow, with a half smile, wondering where she will end up. There is a girl without a single care or a single worry, no darkness and no hopelessness cross her heart, leaving the doom of long shadows. There is a girl. There still is a girl.

1, 2, 3...6 billion

11-January-2001 07:47 pm

When we look at each other, we have a hard time seeing anything inside of the outside. We are judged by our appearance. I mean, initially we are. How many times have you looked at your friend, just looked for no particular reason, and seen someone you have never seen before? It happens to me all the time. All the little details that I never noticed about their face or their hands or their hair or their eyes or ears...all the little things that take a lifetime to take in. When you have that moment, you see the light around someone's head. The glow, the glimmer, the essence.

I wonder if men at war see that light around the head of their enemy just before they take them from the world. I wonder if they do? When you see someone, how could you ever "end" them?

When you finally see the light around someone. When you finally see WHO they are, and you realize that you are with someone that you want to love and that you want to get to know...it is so effortless. The other ones, the ones that you don't see, aren't so easy. Probably because you don't let them see you either.

I Wanna Be a Part of It...New York, New York

16-January-2001 03:04 pm

I have been in NY for the last 4 days. Got home last night at 1 am—3 hours late. Toronto was fogged in of all things. And I mean really fucking fogged in. I could not see my boobs in front of me...and I usually can, believe me.

New York was, as always, an adventure for the eyes and the ears and the nose and the tongue and the very tips of my toes. So much to take in. Watching people should be an Olympic event if indeed the Olympics ever get to NY again. Unbelievably interesting. God. And so many people! So many souls wandering aimlessly. So many sounds coming in and out of your head like flashes of lightning. It's like you are walking through a fantastic book, and the pages are turning and you have to run to keep up turning and turning and turning.

I love New York. Everything is immediate. The food, the newspapers on every corner, fuck! I love that about New York...the NEWSPAPERS!! The headlines and theatre and the lights pulsing like a hundred million red bleeding hearts, dripping themselves onto the sidewalks while we all walk through their oozing, writhing, twisting, sweat-like worms in the rain...(that was a bit much, I know, but so is New York). All the food jumping into your mouth as you casually walk by trying to ignore it...everybody is eating in New York.

The smell of shit and fresh bread all in the same block. The smell of body odour and roasting coffee in the same breath. The smell of gasoline and brewing beer in the next one... New York is indeed a melting pot. Every colour and creed and nation hooking arms as they cross the street. The big first step they all take to go to the other side, like a tightly woven dance that's been practiced for a hundred years. All the horns going off over nothing. The blasting tempers of taxi drivers that are too tired to care who they run over or how they drive. Montel Williams is telling me to buckle up...he should be telling me to pray while I'm at it.

The shopping bags that clip you in the leg as they go by unapologetically. You turn to see them, but they've been eaten up by the throng of bodies going and coming and going again. I saw a few plays. Ate some food. Looked into windows at things no one could afford in their whole entire lifetimes. Walked by Tiffany's and thought about Audrey Hepburn...

jann

My Friend's Dad
23-January-2001 05:38 pm

What is a good life?
Is it its length or its authenticity and valour that make it rich
and worthwhile?
Is it fame and money and fortune and political prowess that
make it good?
To me, it is simply a good deed and a gracious action.
It is truth and friendship and failure and triumph.
It is making wrong turns and righting them.
It is starting over and it is ending without struggle.
It is everything decent in this world.

Reflecting

31-January-2001 01:47 pm

Life does go by. Seemingly without notice, you look in the mirror one day and see someone older and more at peace. You see someone you have to really look at to understand. You look long and deeply into a pair of eyes that are not yours, and perhaps never were yours. Who did I become while I slept?

We have a picture of ourselves in our heads, and it's a picture that is hard to let go of. We all have those moments when we are flipping through an old photo album, and we see ourselves and say, "did I ever look like that?" "Oh my God—look at my hair!" "Look at how thin I was!"

We have a picture of ourselves, different I think than the picture that people see. WE see our faults, they don't. We see every line, they just see us laughing. We see our faces from the inside out, no matter how good the mirror. We never see ourselves. We only see our reflections. I think about that. I can see my hands and my feet and my breasts and my stomach, I can almost see my nose...but I will never ever see my own face other than in a reflection.

I would desperately like to see my own face.

Valentine's Day

14-February-2001 05:06 pm

Love is in the air.
On Valentine's I always think about heartbreak.
I mean, certainly love was involved at some point,
but it's the heartbreak that seems to scratch its way to the
surface on Valentine's for me.
Love the great cliché.
Love the great saviour.
Love the great humbler.
Love the great mystic.
And love the glorious ghost.
The ghost of sweet memories and tender words.
Love.
Drink it in like it is the last drop of water you will ever have.

Didn't Somebody Pay the Light Bill?

16-February-2001 04:27 pm

My power just went out for about 15 minutes, and I nearly, well, er, I did...I panicked. It was so awful. Probably more awful due to living out of the city. Who would hear me if I screamed anyway? The nearest person works at Blockbuster 6 miles away. It's back on now. I am one of the new modern wimps. No blow dryer??? No fireplace that you just click on??? No TV?? I wouldn't have made a good pilgrim. I would have been dead on the second day.

Make that the first day.

Finding Heaven

18-February-2001 02:03 pm

My mother has talked about death very candidly with us kids, since the beginning of "I remember when." She always said that we had to die, but it wouldn't be for a long time. That was of course if we didn't run out into the traffic after someone's turtle???? She would always say that we were going to a better place. McDonald's? Oh, if it could only have been McDonald's. Well, no—actually it's... it was to a place called heaven, and she pointed up there. We would all look with a secret burning desire to see it. Even if it was just a flash or a sparkle of something. I still look up there on a dreary day, or a starless night, and wonder if I am not looking in the wrong direction. I think heaven is inside of me. I am not sure where, but I think that it is indeed a good, if not great, traveller. It goes where I go. With every thought and every dream. Heaven. A compact, versatile, moveable wonder.

My mother to this day talks about what to do with all her stuff. "Oh I hope you kids don't just sell it all." I always say that I will definitely NOT sell any of it...well, maybe those Norman Rockwell mugs. Every time I buy her a birthday present, she says, "Well, this will be yours when I go"...

Lord have mercy.

Eating Meat Again

22-February-2001 01:05 pm

My mother can pack a lot of shit into their motor home. I think she just takes everything out of the house, and crams it into the space just under the bed out there. The bed lifts up, and in goes all the stuff in the house. I swear.

I am going over there tonight for dinner (mom and dad's). Mom always asks me what I want to have. God love her. I always say "Anything..." And then she'll say, "Are you eating meat again?" and I say, "Yes Mother, I have been for the last ten years." We have that conversation every now and again.

What is it we want?

23-February-2001 12:04 pm

We seem to be destined to want to be better than we already are. And I don't mean in a spiritual or intellectual way. I mean our bodies. Period.

We want something that we don't have. What is it we want? And if we had it, would that be the end of it??? I doubt it somehow. I think it is never-ending I am afraid.

The need to be perfect.

I never heard my gram say a word about herself or her body. Never. I am sure she thought about it, but thought it was vain and self-serving to think such things. I miss her every day. It will be a year in May. Lord...

I am fucked-up today. All fiction and very little anything else. I am a bag of wind.

Oh gram...I have your pyjamas at the foot of my bed. I had a dream about you finally, and you were fine, just like you said you would be. Wish you could have seen where I live now. You would have loved it.

The Mountain and the Snow Angel

25-February-2001 01:27 pm

People forget how long it takes to be something. "How do I become?" they say. You just do. You just become. Time tells you who you are. You just have to listen and see. It is a long process, the becoming of anything. A mountain will tell you who it is, just by standing there and not having to say a word. It just became itself.

There is a boy making an angel in the snow. I am watching him flail his arms around him, sweeping his legs, small as they are at his few years, into the biggest arch he can muster. And now all that is left is the getting up. It is always the hardest part, the getting up.

Every soul has the dream of becoming itself. Its true self. So many of us, and yet not so many, all wanting to be someone...to be remembered. It seems simple, but is not.

The angel is gone already; he wiped it out, that boy. He looked at it, and saw that it was not good enough, so he took his wee feet, and stomped it away like it was never there at all.

The hardest part is the getting up.

In and Out of Every Thought

06-March-2001 11:30 pm

There is nothing so sad as a man crying with a crumpled-up tissue in his hand, in the middle of the intersection in a big, fast city. It was a strange juxtaposition of strength and weakness, success and failure, triumph and sincere remorse. Very hard to see.

He has stayed with me all of this day. I wonder what was wrong? Ever wondered what was wrong with someone openly crying in public? I do. I always want to go up to them and say, "What happened?" I wonder what they would say back to you? What, if anything, could you do anyway?

Saw a man later in the day with the "elephant man" disease. It was so remarkable, and so unremarkable. He had his headphones on, and his head as low as it would go. Watching his feet plod one foot in front of the other. I wondered what he was listening to. Did he listen just so he wouldn't ever hear the jeers and the comments that surely must follow him through every day?

I will never forget his head hanging there, like it was not attached to him, or who he was, that it was most certainly not part of who he was.

The Ever-Changing Weather

19-March-2001 04:16 pm

We just had some sort of bizarre blizzard out here. It was the oddest, weirdest thing. Black clouds ate the house. We were a meal for some furious beast of nature. Black and then completely white, all in about 3 minutes. It ended as it began, very peacefully, with a sigh. It is as white out there as I wish my teeth were. Not one blade of grass survived the deluge. We are underneath the storm now. The farmers need the snow this time of year...so my mother tells me every single time it does this. She says, "Well the farmers will sure be happy." Every time.

Doggy Dog??

29-March-2001 01:02 pm

There is a big fat pigeon on the balcony with a French fry in its mouth, now how fucking funny is that? Probably looking for the gravy. Not here buddy. Try Swiss Chalet. Where the hell did he get a perfectly good French fry?? Off he goes.

Life is like that. You finally get yourself a French fry, and don't have a single place to dip the thing.

Every One a Miracle
06-April-2001 04:04 pm

It is interesting listening to people talk about their children. Grown men reduced to tears as they regale us with the simple tale of a child peeing in their eye as they changed a poopy diaper or the time when Jr. walked into the patio glass door and fell down on his bum and cried until snot came bubbling out of his nose..."You don't say?" or the time Jr. went up the stairs for the first time, and said boo! The rest of us listen with mild enthusiasm. "Oh yeah, that's really great, what a story! What an unbelievable accomplishment." God...

Children change people with a determined purpose. To change the world. Children change the world, because they soften us all, and teach us real true love. Pure and simple. Not lust, not romantic, not sexual, not puppy love, but real, true, deep, passionate love. Universal love. Faith. Hope. Mercy. Above all these is love.

Children show us God each and every day. Imagine making a person. Making a person? Is that random? Is that happenstance? Is that evolution or quite simply a miracle, or quite possibly a bit of both?

I look up so many nights and am breathless with wonder. I can't think any one thought without it tangling around my head, and becoming incredible, unbelievable, sensational.

The stars hanging there without time ticking. Without movement. Without worry or strife. Stars looking into my heart and back through my life like I am water. Liquid and shapeless. Fluid and endless. Looking through me into who and what I am.

To think that I am a part of that, and you are a part of that, is so beyond me. Kind of makes you want to cry or laugh, or just lie down for a rest.

jann

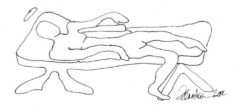

The Way of the Buffalo
11-April-2001 01:06 pm

I want to get a dog. I won't tomorrow, but today, I would like to have a dog. They should give you a dog when you travel alone. You could just get it when you check into the hotel, no? "Here's your dog Miss Arden." They'd sleep at the end of the bed, and go walking with you.

I better go, as I just saw another one of my marbles roll under the TV.

The Auto-Bike
16-April-2001 11:16 am

I watch a lot of infomercials, and I mean in their entirety. I watch them and actually find myself considering ordering the knives and the rotisseries and the hair removal systems and the plethora of different ab-rollers. You name it. I did end up ordering an "auto bike" a few years ago. Don't ask. But I do use it all the time. You never have to change the gears. You just pedal like a fiend, and off you go over hill and dale.

The World IS Better
17-April-2001 04:31 pm

I am now reading Amsterdam by Ian McEwan. I am at a point where I don't really know what to think of it. It won the Booker Prize, although I don't know if that means a fucking thing. Art is subjective, and there are so many books that literally shimmer, but sadly will never win any awards. Literature, I'm afraid, is as political as the music business. At least authors, God bless them, will never be judged on how they look. How big their tits are, or if they are 16 years old perpetually...

Ever Been Goosied?

26-April-2001 04:32 pm

The lake is melting quickly. The geese are finding little spots to land and soak and float. They are as noisy as they can possibly be. I think the Canada Goose would be an effective weapon in any kind of warfare. Perhaps drug growers? We could send a few hundred thousand goosies (I know) to nest and honk and shit all over their pot??? Just a thought. Who'd want to smoke that? Don't answer that question.

The cats spend their days racing around here like it's the Indy 500. Streaks of hair rushing by me with great purpose. "We have a lot of things to do," they scream. Everybody is on the bed with me at night. Either in the crook of my back or under an armpit or on my head. Perhaps they are trying to choke the very life out of me. If you don't hear from me, you'll know the cats have finally done me in.

The Weirdness of Singing

03-May-2001 12:05 pm

Singing is a weird undertaking. It is an out-of-body experience. I hear myself from inside myself. It's like hearing an echo from another version of yourself. I don't know what else to call it. I have my eyes shut most of the time, because that's how I hear it all that much better. I would rather hear than see...or perhaps I can see what I hear.

Something for Nothing

21-May-2001 07:21 pm

My heart just cracked. My head just fell in. The coffee is cold, and I have to throw some towels into the dryer.

The Old Socrates and Plato Story

24-May-2001 03:23 pm

Socrates was killed by the very peers who thought he was a genius, a groundbreaker, and a leader. They made him drink hemlock in front of his friends and colleagues, as they watched him die. In Athens, where he lived, they accused him of introducing new gods, when really he was introducing new ideas. He was getting people to think for themselves, from the inside out. Dangerous these ideas of ours... He was one of a handful of philosophers that changed the world as we knew it then, and continues to change the world as we know it now. This was a man who never wrote down a single word he spoke; his faithful follower, Plato, did some of that for him. (Whether we can credit Socrates with these actual words and accounts is still debatable.)

Nonetheless, Socrates began the journey of democracy. He felt that debate was at the centre of good and decent living. I can't imagine what life must have been like for people then. Exciting and daunting, exhilarating and mysterious. I was happy to read that Socrates felt that knowing nothing was the beginning of knowing anything. I must be on the right track, because I know shit.

Scratch—"Save World"—from To-Do List

25-May-2001 01:45 pm

My horoscope today told me not to bother saving a world that did not want to be saved. Damn, and I was all ready to do that today!

Becoming

29-May-2001 08:06 pm

Memories define us and make us who we are. What we choose to remember creates us. I am what I remember I am. What I have forgotten, I am no longer.

A song on the radio can take me back 25 years, and set me in a field with a beer in my hand and a cigarette dangling from my mouth, and I remember who I was, and who it made me to be now.

The smell of cotton candy and fried onions takes me back 30 years and sets me on a ride at the fair seeing my mom and dad blur past me waving their arms with a camera flashing and teeth locked into the sweetest smiles. I remember having my head out the window of our blue Starsky and Hutch car eating the bugs as they flew into my gaping jaw. How my head blew back and my eyes teared and my breath laboured to come into my lungs. I remember the speed and the smell of the tar on the highways and the gasoline.

Memories are what make me who I am. What I remember of my life is what I can stand on to look over the hills before me. The horizon is endless, and I am endless. There is nothing like the sun on one's face to feel timeless. The brightness lights up your heart with warmth and comfort. You know the darkest days will be lit and burned away if you just keep moving forward.

Odd Jobs
29-June-2001 11:46 am

It is my "job," but yet not my job at all.
It is my pleasure and my passion
my lifeline
my self, my body, my other.
I don't know how to even explain it.
I love singing, but feel endlessly guilty about what I do.
I feel the desire to move on,
and to be something other than what I am.
How do I even talk about that?

I want to be everything.
I want to try everything, and do everything.
I am worn out to the point of nothingness.
I am grateful.
I am.

It's Up to You, New York...New York!

16-July-2001 09:55 am

I know why New Yorkers are so proud of their city. It is everything you think it will be and then some. There is nothing you cannot have here. Nothing you cannot buy or have delivered to you. Once you are used to that, you cannot ever go back without some sort of twelve-step program. You would go through terrible withdrawal. They must think we are asleep up where we are. Even after being here this short while, I can feel it seep into my blood like a glass of expensive wine. Just the scent, the aroma...

and you're hooked.

Eaten by the Dog (or is it Dohg)

24-July-2001 02:48 pm

Mom and dad's phone was off the hook last night for hours. I finally drove over there fearing that they had been eaten by the dog, or even worse, that they perhaps could have been having sex and my father had a heart attack...having sex. I am really kidding. I hope my parents never read this...they don't have a computer, so that helps a lot.

See What I Mean?

16-August-2001 08:11 pm

I seem to be in a bit of an "overload" funk. I am doing too much all the time. Even when I have a spare moment, I don't sit down, and on top of that, I am not eating carbs. I sound like a Hollywood nut now don't I?? No, I am not sleeping in an oxygen tent as of yet.

The sun is out. Not one single cloud. Seagulls float by. Bird shit on the lawn. Cat fur everywhere I look. Ringing phones. People needing things from me yesterday. Wanting chocolate. Feeling full and so empty a second later. No air. Hot. Got to buy candles. Moved a big ugly chair downstairs to the guest room. (That was nice of me don't you think? Let the guests deal with that eyesore??) I want KFC. I want chips and pop. Need to put laundry in the dryer. Shave my legs one of these days please (I am killing myself with my own legs). Would like to have sex more often. Never want to have sex again.

See what I mean??

The Heavenly Spirit on Earth

13-September-2001 01:27 pm

"It is still a beautiful world, strive to be happy."
These were old words found in a church somewhere in the
17th century.
Imagine how horrible times were then,
the disease
and the wars
and the housing
and the filth
and the fear.
God,
imagine the state of Christianity and dentistry!!!!

Life's Pages
14-September-2001 07:12 pm

The sun is in the sky. It is bright and clear and shining down on the earth. A bird flies by with the simple grace that only a flying bird possesses. The wind blows through the now coloured leaves, whispering hello and goodbye in an instant.

I walk to get the mail. It is warm and uneventful. Cars roll by, I wave and they wave back at me. Men pound nails into the roofs of the new houses, and wipe their brows and drink water.

The grass is yellow and dry beneath my feet. There has been no rain for so long. The boats on the lake look forlorn. Their end is near. They will be put away until next summer.

Fall is falling. Winter waits just over there, I can see its breath over the mountains. The patience of winter, how it waits its turn never ceases to amaze me year after year. And spring is crouched neatly behind winter, waiting its turn, and then summer and fall and winter again.

Life is turning its pages. Too many to read, and I am too tired to try.

Like the Sun in the Morning and the Moon at Night

25-September-2001 05:47 pm

The world is moving through space like it always has, and I don't need to tell you how many tragedies it has witnessed in its time. Millions and billions and then some more. There is no punishment for the evil done, and no reward for the goodness and kindness and innocence of the wonderful people.

I truly do believe in peace. I believe it starts with peace of mind. You can't change the world, but you can change yourself. For the most part you don't even have to change, it comes to you like the sun comes to you every morning. It comes to you like the moon comes to you every night. It ebbs and flows. It blooms and withers. It falls and gets up again, life does. Change does. It will come to you while you sleep and give you lines on your face. It will dry and break your bones, and steal your breath. It will take your teeth one by one and make your blood thin. And the funny, fantastic part is this: you won't even notice. You will just simply be old and wise and grey and peaceful. You won't remember yesterday, and how you looked or who you were, you will only know the day, the moment, the second, nothing else. You are here.

All the terrible things will fade. All the wonderful things will glow.

When IT Happened...

14-October-2001 02:26 pm

I see people worrying their lives away right now. Sick with it. Filled with it. Consumed with worry. We should be consumed with wonder, but we are not. Wonder has succumbed to "wondering when" now. I will tell you this; the world is not what it looks like on TV. The world is still beautiful. We don't see much of that you have to remind yourself of everything good and by God, there is more good than bad. Goodness will prevail.

Where the Wind Takes You

17-October-2001 06:25 pm

There are 200 geese drifting listlessly on the lake. They are in small groups, discussing nothing, just floating and paddling. They are what peaceful is. Sweet pea is looking out the kitchen window at them, her head occasionally cocked to one side, pondering what indeed these fuzzy floaters are. They are all drifting north with the wind. They just let it take them; they don't resist and try to stay in the same place. They just go. There is a lesson in that. When you watch the real true living things you see how easy it can be. I let shrodie out a half hour ago and he is in the grass at the shoreline, waiting for one of them to get close enough to kiss...yeah, right. I have to go and grab him, I shall return.

Okay, now that we have doused each other in the laundry-room sink to wash muddy paws, we can continue with this. God, that was a rodeo, and I don't know who won.

I can see myself on an old bicycle, racing down a narrow tar road. I am 10 years old and the world is a good place. Leonard is flanking at my right, and Dale is ahead of me to my left. We have a pack of hounds galloping behind us, tongues dragging between their thin furry legs. We are going nowhere to do nothing. We have made no plans other than to pedal up the hills and let them pull us down them. Bugs in teeth that go unbrushed on this summer morning. No time for that. I have a silver knife in my pocket that my dad gave me. It is my secret treasure. No one can use it, save for me. I have gum in the other pocket, soft and pink and it too is a secret, although I share it later with the boys. We chew it all, and slurp up the sticky, gobby mess like little hungry birds. Dubble bubble. I love my mother for buying a hundred pieces that will never see the light of a Halloween that is only a few days away. You can't imagine how excited we are about going door to door and getting as much candy as we can (I later find out that in Springbank circa 1972, you have to sing for your treats! Unthinkable!!!). The wind is easy, and the sun makes us see the road wobble and fly ahead of us. It's more like a dream than a dream. The clouds are all bears and lions and buildings. We look up at them long enough to scare ourselves to death, and then back to pedalling like mad. We will never be old. We will never die. We will never get sick or sad or cry about friends getting married. We never knew anything. We didn't need to. We were busy letting the wind take us with her, and we were so happy to go.

jann

What We Do To Each Other—Part 1

25-October-2001 11:18 am

I am lucky. So very lucky, I somehow cannot get my head around the luckiness. I am Canadian. I come from a place where passiveness is a custom. Where apologies are a salutation. I am a Canuck.

What We Do To Each Other—Part 2

25-October-2001 11:18 am

I do not like people. I stood on the corner of Yonge and Dundas today for a half hour. I watched people spit constantly. I watched people throw garbage everywhere. I watched as people yelled about God and the coming of Jesus and the end of the world. I watched them all swearing and begging and yelling and hating. I don't like us at all. I don't understand the lot of us. I want to disappear somewhere, and I don't know where that is.

Early Morning on the Road—extended version
31-October-2001 12:20 am

Thank you for coming to the shows. I see your outline in the dark, and I am grateful. I see the reflection of your glasses and hope they are not binoculars. I hear you cheer and I rejuvenate. I hear you clap and I smile with such reward. I hear you laugh and I know that high school was worth the pain (I loved high school). I try to see you and hear you and feel you. I try to wonder where you are from and where you are going.

I am tired now. It's 3:05 am, and I should go to bed. I am wired. I feel like I am on speed or crack or junk or a lot of coffee. Thank you for coming to the shows, and listening to the lot of us. I will remember you.

Hit the Ditch
03-November-2001 10:15 pm

There are so many geese out on that lake of mine. Hundreds. I bet there'll be some poops to dodge out there for quite some time.

I myself like goose shit.

Where the Day Takes You

10-November-2001 03:27 pm

So many things to say, and I don't know what they are.

It Looks Like I Feel

19-November-2001 01:43 pm

It is grey and quiet and cool here. It looks like I feel, which is not a bad thing at all. I feel quiet and complacent. I feel lazy and guiltless and heavy and weak and good. It may not seem like a group of well-adjusted words, but in all honesty, it's the perfect combination of simplicity and serenity. I am content to just be here and think about what it is that I am.

Hard To Know

23-November-2001 02:50 pm

Christmas lights are spattered through the neighbourhood. I still had some strung on the deck from last year. Good idea that...leave 'em up I say.

Life Never-Ending

03-December-2001 12:09 am

I think that groups of souls travel together. In every life, we've known each other. Groups of souls that recognize each other through just a simple glance. I know you, you think to yourself, and they in turn acknowledge the recognition. You feel it when you are reunited with an old adversary, a foe, a friend, a lover, a mother. It is a great and wonderful gift. To remember somehow who you were and are.

I have had the same friends in my life for over 35 years. 35 years. Hard to fathom. I knew them, I know them, and they know me. They are bound to my soul, as I am to theirs. The most exciting, thrilling part of my life is finding the lost souls that seek me too, to find me, and I to find them. Oh to be found! What glory!

It's nice to think of a group of souls together. Bound. It gives me solace to know that we are all going together through the bitter sweetness of life never-ending. I feel emptied out, but that is a good thing. It gives one room to fill up again.

The Sound Of

07-December-2001 05:50 pm

The house is quiet. There are creaks in the stairs, that's all you hear, that and the cat purring, a clock ticking, and the dryer throwing the towels around. I love the sounds of silence. The sounds of nothing. The little nothings that make life liveable. Oh to be! Sounds that make you remember lost days. Bruised legs and snotty noses and a goldfish in a bowl. Easy, careless, endless days. Where the sun hardly ever sets on you. It just lingers in the sky like a dream you can't wake yourself out of. Sounds that form your past. Imagine a blind man's memories...how clear they must be. A single sound that paints the most beautiful picture. A sound with colour and shape and mass. If we could only hear each other, there would be no terror, no Palestine, no Israel, no toppled buildings, no war, no hate.

If we could only listen.

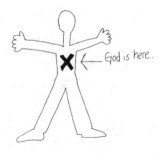

Out In The Cold

13-December-2001 06:04 pm

I drove by my old friend's last night after leaving the diner; the one dying the sad and lonely death of drug addiction. I didn't go in. I just drove slowly by, peering up into her windows. I felt odd about doing it. NO lights on. Not one.

I then pulled around the alley and looked through the sheer curtains on the little worn-out door at the back. I didn't actually go up to it, I rolled the window down and just stared at the motionless withering house and felt bad; the cold air pouring in making me more aware than I wanted to be.

I still knew the house. She still lives there, after all these years—over twenty.

Heavens...I have moved so many times, maybe that's why I find it bizarre that anybody stays in any one place any more. Sounds like a Carole King song. I haven't done anything about her yet. I haven't phoned. Well, she has no phone, it's been cut off like everything else in her pathetic life. I don't know what to do actually.

I am at a loss. I am so afraid to see her. I am afraid that she'll pull me in through the little worn-out back door with the curtains, surrounded with her drug-infested friends, and hold me hostage...how's that for an imagination?? I am afraid that they'll inject me with something, and demand that my parents give them keys to my house. Now there's a story to pass on to the grandchildren. I wonder about my mind most days, but this one day in particular is really making me laugh out loud.

Honestly. I am not at all prepared for her and her problems. Part of me wants to just see her die. Yes, I am saying it. Part of me does. I don't know what part. A dark one for certain. I feel like she is dead already, just her body is still going onward. It doesn't know that it's dead. Drugs strike me that way. What the fuck do I know.

Anyway, I drove off, rolled up the window, and felt emptiness pour into the car, just like that cold air did.

I wondered where she was.

I wondered if she was sleeping.

I was hoping that she was sleeping.

I doubt she has slept in years.

I feel it somehow.

As I drove down the narrow snow-covered alleyway, I stopped the car so suddenly that I scared the groceries in the passenger seat. I saw the most beautiful white rabbit, frozen in its tracks. It was waiting for me to do something. It was hoping that it hadn't been seen. I pretended that I did not. I shut the lights off and watched that gorgeous ball of fuzz hop off into the darkness.

I wanted to cry. I thought of her, my old friend, and I was ripped between the beauty and the ugliness that make up a person's life. And I knew that I wouldn't trade the sadness for anything in the universe. It is what we are. Stardust and ashes and then quiet.

jann

Mental Exercises

16-December-2001 02:54 pm

The wind is ferocious. The windows are clanging and branches are snapping and what is left of the snow is ripping across the frozen lake.

I am having coffee and debating whether or not I am going to work out. Of course I am I say! No you're not...take a rest; you worked out the day before yesterday. Better go down there, or you'll end up bedridden and bloated from eating a bad batch of Twinkies. Oh, just take it easy it's Sunday! Get going damn you!!

So, I am sitting having a debate with my own head. Endless entertainment. Endless joy and interest. I should go back to bed and wait it out I suppose.

Anyway, I had best go work out. My sensible side won out, thank heavens.

Have the Time

20-December-2001 03:53 pm

I have some time to myself. Hard to know what I will do with it. Time seems to have a mind of its own. I bow to it more than I probably care to think I do. Such is life. I would rather just tip my hat, but alas, I must get down on all fours and kiss its tiny feet.

Time tells us what is good. Time tells us what will last.

We cannot know what is good or lasting until time goes by and shows us what is left standing there.

Time tells us what music is indeed timeless...Time tells us how good people were. How grand their actions, or how small and harmful.

Time is a wise healer and a wicked foe. Time is fast and slow, depending on who or what you are waiting for... Time with a lover? Well, that will blast by. A doctor? Well, that will certainly drip like molasses on a very cold day. Time will fade the famous and spoil grand food. Time will bend seasons around each other like kite string. How long is time? Where does it go when it goes? Is it a straight line, or does it bend through the universe and back over us again and again? It could be anything.

Time will tell us all the things we were wrong about in a thousand years. Only we will not be the recipients of that weary news. We will be long gone...or here again and again.

Hard to say.

Time will tell us how silly we were, how barbaric, how archaic. It is hard to imagine what time will bring our way. It is not easy to fathom the road ahead. I am fearful and excited all in the same moment. It feels like a kiss you have thought about in your dreams, and when it finally comes, you are so lost that you don't know who you are or what just happened. So you know, from that kiss at least, that wonderful kiss, that only the moment has any value.

Only the moment holds any truth. Not the past, not the future, but only the present second in which you breathe and breathe and breathe again.

You are not what you did, but what you will do.

You are not what you did, but what you will do.

You are not what you did, but what you will do.

Remember that, if only that. You are always new.

You are a flag on a windy day, moving constantly but never really getting anywhere. That is life. Back and forth. Back and forth. Oh, but the wind in your sails through your heart in your clothes and hair and mouth!!! That makes it all worthwhile.

Time will wither that flag. Time will fade it and break it down, shred its edges and fray its stings. But what a trip to fly, and what a sight to see it there. Pieces will rip away and soar into the atmosphere. Pieces of you and me.

Out there travelling while you are still at the end of that

pole. Moving with the wind. While the rest of you becomes something else. Part of the trees or the ocean or a bird's nest.

We are everywhere and everything. I am looking up at the night right now. The lake is still the lake, but it's so still, so frozen. It's all about time and what it does and what it is. We are time itself. And it never runs out. It just is. That must be true for everything I think.

Shrodie did not last long outside. He is sleeping now. I am sure he never worries about how much time he has. He just is. I wish I were him. I wish I knew that freedom.

That is what I want for Christmas.

jann

So Glad To Be Home

23-December-2001 08:37 pm

They say it will not snow at all in the next few days. Double damn! It would just look so great to have those big slow-motion flakes floating down from the heavens. The kind you catch on your tongue. The kind the cats watch stream by the windows, little paws poking at mid-air. The kind that fill the shakers with scenes of snowmen in hats and Jesus in a manger. Falling.

I have everything wrapped. Love those fucking gift bags. And yes, I do want them back after you've opened them. That's just the way it has to be. My mom always says, I suppose you want your bag back? And I say, yes I most certainly do. Well I want MY bag back then she says. It's all quite funny. Very serious, but funny.

Well, off to do as little as possible. Wish gram were here. She was the sweetest of all peas.

Come and Gone

28-December-2001 02:49 pm

Christmas has come and gone. The lights are a bit dimmer
and the pace a bit slower. I am relieved. The anticipation of
something so elusive, so misunderstood, leaves me tired and
wondering why a lot. The tradition, the pageantry, the cere-
mony, the ritual. Christmas is about family and connecting
and being together. That part I love. That part I hang on to
with all my might. There are so many without family.
Mothers gone. Fathers gone. Sisters, brothers, lovers gone.
The aloneness must take away one's own beating heart. I
can't imagine.

Someday I will be alone. My parents will have left the
world, and I will have to begin to build my own rituals, my
own traditions. I am dreading them selling their house. They
say they will in two years. They will move. I wonder what
will happen to my initials in the concrete by the fire pit?
Will they dig up all the dead dogs we've buried over the
years? Will they find my time capsule from 1972 and wonder
what in heaven's name it all means? Will they plough the
house into the ground and build over 35 years without a second thought? Who will live on the land? What will happen
to all the time we spent living in that place? I hate to think
about it at all.

What about the road we soared down on bikes and

skates and horses and cars and legs running? Will they tear it up and cover the top with concrete and wire? Will they remember what and who was there all that time? I doubt it. I will always live there in my heart. Always. Home will never be anything else but that place. 85th street is burned into my soul more than any other thing or place ever will be. When I was immortal and life never ended, and parents never died, and I would never die, and we would always be together.

I am clinging to this Christmas. Gram gone somewhere good I pray. I am hanging on to my mother's laugh and my dad carving turkey and Pat and Rhona and the kids running about and Charlie sitting in the chair not saying a word scratching his lotto tickets.

I am grasping at the invisible threads that have bound my life together, and I am wondering what the future will bring.

I have suddenly grown up. I am my own. The past is gone. The moment is lingering like a kiss. And we all know kisses don't last forever...

jann

Words—Part I

31-December-2001 07:52 pm

Took the poor ole dead tree down. Swept up a million dead needles and put a thousand glass balls and shiny stars and fat cherubs with harps and little soldiers and diamond-eyed cats all into a box marked "Christmas decorations." Downstairs they all went until I open up that lid a year from now. I'll be saying to myself, my God, a whole year gone by again.

Time doesn't float any more, it descends like a 747, hitting every bump on the way down. Some people love turbulence though, it calms them down somehow. My assistant Janine loves turbulence. She's a riot to fly with; the whole experience is quite liberating really. I figure if she loves it that much it can't be all that bad. She sleeps. I look at her in amazement, gripping the seat and praying silently, and she sleeps. Lord Gordon!

AAAAAhhhhhhhhhhhh...the New Year. Thank God we don't celebrate every new moon. I don't make resolutions. I used to but I never ever kept them. I think I shall resolve not to resolve.

Words, so powerful, so mighty. I love what they do. I am my words. I think I am not, but I am. YOU DO become what you say. That is the power, the mightiness, the urgency of words. Not as simple as we think—words. Speak horrid words, think horrid thoughts...you will become them.

Words, they carry a heavy weight. They are the dream we make. The life we live. The things that keep us from being who we are.

Words—Part II
31-December-2001 07:52 pm

You are a snowflake. A single one floating down from the same cloud and melting into the same puddle of water. So, enjoy your uniqueness while you are floating down, one of a kind, before returning to the fold of the many. This is your time here on the planet. You deserve to be happy. Now be happy. Think good things. I swear to you, it is the silent end-less prayer for the living, and it works miracles.

God bless you all.

Love and health and peace and life.

A Million Shards

05-January-2002 06:52 pm

Shrodie is following me from room to room wondering what I am doing. He sits here by the computer and watches me type. Bumping my hands to pet him. He is watching the kids skate. His little head goes back and forth and back and forth. He is a little man some days, and a wild beast on others. He does not like his bum touched, who does?

I dreamt about tofu because of this show that I watched about China last night. I dreamt about tofu all night long. At one point I made an effort to say to myself, stop dreaming about tofu and go to sleep. Not at all effective.

Could You Sign This For Me?

09-January-2002 03:47 pm

I have spent the last two days in the emergency with mom. They could not get her heart in rhythm for love or money. Poor thing had to get the old "electrical shock device" thing. I don't think I have ever been so scared. Anyhow, they finally drugged her up like a Colombian coke lord and sent us home. Yesterday we had to go up again. God, I'll be glad when this is all over with.

I can't tell you how bizarre the waiting room was. There was a guy named Dave from New Orleans that was hammered out of his ever-loving mind...he was actually panhandling while waiting to be treated for whatever the hell he had. There was a sorry young bloke nearly cut his thumb off with a skill saw...jeeze...he was as white as Janet Jackson's teeth. He must have sat there for two hours waiting to be stitched up, and was still there when we left about 4 hours later, lying on a table having a bit of rest at least. I guess there were more important cases ahead of him... His thumb must have healed itself in the time it took. They had a moaning old lady on oxygen and a young guy with his head wrapped up in gauze and one Indian girl hollering that she "NEEDED TO PEE AND THAT SHE HAD FUCKING WAITED LONG ENOUGH YOU FUCKING BASTARDS   #$$%%^&&^*$%@   #^#$%^&%$#@^%%&

^#%$^&^#%." It got worse.

Mom had me do a walk-by to see if it was a man or a woman. "Pretend you're going to the bathroom, jann, and see who it is."

Still so bloody funny, lying there on her deathbed, so funny. I did it though, and we did laugh about that for what seemed to be an hour. They called security and we never heard another peep out of her (not my mother, but the pee lady). As I waited out there among the throngs of the sick and weary, people slowly came up to me as I paced back and forth waiting for mom, and said that "they knew who I was and could I sign something for them?"

I mean I AM in an emergency ward, pacing back and forth like an expectant father, looking worried to say the very least, but whatever...??? It reminded me of gram's funeral, signing autographs and getting my crying head and heart picture taken. Oh well.

I have to remind myself of everything good about what I do, and furthermore, that people's intentions are good, just misguided and ill-timed. My own mother would have said, "Well, it wouldn't have killed you to sign their little piece of paper."

No mom, it would not have so by God, I signed every last one of them.

jann

Every Word

15-January-2002 01:05 pm

It is 11:23 pm on Monday night. I have been reading your e-mails for 3 hours. I still have a few to go through. I don't even know what to say. I can't believe the things people tell me about themselves. I feel honoured and humbled. I feel empty and full all at once. I feel like I am a puddle and a river and a drop of water. I read the words and try to understand them. I try to understand why it is that people write to me... Because of the music? Because of our common failures? Because of love? Just because is good enough for me. Thank you.

We all have lives that we are trying to piece together. My life is no different. I do the best I can. Fame is a fleeting empty thing. I know that. I live that. I remember that every time I lay my head down at night. I pray all the time for guidance. I pray that someone hears me. Just like you pray. We hope that someone hears us. I love the idea of that. Prayer is all I really have. It is the glue to my soul and my heart. It is the confession that I purge at the end of every day. It makes me want to keep going. I don't care who God is. He is. I am just going to keep talking in my head to Her.

Fuck am I tired. I should go to bed. I thought I would do this now as I am starting to write tomorrow and I am nervous as to what I am going to find in there...my head that is...

or my soul? I don't know if I'll have time tomorrow to do this, so now is the moment. I don't have a clue where it all comes from, the songs I mean, they just do. I am tired of trying to figure it out. I am trying to write when I can. I don't always feel like it. Sometimes I just feel so quiet. Even typing sounds loud and horrible.

jann

On the Tip of My Tongue
18-January-2002 07:32 pm

The ice is not safe. It has been so warm here. It makes me nervous watching anyone, never mind the kids, skate or walk on it. I don't know if I would jump in after them if they were to suddenly break through...I think I'd scream a lot. My mom said to push out a ladder. What ladder? I don't own a ladder. That's what she would do, she said. Send out a ladder. I have a footstool. Would a footstool work? How about an extension cord? Well, as long as it's not plugged in, she said. I figured as much, I said. You never know with you jann, she said.

Matters of the Heart

21-January-2002 06:30 pm

Oh the heart. What a thing it is. So full of love and fear and blood and grief and nerves and fatigue and joy. The heart holds an endless sleepless ocean. It pounds the shores and grinds the pebbles into sand. It wears itself down to nothing. Just when you think it will not beat one more day, it does. So you have to keep thinking and feeling. Our humanity is our thoughts. Our secrets. Our language. Our dreams. Our humanity is our words. Our tears. Our humiliation. Our shame. Our sin.

A cat can sleep all day and not feel guilty about it.

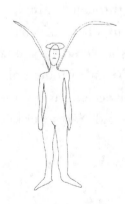

Floating on the Wind

22-January-2002 06:47 pm

It is a black day here, in my head at least. Black and slow like an old sad movie. I am playing the part of the heroine, and I am dying from some unknown disease, and my lover cannot find me, because I do not want to be found. I hear my name being called; it is floating on the cold wind. A long drawn-out

JJJJJJJJJJJJJAAAAAAAAAAAANNNNNNNNNNNNNNN.

Only I have changed my name to Pepsi. So I don't answer.

Chair on the Moon—Part 1

23-January-2002 03:35 pm

The two houses across the lake are almost finished. Funny thing building a house. It's people building lives I suppose. Every nail signifies a day. Every board an incident or a memory. We build houses so that we can live our lives in them. We gather up all our things and put them around us to say to ourselves that we are indeed here.

I often picture the world from the moon. All of us racing around doing tasks, endless tasks, never asking ourselves why we do them. We hardly notice each other. And when we do notice each other, we are so amazed that we have feelings and that we care, we think it's a breakthrough, when it's more like a breakdown. We break down our barriers so cleverly built up to hide ourselves from ourselves. We think we do it to protect ourselves from others. It is our own souls that we deny. We don't really want to see who we are. We drink and eat and work so we don't have to look too deeply or too long. I don't want to live in oblivion. I want to feel myself rise and fall and at some point, wither away like a deep sleep. It is how I choose to live.

I am not going to live what is expected of me, but what I create out of my own heart and mind. We make things happen. We dream them. We cause them. And others do the very same. They make their lives. Sounds good doesn't it?

And then I see the world from my chair on the moon, and I am dumbfounded by the pain, and the struggle, and the misery, and starvation, and I can hardly breathe. No one need live like that, but WE let them, because our walls will protect us. We let part of ourselves die, because we are them. They are us. It is not our problem.

If we knew we would never die, what would it change about humanity? Would we be worse or better?

It is in dying that we all become equal. No other thing will give us that level ground. Nothing in this world can. Only dying makes us the same. Our differences here kill us very slowly. Prejudice and hatred and religion. They all kill. Death lets us live again, with fairness, without colour, without pride. Free.

Chair on the Moon—Part II

23-January-2002 03:35 pm

Ten minutes into a new day, and I am already lying. Lord...

Footprints in the Snow

27-January-2002 07:59 pm

For two days, I have gone out to shovel my driveway, and for two days, two different men have appeared to help me with their snow blowers. They just slip out of a cloud of white onto my drive with a simple tipping of the toque, and proceed to clear away the piles of powder. They have huge smiles on their faces as they change the gears and roll their great machines back and forth like some kind of ballet, clearing away everything in their path. It's so nice of them. There are good people everywhere. Then, as quickly as they appeared, they disappear with a wave, down the road to the next house in search of more snow.

Imagine

06-February-2002 01:07 pm

I drove through Times Square the other day, and looking out the window of my cab on the way downtown, I saw a huge white sign on a building that quoted John Lennon. It said: Imagine all the people living life in peace. As I watched that go by, strains of my cab driver's whistling came slinking through the protective plastic cage into the back seat; he was whistling a beautiful Christmas carol. I thought it was the oddest of moments. I felt like I was in a German black-and-white film from 1948. It was one of those rare moments in life that leaves you wondering if life is actually real, and are you really actually alive? Or are you part of a giant dream that we share with the consciousness of the universe?

New York is not the same. I am so glad to be here again, seeing it all for myself. Today I am wandering down to the site. I need not say where that is as there is no point, you already know. I know it will be terrible. The mass grave that holds the thousands of hopeful hearts. Hopeful that they would have babies and see movies and travel and love their wives and husbands and be mothers and fathers and sisters and brothers.

Hopeful that they would count the sunrises and have hot dogs on Coney Island and go for Sunday-night drives to any-where but here. Hopeful that they would find something they liked to do in life and hear beautiful music and wish on stars falling and make love and read old books and sit in favourite chairs and close eyes to dream dreams. They won't now. Thousands of hopeful hearts scattered from here to Brooklyn to China to California to the Queen Charlotte Islands to Cuba and back around again. Thousands of hopeful hearts dusting the planet with loss and gratitude that WE are still here and that WE did not perish and that it was not US who died. That is human I am afraid. As human as human can be.

These days I think it may be wise to pray. On your knees. On the ground. With purpose and with thanks.

The world has been here for millions of years and we have managed to practically destroy everything in it and on it in about a few thousand of them.

I will never forget seeing that sign and listening to that man whistle. Everything slowed down. My heart slowed down, my breath, my thoughts. I hung on to a moment and knew that every moment was just that special. Every moment needed to be slowed down. Every moment needed to be wrung of its essence and folded up neatly for the next day. New York is quiet. It is eerie. Perhaps the people here think it is pretty normal, that it seems like its old self. But it is quiet. Sad. The lights don't sparkle quite as bright, the singing is not as high and clear, the stores not as eager to take your money from you. It has ghosts wandering the streets looking for buildings that are not there any more. Just like that.

Imagine all the people living life in peace. I hate to say it, but I doubt that in my lifetime or any other we will live life in peace.

jann

Cleaner Than

17-February-2002 12:54 pm

Saturday night, and I ain't got nobody...I just had some kind of chicken sausage and a can of beans. It was actually not all that bad. Sometimes you just gotta open a can and eat with your mouth open. I have on my favourite pyjamas and I am about to slip into bed to finish reading Anita Diamant's The Red Tent. Pretty good book. I certainly know enough about "biblical periods" to last me a lifetime. I did wonder from time to time what indeed women did on the new moon. Now I know. Boy do I ever know. I have to say that the tampon is a small miracle. I had a friend growing up whose mother always said that tampons were for married people. What the hell? How the fuck big were the tampons in that house?

Took my car/truck/what-have-you to a coin-operated washer thing. I nearly blew my lid off with the power nozzle. Sweet mother of God!!! I wasn't quite ready for that kind of power. The "foam brush" was right out of a Peter Sellers movie—and it too was out of control. I laughed my fricken head off in there, all by my lonesome. The foam was shooting out of there like a bad date. I am cleaner than a nun's undies now.

A Busy Streak

18-February-2002 12:58 pm

I have a busy streak closing in on me. I watch it creep into my every thought. I pack and unpack my suitcases in my sleep. I am getting ready for the rush of sounds and lights and constant talking and constant attention. You have to prepare for that. It takes your breath and sits on it for months at a time. I am apprehensive. I am eager and nervous. I want to go and I want to stay. The stage is not my life. You have to keep most of yourself in a box somewhere when you're on it. If you don't, it'll take you and make you hopeless and untrue. You won't remember your life or your friends or your own heart. It is a fine balance. Two worlds— one real and one not. Which is it? That is the trick one has to master every day. The life and the dream. Making one the master and one the slave.

I can hear the wind whining. It's haunting. I know that it's some kind of song, but I can't make out the words. Just as well.

Heavenly

20-February-2002 07:46 pm

Pick-up time for radio press that morning was a dashing wondrous 5:30!!! Needless to say, I was a bit blurred. May as well have been drunk. Nothing like morning radio and its various shenanigans to get you thinking that you'd rather be sleeping. I do however love doing those shows. Good people, good fun and besides, I got a brand-new Frosted Flakes plastic watch. It seems to be working a whole day later. God, couldn't it be morning still around noon?

What a nice day. Shrodie caught a mouse. It's at the front door until I get on some rubber gloves and have a proper funeral. My cousin Tommy and I always played funeral. We had a blast. Saying the prayers and all the moaning going on. It was a sign of things to come I guess. We were always happy to have a little bird to bury rather than an old mouse. A squirrel was heavenly. Anything that had some size to it was all the better.

You don't think of death as anything permanent when you are a kid. Everything is just sleeping. It will just get up and walk away while you're sleeping. When you find out that that is not the case, that little things and people die, you are not young any more. It is the end of innocence.

Cheese, Pickles and Yahtzee

25-March-2002 04:54 pm

The weather has changed every day. It is summer and then it is the dead of winter and then it is everything in between. I brought all the wrong clothes. I have two puffy vests and one toque that says "new york fuckin city" on it. Lots of socks. That's it.

I feel like a four-year-old packed my bag for me. Man, that hat. It was six dollars. I keep wondering what people are looking at as I pass them in the street. And then I realize that I am a walking profanity. I quite like it.

I had a wonderful friend come up from New York to see the show two nights ago. She had a great time. Brought us all Krispy Kreme donuts. Some of the boys had never had one. I had two.

God help me.

Not a Rock At All

28-March-2002 06:06 pm

The wind blew me over the island of Newfoundland today.
We went, the seven of us, in a rental van to the most easter-
ly point in North America, they tell me, to look out over the
sea. The rain blasted us sideways and the waves crashed into
the rocks like drunken men in the pubs do here. There is
more beer than there is sense and more good people per
capita than anywhere else on the planet. There are more
"God bless YOUs" said in a single day than I have ever heard
in a year any place else.

I love it.

Houses are painted with adventure and a little genius
here and there. Pink and red and yellow and bright boy blue.
The Maritimes are colour and more colour. Art hangs on
every wall. Every nook is a memory here. Every one notable.

Not a rock at all.

A big beautiful ship heading out to sea every morning
and back home to the harbour at night. I saw the world's
saddest sweetest graveyard. Lopsided stones with long-gone
names worn out by the sun and the water and the wind.
Little houses that serve as churches on Sunday when a cross
is hung on the back door. Old boats washed up onto the
rocks that serve as a reminder of how big God is.

This is a wonderful place. It's full of people talking a new language. I say pardon me ten times a day, and I can't wait for the dear soul to repeat what in the heck he said. It rolls off of their tongues like rum and lime on a hot day.

You stand on the cliffs and look out at time and you realize how silly it is to count it. You have to just weather it. You have to just stand and watch it and try not to get it caught on the sleeve of a sweater for fear you'll be dragged away.

Part of me will stand here, and be watching the waves for the rest of this life.

jann

Let it Soar

05-April-2002 04:56 pm

You can smell it on people's clothes as they pass you in an aisle of a grocery store. Their distinct unhappiness. The trail of discontentment. We all have shadows that follow us our whole lives long. We all have the voices that tell us we are no good. When you add another voice to that drone, it can really overpower you. That is how a boyfriend or a husband or a girlfriend or a wife can undermine who you are. They will prey on your own voice, the one that is never quite sure what it is doing. If they are doing anything short of encouraging you, it is a tragedy, an injustice to the human spirit.

Oops

09-April-2002 04:02 pm

I just erased everything I wrote. Holy crap. Holy f***ing shitting hell. G. D. Christ almighty. You get my drift. I hit the fu##ing shift button. Well, this will be short then, because I have things to paint.

Apparently George Clooney was staying in my hotel. I bet they said to him, hey, you're staying in jann arden's hotel.

Forget I said that.

Hello To Wally

16-April-2002 12:25 pm

I want to say hello to Wally. He was a young lad who waited endlessly for an autograph or two, and a ticket to go see the show. He apparently waited 8 hours at a mall for a chance to win tickets, and dialled a radio station a million times to no avail. Niks had three spare tickets for one reason or another, and she told me to give them to him. It honestly made me want to bawl. He was so touched. It was like seeing Willy Wonka and the chocolate factory for real. I will never forget his face and how happy he was. Wally made me remember what music is. Why I do it. What the magic is. How important people are. Relationships are paramount. There is no other meaning in life but US.

Old Memories

17-April-2002 05:19 pm

When you leave someone, you hope that somehow they will never ever get over you. You do. You hope that you will leave a hole in their life that never grows over, and that the wind always blows through it, that there is a kind of whisper that lives in their bones repeating your name over and over again.

I know of a few people that have done that to me over these past 20ty years. They never go away. They leave behind an arm or a leg...or a lip. You hear them inside of you, taunting you, making you ache. It feels so bad that it kind of feels good. You know for sure that the lost love continues to twist inside of you. Eventually, you learn to live with all the people rattling around your heart at night.

With the Wave

19-April-2002 03:38 pm

I had a pacemaker for 17 years, and I seem fine (I had them take it out three years ago...long long story). It was the size of a small car, and set every airport security guard running in my direction. No more of this, I said to myself one day. My doctor agreed that its time had come and gone. Out damn spot!! The first night without it, I phoned mom to say good night. She said that if she didn't hear from me, she would assume that I didn't make it through the night. I said, Dead you mean??? Yes, she said, dead.

History Lessons

03-May-2002 02:06 pm

History will tell us what was good. It will tell us what was terrible and what indeed was lasting. History can tell us who we were and are with greater ease and precision than the present ever will. We are what we do, not what we say.

History will give us music that was important and vital and brilliant. The present cannot do that. History will tell us what decisions were the right and just ones. Today is unable to do so. To look back is the greatest of lessons if we apply it to looking ahead. We see clearly that war accomplishes—nothing. Less than zero, and yet we continue with great purpose to fight. My God is bigger than your God. Allah. Yahweh. Jesus. Mary. Buddha. Jehovah. Krishna. There is but one God. He is your vision, not anyone else's. She is your idea, not mine. Mine is mine. NO right. NO wrong. Omnipotent. Everywhere. Everything. One white flag. One God.

It seems we have, with madness, severely split the vote. No clear winner here. God has been voted out.

Duck Bums and Fowl Language

05-May-2002 02:21 pm

Some kids just walked across my back lawn. They are peering in as if they are trying to catch a glimpse of me sitting here writing. I don't even know if they know that this is even my house. I hope not. They have paused a long while... Should I run out there and scream like an old crazy lady and scare them all half to death? Nude even? That would be good fun.

I'll probably move next summer. I'd like an acreage. I think mom and dad may build on it with me. It would be nice for all. Mom says I'll have a house for all my servants when they die... She really is something else. You did say that mom, if you're reading this at Ronnie's (my parents don't have a computer, but they check the site when they visit friends). I got shit the other day for saying fuck so much. Whoops.

where I live

Snow Day

06-May-2002 08:31 pm

I woke up inside of a cloud. White mountains of crystal ice. It looks like a wonderful dream sequence in a romance movie. I keep hoping Clint Eastwood will ride out of the mist on a chestnut stallion, rearing into the sky as he yells for me to get my things and leave with him for some far-off place.

GO WITHOUT ME CLINT!!!!

I HAVE TO FEED THE CATS!!!

I am a bit lost, but that's the road I'm afraid. No one is quite exempt from that little glitch. I am a bit lost. You hope someone finds you in time for dinner.

Your Last

07-May-2002 02:39 pm

There is literally a foot of snow, if not more, outside this window. I am NOT touching my driveway—fuck it. It can melt itself away. 3 people had heart attacks here yesterday shovelling. One guy died. Poor guy. You just never know...it could at least have been during sex...but no, shovelling...shit. Choking on KFC...but no...shovelling.

Every day is your last day. If you can think of it that way, I think you have a better chance at a happy life. This is my last day, who do I really want to be? What do I really want to do? Who truly are my friends? What do I like to eat? Who do I love? Who loves me? Who am I? What do I want to be?

Today is your last day.

I have a perfect chance to get it right.

Yesterday Again

12-May-2002 02:49 pm

I stuck a frozen pan of lasagne into the oven at 385. I have no idea how long it will take to re-cook itself. I don't want to talk to, or see, anyone. I don't want to walk or even lie down. I don't seem to know what to do. Up down, no way at all. I feel confused. It is a temporary predicament, but one I am not savouring no matter how short it may be.

I wish it were dark. The darkness, though, is hours away. I wish I were someplace else. Home is hurting me today. I guess it's because I don't really know how I feel at the moment, therefore, I know not where I am or where I want to be. I don't know how to be here. With you. Without you. There is no respite from living life. You do, or you do not. The movie is playing again. I am the only one in the theatre. The movie is black and white, and it's streaked with sounds of trains and sirens and wind blowing. It is always night, it is always in an alleyway, cats crashing into garbage cans in search of a meagre supper. It is always raining. You cannot see crying in the rain. We all take solace in that.

Flew all morning. Read the paper and have not a clue as to what is going on in the world. I read but didn't take note of a single sentence. Things are no clearer thirty-seven-thousand feet above ground.

I want out of myself for a moment I want to look back

and remember who I was to see who I am and what I have. I need chips and dip and gallons of cold beer. I need tea and shortbread. I need butter and popcorn from one of the big movie machines. I need warm water and skin surrounding my every breath. Smothering whispers and kisses that make your bones ache. Soft sounds of a familiar voice and for time to just go back to the way it was. The old house. The green leather couch. The path by the river and driving you home every night after night after night.

I know I cannot do any of that. Forward is the not knowing, that is why behind seems easier, and my heart tells me nothing of any use. It is sad and mournful. My heart cannot help me, only my good sense. I don't mind it somehow, the dreariness of my own self. The pitiful face I gaze at as I slather cream onto it, brushing teeth, heading for bed, reading book. Going back over the same paragraph again and again, because I am not here. I haven't been here for quite some time.

I should check the lasagne. It wasn't very good the first time, so I doubt somehow it has improved with age.

I know I haven't.

jann

Bittersweet

14-May-2002 03:01 pm

People seem to pour through my hands like water. I cannot hang on to anyone. I cannot seal the endless cracks my fingers make. They slowly leak out. I find myself looking at the ground, trying to see the faces, trying to pick out an eye or a hand. Just a puddle. A memory that dries up with the sun and the wind. It's romantic in a terribly painful way.

Bittersweet.

There are other times when the water overflows, and your hands cannot hold it all in. Those are good times. Those are the times you cling to.

Rainy Day Dreams

08-June-2002 05:01 pm

I am staying in all day. I am going to sit in the bath and stare up at the skylight, and think of all the things I want to be. I am going to make grilled-cheese sandwiches and tomato soup and popcorn and crystal light. I am going to order movies and watch soccer and cheer out loud here all by myself. I am going to sneeze and not cover my mouth. I am going to sit nude on the couch for at least 60 seconds and dry off without using a towel. I love doing that. I am going to chew all the pens in the house (if I can find one). I am going to feed the cats tuna out of a can. I am going to light candles and watch the sun go down. I am going to phone my mother (she was fast asleep an hour ago when I rang) and talk for half an hour. Why do people say fast asleep? Why fast? I am going to nap on and off and on and off again. I am going to phone my friend in New York and see what's new there. Poor old New York. Poor old world. Shrodie is watching the rain with me. His little head follows a single drop, and then he loses it and starts on another. I am going to read until I cannot keep my eyes open any more. I am going to pray until I fall asleep.

Fast asleep.

All is Well

03-February-2002 01:53 pm

Anyway, not much else new here. I am writing. All is well.

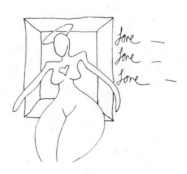

ALLISON HEWITT IS TRAPPED

ALLISON HEWITT IS TRAPPED

A ZOMBIE NOVEL

Madeleine Roux

St. Martin's Griffin ❧ New York

For my family

ALLISON HEWITT IS TRAPPED. Copyright © 2010 by Madeleine Roux. All rights reserved. Printed in the United States of America. For information, address St. Martin's Press, 175 Fifth Avenue, New York, N.Y. 10010.

www.stmartins.com

Book Design by Rich Arnold

Library of Congress Cataloging-in-Publication Data

Roux, Madeleine, 1985–
    Allison Hewitt is trapped : a zombie novel / Madeleine Roux.—1st ed.
        p. cm.
    ISBN 978-0-312-65890-8
    1. Young women—Blogs—Fiction.   2. Zombies—Fiction.   3. Blogs—
Fiction.   I. Title.
    PS3618.O87235A79 2011
    813'.6—dc22

                                                                2010037783

10 9 8 7 6 5 4 3 2

The New University of Northern Colorado
10 South Sherman Street
Liberty Village, CO 80701

August 3, 2108

The Witt-Burroughs Press
University of Independence
1640 Johnson Avenue NW
Independence, NY 12404

Dear Dr. Burroughs:

Let me first express my sincerest admiration for your continued interest in our humble university. Your devotion to high academic standards and the rebuilding of our great nation is to be commended. Secondly, allow me to direct your attention to a certain individual whom you may wish to add to your new book.

A colleague of mine mentioned that you are interested in publishing a collection of biographical essays of important personages from The Outbreak. Allow me to put forward a candidate for this exciting new venture of yours. How appropriate to commemorate the 100th anniversary of The Outbreak with an assemblage of inspiring stories dedicated to the memory of those brave souls to whom we are most deeply indebted. The individual I speak of is not widely known. In fact, I can say with some certainty that you will have never heard of this woman. I am, however, equally certain that you will quickly discover that her story is one that many of us can relate to. I feel that she, through her bravery and sacrifice, deserves a spot in your collection.

I can promise that this woman is held in the highest regard among our small community. Before her sad passing she was recognized as one of the foremost leaders and innovators in the state. While she is not as famous or recognized as individuals such as Simon Forrest, architect of the memorable Victory Gardens, nor as gifted or prominent as our current poet laureate Shana Lane, I feel strongly that Allison Hewitt deserves a place among the pantheon you wish to create. Her struggle, painstakingly catalogued during the very worst of The Outbreak, is a snapshot of the horrific danger and destruction caused by The Infected.

It has been my personal privilege and honor to re-create the record she left behind. We know now that she was taking advantage of SafetyNet—or SNet as it's more commonly referred to—the military's emergency, nationwide Internet service. As I'm sure you know, SNet allowed many of our armed servicemen and -women to organize, meet, and eventually turn the tide against The Infected.

I have only recently learned from my father's journals that Ms. Hewitt kept an online record of her journey during The Outbreak. Many hours of research were required to re-create Ms. Hewitt's adventures as the Web provider hosting her story had long ago taken down the blog to conserve space. Only through constant petitioning and many frustrating hours did I succeed in gaining access to these lost pages. I have, to the best of my knowledge, collected every one of Ms. Hewitt's postings and I have attached them for your perusal. I'm perfectly aware that including the entirety of Ms. Hewitt's story would be impossible, but I implore you to consider an abbreviated version of her story for your collection. Let her stand as a symbol of the public's struggle, to give a face to the faceless masses, and to endure as an example of the dear cost of survival. Her story, I think, is worth remembering too.

Best good wishes,
Professor Michael E. Stockton Junior

September 18, 2009—Heart of Darkness

They are coming.

They are coming and I don't think we will ever get out. If you're reading this, please call the police. Call them now; call the cops if there are any cops left to call. Tell them to come find me. I can't promise we will be here tomorrow or the day after, or the day after that, but tell them to rescue us before it's too late. Tell them to try.

If they ask for a name, tell them my name is Allison Hewitt, and tell them that I'm trapped. Allison Hewitt and five other missing souls are holding out in the break room of Brooks & Peabody at the corner of Langdon and Park. We are all in relatively good health. Most important: none of us are infected.

If they ask what exactly you mean by all that, tell them this: on the evening of September 15, 2009, just before closing time, the Brooks & Peabody shop on Langdon and Park was attacked by the infected. I don't know what else to call them. The infected? The damned? I guess I'm not sure if it's a virus or disease, but I know it spreads and I know the kind of destruction it brings.

Our phones don't work, not the landlines or the fax, and our cell phones began running out of batteries yesterday. No one thought to bring a charger to work or to keep one in the break room. Phil, my manager, swears there's a charger in the stockroom around back but that's all the way across the store from here and none of us are brave enough to try for it. I think eventually we'll become desperate and have to go out into the store. The food in here won't last forever and I never thought I'd be so sick of beef jerky. The only electricity we have comes from the emergency generators that Phil bought last year when the flooding was getting bad and everyone was worried about losing power during the end-of-school sale. I don't know where the wireless is coming from—it's something called SNet. I'd never used it before. It could be coming from the little row of apartments that sit on top of the store. Maybe someone is alive up there; maybe they're trying to contact you too.

We're living behind a solid, safe door. The lock is industrial grade. The safes are housed back here and the doors are very heavy and reinforced. It was the logical place to hide—no windows, a refrigerator with some food, and most of all *the very heavy reinforced doors.* I can't stress that enough, how much we rely on that door, how that one, metal door has come to symbolize, over only a matter of days, survival.

If there are no windows and only one door, you might ask, how do we know they are coming?

We know because of the security cameras. They must run on the emergency backup generators because they still work, and the one and only monitor to view the feed is in the safe room. The safe room is just off of the larger area with the table and chairs and refrigerator. Sometimes when I can't sleep I go sit in that room (it's not locked anymore, I don't think money will mean much now and none of us has even tried to steal any of it) and watch the monitor. Thank you, Brooks & Peabody, for installing those cameras. Those cameras allow us to see almost the whole store. The picture is black and white and not very clear, but I can see them, and I watch them scrape around the store, winding through the bookcases, passing the Mystery and Science Fiction sections, lumbering by the reading lights and bookmarks. They will not leave, not even after everyone in the store is gone or dead or becoming *one of them*.

What are they looking for? *What do they want?*

Sometimes I see them disappear out of frame and I know they're just outside the break-room door, moaning at the barrier, thumping their heads and their rotten fists against the steel. It's unfair, I begin to think, because the others are trying to sleep. What do they want? Do they think we'll answer the knocking and thudding? Do they even have the capacity to think, or is it something else making them claw at the door?

One of the other grad students in my apartment complex had a greyhound. His name was Joey. Joey was the nicest dog I think I've ever met. He was rescued from a racing track, from the kind of place dogs don't ever want to be, where they're abused and treated like objects. You can drive a car around a track day and night and it won't complain; greyhounds are the same way. They don't complain, not ever, they just look at you with those big, bottomless eyes and beg you to be nice, to show a little mercy if it's convenient. Joey didn't seem like the kind of animal that could hurt even an injured fly, but one day he bolted past me out the lobby door. I don't think there was even a foot of space but he just zipped right outside and into the yard. He had mauled a rabbit before I could even get his name out twice. He was so fast, so efficient, so completely unlike the couch potato Joey I had come to know.

It wasn't Joey that killed that rabbit, not really, it was his instinct, his prey drive.

Prey drive.

That's what waits outside our door, insane with hunger, driven forward not by intelligence or understanding but a blind, consuming need for what we have . . .

I'm trying to stay extremely calm. I hope I'm doing an okay job. In a weird way, it helps to write about it, to talk about it. Somehow that makes it less real. Now it's just a story I'm writing for you, a tale I'm spinning, and not a cold, vicious reality underpinning everything I do and say and think. It's nice for a change, to do something I want . . . And I think that's what I miss the most: making choices.

There aren't any choices to make anymore, just survival, just what needs to get done. Soon we'll have to go outside that door to get food. There are some bigger refrigerators and a dozen or so bags of potato chips out by the registers. We'll need to get to those soon. We don't have a choice. I didn't choose to be trapped with these people, these coworkers and strangers that I never wanted to know beyond their connection to a part-time job. I didn't choose to be taken away from my mom, the only family I have left. She's already sick and now I won't even get to be there at the end . . .

I was studying to be someone but that's over now. Now it's just these people I don't really know and the constant, crippling fear and the drive of the infected. I understand it, I suppose; I understand the reason those things groan and shuffle around outside the door, and the reason Joey murdered that rabbit. It's in our blood, in our hearts, the hunger, the ambition, the out-and-out need to survive. I just wanted to work here, to make a little cash, and now, suddenly, I will die here.

Maybe I'll write again. At least it's some small comfort to look forward to. I should close my laptop and get some sleep. I should stop staring at the glowing screen but it's hypnotizing and I can't look away. But I'll force myself to go to bed, to close my eyes and cover my ears.

They are coming.

They are coming and I don't think we will ever get out.

COMMENTS

anonymous says:

September 18, 2009 at 11:03 am

the city is overrun. chicago gone too. get out of the city, get out as fast as you can.

> **Allison says:**
>
> *September 18, 2009 at 12:08 pm*
>
> Overrun? You mean for good? How did you get out? Tell us if you find somewhere safe.

Luis Wu says:

September 18, 2009 at 1:36 pm

Hey Allison,

You still out there?

We have been checking on your blog silently so far. Can't disclose our location—sorry—as there are some marauding survivors about in our area. Take good care. Are you using SNet? That's the only network that seems to be up. Hope you manage to keep your head above the water.

> **Allison says:**
>
> *September 18, 2009 at 2:01 pm*
>
> I understand. Don't give yourselves away: stay safe and stay smart. SNet has had a pretty stable connection so far. Let's hope that doesn't stop anytime soon! Update me when you can.

September 19, 2009—Hatchet

For the most part we're not what you would call athletes. I'm not certain "survival of the fittest" really applies in this case, but only time will tell I suppose.

First there's Phil Horst. Phil takes the definition of meat and potatoes to the lumpy, Green Bay Packers–loving extreme. He's not just the manager, ho no, he's very much a gleeful retail sort of fellow. Most of us work here without complaint, going about our menial tasks with competence, but Phil is the only one who seems to really enjoy it. He loves this place. There is no limit to his enthusiasm for inane mystery novels and bestsellers. He's gulped down the Kool-Aid and can't wait to hand out free samples.

Phil, Philsky, is a big guy, tall and solid, but not particularly fast or agile. Imagine the captain of your baseball team, and now imagine him fifteen years down the line with kids, living on a steady diet of cheeseburgers and soda. Now imagine he believes himself to be the lovable papa bear and best chum of everyone he employs.

He has a habit of yanking up his pants by the belt, shimmying the hem up under his belly while drawing himself up like a Kodiak getting ready to attack. Primarily he does this when he's faced with an unpleasant request or annoying customer.

Phil's our own roly-poly spokesperson for Midwestern living. He's the type of guy you expect to see tailgating every weekend, the type of guy who says things like "drawring" instead of drawing and "donesky" instead of done. This has earned him the secret nickname of Philsky.

Sometimes I'm certain he and I speak different languages. Teach me your customs and your traditions, Oh Great Philsky, teach me the way of the domestic beer.

Believe it or not this man was a philosophy major.

It's good to know that if things ever return to normal, Brooks & Peabody will emerge with its managing staff completely intact. The two assistant managers are here with us too, spending most of their time huddled together over the same *Newsweek* we've all been reading over and over again. They too haven't had a hard time adjusting to our bizarre diet of junk food and diet sodas. It's familiar territory for them.

Janette is probably my favorite person to work with. She's laid back; she sipped the Kool-Aid and dumped the rest out in the trash. She and the other assistant manager, Matt, are nerds in arms. They're the only employees that actually see each other outside of work and although they're both married, I've always had this secret inkling that, were things otherwise, they would date. They give off that "You bother me so much but oh God take me" vibe that so many odd couples exude like an awkward, fumbling, sexually charged musk.

Matt is our resident discerning snob when it comes to books. Miraculously, he's never realized that having expertise in only one area of literature pretty much makes you ineligible for that position. But he's nominated and voted himself into the role and none of us have the energy or perseverance to pick a fight. He never outright sneers at other people's taste in books, he just has this one tendon that works in his jaw; he thinks you're a plebeian. It means he is secretly spitting all over the cover of whatever book you mentioned.

Neither Matt nor Janette is particularly out of shape, but I'd wager most of their adventures take place safely in their minds. I'm not sure if any of Janette's cosplay outfits involved a katana, but if so we could really use it now.

Holly and Ted are here too but they're not employees. They hang around in the store so often that I recognize them whenever they show up. I've helped them order enough stuff that I know their names and the kind of books they like to read, but otherwise we're strangers. Holly is a petite redhead, very quiet and mousy, with a little pattern of stars tattooed on the top of her right hand. She looks like a lot of the girls I grew up with as a child, the girls next door, but Holly is clearly going through her undergraduate rebellion phase. She and Ted dress almost identically and both of them have innocuous tattoos that aren't quite hard enough to be considered badass.

These two are dating, or are—more accurately—in a state of symbiosis. And so Janette and I have taken to calling them Hollianted. They are never apart. They are one word. We now call them this to their face, which they find a little insulting I think because they want desperately to be individuals and have meaningful identities. I've told them that when and if they can tear themselves apart for ten minutes we will consider assigning separate names.

"Until then," I told them over a meager lunch of salted peanuts and Crystal Light, "you're Hollianted."

I really don't think it's so mean. It sounds like a religious holiday to me. Janette agrees. We like to tease them by asking each other things like, "What are you getting your dad this year for Hollianted?" or "What are you giving up for Hollianted? I think I'll give up chocolate."

Ted is a Chinese exchange student. I couldn't for the life of me figure out why he chose Ted as his American name. Then he tells me his mother gave him teddy bears every year for his birthday, and that he has a huge collection of bears from all over the world at his parents' house in Hong Kong. Suddenly I see why he chose it. Alone in the U.S., starting college and living with a complete stranger in a ten-by-ten closet . . . I would choose a name with a warm association too.

Huh. I guess that would leave me with the name Emma or Hermione.

Ted is an undergrad studying biochemistry at the university. He has that look about him—the studious, terrifyingly intelligent look that we literature majors, even the grad student–level ones, fear. Like Phil, Ted seems to me like he's come from another planet. He mumbles formulas in his sleep. He says it helps him drown out the banging and groaning outside the door.

C-six, H-six benzene, A-G-two-O silver oxide, C-U-Fe-S-two copper iron sulfide . . .

Iron. That reminds me: we only have two weapons.

Two doesn't sound like much, but I'm actually impressed that we managed to find that many in this store. We don't even leave the box cutters in easy-to-reach places. Someone held up a bakery down the street with a pair of garden shears last year and ever since, Phil has been paranoid about keeping sharp objects hidden. This paranoia may have cost a few people their lives the other day. Thankfully, in the back storeroom I found a little treasure I had walked by and ignored for months and months. A fire alarm and a glass case with a bright red ax become part of the landscape after a while.

You just don't notice these things until there's screaming from every direction and windows shattering and blood creeping down the green and ivory–tiled aisles . . .

Well, I noticed it. I noticed it just in time. Phil put me on one of the most unpleasant tasks in the store: cleaning the storeroom shelves. The shelves go right up to the ceiling with about a foot-and-a-half gap between each one and they get unbelievably dusty after weeks of neglect. I have no clue where all the dust comes from, but 90 percent of it settles on these fucking shelves. Phil doesn't care that I have dust allergies; he won't make the assistant managers do the chore so it's me, only me.

Sending me to the back room probably saved my life. It put me by that fire alarm and just a few feet away from an old, forgotten ax.

When I sit and watch the monitors there's an infected creature I recognize. I recognize her for three reasons:

1) Her name is Susan. Because she was—*is*—a regular. She bought six copies of *The Shack*. Six. I shit you not. She is shaped like an old, bruised pear and she wears the ugliest pair of glasses I've ever seen; these babies would look more at home on the Hubble than a human face.

2) The Thing-Formerly-Called-Susan was in the Christian section when it all started. The floor-to-ceiling window behind her imploded, sending shards of glass the size of stalactites crashing onto the floor. I watched her try to run toward me, through Biography and Home & Garden. She didn't get very far. Some of the glass had hit her ankle and she was bleeding all over and limping. A gnarled, dripping gray thing came in the window and caught up to her, limping harder than Susan, propelled forward with a terrible kind of hungry speed. It draped itself over her neck and they fell to the floor. I saw clumps of her hair flying between the bookshelves and her blood seeping fast toward me across the grout in the tiles. The blood overtook the book she had been carrying and it tumbled out of her arms and landed with the spine mangled and open.

The Longest Trip Home.

3) Susan should have been dead. You don't lose that much blood, and that much of your neck, and walk it off. But she did exactly that. She just sort of shrugged off the decaying person on her back and got to her feet. Shuddering, she inflated like an accordion pulled up off the floor by its handle. Her legs straightened unnaturally and then she slumped down, hunched over with a big, raw hole torn down the side of her neck.

It's hard to remember too many details, but I know I could smell the coppery too-sweet stench of the figure at her back. Suddenly I didn't mind that she bought so many copies of *The Shack*. I wanted right then to take her up to the register and help her buy six more. But she slid past the book she had dropped, smearing her own blood across the floor with her feet, feet that were turned in too much. She was walking like a toy duck that had been hastily assembled by a two-year-old. Susan came at me, not fast, but my brain was still trying to compute what I had just seen. Then there was a little flash of red in the corner of my vision. It was the ax, the dear, beautiful ax with its highly polished, gleaming handle and red, curved head. It was so bright, so perfectly red, like a new coat of lipstick just before a night out. There was a hard little hammer hanging down next to the glass case—BREAK IN CASE OF EMERGENCY. Fucking hell, I thought, this certainly applies. Like I said, the memory is fuzzy from panic, but I think my fist did more of the breaking than the hammer. Still, my hand didn't feel a thing, not until it was gripping the ax. And then I had both hands on the handle and I was running for the front of the store but Susan, poor, ugly Susan, was in the way. I swung, hard, a big, overhead swing that came down at her shoulder. I took off her right arm at the joint and it came away easier than I had expected. She seemed soft somehow, hollow and boneless.

I didn't stop to see if that had finished her off. I kept hold of the ax and sprinted to the front of the store where Phil was ushering Matt, Janette and Hollianted toward the break room. I remember now that Phil had a bat. I never knew we had a bat in the store. I found out later that Phil hid it under a loose board in the cabinet beneath the cash register. Phil swung the bat wildly as he caught sight of me, beckoning me with a bloody hand. I never thought I'd be so happy to see that silly bastard waving me over. He was shouting at me; screaming, actually. I knew what he saw behind me, I knew Susan wasn't down for good.

Now I see Susan on the monitor from time to time. We don't call her Susan anymore, we call her Lefty.

Tomorrow I'll have to confront Lefty again. We're running out of food and we need to raid the refrigerators out by the register. We might even need to ransack the café if we can get that far. We'll have to leave the safety of the door. We don't have a choice.

September 20, 2009—In Defense of Food

"Do you think we should save him some Doritos?" Ted asks.

In unison we glanced at Phil's office, the closed door, the quiet man hidden inside. "No," I tell him. "He'll come out for food when he's good and ready."

I'm really starting to miss Phil's go-getter attitude.

Phil's become suddenly vacant, as if all the goodwill and energy he had saved up from many blissful years of excellent customer service has deserted him. I was expecting him to volunteer for Recovery Duty (which is the very serious and important name I've given the task), but instead he's been sulking in his office all morning, scrunched up against the cupboards, clutching a framed photo of his kids. Janette and Matt are silent on the subject but Ted can't seem to shut up about it.

"He's lost it."

"You know what, Ted? How about you lay off him and get back to me when you have kids of your own to miss," I say. He turns his head away, pushing his glasses up his nose. Ted wears tortoise-shell Oliver Peoples glasses. I can't quite tell if they're supposed to be an ironic statement. One of the lenses is cracked and it makes him look like a battered child. His inky black hair falls in messy shocks over the rim of his glasses, dangling like a beaded curtain over the lenses.

"Look, I just need one other person to come with me," I go on.

Janette, Matt and Hollianted were all sitting at the round conference table. I stood near the door, the trusty ax leaning against my
knee.

"We can hold out for another day," Matt says. He wears glasses
too but they are definitely not an ironic statement, they are thick
and bookish. Matt has all the riotous energy of a basset hound,
which is to say none, and he also has the drooping eyes and down-
trodden expression. I don't doubt Matt cares about some things,
but that passion is pure speculation as he never raises his voice
above an indifferent mumble.

"And what about after that?" I ask.

"After that someone will come for us," Holly says matter-of-
factly, speaking without prompting for the first time in memory.
Ted looks at her, a strange light in his eyes.

"Holly," I say, "I agree that we shouldn't give up hope but . . .
we need food, we need to stay healthy and strong."

I don't want to point out to her that the streets outside the
building are ominously silent. The first hour or so after the infected showed up you could hear police sirens and fire engines
screaming down the street outside. After that the noises stopped
except for the occasional scream and what sounded like a car accident. From what I could make out on the monitors (only one of
which caught any of the world outside the store) there wasn't
much to see except a rolling pillar of smoke that filled up the
space between our store and the other side of the street. It's impossible to tell whether it's sunny or overcast, rain or clear.

"Phil should go," Ted points out, nodding and placing his open
palm on the tabletop. It's meant as a solemn gesture but Ted
doesn't have the kind of adult authority to pull it off convincingly,
especially with his silly cracked lens.

"Yes, Phil should go but he's indisposed at the moment," I say.
Without planning it, all of us turn to glance at his office. Through

the window only the top of his dark head was visible. "So I'll need someone else to volunteer. I'm sure one of you can swing a baseball bat well enough."

"I guess. I did judo for six years," Ted says, shrugging his bony shoulders. He was skinny before, but a few days of nothing but diet cola and rationed snack food has made him absolutely skeletal. Sparrows have meatier frames, and with his fluffy black hair he's looking more and more like a bespectacled scarecrow.

"Congratulations," I tell him, "you've just volunteered yourself."

Ted rolls his eyes but gets up anyway. I get the feeling he wanted to go but didn't want to look too eager. Holly makes a grab for his wrist, her big amber eyes filling up with tears. We're all emotional these days but Holly's demeanor turns on a dime. One minute she'll be whistling show tunes to try and keep us optimistic and the next she's bawling into Ted's arms.

"He'll be fine," I say, grabbing Ted by the other arm and giving a tug. "I checked the monitor this morning, there's fewer out there than ever."

I don't say the obvious thing, the thing I know she's thinking: zombies, there are zombies out there.

"I really don't think this is a good idea," Matt says, getting slowly to his feet. His beard has come in shaggy and uneven and he looks like a retired lumberjack in his faded plaid shirt and ill-fitting jeans. He's using his assistant manager voice, the one with the snide sarcastic bite.

"What's the alternative?" I ask.

"Yeah, what's *your* brilliant solution?" Ted asks. I like Ted more every minute.

"I don't have one," Matt replies, "but I think we should all just stay here. We don't know anything about those things. We don't know how it spreads. It might be something in the air."

Matt, unfortunately, is a conspiracy theorist. This is not the appropriate time for him to regale us with his interpretation of which government is responsible for the infected. But he's going there, I can feel it. I mentally recall our heated discussions of the pyramids and the Aztecs and decide that this is a conversation that must be avoided at all costs. He's glaring at me now over the top of his glasses. He has what we employees affectionately call a "death stare," which means that he has a shifty, deeply unnerving gaze that says he not only knows that you did, in fact, do something wrong, but that he will rain down furious punishment for said infraction.

"I appreciate the concern, Matt, but we have to eat."

"Don't go out there with your mouth and nose uncovered," he says, unbuttoning his shirt, revealing a stained white T beneath. "It's a bioweapon, it's probably in the air." He hands the shirt to Ted and when Ted won't take it, Matt comes over and begins wrapping it around the kid's face, squishing Ted's broken glasses into his eyes.

"Well, considering the vents in here aren't sealed we're all pretty much fucked already then," I say. I'm hoping Janette will say something, that she'll make Matt sit down, make him shut up. But she just sits there staring up at him, her expression blank and frozen, her dirty blond hair hanging limp around her hunched shoulders.

Ted, putting his expensive biochemistry degree to work, weighs in with, "Shit, man, it's not a bioweapon. No one on earth has the technology for this kind of bullshit."

"Oh, is that your *expert* opinion?" Matt asks and I know he's prodding.

Holly stands up then, going to stand beside Ted in solidarity. "He would know!" she shouts. She takes the shirt off Ted's face and fixes his glasses.

"Wow, okay, let's keep it down," I say. "We don't know what

gets them excited and since Ted and I are going out there, we need it as clear as possible."

"Fine, whatever!" Matt says. "I'm just stating for the record that I think this idea sucks."

"I'll keep that in mind when we get back and ration the food."

It only takes us a minute or two to get ready. At Matt's continued urging we agree to cover our noses and mouths; it's really not a half-bad idea since we might have to defend ourselves. The last thing I want is their goo flying all over my face and Matt is, admittedly, correct in pointing out that we don't exactly know how the infection spreads. I get the feeling Matt is angry and frustrated, but—like always—he's all simmer and no boil.

I tell Ted to make sure his mouth is covered and I put on a pair of sunglasses from the break room. We look ridiculous, Ted with Matt's flannel shirt wrapped around his head, his cracked brown glasses peering out, and me with Holly's studded black sweatshirt wrapped in the same way.

Hollianted cling together before we leave. It should be a romantic moment, and it might have been, but Ted looks so outrageously stupid that it can't be taken seriously. This is the new face of romance, I think, giving his shoulder a gentle squeeze of encouragement. He peels himself off and we remind Matt to stay by the door and listen for our knock, which he agrees to do, lording over the sacred keys with his furious grimace. Matt's keeping the keys in case anything happens to us, the discussion of which plunged Holly into another wail of agony.

Ted takes up Phil's bat and I grab the ax and we're ready to go. We've each got four empty plastic bags to fill with loot. I feel like a boxer waiting in the corner of the ring: I want to go, want to start, but half of me wants to stay behind and cower.

Two steps out of the door and I see her.

Lefty.

Sorry, old girl, I'm not going for a limb this time.

Ted and I have come up with a vague strategy: go for the head—barring that, the chest. I'm not entirely confident Ted has a strong enough arm to really do much damage, but he acquits himself admirably with Lefty, slamming her in the chest while I take a sloppy swing that connects with her neck. Her windpipe collapses with that same, weird hollow feeling. It doesn't even feel like I'm hurting a person—no human is that soft, that destructible.

Lefty's decaying, oozing head stares up at me from the ground while her body crumples into a headless heap. She's still wearing that damn T-shirt, the one with the dancing daisy and the words "World's Best Mom" in little kid's handwriting scribbled underneath. I know I should keep moving but I can't help looking at her eyes. There's no person there, no identity, just a startling hunger that persists even after I've lopped off her head. Ted pulls on my sleeve, the end of his bat coated in a black sludge. He nods to our right, to the short staircase leading up to the cash registers and the coolers.

Our destination.

I glance out the windows on our left. Most of the glass is gone and what remains is just a jagged barrier along the bottom edge. There's a pile of shards on the floor just inside the store and I can make out the letters BRO and ODY from the shattered sign. Outside, the street is almost completely obscured by a haze of thick, ashen smoke. The smell, even through the head wrap, is indescribable. I can't help but imagine a graveyard, a cemetery with all its graves and tombs opened up at once and the decay and death thrown into the wide-open air. It chokes and stings.

Ted and I bound up the stairs and immediately two more zombies come at us. One is Mr. Masterson, the dementia-ridden golden oldie who lives above the shop. He's got his baseball cap and tan

Windbreaker on but it's stained black and gray down the middle, and part of his lung is trying to escape through the gaping hole in his chest. He sees us—or smells us, or whatever it is these things do—and lurches toward Ted, groaning as if Ted is the most desirable piece of ass he's ever seen. I intercept him with a blow to the legs. He's tall and this gets him on my level, a perfect position to go for the head. Ted's now somewhere else, taking care of the monster teetering around behind the counter.

Mr. Masterson is laid out and I jump over his squirming, headless corpse to the cooler in front of the counters. It's mostly intact but a few bottles of water are missing. I'm amazed the thing hasn't been pillaged altogether. I go for the water first and then the diet soda and the juice. There are some sports drinks in there too so I grab those and the monstrous vegan cookies that are, thank God, still in their wrappers. Ted is having trouble with the zombie behind the counter so I go to help him. Together it's not a problem, and soon Ted is going for the upright cooler behind the counter where we keep the extra bottles.

"Water first, moron!" I shout through the muffling of the head wrap. He was reaching for a Mountain Dew.

While Ted fills up his bags, I go back out around the front of the counter where there's junk food. I reach blindly for whatever I can get, shoveling candy bars and gum and chips into a new plastic bag. Once the display is empty I turn to help Ted. Out of the corner of my eye I see something, something I can't resist. It's stupid, I know it is, but like one of Pavlov's dogs drooling over the mere tinkling of a bell, it can't be helped.

Just to the left and around the cash registers is the rest of the store and, more importantly, hundreds of bookshelves filled with books. The nights of unbridled tedium come tearing out of my subconscious. My focus is gone, I can't concentrate. *I need to get the books.*

I set down the full bags. That's my first mistake. With a quick glance in Ted's direction I can see that he's still busy with the cooler, so I jog over to the nearest bookcase and begin shoving books under my left arm, squeezing them against my side. It doesn't matter what books they are, I just need them all. Dante, de Laclos, Austen, and Dickens—all of them are in my arms and the weight of them, the feel of the new, glossy covers on my fingers is beautiful.

Then I hear a sound, a terrible, hoarse sound from just to my left and I acknowledge then that I've made a stupid mistake. There are three more of them, bigger than Mr. Masterson, and they've somehow managed to stop groaning long enough to surprise me.

Oh fuck, I think, feeling the sweat pop out all over my face and neck. I can't find the ax. I've left it out of reach. It's back by Ted with the bags of food.

And everything was going so well.

I throw the nearest thing, a monster copy of Whitman's collected works, and it hits a zombie square in the face. It doesn't stop it but it sure as hell slows it down. The tragedy of it is, I can't keep all the books in my arms, an unforgivable oversight. I scramble back toward the cash registers and the food, panting like an idiot underneath the sweatshirt around my face. The other two zombies are slow, hungry maybe, and it's made them sluggish. It's hot as all hell in there and the sweat is pooling at my temples and dripping down my neck, joining the perspiration on my collarbone and the deafening thunder of my pulse.

"What the *fuck*!" Ted screams, yanking me forward by the front of my shirt. I grab the ax and my share of the food bags. We break into a sprint, going back down the stairs. He's just barely managing to carry the heavy, full bags and the bat but we get down the stairs safely. Neither of us bother to dispatch the monster shuffling toward us from the broken windows, we're too close, too near to safety. Ted pounds on the door with the bat and I can hear him whimpering inside his head wrap.

"Where are they? Where are they?" I'm shouting. I don't know why I'm shouting since Ted is right there in front of me, his black hair trembling above the face wrap. The door isn't opening, I can't hear anything inside. I glance over my shoulder and the zombies are right on top of us, grunting and staring and if there was any humor in their eyes, then they're laughing at Ted and me, who are flailing like idiots against the locked door. That door, *that fucking door*, the door that kept us safe.

I drop all the shit in my arms and pick up the ax and swing and swing, blindly, feverishly. There's blood and gray, smelly globs flying in every direction. I don't know if I'm chopping up one or two or three of them but it doesn't matter, I just keep swinging until I hear the sweetest sound in the world: a thump and a click and the door opening for us, just for us. I turn and kick the bags inside. I kick until someone grabs me by the arm and pulls me inside.

The door shuts and I'm home, safe, *alive*.

- -

COMMENTS

Isaac says:

September 20, 2009 at 2:24 pm

If you heard sirens in the area, it's possible that a police car or a different emergency services vehicle has been abandoned nearby. And if you guys are brave / foolhardy enough you could strike out a couple of blocks. Ambulances carry medical supplies—you haven't mentioned them so far in your blog, so I assume you haven't got any, and sooner or later someone is going to get hurt. Firefighters' jackets would be okay for makeshift armor; thick clothing protects from bites. And of course the police have guns, so any officers who didn't make it could have pistols or better with them. I know it sounds cold, taking stuff from the dead, but this is life and death.

Also, I doubt the virus (or whatever) is airborne; you would definitely have caught it from such close proximity to the infected. An exchange of fluids (like a speck of blood landing in your mouth or eyes) is probably what you should watch for. The depressing thing is, it seems despite the zombies, humans are still their own worst enemies.

Allison says:
September 20, 2009 at 5:37 pm
Thanks, Isaac. I'd tell you to be safe but it sounds like you're more prepared than we are. We've got a few first aid kits but nothing substantial. We would strike out but I don't know how the others would feel about it. Ted might go along but I'm sure Matt would come up with some reason for us to stay inside.

September 21, 2009—The Botany of Desire

And now, with absolutely no ado, *5 Things I Would Literally Prostitute Myself For*:

1. A hot shower (At least ten minutes—come on, I'm selling my body here.)
2. A vegetable. Any vegetable (maybe not beets)
3. Toothpaste and a toothbrush
4. A functioning goddamned toilet
5. A Panzer VIII Maus

COMMENTS

Isaac says:
September 21, 2009 at 12:46 pm
Add a few pounds of bandages and Neosporin and you've just about got my list.

> **Allison says:**
> *September 21, 2009 at 1:09 pm*
> You're thinking too practically, Isaac. This is the end of the world, right? Tanks and toilets, my friend, tanks and toilets.

Mel says:

September 21, 2009 at 2:35 pm

New Orleans gone. Attempting to escape by water and hoping Cuba is untouched.

D.J. says:

September 21, 2009 at 3:08 pm

Is there a way to reverse this? Amputation? Medicine?

> **Isaac says:**
>
> *September 21, 2009 at 5:59 pm*
>
> I wouldn't trust it. If someone is infected you should quarantine them or, if you can stomach it, end it for them.

September 23, 2009—Pandora

"Good night survivors, Isaac, D.J. and Mel. Good night sun, good night moon, good night laptop, I think we'll all be gone soon."

Nope, nothing, not a drooping eyelid, not even the softest suggestion of a snore. Nothing seems to work, not even a cheerful little lullaby can put me to sleep. I've become an insomniac.

It began innocently enough. It started with a strange coincidence. After Ted and I returned with the loot, we rationed it out. I feel something happening with Ted, something like friendship or solidarity. He didn't mention my complete lapse of judgment, the lapse that almost led to us being zombie snacks. I don't know why he did it, but it made me glow a little with relief.

We've worked out the rations to roughly this:

2 Bags of chips per person per day
2 Drinks (juice first because of the expiration date) per person per day
3 or 4 Candies per person per day
2 Cookies each, to be eaten at the owner's discretion

It really isn't much but it's the best we can do. There are still a few sticks of beef jerky left in the refrigerator and an old cling-wrapped muffin of indeterminate origin that no one has been brave enough (or dumb enough) to eat.

After we finished rationing the food we sat down to eat. Ted and I kept mum for the most part. Janette seems extremely fragile these days; she's never handled gore well, not in books or movies, and so we spared her the details of our expedition. Poor Phil ate in his office still curled up on the floor like a child silently enduring a time-out. He mumbled a quiet "Thank you" when I handed him a bag of Doritos and a soda.

The rest of us ate at the table, sitting beneath the pale, buzzing glow of the emergency lights, crunching and chewing, each of us wrestling with our own tangled thoughts. Matt has been much more cheerful. I think he feels bad for voting against the mission in the first place and he's demonstrated what one might almost call "enthusiasm"—or as much as his droopy basset-hound face can muster.

It was after dinner or thereabouts that I noticed the remarkable thing on the floor. It was wedged beneath the counters across from the door. At first I thought it might be a packet of papers or an old "Team Work" pamphlet that had been dropped and forgotten long ago. I waited until the others had left the table, separating to opposite corners of the room. Hollianted generally try to keep their distance so they can cuddle and make out in peace. Janette and Matt started up a game of poker with a deck of old cards they had found. Matt was officially out one shirt; it was spattered with grime and zombie juice.

I pretended to knock the shirt off the counter and bent down, grabbing the thing wedged under the counter and shoving it into my jeans pocket. Matt looked over at me as I put his shirt back on the counter, staring at me as if I were a fly he had just noticed hovering over his head.

"Sorry. Clumsy," I think I muttered.

Matt turned his attention and seething death glare back to the card game, and I grabbed my laptop and shuffled into the safe room. That's where I am now, my screen propped right next to the television monitor. The store is quieter these days. Whatever commotion Ted and I had stirred up settled, and fewer and fewer hunched figures drift by the cameras.

And I've been too distracted to give them much thought. What did I find in my pocket that night? A book. Miraculously it had made its way into the break room, kicked inside during the scuffle. I must have dropped it just before Matt opened the door and somehow managed to knock it inside. The damn thing made it, the lone survivor, the shipwrecked castaway. This alone might not seem very exciting or remarkable, but when I took the book back to the safe room I couldn't believe which one it was.

The Awakening—my mother's favorite book.

Elation . . . Joy . . . Complete disbelief . . . Here comes the crazy train, pulling into the station. Toot toot!

I don't believe in a higher power, I never have, but I must admit that for a quick, flashing second I felt the presence or maybe the interference of something supernatural. It just seemed too coincidental, too perfect. For a moment, I sat with the book sitting on my open palms, just staring at the cover as if it were an offering, a bowl of blessed incense. From that point on, from the moment the book came into my possession, I stopped sleeping.

Look, I know this isn't exactly the hand of God reaching down to give me a sign or something. When I was in grade school my friends and I would play that Ouija board game at sleepovers. We would scare ourselves witless, watching in openmouthed terror as the little pointed marker spelled out D-E-D. Close enough for us, close enough to keep us up all night wondering which of us would die during the night. Years later a boyfriend would explain to me why those board games worked. Tiny, minute vibrations in the fingertips communicated the desired outcome. So your conscious mind might not be thinking G-H-O-S-T but your subconscious is. That's all it takes to move the marker slowly, slowly, centimeter by centimeter across the board.

Maybe it was my subconscious at work. Maybe I had grabbed *The Awakening*, shoved it beneath my armpit and locked on, determined no matter what not to let it go. Either way, divine intervention or trick of the mind, I had the book now. I don't know why I guarded it so jealously, not allowing the others to see that I had found it. That's stopped now and they've been passing it around for the last few days, taking turns reading and rereading it.

But the first night I had it, after we had rationed the loot and had dinner, I went to the safe room to be alone with the book. I read it front to back and started over again. Then I began to get drowsy and decided to get some sleep. I drifted off, the neon light of the monitor covered my face and hands as I made a cradle for my head to rest on.

Maybe the book didn't start the insomnia, maybe the dream did, but the book started the dream so the exact culprit doesn't matter. The dream went like this: I was back out in the store with Ted, swinging my ax around and grabbing food. Then something rears up behind me screeching and rasping like a banshee. I turn and it's one of them, one of the undead, and it looks like it should be Susan but it's not. It's my mom and she's wearing that fucking shirt with the sloppy, little kid handwriting . . .

WORLD'S BEST MOM.

I can't move. I can't stop looking at her face but I want to run, get away from those hollow, glaring eyes. They're not my mom's eyes anymore. Her hands are clawing at me, the flesh gone, showing the gleaming bone beneath. Her skull is peeking through the sagging holes in her face. She's bald, of course, the chemo took her hair months ago, and there are garish purple spots all over the top of her head. Her fingers are ripping through my shirt. She's tearing at my skin but there's nothing I can do. I can't kill her, I can't swing the ax at her neck, I just stop and wait and let her rip me apart.

I wake up in a cold, shivering sweat. There are little beads of moisture on the counter and the backs of my hands are slippery and wet. The monitor flickers and shifts for a minute and then the camera fixes on Susan's headless body, still there, still wearing the T-shirt.

It's after that, after the dream ends, that I can't sleep.

And now, writing this, my hands are shaking because I can't control my nerves. My eyes hurt and they feel sandy, filled up with grit and blurry from hours and hours spent in the dark, wakeful night. I'm clammy all over and I know it would go away if I could just rest, just sleep for an hour or two but I can't. Something in my brain won't let me. I think about sleep constantly and I try to read to stay distracted, to keep my mind off the fact that when evening comes nothing will happen; I'll close my eyes and feel perfectly, horribly awake.

It has to stop. If I go on like this much longer I'll be useless, weak, dull and sick.

It has to stop.

COMMENTS

Isaac says:

September 23, 2009 at 10:33 pm

You're not insane. Stay alert, try to create a routine and stick to it. It'll be easier on your body if you can find a rhythm. Don't let your immune system get too weak.

Mel says:

September 23, 2009 at 11:20 pm

Boat leaves today and I'll be on it. We saw a few of the creatures in the water but they looked slow. I think we can make

it. You won't hear from me again, Allison but I'll be thinking of
you. Goodbye.

Allison says:

September 23, 2009 at 11:55 pm

Good luck on the waves, Mel. Send us a postcard from
Cuba and some rum. Lots and lots of rum.

September 25, 2009—The Curious Incident of the Dog in the Nighttime

Knock, knock . . .

(Come on, say it.)

Fine. Who's there?

BLAGRRUUGGHHEEEFGH.

"You're fucking losing it too, aren't you?" That was Ted's enthusiastic response to the joke. I think he laughed though, later, in secret. "First Phil and now you? Do you like stay up all night thinking this shit up?"

"No," I replied sheepishly. "Not *all* night."

Sorry. That's the kind of moronic shit that passes for humor around here these days. It's bleak. Somewhere between my twentieth bag of Lays and my tenth SoBe, I must have started to get a little depressed. Yes, it's official. We've lost that loving feeling, our chutzpah, our joie de vivre. Not that we were ever chipper about being holed up in a beige corporate break room, but at least there was no complaining, no dull, empty staring.

I never thought it would get so bad so fast. Janette and Matt have lost their taste for cards and spend their days playing nonsensical word games and endless rounds of Would You Rather. Phil literally will not come out of his office unless it's to use the bathroom, which brings us to our most recent situation: the house of unspeakable horrors that is our bathroom.

There is no running water, limited toilet paper and no working ventilation. I'll let you imagine for yourself what the smell is like because if I try to describe it our tête-à-têtes will come swiftly to an end as I destroy my laptop beneath a fountain of neon orange Dorito vomit.

Really, we stink.

It's something we can no longer blithely ignore, not only because it's an astronomically bad odor that has begun seeping out from under the restroom door, but also because we're all too crabby and sullen to bother with manners. Between the vicious gas we're all suffering from and the nearby sulfurous death chamber just waiting to unleash a new round of villainy every time someone needs to take a piss, it's become a code-red situation.

Thus, a meeting is called.

"All right, guys," I say, trying my best to keep a straight face. I'm constantly in danger of bursting into giggles. For one because we're having a group heart-to-heart about farts, and also because I haven't slept in days. I'm a giddy, shadowy shell of a human being. I know that the smudges beneath my eyes are beginning to resemble army-issue duffel bags but this matter demands our immediate attention and I'm determined to get it straightened out. I can see Ted is about to start laughing any second so I shoot him a suitably grown-up look.

"I don't think I need to point out to everyone how fucking awful it smells in here," I say, putting my hands on my hips, striking a serious pose. "We need to figure something out because I'd rather be eaten by those god-awful things out there than let this get any worse."

"There are the bathrooms out in the hall," Matt offers, tearing open a bag of Cheetos. He's looking less like a homeless lumberjack these days.

"Yes! Exactly my thought! We need to start using them, but wisely, okay? And I know this is gross, but we need to empty the toilet in here. We'll do it in shifts so no one passes out. There's a bucket in the maintenance closet at the end of the hall. I don't think the zombies will mind a little shit and piss so we'll just toss it out into the store," I explain. At this, Phil's head jerks up as if someone's socked him in the gutsky. "Yes, Phil, what is it?"

"We can't do that," he says with surprising vigor. He doesn't have bags under his eyes. He sleeps more than all of us put together, more than a narcoleptic old cat.

"What do you mean?" Ted blurts out, sitting up farther to be able to see Phil. Ted has been eating well and he's starting to put on some weight. It suits him. Unfortunately, his broken glasses and untamable hair still leave him looking like a Boy Scout. "We can't let it go on like this, man, it's fucking gross."

"Ted is right," I say. "He's absolutely right."

"But it's *the store.*"

"Oh for *Christ's sake,* Phil, I don't think we'll reopen for at least a few months, okay? Don't worry about it, please. You're fucking overruled." I can't really explain how good it feels to tell him to shove it. He hasn't made a nuisance of himself but he certainly hasn't been much help either.

"Just . . . Just try to throw it close to the doors, okay?" I add, and this seems to calm him down a little. "From now on, we'll use the bathrooms across the hall. Never go alone, check all the stalls and make sure someone is keeping guard. Every three days we'll empty them out."

Matt and Janette amble to the door, looking dour as they prepare to retrieve the bucket from the maintenance closet. This behavior is expected of Matt, but I was hoping Janette would perk up a bit at the thought of helping the group. Phil wanders back into his office and slams the door, making the photos on his wall rattle and dance. Hollianted come to stand by me and I'm glad for their smiles, even if they look exhausted and strained.

"Well, I think that went well, don't you?" Ted asks, grinning. He's wound a bit of electrical tape around the joint of his glasses. The effect is charming.

"Swimmingly."

I take the first Shit Shift, which is what Ted has christened the chore. This is a much worse task than I envisioned and it takes absolutely forever. Let me tell you, when you've got a bucket teeming with murky fecal matter, you take very great pains to make damn sure you don't spill it on yourself, the floor of your living space, or anyone who might get in the way. This means that the going is slow and stressful. All the while you're gagging and trying your best to breathe through your mouth *but even then it's like you can taste it.* Shit particles. Pee vapor.

Christ.

I'm on my last leg of the shift when it happens. Ted has been keeping watch for me while I run my insane little relay, scooping the bucket into the toilet in the break room, carefully walking at top speed through the conference room, out the break-room door and into the store, then across the floor to the broken windows. I've been tossing most of the waste out the windows. Phil was kinda right—there's just something weird about dumping crap on the floor of the store. So to make him and, I think, everyone else happy, I fling the contents of the bucket out the broken windows.

It's also a chance to get a look at the outside world, which is something you really can't pass up. The rolling parade of smoke has cleared some and now you can see the building across the street. The windows are broken there too. It's almost satisfying to see that overpriced, snob-factory of a boutique run-down and gutted. Almost. There are a few zombies wandering the streets but they all seem to be heading in one direction, west toward the university campus. There's no sign of human life, no trace of other survivors, just overturned cars in heaps, the carnage of a sudden battle, scorch marks and tire treads painted down the streets . . . It looks exactly like a movie set.

During the relay race Ted and I have begun sharpening a theory. We posit that there are two kinds of zombies: Groaners and Floaters. They're both dangerous, for obvious reasons, but they're actually quite different. Groaners are loud, they groan (duh) and moan and squeal as they come for you. They're faster, more determined, more desperate. Floaters are arguably more dangerous because they're quiet, weirdly quiet, and they can sneak up on you. But they're slow and they don't seem to react very fast. Ted and I think that Groaners are hungry, so they've gone a little wild. Floaters are running on a full tank so they don't care as much about getting their bony claws on your face. During the Shit Shift we have encountered a few of both, but mainly Groaners. I have to say, I prefer Groaners—they let you know they're coming, they announce their arrival.

I'm feeling tired, so run-down I can hardly focus my eyes, but I'm going to finish this last trip to the windows if it's the final fucking act of my life. Setting a good example, I've come to see, is key to leadership. If I empty the toilet first, then the others will do it without complaint, and if I do a thorough job then I'll set a good standard.

Like I said, this is when it happens: I raise the bucket, holding my breath as I wind up to toss the waste out the window. Then I hear this sound. It's one I haven't heard in a while, a sound that will make any human being with a pulse stand up and take breathless notice.

Woof . . . Rerr . . . Woof, Roof!

It's a dog, a mutt, and it's staring me down from the middle of the road. Maybe staring isn't the right word—regarding, lovingly, sweetly, begging with its big chocolate eyes. It's got dark, pointed ears and one is standing straight up, the other is flopped over. His nose is marbled pink and tan and he's got a sturdy, if starved, body. There has to be German shepherd in there and maybe some pit bull. He's mostly black and orange, with the biggest tongue I've ever seen hanging out the side of his mouth.

"Come here, little man!" I call.

"What are you doing?" Ted growls.

"I'm calling to the dog, what does it look like?"

"You can't, Allie, what if he's infected? And he's probably hungry. He'll eat all our food."

"Don't be so heartless, asshole. We can't leave him out there! Come here, we won't hurt you."

The dog takes a few slow steps in our direction. I decide then and there that he is a smart and good dog for not charging into the arms of a human with a bucket of shit poised at the ready. I gently slop the waste down the outside of the windows and set the bucket down. This seems to be the signal the dog was waiting for and he pads over, snuffling up my pant leg and licking at my belt buckle.

"I love you too," I say, patting his broad, matted head. "Come with us, we've got yummies."

Everyone takes part in Shitgate '09 with unmitigated eagerness after the dog arrives. What the hell is it about a happy mutt that makes humans forget their worries, their massive troubles, and soldier on? He's done something to Phil, given him new life, new purpose and it's the same with everyone else too. Holly never struck me as a dog person and I know Janette only had cats, but Dapper (that's his name) has won them over. Sure he eats, he's another mouth to feed and water and take out into the store for the bathroom, but he makes us all a little less cranky.

And I'm sleeping again. Dapper sleeps with me, curled up on my feet, his cold nose pressing into my shin. Sometimes he licks my feet. I think he knows we could all use a bath. He doesn't complain. He doesn't tell me it's hopeless, that we're stuck here forever until the food runs outs, until the undead somehow find a way in. He just looks up at me with those huge, accepting eyes.

He's grateful and he's gentle and he's mine.

COMMENTS

Isaac says:
September 25, 2009 at 8:28 pm
Usually a new dog makes you *lose* sleep with all but whatever works I guess. The Dakotas are a wasteland but I'll take quiet over those creatures any day. Rural life seems to be the way to go, hardly any creeps around here to kill, just the occasional neighbor that wanders over from the next farm. You might want to start boiling your water if sanitation is bad and if someone is ill keep them away from the rest of you. Glad you're sleeping again, keep us updated.

> **Allison says:**
> *September 25, 2009 at 9:51 pm*
> Yeah, dog as cure for insomniac, who knezzzzzz-
> zzzzzzzzzzzzzzzzzzzzzzzzzzzzz . . .

September 26, 2009—The Dirty Girls Social Club

"But I'll look like a boy!"

"You won't, I promise, and besides, aren't you sick of *smelling* like a boy?"

"I don't care," Janette says, crossing her arms stubbornly. "You're not touching my hair. . . . And I don't smell."

"You do smell, dude. Trust me." She's not budging. "It's not a fashion show, Janette." Oh Jesus, I think my mother used to say the exact same thing to me in high school when I'd wander downstairs in a hideous black mesh T and neon pink high-tops.

I don't give a shit about Janette's feelings right now. Something's got to give and that means one thing: mandatory haircuts today.

I'm not bothered by it. I've had short hair for a few years now. I used to rock that long, layered look with a few lowlights and then my mom and I decided to chop it all off for Locks of Love. This was before she got cancer; kind of ironic, I guess. Or is that Alanis Morissette "ironic"—as in, not really ironic but just coincidental? Anyway, we both found out at that point that we liked having short hair, so we just kept it. When Mom was diagnosed I shaved my head in solidarity. It's grown in again but today we'll chop it off.

I used to joke that maybe the wig my mom got from Locks was

made out of her own hair, or mine, or it was some Frankenwig hybrid of both of us. She never wore it much. She looked good with a Q-ball and I think owning it, embracing it, gave her strength.

Anyway, Janette and her insecurities are irrelevant. I'm worried that we'll get fleas or, worse, lice. Without a functioning shower it's impossible to stay even moderately clean. I think this is the first step. Holly takes it like a champ and really, she could look worse. Janette's long, strong-chinned face isn't exactly flattered by short hair, and she looks like someone, something, I can't put my finger on it—but she certainly doesn't look like a boy. Not an ugly one, at any rate.

I can almost feel us bonding, like spending a day at the most backwater, run-down salon imaginable. There's no exfoliating mask or sea-salt scrub, but we look and feel different—better.

Peter Pan. That's who Janette reminds me of, that chick who played Peter Pan onstage. I'd tell Janette but I don't think she'd take it as a compliment. I wish she was Peter Pan. I wish she could fly up and out of here and find us all some help.

- -

COMMENTS

bruce says:
September 26, 2009 at 4:56 pm
Haircuts, that's a good idea, also one less thing for Them to grab onto. We've been trapped in a library for a week now . . . only three of us left out of the original 37. Mostly 'Floaters' in this area, as you call them. Books are the only thing keeping us going. Won't last much longer, we have no weapons and they are slowly breaking down our defenses. Hope you have better luck than us.

Allison says:

September 26, 2009 at 6:01 pm

Bruce! You're a genius! I hadn't thought of the safety benefits. I'll pass that on to Janette; I'm sure she'll be jazzed to hear that short hair makes her a zombie-dodging ninja superstar. Good luck in the library. And what's this about no weapons? Get yourself a solid dictionary and throw that sucker like it's the motherfucking Olympics.

September 27, 2009—The Bloody Chamber

"Tell them. Go on. Tell them what you told me."

"Can't I plead the fifth or something?"

"No, no you can't, Allison. Tell them now or I'll do it for you."

I'll paint the picture for you: I'm standing in front of the assembled group sweating like a hog, a stinky hog with a string trimmer haircut. They're glaring at me because they've read Ted's expression and know now that I've done something bad, really bad, time-out in the corner bad. It's elementary school all over again. Show and tell, the mortifying gauntlet of raised eyebrows and pursed lips. Everyone is even grumpier than usual, as if Matt's sour attitude has spread like its own miniature undead plague. It's late September now and it's starting to get cold. It's creeping through the walls and causing the clammy dampness of our tiny world to change into something more sinister. Holly has a cough. I've learned now where Brooks & Peabody's priorities are at: the security cameras run on the emergency power—but not the much-needed heat.

I don't know. I fidgeted. I think I cleared my throat.

"I've been keeping a blog for a while now. It started out as a cry for help but then I . . . I don't know, it felt good to talk about what was happening so I kept going." I don't know why it's hard to say it, but it feels like a betrayal and I can see Holly is on the verge of tears. "There's good and bad news. The good news is that there are still other people alive. They're out there, they wrote back to me. The bad news is . . . They're just like us, trapped, helpless."

"I don't suppose any of them were policemen or EMTs?" Matt asks dryly, rolling his eyes at me.

"I don't know. But that brings us to another point." I look at Ted, who nods solemnly. Ted and I have discussed this, convened our own private congress and voted, unanimously, to take action. And we've come to a decision; now it's time to tell the group and I know already it's not going to go well. At least Dapper was there to sit quietly at my feet like an old wise statue, a talisman against the anxious glares pointed my way. "Ted and I are going up to the apartments today. Food is getting low again and we all need to think about finding something more permanent."

"More permanent?" Holly echoes. Her face has gone completely white and her fingertips are hanging off the side of her mouth. She'd started chewing her nails a lot lately.

Ted and I exchange a look.

"The thing is, the news coming in from outside isn't good. Chicago is under attack too, and—"

"Under attack?" Janette asks, her hand clutching Matt's knee. I start to wish they would stop repeating everything I say and contribute, but that's asking too much. It's my fault—I should've phrased that better, I shouldn't have given her hope. I mean, I suppose an attack could imply a resistance, I know that's where her mind went. It's where mine would go too.

"Overrun."

There's a long pause after that. I watch tiny particles of the full truth settling down on their faces, melting over them in a horrifying fog, putting creases in their foreheads and then drawing their mouths down in fear. Holly covers her mouth and makes a raspy, strangled sound.

I should be angry. This is really all your fault—Isaac, and you,

Mel, and you, you, anonymous and you, Bruce. You should all be ashamed of yourselves. When I saw someone else was out there, I almost spat out my Sierra Mist all over the keyboard. And then, in my exuberance, I told Ted about you and subsequently outed my sad little secret Internet life. Ted, understandably, was not pleased.

"What were you *thinking*? Using your fucking laptop! You're wasting energy," he snapped, scowling at me. He had refused a haircut and now his fringe was starting to overtake his glasses. He pushed it out of his view with an angry little huff. "I can't believe you. Why didn't you say anything?"

"This is a good thing, Ted, I can feel it. Look, if there's still wireless then there are still people *doing* things, right? Normal things! Or at least, not everything is fucked, you know? I mean . . . Right?"

"You have to tell the others," he whispered, frowning and shaking his dark, moppy head. "They deserve to know. *I* deserved to know. I wish you had told me what you were up to."

"Well, now you know. It wasn't . . . *intentional*, I just didn't think anything would come of it, you know? It felt more like therapy than an S.O.S. No more secrets from now on, Ted, I promise."

That seemed to calm him down a bit so our congress of two moved on to a new topic: Dapper. Dapper doesn't bark. He hasn't barked at any of us for any reason. Maybe he's intuited the danger we're all in; maybe he's just trying to fit in and be as likable as possible (which has worked, by the way). But last night after haircuts, we started to notice noises up above us, loud, scraping noises like furniture being moved around. At first we didn't think much of it but then Dapper started barking his head off, jumping up and flashing his teeth at the ceiling.

Ted and I have determined that this is significant. The barking coupled with the noises . . . We think there might be survivors up there. It's entirely possible too, considering they're on the second floor. I have no idea how agile those undead things are. They might not be able to handle stairs very well and if stairs slowed them down then maybe the tenants upstairs managed to hold them off. We wonder if maybe Dapper came from one of the apartments upstairs and this is his way of telling us to go up.

And that brings us to the unpleasant task of asking, yet again, for volunteers. Ted and I are less certain that we can safely get through the store, out the back and up the fire escape with just the two of us. A third person would be nice, someone to keep watch in the back, just one more pair of eyes on the lookout. I can see Matt is rousing himself for an argument and he's shifted forward a little, as if putting himself between us and Janette. Matt has taken the long, thoughtful pause to organize his thoughts and prepare for the inevitable showdown, his death glare booted up and set to disintegrate.

"No," he finally says, predictably. "No way. It's suicide."

"It's not suicide, Matt. Don't be so dramatic."

"You have no idea what's up there, how many of them are up there."

"But what if it's not so bad? What if we can clear it out? We might actually be able to live like real human beings with couches and countertops and beds!" I say. This is getting bad—if he keeps the doom and gloom going then no one will volunteer to help us.

Then Janette, wonderful, gorgeous, Peter Pan Janette, murmurs very quietly, "A bed would be nice."

Matt balks at her, appalled and utterly betrayed, and then sits back hard against the cupboards. He crosses his arms over his chest and looks in the other direction. I'm hoping this means Janette will join us, but she's silent again. Ted and I glance at each other and I shift awkwardly from foot to foot. I can feel the frustration building. I want to shout: *Don't you get it? Don't you see what's happened? We just have to get along! That's all we have to do, just fucking get along!*

"Please?" I ask, sighing.

"I'll go. Damn it, yes, I'll go."

It's Phil and he's standing up, looking down at his comrades with a slight sneer. He's woken up at last. He nods, either to bolster his own confidence or ours, I can't tell, and then strides to the door. "Well? What are you waiting for? Are we going out there or not?"

"Yeah, of course we are, but let's take a minute and get ready, okay? No rush." Ted pulls Matt's shirt off the counter. He looks skeptical, chewing on his lower lip, and I can see why: Phil's just a bit too enthusiastic.

Phil refuses to go out unless he can use the baseball bat. Fine. We get the fire extinguisher down from the wall in the safe room and give it to Ted. We figure he can at least slow them down if any get too close. I'm not sure how much damage a fire extinguisher blast to the face does, but none of us are willing to experiment.

The plan is to move fast, to not get bogged down in one area of the store. Keep moving until we make it out the back. We hope that once we make it onto the fire escape, any Groaners that have decided to follow us will disperse by the time we come back down. I've checked the monitors and the store looks nice and quiet. Between taking Dapper out to go toilet and trips across the hall to the bathroom, we've cleared out most of the trouble in the immediate area. I'm less confident about the back of the store, where there are plenty of bookshelves for hiding and skulking and ambushing.

But my real fear is about going outside. Once we open the very back doors, the ones leading out from the storeroom, there's no telling what we'll see.

We've wrapped up our heads and reminded Matt to keep a close ear to the door. Secretly, we've asked Holly to listen for us too. Of the three of us, Phil looks the most outrageously stupid. He's using an old Windbreaker for a head wrap and his glasses are poking out, resting a little on the fabric. His white polo shirt is now more off-white or yellow and his khaki pants are hopelessly wrinkled. Grunting, he scoots up his pants and nods to Ted, who has his hand on the door. When we go out, it's pretty anticlimactic. The area outside the door is empty and there's nothing but the sound of a distant car alarm.

I go out in front with Phil and Ted takes the back position. We turn right, going up the stairs and past the empty refrigerators and cash registers. It's hard to resist the bookshelves when we get there, but I've learned my lesson and I know that behind any one of them could be a whole mess of undead. Before going out, Ted asked me to please only grab one book on the way back if I had to, two at the most. Cheeky bastard.

Once you get past the cash registers there's about twenty or thirty feet of bookshelves before you get to the back storeroom. We stay hard to the right, leaving only one side open for an attack. There's a low grumbling from the left and Phil whirls around to face it, ready, poised, and he's raised the bat and taken a hard, crashing swing before I even have time to warn him. I glance at Ted, who seems less skeptical now, even through the barrier of Matt's flannel shirt.

The floor is littered with books, stained, ruined books with pages glued to the floor by God knows what. I ax down a few Groaners right before we take the right turn into the storeroom and I can see that in the bookshelves across the room, there are more and they've noticed us. But the plan is to keep moving, so we do, and we maintain a fast, shuffling walk that turns into a jog when we make it into the back room. The storeroom is a big, open area with a few long tables for organizing shipments that come in. There are two areas, the first large room which has mostly empty shelving units and restocking supplies, and then the very back room which has the doors leading to the outside world. We make it to the very back and I know it's grim before we even get there—the noise, the grumbling, pained noises of dozens of undead shifting around. They've anticipated our arrival and begin slowly meandering out to meet us at the doors.

Phil is still focused and on point and cracks a few right on top of the head. I don't recognize any of these Groaners, which makes it a little easier to clean up Phil's work with a few well-placed swings to the neck. The hardest part is keeping a good, safe distance from Phil, who throws himself into the work with a real admirable zeal. Ted hangs back, shooting out loud jets of foam with the fire extinguisher, pushing the oncoming undead back so Phil and I have time to dismantle each one. We work out a rhythm.

When the storeroom is clear and the floor is covered in a sticky, black sludge, we take a moment to breathe. Phil's shoulders are shaking from the exertion, and he leans over to rest his hands on his knees and pant. I forget how lazy we are, how we sit around all day passing around the same book, the same magazines, playing cards, eating junk food and sleeping.

The back storeroom isn't anything remarkable. There's a long table and a few ancient computers for checking in shipments and a few more shelving units. I can see that the back doors are open a crack; a thin, ghostly line of sunlight runs down the middle of the floor. Phil staggers upright and soldiers on, boldly striding toward the door. It feels like something big, something important. We've conquered something, reached a goal that was once just a vague, imaginative "there."

I'm worried about Phil. I know he's a grown man and he can take care of himself, but I'm not sure he's prepared for what he'll see when those doors open all the way. I'm not sure I'm prepared either. Phil pushes hard against the heavy door and it lets loose a long, metallic squeal. The world outside is gray, punctuated by a few slender shafts of sunlight bleeding through the clouds. It's colder than I expected, late September, chilly and overcast and crisp. It's the kind of weather I used to love, sweater weather, sit outside bundled up in a blanket weather. But there's no lush, amber scent of burning leaves and no squirrels frolicking in the trees, just abandoned buildings in the distance, standing like forgotten monuments, the lights out, the people gone.

I can hear that car alarm again but no running engines, no mysterious rescue vehicle en route to save us. It's ghastly and quiet. The cement landing outside the door is empty. There's no greeting party of undead to interrupt the horrible, aching calm. This was a city once, a living place, and now it's gone muted and gray. Phil stumbles out onto the landing, heedless of the cold, but I can see the hairs on his arms standing up and goose bumps. I go out too and then down the steps. The big recycling Dumpster and the garbage Dumpster are open, riffled through, papers and boxes scattered across the pavement. Ted is jabbing at my back urgently. I turn and see he's pointing at something. It's a car, Phil's car, and suddenly everything becomes clear.

Phil's running toward his old maroon LeSabre before either of us can put out a hand to stop him. Even if we had, Phil is a huge guy, with linebacker shoulders and enough weight to throw us off without effort. He's sprinted down the stairs and over to the car, but he doesn't even make it to the door before he's stopped.

I can't explain it. Everyone knows it's uncomfortable and heartbreaking to see a grown man cry, but it's worse somehow when it's your boss. He's fallen just short of the car and stumbled down to his knees; his entire body is jolting forward and back as if he were being electrocuted. The gas cap is open, hanging down. It's the same with the car next to his, Janette's. There's no gas. It's been siphoned, stolen.

He came with us to escape. That's clear now. I should've thought of that possibility. I want to be mad, I want to stand him up and shake him hard and then slap him across the face. But I can't. I want to ask him: *Where would you go? Where do you think there is to go?*

Instead, I walk over to him and gently put my palm on his shoulder. He's tense all over, one big knot of nerves and frustration. "It's okay. I won't tell the others."

We need to keep going, to push forward, but I don't know how to rouse him from the grief. It's just another wave of horror, another in an unending series of unwelcome surprises. Phil stops shaking after a moment and gets to his feet, slobbering across the back of his hand as he tries to wipe the tears and snot off of his cheeks and chin. There's a tear caught in his goatee but I don't say anything about it.

"There are golf clubs in the trunk," he says in a sad, calm voice. He pulls a key ring out of his khaki pants and goes to the trunk. Inside, a big bag of golf clubs wait, sleeping in the gleaming leather bag, their fat heads covered in hoods like executioners. Phil reaches over and carefully, lovingly pulls out one of the clubs. "Ain't she a beauty?"

She is.

"Here, one for each of us."

Phil hands me a club. He tells me it's a "driver." It's light, unnaturally light considering the enormous metal head. I pull off the cover and even in the dull, overcast light the silvery metal gleams. DIABLO is etched across its face. "We'll take the drivers and the woods," Phil says, handing Ted a club and keeping two for himself.

He seems to be composing himself. I think just holding the clubs again brought him back to a state of normalcy.

After that it's time to keep moving. I'm getting nervous standing out in the open for so long. I keep imagining that just around the retaining wall to our right is an entire army of Groaners scuttling toward us. We go back to the cement landing, where Ted slaps Phil on the back and thanks him for the clubs.

The fire escape hangs down from the apartments above, ending a few feet above the landing. I'm too short to make it up to the top rung by myself, so Ted gives me a boost with his hands cupped into a stirrup. I'm not excited to go first up a ladder that could very well take me right into a room full of undead, but there's a shiny new golf club hanging from my belt loop and I'm itching to try it out. Not that I've grown tired of the ax, it's just nice to know that I've got a backup.

The wrought iron of the fire escape is freezing cold and covered in little pits that hurt my hands. I go as fast as possible, hoping to get to the top and inside a window before the creatures waiting inside have a chance to anticipate us. We still don't know how they find us—is it scent? Is it something worse, some evil gift acquired at the moment of death?

I reach the slatted metal landing with my teeth chattering from the cold. Once your adrenaline drops, the freezing temperature moves in, shimmying inside your clothes and making your bones ice over. The window immediately in front of the fire escape is wide open. Not a good sign. Whoever lived inside must have tried to escape, and why would they do that if they were tucked away safe and sound in their apartment?

Once Ted and Phil are on the escape with me I peek inside the window. I'm looking in someone's kitchen. It's been totally ransacked. The drawers and cupboards are open or yanked down onto the linoleum; silverware and plate fragments litter the ground and countertops, and the refrigerator door has been propped open. Not seeing any immediate danger, I climb inside and then open the window wider for Ted and Phil. They struggle through the small opening, sighing and grunting as they wedge themselves through the window.

It's cold inside, and filled with the kind of eerie silence that makes you think of ghosts. Nothing happy could've happened here. There was never any joy or laughter, not when the feeling of death is creeping and crawling over everything. Even the bright, cheerful yellow paint job can't keep the chilly fear at bay. I check the cupboards to be sure, but there's nothing, not even crumbs. Someone has already come and cleaned out the apartment. There's no food, not the edible kind, and the refrigerator stinks from mold and spoiled milk. I shut it and continue on into a narrow, poky hall. The framed photographs are still there, knocked onto angles, but intact. I try not to look at the posed family photos, the hopeful smiles and cheesy sweaters.

"Fuck," I hear Ted murmur. I was thinking the same thing. When you live in almost constant fear, your instincts become better, sharper, and you can tell when something is terribly amiss. I get that feeling in the living room walking over the suspicious red stains on the ivory shag carpet, and I get that feeling again when we've finished walking through every room and find no one, just mess after mess, open drawer after open drawer, a phone hanging off the line with no dial tone.

We leave that apartment and go out into the hall. Here we meet a few of our undead friends and Ted and I get to practice our golf swings. I've never cared for golf much but I could certainly learn to love it. The driver is light but vicious. It takes a hefty chunk out of the first Groaner's face. I prefer the ax, it's more reliable, more deadly, but the driver is easier to swing and much less tiring. It's easiest just to knock them over the banister down onto the stairs below, so we do and listen to the satisfying crunch of their soft bodies hitting the ground floor.

The hall is dark, the walls covered in striped, rose pink wallpaper with a floral border. There are other doors hanging open and a shiver jutters down my spine. I don't want to go inside them, but I know we should. The first two are almost identical to the other apartment—ransacked, cold, empty and filled with the pervasive fog of troubled souls. There are two apartments left after that, and only one of them has a tightly shut door. We enter the open apartment first.

I thank God for the cold, cold weather.

He's there, a middle-aged man, probably no more than thirty-five. He is—was—sitting on a rocking chair. It's oddly placed in the middle of the living room, pushed away from the sofa, entertainment center and grandfather clock. The backside of the chair is red but it shouldn't be. His head is thrown back, his very dark curls cascading over the edge. I walk closer. Phil and Ted have stopped at the door and I can hear Phil retching in the hall. The man's neck is open, gashed, not by teeth, not by the undead, but by the clean, sharp sweep of a knife.

"No, this isn't right," I say, shaking my head. His eyes are open, staring, milky white where the blue should be. The room is so cold that he hasn't begun to decompose. The same thought keeps occurring to me every few seconds: even if we clear this place out, even if it's safe, *how can we live here?*

Then I'm running into the hall and vomiting over the staircase. I can't help it, it's worse, so much worse than the other things, the walking, unliving things. You can feel him trapped in there, the silent scream, the wide-open mouth begging for life.

"We have to get him out of there," Ted says. I agree and my esteem for Ted grows a little more as he and I carefully pick up the body, me the feet and Ted the shoulders. We're not sure where to take it, but we settle on the opposite end of the hall, in a quiet corner by a closet door. He's heavy in our arms, even without his blood, and I can't keep my eyes off the raw, red ribbon sewn across his neck. After putting him in the corner we go back in the apartment and find a clean sheet in the man's linen closet, one of the few things that hasn't been taken. We put it over him and watch the white speckled fabric settle over his body, shrouding him like a martyr at peace.

I think about the red stains in the first apartment, the ones on the carpet. I wonder where the bodies are.

There isn't anything to say, so we silently go to the last door, the closed one. It's locked so I take the knob off with the ax. The windows in the living room are open a little and a murmuring breeze rolls in. It's chilly here too and again, I'm thankful. There's another body here, an old, frail woman with hands covered in brown age spots, the skin so ancient it's stretched across her bones like parchment. She looks happy, okay, sitting on her overstuffed couch with closed eyes and a wan smile. I wonder if she had a heart attack, if she saw the commotion outside, staggered over to the couch and simply died. She's easier to carry, but so light and fragile I'm worried we'll crush her into dust. We put her beside the man and cover her too.

Phil keeps a lookout from the door, his baseball bat and gleaming club at the ready.

When we go back in her apartment we find everything where it should be: the china, silverware, pots and pans and towels and bed linens. Everything is very clean but there's a faint smell of dust, as if all her possessions were old, from a different time. I pick up a piece of junk mail on the front desk. Ms. Jane Weathers. I go into her kitchen and it's painted bright green. There are a few plants on the windowsill, but they've begun to shrivel up and wilt.

When I open up the cupboards beneath her sink I have to keep myself from laughing. I'm trying not to chuckle, I really am, but it's just too damn much. The apartment could be a model for

emergency survival. Poor Ms. Weathers was undoubtedly a prod-
uct of the "duck and cover," fallout-shelter-in-your-backyard era. It
shows. Ted finds two generators in her coat closet and an ancient
AM/FM portable radio with numbers on the knobs that are probably legible from outer space. In the cupboards I find all the
canned crap that languishes in the very back of your pantry—
green beans, baked beans, peaches, instant mashed potatoes.

"Well, looks like we're going go be living it up *Leave It to Beaver*
style," I say, holding up a can of creamed corn for Phil to inspect. I
can't remember the last time I ate any of these things, but they all
sound better than Cheetos. The apartment is perfect: clean, spacious and well-stocked. I don't know if we can all fit, or if we should.
There are other apartments, but I can't stop thinking about the
bloodstains on the carpet . . . That apartment is the most logical
choice. It has the handy fire escape. We could put a rug over the
stains, we could do something . . .

"Incoming!"

Phil is shouting, and in the doorway he's whacking away at the
shuffling creatures trying to get in. I see a decrepit arm with three
fingers reaching in for him and reach the door in time to lop it off.
Ted is there, the fire extinguisher puffing away, screaming past
my ear. I take a brown paper bag and fill it with canned items and
a can opener and rejoin the boys, who have cleared a path back to
the apartment with the fire escape. We sprint inside and I push
the bag into Ted's arms. He and Phil go down first and I cover their
escape, hacking away at two Groaners who have followed close on
our heels. I shut the window on my way out, leaving it open just
a crack.

Inside the store it's quiet, and we move a little more slowly. On
the way by the bookshelves I grab a few books and toss them into
Ted's bag. I restrain myself and he pats me on the back. Holly
greets us at the door, tears of relief shimmering in her eyes. I

never noticed how beautiful she is, how her new haircut shows her pretty face to advantage, how her cheekbones are high and regal. I'm just glad to see they're all alive and glad to have Dapper dancing at my shins, doing laps around my feet as I take off the head wrap and wipe down the ax and golf club.

"We found some golf clubs in the apartments," I say in response to their curious looks.

Phil shoots me a grateful glance and we all sit down to a dinner of beef jerky, Pepsi and cold green beans.

Now I'm alone in the safe room. I'm exhausted and so afraid.

The monitors are quiet, everyone is asleep, but I can't help thinking . . . Maybe we shouldn't live in the apartments. It seems wrong somehow, to take over a place we have no claim to, but what choice do we have? The break room is too small and I'm desperate to sleep on a bed again, to feel something soft underneath my head at night, to return to some semblance of civilized life. But something nags.

I don't know why we feel bound to this place, but it seems impossible to leave.

I turn on the radio we found in Ms. Weathers' apartment. The batteries are still good. It smells like old, wet books and there's dust collecting in the knobs and grooves. I tune it around, looking for signs of life but there's only static, static, static.

COMMENTS

CptCrckpot says:
September 27, 2009 at 7:09 pm
Things aren't much better in Texas, if you were having any thoughts about trying to make your way here. I'm in an office in an industrial park between Dallas and Fort Worth. I worked the

night shift doing customer service for a small company. Things had only just started when I came in to work, not even any mention on the news. I heard some sirens shortly after I got here, and later on I could hear cars crashing and gunshots in the distance, but that was it. Good thing our office is the last one in the last industrial park going north on 360 out of Arlington. I've spent the past week just laying low here in the office, and have fortified things as best I can.

> **Allison says:**
>
> *September 27, 2009 at 7:34 pm*
>
> Captain, we wish you luck. Are there other survivors with you? There's strength in numbers, so see if you can find some coworkers to help with the fortifications.

Isaac says:

September 27, 2009 at 7:56 pm

Supplies are low here and with winter coming there's no time to plant anything. I just hope we can hold out on the canned rations we have left. It makes me nervous sometimes, not seeing any of those creatures for days and then BAM, one drifts into the yard and starts pawing at the windows. I've got a hunting rifle but I don't shoot unless absolutely necessary. An ax, as you know Allison, works just as well and doesn't waste ammunition. Do you have anything to defend yourself with, CptCrckpot?

> **CptCrckpot says:**
>
> *September 27, 2009 at 9:03 pm*
>
> Not really, no weapons here except some fire extinguishers and letter openers, and the wireless is becoming erratic. I don't think we'll have it at all by the end of the week.

September 29, 2009—Little Children

"Couches, windows, actual places to sleep . . . It's the best choice, Allison, and you know it. I think we should move upstairs."

"We have to talk about this, Phil! We have to decide together, as a group. You can't just decide for us, it's not a Philtatorship."

"*What?*"

"It's from . . . Forget it. Look, what's important is that we discuss this like adults." Phil's giving me an empty stare. He's not even listening. "No one is in charge anymore. This is bigger than what you want."

Something strange has happened. Phil is suddenly a trusted voice of authority.

Ted and I expressed our considerable doubts to each other, our fears that, while the apartments upstairs were nice and a general improvement, we still weren't sure about making a permanent move. There were more pros than cons to moving, but like me, Ted wasn't fond of the general malaise of evil that hung around the place. But Phil, the son of a bitch, went right ahead and gushed to Matt and Janette about Ms. Weathers' apartment. It had a good view of the street, it had generators and silverware and peas!

Matt and Janette, accustomed to taking orders from Phil, jumped on board the train, leaving Ted and I to voice our doubts.

"But it was your idea to take a look around up there," Matt

protests, rolling his eyes at me for probably the fifth time that morning.

"I know that, but you have to understand. . . . It's just, I feel like maybe we should talk about it some more, maybe take a vote."

Conveniently, Phil hadn't told them about the dead body with the slit throat. I think he may have mentioned something about moving Ms. Weathers out of her apartment, but that didn't seem to bother Matt or Janette. It was tempting, so very tempting, to let them know that Phil had been ready to abandon us at a moment's notice. When the scent of freedom was on the air, even briefly, Phil had taken a big whiff, rounded third and dove for home face-first.

I was hoping that they'd go for the vote idea. Holly would vote whichever way Ted did and then we could pronounce a stalemate and stall for a while.

"Fine," Phil says, throwing up his hands. "A vote it is. All in favor of moving upstairs raise your hands."

One, two, three and—what's this?—*four* hands go up. Ted and I whip around to glare at Holly in unison and she takes a step back, shrugging her shoulders. "I just . . . I think it would be nice, don't you? I'm sick of it down here."

I elbow Ted, hard. "Control your fucking woman, dude."

"Hey!" Holly shouts.

"It was a joke, Holly. Pipe down," I say, pinching the bridge of my nose between thumb and forefinger. I can hear Phil laughing, chuckling at my frustration. Democracy is overrated. I should've just barred Phil in his office. Briefly, I consider telling them about the murdered man in Apartment D but decide against it. I haven't seen Phil, Matt and Janette this happy since before this stupid shit storm began.

"It's going to take a lot of work," I remind them, tugging at my side of the power-struggle rope. This wasn't going to be easy, but

Phil still had a ways to go before the rest of the group looked to him for tasks. "We encountered some Groaners up there so we need to be vigilant. I think we should stick to two apartments, divided up however, but we shouldn't spread out too far."

Having won the argument, Phil is practically exuberant as he goes about hauling what's left of our food upstairs. We organize teams, only one team taking a trip at a time, two people on the look-out while one person carries food or books or cleaning supplies. It takes three trips to get it all upstairs.

I wait to go on the last team, lingering in the safe room. We have to say good-bye to these monitors, these little beacons of information. Dapper is whining and hungry and I know he doesn't want to leave the break room. I should be more confident, more optimistic, but it all feels too hasty. This is how mistakes are made, I keep thinking, this is how we end up cornered and fighting for our lives.

Hollianted and I will be taking one apartment, the other three are inhabiting the other. They're right next to each other, so I take the initiative and take the ax to the drywall. It takes a few hours on and off of work, but eventually Ted and I have got a respectable hole straight through the shared wall. We have no phones, no walkie-talkies and we need a reliable way to stay in touch across the apartments.

There are several things preoccupying my mind, but one in particular: it makes me sincerely nervous that I still haven't found the source of the wireless. With Ted and a golf club, I scoured every apartment looking for the router. I've come to the conclusion that it might be in the maintenance area midway between the store and the apartments, the sort of no-man's-land at the bottom of the stairwell. We've decided to leave exploration of that room for another day; it's likely to be very dark and cold and we only have a few candles and one flashlight. Luckily, Ms. Weathers kept a healthy supply of batteries around. We hope this will be enough to power the flashlight and the radio indefinitely.

And there's something else that worries me: as soon as we arrived and started settling in, Dapper began barking and growling, turning in circles and baring his teeth. Ted and I are trying to keep the nervous, meaningful glances to a minimum, but we couldn't help a shared moment of anxiety when we noticed Dapper's strange behavior.

And so we've moved upstairs. In a way, it was easier than I expected. Matt, Janette and Holly took the journey well and they really didn't have to see much of anything. We told them to keep their eyes forward but I'm sure they glimpsed the trail of carnage in the back storeroom. Most of the undead were still cleared out from our adventure the other day. They've each been given a golf club which, in a matter of hours, ended up coming in handy.

Moving apartments wasn't nearly enough excitement for one day.

Not three hours after we'd handed out the golf clubs, I hear a scream come from the other apartment. There are many kinds of screams—horrified screams, pain screams and surprised screams. This was one of the latter. I peek through the jagged hole in the wall to see Janette covering her mouth, her golf club on the floor and a man I'd never seen before kneeling there with his hand rubbing his forehead.

Hollianted and I sprint into the other apartment, where Phil and Matt are just coming on the scene too. The man isn't dead and certainly isn't undead, but he does have a reddening bump on the right side of his forehead.

"Who the *fuck* are you?" I ask, in what I believe to be a remarkably calm voice given the circumstances.

"Jesus, I was thinking just the same thing!"

Ted is raising his golf club up over his head, winding up for a big, brain-bashing swing. The stranger flinches, covering his blond, curly head with both arms.

"Don't! Fuck, don't hit me again. I'm not armed."

Phil races forward to confirm this, lamely patting the stranger down, mimicking whatever he had seen them do on *Law & Order*. When he steps back, he nods solemnly, giving a little comical grunt of acquiescence. I ignore this and put myself between Ted and the newcomer.

"Why the hell were you hiding in a linen closet?" I ask, crossing my arms over my chest. He's still kneeling on the ground, which is good. It makes me think he at least recognizes who has the upper hand here.

"I live here," he retorts with a laugh of disbelief. "But I heard all these noises and voices so I got scared." He swallows a big lump in his throat and glances to his left. Something is wrong. An idea comes to mind and I know I have to get him alone.

"What's your name?" I ask, trying to sound gentle.

"Zack, my name is Zack, but we can't stay here. There's a—"

"We've cleared them out, checked everywhere," I interrupt him, widening my eyes to let him know that whatever it is he wants to say, he'll have to save it.

"Apparently not!" he mutters, rubbing the bump on his head.

"This is really your apartment?" I ask.

"Not this one, Apartment D. It's my brother-in-law's place," Zack replies. I look at Ted. D is where we found the man in the rocking chair.

"So why are you in here then?" I ask.

"I couldn't . . . I couldn't stay there! Not after—"

"They got your brother-in-law," I finish for him. He squints at me, tilting his head to the side. I can hear Phil squishing around on the carpet behind me, fidgeting. Through the hole in the wall I can hear Dapper yowling. I don't want the others to know about the man in the rocking chair. It won't help anything to put them in a panic.

"Can you stand?"

Zack nods slowly and then digs his heel into the carpet, lifting himself to his feet with one strong push. He stands and looks around at all of us, his eyebrows meeting over his anxious gaze.

"I guess we can't kick you out, seeing as how you live here and all."

"Um, Allison, could I have a word?"

"Sure, Ted."

He hands the golf club to Phil wordlessly. I follow him to the master bedroom and he shuts the door. His hair is getting in his eyes again so he pushes it away and glares at me.

"What?"

"You know what. We can't take him in. It's out of the question."

"Really? And why is that?"

"We don't know anything about him. For all we know he could've killed that guy!"

"His own brother-in-law? And why would he stick around? Murderers generally don't hang around after they kill somebody. I mean, serial killers like the attention and stuff but that's totally different. Not to mention, he was hiding in the linen closet. If he was gutsy enough to slit someone's throat, why would he hide from us?"

"Because he's outnumbered? Because we have a dog? Any number of reasons!"

"It just . . . It just doesn't seem right to kick him out. How can we do that? You know as well as I do that he'd probably die out there on his own," I explain. "And besides, do you really want to make enemies?"

"We know there are other people out there. We know that now, you said it yourself. Those people, whoever, on your, whatever . . ."

"Blog?"

"Yes. Look, if we didn't know there were other survivors then maybe it would be different, but the way things are . . . I just think it's a bad call."

"Our food supply is better, we have room. I can't in good conscience send someone out to their death," I say. I lean forward and grab Ted around the collar and yank him toward the window. The chintz curtains are closed so I push them back. "Look. Look at it down there. There's nothing left. Where would he go? We can't be barbarians, Ted, we just can't. What if it was you hiding in that closet? Or my mom? When things get back to normal little acts of kindness will add up."

"Jesus, you sound like my girlfriend."

"Is that such a bad thing?" I shout. I'm losing my temper; I try to breathe. Just a few deep breaths and everything will be easier to handle . . .

"You just want him around because he's good-looking."

"I—*what*? Are you completely insane? What does that have to do with anything?" The deep breaths aren't working now, nothing is working . . .

"Well if it turns out we need to repopulate the Earth he's a big upgrade from Phil."

I don't mean to, I don't think I even wanted to, but I slap Ted, hard, right across the face. He reels back, holding his cheek, his glasses askew.

"When have I ever made a decision out of purely selfish motives, Ted? Do you think that by only considering myself we would be where we are now? Do you? *Answer me.*"

"It was a stupid thing to say. I'm sorry."

"He stays. Get it? He just . . . He just fucking stays."

I leave Ted behind, letting him hold where it smarts. There's something ugly inside of me, it's not just my temper. It's something worse. I can feel all of the questions, all of the doubts, swirling into one terrible mass of anger. It's too much to handle, too much for one person. And it's worse because I know if my mom were here she could help. She would know what to do. She was always so strong, so put together . . . She would know just what to say to me. Maybe my instincts are wrong and maybe Ted is right, but I'll be damned if I start acting like nothing and no one else matter. It all matters, every little last vestige of humanity matters now. The books, the radio, the people . . . We have to carry it forward.

In the living room they're still standing around, useless, staring at Zack like he's Zombie Santa Claus just fallen out of the chimney. I push through them, through the wall of Janette and Matt, and take Zack by the wrist.

"Everybody, this is Zack. Zack, this is Janette, Matt, Phil and Holly, and the guy in the other room is Ted. I'm Allison. It's good to have you with us."

Zack is staying in our apartment because the suspicion and dislike rolls off of Matt in a pungent, snappish wave. Ted is doing his very best, but I know he's swallowing his pride and his frustration. Holly, of course, is affable and kind. She's an asset to us, I can see it now. When everyone else refuses to smile or laugh, Holly is a bright ray of sunshine bouncing down the halls. She's even begun an art project in the living room of our apartment, something to make it look a little cheerier and more like home.

Zack has volunteered to sleep in the bathtub with some pillows and a comforter, which gives me the bedroom all to myself. I can hear Zack's elbows bumping the walls next door, and Dapper is stretched out on the end of the bed, but otherwise I have solitude, a quiet place to write and rest. Hollianted use the hide-a-bed out in the living room. I think they're grateful for the privacy and I envy their relationship. I hate that Ted is a little bit right. I'm lonely, and he can see it. Maybe everyone can see it.

COMMENTS

Brooklyn Girl says:
September 29, 2009 at 3:37 pm
Bed Stuy still here. We've managed to block the stairs to our apartment and use the fire escapes to go out for supplies. So far the fires have managed to burn away from our block, but the smoke is making visibility horrible. You don't see the things until they're right on you. We're raiding the bodega down the block tonight. Keep the faith.

Allison says:
September 29, 2009 at 5:51 pm
Thank god. I thought NYC would be the first to go.
Is Manhattan history?

Rev. Brown says:
September 29, 2009 at 5:58 pm
Let your faith be your shield! Your arms will tire, your blades will dull, but the Lord's light will carry you past harm.

Be not afraid! His righteous judgment has fallen on this world of sodomites and non-believers, and only we, the faithful, will be taken up to heaven after he has culled this herd. As the dead marched on Jerusalem when Jesus was hung upon that cross so too do they march on us in this final hour.

When the rapture comes—and fear not, it will, and soon— the Lord will see the faithful into Paradise while leaving the

satanists, atheists, and homosexuals behind to eek out an
existence before being consumed by the fires of hell.

Bob in Rhode Island says:
September 29, 2009 at 6:32 pm
Try to make it to a supermarket if you can, there won't be much
left unless you hurry.

> **Allison says:**
> *September 29, 2009 at 7:07 pm*
> I'm aware, but right now venturing out is risky. I'm just glad
> we managed to move into the apartments without incident.
> I mean I guess Zack qualifies as an incident but that might
> hurt his feelings. ☹

S.W.A.T. SGT. jason jeffery says:
September 29, 2009 at 7:45 pm
I live 30 miles from Arlington in a small town, so its not so bad,
my guys scott and jerrod are the only survivors I found, and
we 3 are holding up pretty good at scotts house, keep posting,
you're a light in the darkness.

September 30, 2009—Breakfast of Champions

"Happy Last Day of September!"

I wake up to breakfast in bed. It's the first hot food I've had in weeks: oatmeal with maple syrup and chocolate chips. There's a little fabric posy on the side of the plate, a flower no doubt clipped from one of the many fake bouquets decorating Ms. Weathers' apartment.

"What's this for?"

"I wanted to say thanks, you know, for saving me from the dreaded death by golf club."

"You're welcome. I don't believe in cruel and unusual punishment. I do, however, believe in chocolate chips."

"Lucky guess, I suppose."

"How did you manage to heat this up?" I ask. Zack is sitting a safe distance away on the edge of the bed, forcing Dapper to move over. The dog glares at him and then rolls over and goes back to sleep. I would be embarrassed, but we're all so filthy and disheveled that I won't look much different later in the day.

"That's the other thing I wanted to thank you for . . . My brother-in-law . . . I know you moved him. I couldn't. I couldn't touch him, couldn't look at him," Zack says, staring down at his palms. He's wearing faded jeans and a dark green thermal long-sleeve T. "I saved some things from his place, before the thieves showed up."

"So that's what happened," I say quietly.

"They took everything and one of them . . . You saw. I was trying to warn you. I'm worried they'll come back. They couldn't get into this apartment and I wouldn't be surprised if they returned," he says. "Everyone is so desperate. They do terrible things."

"We'll be ready for them," I reply, forcing a smile. "I'm sorry for cutting you off yesterday. I don't want the others to know about your brother-in-law, about what happened to him. It was hard enough just to get them up here in the first place—you'd think it was halfway around the world and not just upstairs. I'm not sure how they'd react to something like that." Zack doesn't need to know I wasn't big on the move in the first place. We're talking in generalizations, euphemisms, but I'm too nervous to say the word "murder" in front of him. I choose to leave out that once Phil stepped in, the move upstairs happened relatively quickly. "That still doesn't explain the hot oatmeal."

"Oh!" he says, brightening up. The curtains are open and the light coming in is pale, milky. It casts a glowing light that makes the room feel sleepy and comfortable and soft. Zack's green eyes glimmer in the dim haze of yellow and he smiles. "I rescued a hibachi. There aren't many coals left, but enough for a few meals. I've never tried lighting it up with just newspaper, but we could try that."

"A hibachi? Phil will positively die of happiness. Unless it comes off a grill he doesn't consider it real food."

"I'd have to agree with him there," Zack says, chuckling. "I mean . . . Well, all right, I have a confession to make," he says, his smile fading. I don't know why, but the expression makes my stomach flip over. He sighs very slowly, his chest inflating and collapsing like a baster balloon. "I was the sous chef at L'Etoile, so hot oatmeal doesn't exactly present a challenge."

"See? I knew there was a reason I stuck my neck out for you,"

I tell him, smiling. That feeling in my stomach fades. Out in the living room I can hear the first evidence of Hollianted waking up. There's shuffling and the scratch of a can opener across a countertop.

"It's cute," Zack says.

"What is?"

"How you worry about them. You're the mother hen around here, aren't you?"

"I—oh, it's that obvious?"

"You sure you don't want to tell them about the thieves?" he asks. I want to eat the oatmeal but it's hard to dig in with him scrutinizing my face. "It doesn't seem right, ya know, to leave them in the dark."

"Let me worry about them. Like you said, I'm the mother hen."

"You don't think they have a *right* to know?"

It's touching that he's worried about people he's only known for a matter of hours, but it's hard not to snap at him. That's something I need to work on, the urge to start a fight at the first sign of disagreement. I don't know what's got me so touchy, maybe it's the tantalizing food just inches away that I haven't been allowed to touch yet. The proximity of the hot food must have made my mind fuzzy. My memory's not perfect, but I said something like, "Everything is so fucked, Zack. Who knows what will happen tomorrow or the next day? It seems like leaving it open, letting them think there's a chance for something good . . . I just can't add another reason to worry. Not now. Not yet."

"Fair enough," he says, holding up his hands. "I'll leave you alone. If you've gotten them along this far then you must know what you're doing."

"Thanks," I say. "I just want everyone to get along." The oatmeal is perfect, gooey and warm and remarkably well-textured. It does not taste like it's come out of a cardboard box. "This," I say, holding up a spoonful of the oatmeal, "is probably your one-way ticket to their hearts and minds."

It only takes a few hours for Zack to start fitting in. I don't know why I was so worried about it; it's how we live now. Another human, another living creature, you learn to accept them and like them and take them into your family. It's not even a conscious process, but an unavoidable survival technique. None of the usual friendship rules apply—there's no slow, intermediate zone where you're just starting to know someone. You're living in close quarters, you sleep, eat and live in the same small, cramped apartment and you discover quickly how to fit that new person into your routine.

Zack helps with dinner and somehow we make a kind of fried casserole out of cocktail weenies, baked beans and canned corn. Now he's helping Hollianted clean up the dishes. I'm back in my room, sitting on the bed with the curtains open. I can see the city. I can see what's left of it. In the distance, smoke lingers on the horizon, buildings black and charred as they burn slowly from the inside out. I wonder if it will all end in fire, if we will live to see this apartment, and the store, in flames. And I wonder where my mother is, if she's alive, if she found a group like I did, a broken little family to cling to.

I've been tinkering with the radio. Sometimes I think I can hear voices, a single voice, humming beneath the static. I'll find it for a minute and then it's gone. I want so badly to hear someone out there that I think sometimes I'm imagining the ghost of a voice.

Update: October 1, 2009—Approximately 1:30 A.M.

Ms. Weathers' wine supply has been discovered. Ted and Zack now best friends. All of us now best friends. There's no more room on the bed, there are bodies sprawled everywhere. Dapper insists on taking up 1/3 of it for himself. Dog not drunk.

Zack has requested—nay—*demanded* I provide a portrait for you all. I oblige. Behold:

(Note to reader: Zack insists I point out the following: that his hair is not, in fact, made of macaroni noodles, that he actually has a bit of a beard and not the pocks, and that he is jubilantly swigging from a bottle of Chianti, not a giant's used tampon.

Also that his eyes are not wildly out of whack as shown in portrait.)

And again. Cubist:

And finally, Holly's contribution:

Ceci n'est pas Zack.

Spot the art major.

COMMENTS

Mom says:

October 1, 2009 at 2:27 am

Allison sweetie, is it really you? Stop getting drunk and respond to this, please. I need to know that you're okay. Your aunt is here with me and the neighbors too. I'm afraid there isn't much food left and we'll have to leave soon. Can we come to you? Do you think it's safe? Oh thank God you're okay. I love you so much and I want to come to you.

> **Allison says:**
>
> *October 1, 2009 at 2:57 am*
>
> Holy shit, I'm the worst daughter ever. Mom? You there? How did you find this? Whatever, it doesn't matter. Is everyone okay there? Can you take the side streets? I think you should avoid Main Street, it's clogged with cars and those things. Don't try for us unless you think you can make it. I love you too, I love you and write back soon.

> > **Mom says:**
> >
> > *October 1, 2009 at 3:08 am*
> >
> > That's it. We're coming to you. Give us three days. It should be more than enough. If you don't hear from us by then . . . Then I don't know, but don't come looking, Allison. I need you safe and sound. I'll be seeing you soon, sweets.

October 1, 2009—Other Voices, Other Rooms

"Ho-ly shit. Holy shit, holy shit, holy shit!"

"Wow. That's almost word for word what *I* said."

Upon hearing the news, Ted graced us with a rousing rendition of his happy dance (not to be missed, trust me, like a Maypole doing the Electric Slide), ecstatic that my mother is both computer literate and a total badass. The others had a more measured response, especially Zack. I think he knows it's rough out there and he doesn't want me to get my hopes up too high. But my hopes are up now and they're not coming down: my mom is alive and she's coming to me. But that's not all, that's not nearly all.

There are voices that you never forget.

They don't come often but when they do, they implant on your memory like a soft, invisible polyp. You might not hear the voice for years and years but when you hear it again, your mind sparkles to life, activates, and the voice becomes as real as a warm stone in your palm.

Your mom (w00t), your dad, Frank Sinatra, Billie Holiday, Dick Clark, Bono . . .

My dad died when I was young, really young. I shouldn't remember his voice; I didn't even get to know him really. But I can conjure the sound of his laugh, the way he made a soft hmm'ing sound when he thought, with just a skip into memories. I can hear him, I remember him. He will always be with me.

There's a new voice now, a voice I know I will never forget. It may as well be God or Buddha or a great, unknowable deity too gentle and perfect to perceive . . .

The radio is working. *And someone is out there.*

The Lord's light will carry you past harm . . .

Maybe you're right, Rev. Brown. After all, believers find God's touch, His work in every infinitesimal thing. And now there's a new light for us to cling to, something to strive for, to use as a shield against the daily doubts, the pessimism, the fear. Maybe it isn't religion, maybe it isn't God, but it's something good and beautiful to believe in.

91.7 is the magical number. I found it in the dark, thick time of night when you know morning is still far off and you crave rest, but you know too that you won't be getting back to sleep. It's the kind of lonely, empty time when you need something, anything to occupy your mind. I started fiddling with the radio, keeping the volume very soft so as not to disturb the others. Dapper stirred at the fizzling, constant static, wriggling his way over to me across the valley of irretrievably wrinkled bedsheets. His head was resting on my calves as the little line indicator went up and down, up and down, searching across the bleak airwaves until finally, after an hour of idle tuning and flipping between AM and FM, twiddling the antenna in different directions, the voice crackled to life.

". . . down to us, if you can manage it, we have food, shelter and limited medicine. We have nurses and volunteers at the ready to help you if you are injured. I repeat: the university campus is open. We have gathered in the gymnasium. If you can get down to us we have some food, shelter and limited medicine."

I scooted closer to the window, breathless, euphoric, and stuck the antenna as close to the glass as possible. The message repeated, this time more slowly. I wondered if perhaps it was a recording, but then, as if reading my thoughts, he said something else:

"I don't know how many of you are listening, or how many of you are still trying desperately to survive, but I want you to know this: all hope is not lost. You have somewhere to go, somewhere to seek. It's late and you feel afraid, hopeless, but don't despair. Just today a woman came to us. She was starving, injured, terrified, but she crossed ten miles to get here. She heard us, she persevered, and she arrived in one piece. Her name is Melissa. She came with her two-month-old daughter and she told me that the radio, the broadcast, inspired her to continue. And so to honor Melissa and her courage, I've chosen to read from her favorite book this evening. So dear listeners, close your eyes, let the worry drain away and listen."

I couldn't believe it. I was hallucinating, I just had to be. It wasn't possible. I get word from my mother *and* confirmation that others are out there—close—in the same twenty-four-hour period. The university is only ten blocks away, a ten- to fifteen-minute walk at a leisurely pace. But to go out—to risk it . . . That ten blocks would be dangerous and filled with undead. The university is at the heart of the city, a populated place. It could be absolutely crawling with those things . . .

Jesus, Mom, be safe.

She's probably already left and won't be able to read this but I just can't stop thinking about her out in the open, trying her damnedest to get here.

There will be time to worry about that in the coming days, discussions to start, arguments to endure. For now, I wanted to stop worrying, fretting, and just follow directions. And so I did as the voice said, I sat back against the pillow, put my hand on Dapper's head, closed my eyes, said a prayer for my mom's safety and listened.

"'It was the best of times, it was the worst of times, it was the age of wisdom, it was the age of foolishness, it was the epoch of belief, it was the epoch of incredulity, it was the season of Light, it was the season of Darkness, it was the spring of hope, it was the winter of despair; we had everything before us; we had nothing before us, we were all going direct to Heaven, we were all going direct the other way. . . .'"

There are voices that you never forget.

Sleep tight Isaac, Brooklyn Girl, Reverend, *Mom*. There are voices in the darkness, sweet beacons of radiant possibility, and they offer the chance to each and every one of us for survival.

COMMENTS

Isaac says:
October 1, 2009 at 10:08 pm
Congratulations on finding your mom, Allison. If only all of us could be that lucky. I've got my fingers crossed for her journey.

> **Brooklyn Girl says:**
> *October 1, 2009 at 10:34 pm*
> Add another pair of crossed fingers! Let us know the minute she gets there.

> > **Allison says:**
> > *October 1, 2009 at 10:48 pm*
> > Thanks for the support guys. I'm sure, wherever she is right now, my mom appreciates it!

October 3, 2009—Paradise Lost

"Who the hell needs this many Christmas ornaments? Did she have a different tree for each of the twelve days of Christmas? This has to be a sign of mental instability, right? I mean, it's beyond compulsive," I say, holding up just one of a gajillion glass Christmas balls. "Beyond tacky."

"They're hideous," Holly confirms, shuddering.

"Do you think we could rig them somehow? Turn them into bombs? Couldn't you just see these raining down from the window, taking out a whole legion of those creeps?"

"Worth a shot," she says.

Today we continue the task of organizing all of Ms. Weathers' things and finding a place for them. She really has a lot of clutter. It takes up most of her closets and even part of the hallway. Most of the stuff she's saved up and packed away is sentimental junk. Nothing is labeled, so Holly volunteered to help me go through the boxes and sort out the ones with useful items and the ones that could be set aside for later.

It's hard to focus. There's no sign of my mom yet and I'm picking up old watercolor paintings, no doubt by Ms. Weathers' grandchildren, and having a hard time remembering what box I pulled them out of. I haven't told anyone about the radio yet. I know it seems selfish but there's a reason for the omission.

Holly is cooing over something she's found. It's an old photograph, faded and orange and covered in water spots. The frame is still in good condition and the photo is of Ms. Weathers and presumably her husband or an old boyfriend. He's in a sailor's uniform, dressed as a cliché, and they both look positively carefree. I take it away from Holly before she can get too attached.

"I know it's hard to get rid of all this stuff," I tell her, burying the photograph in the bottom of a box. "I know it feels wrong, like robbing her or something. I hope she would understand. We're all still young, we don't deserve to be struggling to live."

"You're right," Holly says quietly. Her short red hair sticks up in every direction. It's really quite endearing.

"Here," I tell her, pushing another box over, "try this one. Let's hope it's not more expired coupons."

I can't guess if Holly can tell I'm distracted or if she's distracted by something too. I mean, she knows I'm worried about my mother but she has no idea about the radio yet. There's a mean, aching trouble gnawing at my stomach and it's not hunger. I open another box: candles and air fresheners. Not bad. I keep meaning to investigate the maintenance room downstairs and a solid supply of candles is just another reminder. Maybe I could actually do something productive if the voice repeating in my head would shut up and go away.

You have somewhere to go, somewhere to seek.

I should just tell her. I should tell everyone. Something is standing in my way, a question. It's that one word, "seek." What if I don't want to seek? What if I'm done with seeking? Even if we made it to the university, then what? Would we stay there forever or would there be another destination after that, and then another, and another? We've found a good thing here. It's not perfect, it's not glamorous, but it feels manageable, sustainable. Phil, Janette and Matt have already slipped into the old pattern of life; they ignore us and we ignore them. Maybe that symptom alone is enough to convince me that we've discovered a semblance of normalcy—why risk it? Even if it's only ten blocks away, why uproot again just to live in a crowded gymnasium with a new set of strangers? But if I don't tell them it feels like lying, like just another betrayal.

"Allison?"

"Hm? Yes?"

"Are you okay? You've been staring at that Glade PlugIn for five minutes now."

Fuck.

"Oh, oh yeah, I'm fine. Sorry, just had a thought, that's all."

"Is it your mom? Want to share?"

Sure, I think, looking at Holly's wide-open face, why not? It's not that she's stupid, she's just very, very trusting. I can't imagine she'll prod for my true motivations.

"Holly," I begin, clearing my throat, "do you like it here? I mean, if you had the choice, to stay here or go somewhere else, what would you do?"

She shifts from sitting cross-legged to sort of resting with both her legs crooked to the side. The miniature snow globe in her hands began to travel up and down, tossed from palm to palm as she sticks out her tongue a little and considers the question. At least she doesn't have an immediate answer. Maybe my hesitations aren't so strange after all.

"I guess it depends," she says at last, shrugging.

"On what?"

"On where it is."

"Yeah, that's a good point."

"Why do you ask?"

"I don't know; just curious, I guess. I mean, this place isn't so bad, right? We've sort of carved out a bit of a niche, don't you think?" She looks away as I ask the question, molding her palms around the curved dome of the snow globe, pressing it together until it looks ready to shatter in her hands. "Holly?"

"It *is* good here. I . . . I like it."

With that, she turns back to the boxes, conversation terminated. I watch her as she gets up on her knees to reach across for a big, heavy, unopened box. She grabs it by the flaps but it's too heavy and the box tumbles out of her arms, landing askew. A cascade of tinkling Christmas ornaments lands across our feet, red and green and gold, smelling like dust and pine. One of the green ball ornaments has broken, cracked open on its end like an egg.

I reach to start cleaning it up and without warning, Holly is in tears. She covers her face with both hands and sobs, hard, her whole body shaking with the effort to stop, to recompose. I gently touch her knee, wondering if my question was too much, went too far.

"Hey, it's okay. Only one broke, we'll just clean it up, no worries."

"It's not . . . i-it's not that!" she says, forcing out the shuddering words between sobs.

"Jesus, hey, don't worry. What's going on?"

I brush the broken glass to the side and move closer to her, hoping a human presence and a shoulder to cry on is what she's looking for. Holly stays still, hiding her face for a moment before her fingers slowly wipe down her cheeks.

"It's Ted," she says, stumbling over his name. My first thought is that he's broken up with her and my second is that I'll have to break his face. "He's . . . he's proposed. He asked me to marry him."

"That's great!" I shout, maybe a little too enthusiastic. Holly stares back at me, mystified.

"It is?"

"I mean . . . yeah—isn't it? I thought you two were . . . ya know, in it for the long haul."

"It's not that. I love him, I really do, but I just don't like it. . . . It feels like he's only doing it because of this, you know, because of everything that's happened," she says. The tears have stopped, coming to a slow rest on the curve of her cheekbone. She sniffles, wiping her nose with the back of her pale hand. "So I asked him: would you be asking me this if we weren't stuck here together? And he said no!"

I knew Ted was no Casanova, but that's pretty inexcusable.

"Well, I'm sure he means that . . . that the circumstances being the way they are, well, things are uncertain. I'm sure he would have proposed eventually, so what's the difference if he does it now?"

"I don't know. See? I just don't know! I should be happy, part of me is. I thought he would never get up the courage. He was so shy when we met and I know his parents would never ever approve of us, but that's just it! It means he doesn't think we'll ever see his parents again. I think he's given up."

"No," I tell her firmly, squeezing her knee. I mean it. "That's not true. He wouldn't have asked you to marry him if he'd given up hope. He has hope for the two of you, for a life together. That's not an insult, Holly. I just wish you knew how lucky you are."

She rests her warm hand over mine and nods, a smile tugging at her lips even as the tears finish sliding off her chin. Carefully, she picks up a jagged piece of the broken ornament and turns it, letting it catch the light, crackle to life and sparkle.

"You won't tell him, will you? That I was mad?" she asks, dropping the piece of glass. I can't stop looking at it.

"No, of course not," I say, laughing. "It's our secret."

I had a visitor just before getting into bed tonight. Zack came to chat. I hadn't seen much of him or Ted today; while Holly and I worked on sorting Ms. Weathers' belongings, Zack and Ted volunteered to sweep the other apartments more thoroughly to locate useful items and to check and double-check hiding places. The cold has seeped in through the windows; Zack shuffled in draped in a chunky afghan.

"Busy?" he asks, nodding toward the laptop perched on my knees. Dapper rolls over a few feet, anticipating that he would be asked to move.

"Not really," I reply, shutting the monitor. "What's up?"

"Is everything okay with Ted? He seemed weird today."

"Weird how?"

"I don't know. . . . Jumpy . . . Irritable," he says, sitting down at the foot of the bed. "I know he's not my biggest fan, but it was strange."

"I'm sure he likes you just fine," I say. "It's just stress. I think he and Holly are having issues. Best just to leave it alone."

"Ah," he says, "I see. . . . Trouble in paradise."

"So you would call this paradise?"

He looks over at me, squinting like I'm miles away. I try desperately to keep my face neutral, to stop my cheeks from turning a bright, burning red. Getting a sneaky question past him will be hard, much harder than with Holly.

"What are you up to?" he asks, scooting closer.

Well, here goes.

"I heard someone on the radio last night," I tell him. His eyes double in size. "It was a man at the university. They've set up some kind of relief effort there. He also read me to sleep."

"Really?" Zack replied, arching an eyebrow with a smirk.

"Not like that. It was . . . nice, but odd, ya know? To hear someone out there, someone with some kind of authority. He said they had food and shelter."

"He a cop?"

"I don't think so, he didn't say anything like that," I reply. He looks away, down at his fingernails. "So?"

"So what?"

"So do you think we should go?"

"It's not so bad here."

"That's what I was thinking too. The last thing I want is to be milling around with a hundred sweaty college kids, or my own goddamn professors," I say, shaking my head. "But we might run out of food here, especially if my mom is coming and bringing people, or the cold. . . . I just think it's worth discussing."

"Look," he says, taking my hand. "Food can be found. What we have here . . . It's like a home, a place of our own. If we go to the university who knows what we'll find. It might sound good now, but it will be harder to leave once we're there."

"I know," I say, "but I'm not good at keeping secrets. I think I should tell the others."

"Do it," he says, nodding vigorously, his curls bouncing. "But I guarantee you they'll say the same thing."

"Thanks for listening."

"Mind if stay? I could use a bedtime story."

We turn on the radio and blow out the candle. The voice is there, the stranger. We lie perfectly still in the dark, both of us on our backs, listening to Dapper breathing and to the low, rhythmic voice coming to us over the radio. I can't help but wonder at the miracle of such things, of technologies I've never cared about or considered before. It's as if an entirely new person is there with us, a man I've never met but that I know will become familiar with time. He's there, reading, his voice separating into a million pinpoints of light, carrying a story, words, warmth. We lay quiet and still and I feel my breath going out of my lungs, lifting out and over to the radio, traveling through the speaker, across the invisible airwaves to visit the stranger with the mesmerizing voice.

The voice reads from *The Awakening* and I can't help but think of my mom. I wish she was here to listen, to put me at ease. It would be much easier to just relax and enjoy the radio if I knew she was still alive, if I knew she would make it here to read it to me again the way she used to. She's out there, I know she is. I just hope my urgent thoughts are enough to see her safely through.

- -

COMMENTS

Isaac says:

October 3, 2009 at 9:08 pm

Any word from your mom yet?

> **Allison says:**
>
> *October 3, 2009 at 9:29 pm*
>
> Nothing yet. I'm trying not to panic but it shouldn't take her long. On a normal day you could get here from her house in forty-five minutes. I guess that distance doesn't mean much anymore.
>
> > **Brooklyn Girl says:**
> >
> > *October 3, 2009 at 10:09 pm*
> >
> > Hey, if we're still here hanging on then she could definitely make it. Don't give up hope, Allison.

October 4, 2009—Sense and Sensibility

"Anything?"

"Nothing. Not a peep. There are some Floaters milling around outside but no sign of her."

Ted puts a hand on my shoulder and squeezes. I don't know what to do. If I cry it's like I've accepted she's not coming. I won't cry, I won't. I need to focus, focus and lead.

And so the meeting goes about how I expected.

No one in particular is jumping at the idea of leaving the apartments quite yet. Phil brings up the possibility of finding lost family members among those assembled in the university gymnasium. Janette finds his idea promising and exciting. Matt points out that a single mother carrying a child and traveling ten miles through dangerous country was an anomaly, not something to be expected. This, of course, is his way of saying that it was highly unlikely that Phil's chubby, well-meaning wife (or their two kids) had made it the more than ten miles from their tan rambler to the university. Phil throws a bit of a tantrum, but something tells me he felt Matt was right.

Ted, who has spent most of the meeting glowering at me from the corner of the living room with his glasses still skewed slightly to the right, corners me after the others have left to start on dinner. We stand alone in the living room, the low, glass surface of the coffee table between us. I can see he's gunning for a fight but that he's hesitating to start in with too much heat.

"It's okay," I tell him. "You can just say it. Go ahead. I know what you're thinking."

Ted refuses to speak, his lips pursed so tightly they look like a starfish all folded up and suffocating. I can see the thoughts flickering in his eyes, the decisions, the careful weighing of the options. He pushes his glasses up the bridge of his nose and tosses his hair around like an impatient stallion.

"I don't want to fight," he says.

"Yes you do, and that's okay. Just start now before I get too hungry."

"Fine," he snorts. "Why didn't you tell me? I thought we had . . . I know you're fucked up worrying over your mom, but I thought there was an understanding, you know? We hash things out and then take it to the group. What happened to that?"

I kinda knew this was coming, but knowing doesn't make it any less obnoxious.

"It's not a decision I can make, or we can make, get it? It's a group decision, everyone is involved."

"Everyone?" he says. He's lowered his voice to his serious register. When he starts to get angry his accent becomes thicker and his shoulders hunch over as if he's readying for a fistfight. I don't think it will come to blows, but he still looks like a warthog kicking at the dirt, coiled up, tensed, a ball of fire seething right in front of the gold-framed Thomas Kinkade print.

"Right. Everyone. Everyone meaning you and Zack, right?"

I didn't *know* this would happen, but I thought it might. I cross my arms, puffing out my chest to mimic his ridiculous, dominant posturing. I keep silently insisting there's no drama here. I keep telling myself this is about a power dynamic, not about Ted being a jealous, whiny little prick.

"Does Zack know?" he asks, much more to the point.

"Yeah, I guess so, yeah. But, come on, in my defense he wheedled it out of me."

"Is that what they're calling it these days?"

"You know that saying, how does it go—I hurt you because I love you? Well, that saying doesn't apply here."

"Is that one of your kinky sex games?"

"Look, asshole," I mutter, taking a big step toward him, "I'll slap you again if I have to. Don't make it seem so appealing."

I can feel it surging, that clash of the titans—hot, angry, boiling temper that's just dying to rip right out of my throat and through the palm of my hand. I still don't know where this is coming from. Best guess? Ted's goddamn fucking attitude and the fact that my mom, the most beautiful woman in the entire world, is missing and maybe, just maybe, dead.

"Fuck it," I say, deflating. "This is a waste of time."

"Yeah."

"Do you think we should leave? I mean, when my mom gets here, do you think we should go?"

It takes Ted a moment to answer. In the meantime, we both take a seat on the big, calico couch. It's covered in handmade afghans that take up so much space that the couch itself is barely visible beneath all the crafts. Everything in this place smells like cinnamon. Cinnamon tinged with sweat and shit, the smell we seem to carry with us everywhere. We can't get rid of it—no matter how careful we are about cleaning the bathroom we always seem to reek just a little.

Ted rests his right ankle on his knee and shoves his hands deep in his pockets. I'm tempted to interrupt the silence with a bit of a heart-to-heart about Holly but I keep my mouth shut. I think I like Holly's new allegiance, the way she grins at me like we're twins separated at birth. I can't read her mind but I can take a pretty accurate guess.

"My gut says yes," Ted replies at last. "But that's a big change. Who knows if it will be that much better. Still, to see people, new people, hell, lots of people . . ."

"I know. That's how I feel too."

"It could be a madhouse," Ted says, smiling crookedly. His foot bounces rhythmically in the air. "And super-unsanitary with all those people in one spot."

"I think we should stay," I tell him. The tension melts away, leaving behind the same old easy friendship that existed before. It's as if the radio, Zack, our disagreements never even existed.

"Really?"

"Really. What's the point? Searching, searching, never happy with anything . . . When does it end? It exhausts me just thinking about it. Buddha taught that desire never learns, it never wakes up to its own foolishness, it drives us on endlessly—and for what?"

"Hmm, well, Confucius say: 'White girls who sit on tack get point.'"

"Right, never quote Buddha to a Chinaman, I forgot."

"Cracker."

"Infidel."

"Honky."

"*Oriental.*"

"Forsooth! That stings!"

"If you think we should go then I'll think about; if not then I think the case is closed," I say, brushing the jokes aside for the moment. Ted looks at me. He really needs a haircut.

"I just can't help but think about Phil and his kids, and Janette . . . and, you know—please don't hit me—maybe even your mom. If she doesn't make it here then there's a chance they made it to the university."

"I'm trying to get over that. I don't want to cling to hope for too long. She said three days and that should be long enough but . . . We have to give her longer," I tell him, forcing a smile. "After all: woman who fart in church sits in her own pew."

"That doesn't even make sense. What is wrong with you?"

I reach across and punch him in the shoulder. It's better than a slap; it makes him fall over, groaning theatrically and clutching his arm. Outside, through the curtains, through the glass, I can hear the undead making their slow, determined march down the street. I know what direction they're going. West. West toward the campus. I wonder if they can sense the bodies there, the feast to come . . . Or maybe they're mustering outside our door, coming for us instead.

Or maybe they've found my mom and her fate is already sealed.

We stay. For now we stay in here, safe, uncertain, huddled for warmth.

Tomorrow is Phil's birthday. Holly and I are going to try and make a cake somehow. Zack has asked if we can listen to the radio together again. I can't for the life of me think of a good reason to turn him down.

- -

COMMENTS

> **Brooklyn Girl says:**
>
> *October 4, 2009 at 8:36 pm*
>
> Lost one of our own today, my cousin. I couldn't do it. I couldn't kill him so we locked him outside. He's scratching to get in, to . . . It doesn't matter. He's not himself anymore.

>> **Allison says:**
>>
>> *October 4, 2009 at 8:55 pm*
>>
>> Condolences, that's the worst. You can't help him now but that doesn't make it any easier. Are your supplies holding up? Did the bodega deliver?

Brooklyn Girl says:

October 4, 2009 at 9:10 pm

Rations are fine, especially now that we're down a man. I'm worried we didn't check the apartment stairwells thoroughly enough. We'll tackle that tomorrow. Hopefully by then Gary will have stopped trying to get back in.

> **Isaac says:**
>
> *October 4, 2009 at 10:23 pm*
>
> Put Gary out of his misery. He can't thank you but he would if he could.

Isaac says:

October 6, 2009 at 7:26 am

Allison? Everything still okay?

Brooklyn Girl says:

October 6, 2009 at 10:23 am

Damn. Losing Gary was bad enough. Please tell me you guys are still going strong!

October 6, 2009—Things Fall Apart

Sorry, guys. My long silence wasn't intentional. When the shit hits the fan I can't exactly dash off an entry. It's hard to be coherent when you're chopping at a zombie with one hand and typing with the other. So I'll try to catch you up. Please forgive any omissions or foggy bits; my mind is still reeling.

"Any sign of her yet?" Ted asked. This was yesterday.

"Jesus, no, okay? Don't you think when I see her I'll say something?"

"Sorry. I just thought . . . I don't know."

"She'll make it. She has to. Maybe I've jinxed it. I have to stop watching the street."

I appreciated Ted's concern but it was getting exhausting. I know that soon I might have to confront the possibility that my mom is gone, that she's never coming to find me. I'm not ready for that yet. I know my mom and she's a fighter and if I'm the prize at the end of the rainbow then she won't give up without a struggle. She wouldn't want me to dwell on the possibility of death, not when there's so little life left to embrace.

And it's not that I'm morbid, really—I just have a healthy outlook on death. Even as a child I didn't see what the big deal was. I had confronted death early on. My dad and older brother died in a car crash when I was three and a half. It was then that I learned the phrase "They didn't suffer" meant something, but the phrase "They've gone to a better place" did not. I didn't for a moment, even at a very young age, believe that wherever they had gone was better than being alive and with us. It seemed insulting to me that people could say that, that strangers, even well-meaning ones, could smile and pat my head and imply that my dad and brother would rather be in heaven than with Mom and me.

And so I learned an important lesson: things were and then they simply stopped being. I didn't agree with the popular opinion that death was something to get bent out of shape about. But I've reversed that stance on death. I no longer think that it's okay, that it's not something to get worked up about.

We lost one of our own, one for sure and maybe more.

Holly and I started in on Phil's birthday cake bright and early that day. We weren't sure how many attempts we would need so we decided that it would be best to leave the entire morning and afternoon open for trial and error. Don't ever attempt to make a cake on a hibachi. Just don't. Anyway, we did. The batter part of it was easy, really, since Ms. Weathers was apparently a proficient baker. Flour, sugar, salt, baking soda, vegetable oil—all of that was easy to find. Eggs and milk were trickier, but they magically appeared at midmorning.

Zack came into the kitchen breathless, his arms full to overflowing with cans of Parmalat and a broken off carton of eggs.

"Where the hell did you find that?" I asked, watching him carefully drop the milk and eggs down onto the counter. He wiped the back of his head with his sleeve. I remember he was sweating despite the intense cold that persisted everywhere—outside, inside, in your bones. His green eyes flashed with mischief as he nodded vaguely toward the window.

"Out there."

"*Out there?* You're telling me you went out to get this shit for a birthday cake? Are you insane?"

"You needed them, right? You can't make a cake without eggs and milk."

"Well . . . *yeah*, but . . . Christ . . ."

"Come on," he says, touching my shoulder, "don't be like that. I'm fine, see?" He turned a cheeky little pirouette, the afghan bundled around his shoulders swinging out like a cape. Holly stared wide-eyed at him and I can't say I blamed her. To be out there, alone, among the undead . . . But if Zack could go out and come back then my mom could too.

"Are you sure you're okay? You didn't get scratched? Bitten?"

"I'm fine," he repeated, his smile fading. "A thank-you would be nice."

"Thank you," I blurted out, shaking my head at his stunt. "But don't do that again."

He leaned in and kissed my cheek. His beard rasped and it made me go cold all over. Holly moved closer; I didn't notice it until she was practically breathing down my neck. Zack disappeared down the hall and we were left standing there, straining to breathe, to say something. I still can't imagine him darting between the overturned cars, the fallen lampposts, the broken mailboxes . . . It seems absurd, impossible, and all of it for a cake.

I think that's when I felt my first premonition of danger.

"Are there any clean bowls left?" I asked Holly, turning away from the hall. I didn't want her to see how shaken I was but it was too late.

"We can take a break," she told me gently, rubbing my back.

"No way. Third time's the charm, right?" I said, trying to brighten up. We dumped one of our failed experiments into a plastic bag and measured out the sugar, flour and salt again. I could see her hands shaking as she cracked two eggs into a bowl and whisked in a few cups of milk. I made frosting out of milk and powdered sugar and set it by the window to keep it cool. From the bedroom I could hear the radio. Ted kept it on all morning, fascinated, obsessed with listening. They'd started playing music intermittently, mostly cheerful, inoffensive oldies. No one needs the Cure right now.

Phil, Matt and Janette were playing cards next door. I could hear them through the wall, laughing, shouting, throwing bad hands down on the coffee table. In my memory that sound is muddled and faded, like a television playing in a distant room. Everyone was dedicated to keeping Phil in high spirits, distracting him from the fact that he'd spend his birthday in a gutted, stolen apartment eating a cake made on a hibachi. From down the hall I could hear the Everly Brothers crooning about dreams. Holly and I opened the curtains in the kitchen and living room to let in some of the overcast, milky light. There was a threat of rain in those clouds, a dark heaviness casting long shadows down the street.

"Should I use the whole bag of chocolate chips?"

"Hm? Yeah, go for it," I said, turning to see Holly holding the open bag above the batter bowl. "But go easy on the walnuts." Ted spent the morning organizing all of our foodstuffs, carefully putting them together in neat rows, arranging them in a few labeled boxes so we could easily find corn, beans and fruit without searching through the pantry. Holly and I dodged the boxes as we moved around the kitchen. Dapper made himself a nuisance as usual, tangling in our feet as we tried to bake.

Zack joined us to help with the actual baking. We poured the batter into a deep pan and lit one half of the grill, covering the cake with foil and leaving it to cook on the unlit side of the grill. Zack's theory was that the heat would be just enough to cook the batter without burning the sugar and the foil should keep out most of the smoky flavor. For the next hour we took turns checking under the foil, poking the top with a fork. Despite our best efforts, the damned thing smoked out the entire living room and we waded through a haze of burnt vanilla. In the next apartment they could smell the burning and made a lame attempt to keep it out by taping newspaper over the hole.

There were no birthday candles so we frosted the cake and arranged a ring of candles around the pan. It looked a little black on top but the middle seemed okay. Janette and Matt brought Phil in and we sang "Happy Birthday," huddled around the candles for warmth. The room was colder than usual and this was about when I noticed the kitchen window was wide open. Someone must have opened it to air out the smoke.

As we sang, I saw Holly was about to cry. That part is strong in my memory right now. It reached me too but I held it at bay, feeling too cold, suddenly too afraid to find the depth of feeling. Phil clasped his hands to his chest, his stained polo shirt replaced with a big zipped-up pullover. We were all wrapped in blankets, a group of mismatched druids holding our sad and arcane ritual, singing and shivering and glowing in the candlelight.

Phil got the first piece. Matt, his droopy basset hound face perking up, chanted "Speech, speech!" but thankfully Phil ignored him. He didn't need to say anything about the cake, about the sentiments. We could all intuit his gratitude by the big, dopey smile on his face. I wished he would shave—he was starting to look like a caveman. No one had anything to give Phil but we started up another card game. I picked the chocolate chips out of a piece of cake and gave it to Dapper, who ate it all in one bite. Zack, Holly and I sat out. Zack stared at me until I caught him doing it. I didn't know why he was watching me, why his eyes were so intense, so persistent.

The cake was gone and the first game of poker was over when it happened.

I didn't see most of it, not really, just a blur, a scream, a crash of dishes and silverware. When I first heard Holly cry out I thought she'd burned herself on the grill, but when I turned to help her, there was something wrapped around her neck, something brown and mangy, like a rotten muffler. Dapper lunged for it, but I grabbed him by the collar and dragged him back. If he bit that thing he'd be history too.

But it wasn't a mink or a fox, it was a squirrel and when it leapt off of Holly it took a trail of blood with it. Without thinking the ax was in my hands and I chased after the thing, cornering it against the couch and the closet. It wasn't alive, wasn't normal. I could see the shiny wet skull through the torn fur of its head; both ears were missing, chewed away. The ax took it in the middle, separating it cleanly in half. I took off its head too, just to be sure.

Too much excitement and too many distractions. I never even noticed the window was still cracked open.

I expected more talking, more shouting, but when I returned to the others there was only silence. They'd formed a tight ring around the struggling girl on the floor, the futile clawing at her own neck. It was a small bite, just a little tear in the skin, no bigger than a bad fingernail scratch, but it punctured her veins, and we could all see that. Already her eyes were changing, becoming greenish, her skin molting its healthy pink color.

Ted rushed forward, holding her, whispering her name over

and over. I put out my hand. I wanted to pull him back, to save him before Holly took him. But there was no fight in her yet. He stood, pulling her gently to her feet. Holly looked at me. I stared deep into her and watched as she stopped recognizing me, as the cruel unknowing slipped over her face like a Halloween mask. We broke the circle and Ted went past with Holly limping, slumped against his shoulder. I couldn't see his face; he wouldn't let me see it.

I offered him the ax. He'd gained a little weight. There was a hardness to his cheekbones and a square, iron set to his jaw; I saw it clearly now. He was growing up right there, right on the stained, faded carpet of a house we didn't own, in a life we no longer recognized.

I trailed them as they went to the door, out into the hall. The door slammed in my face. None of us said anything, not even good-bye. I worried for a moment that Ted would do something stupid, that I wouldn't see him again—or that if I did, it wouldn't be a Ted I knew but a Ted I'd have to annihilate. I almost wanted Zack to put his arms around me, to tell me it's okay but I knew it wasn't. I knew everything was completely fucked now.

Then there was that sound like dropping a barrel, followed by a kind of fast, soft crunch. I was at the door when I heard that sound, my palms flat against the wood during what I knew was Ted's last moment of peace. I looked back at the others. Janette and Matt were clinging tightly together and Phil was at the window, staring at it as if the window itself committed the crime.

He's done the right thing, I remind myself. He's one of us. He knows what must be done.

Then there's a sound I'm not expecting, not hoping for: a cry, a wail, not of sadness but of absolute frustration. Ted opened the door and I was there waiting. I could see his face now—there was nothing left, none of the spry, wicked Ted that lurked beneath the sober, nerdy exterior. It was wiped away, cut off with the same sweep of the ax that ended Holly.

"If any of you want to say good-bye, you should follow me."

We filed out into the hallway, Dapper included, our heads bowed, our mouths sticky with tears that hadn't fallen yet and words no one had the courage to speak. Holly wasn't in the hallway, but there was a fresh stain on the floor and on Ted's hands. Her sweatshirt hung from the stairwell banister like a wreath of flowers slung around a gravestone.

Ted wasn't saying anything and I wasn't sure I could speak, but I took his hand and held it and squeezed it until I could feel him squeeze back.

"It's not fair," I whispered. "It's so fucking unfair."

Janette began to cry and Phil was sniffling, trying hard to be brave. I don't know how long we stood there—bowing our heads toward that sweatshirt, waiting like comrades of a fallen soldier, waiting for some sign to go on, that things wouldn't just end altogether—before we finally found the strength to raise our heads. Part of me wanted it to end, because if someone as sweet and well-meaning as Holly could be destroyed by something so random, so coincidental, then what was the use?

Ted let go of my hand and turned, leading us back into the apartment. That's when I noticed that Zack hadn't been standing with us and I couldn't remember when he stopped being there. I let it go. I let the focus go for one minute and he was gone. I knew something was really wrong when Ted slammed the ax, headfirst, onto the countertop.

"No," I told him. "No, search, search everywhere."

He ran out of the kitchen, Phil and Matt sprinting into the other apartment. We were not looking for Zack; we were looking for the boxes, the neatly labeled boxes holding our food. All of the food.

Ted walked into the kitchen, his face blank, bloodless. I could tell from his voice that we'd lost everything.

"There's something you need to hear, Allison."

It was the radio: I could hear it trickling out of the bedroom and down the hall. It was The Voice, the stranger I had come to rely on. "—is an alert, be on the alert. He is five-eight, blond, green eyes, about one hundred and seventy pounds. We know him only as Jack. Staffers are reporting stolen goods and equipment."

"Get your bat."

"Allison!"

It was Janette, in the living room screaming her head off. Ted and I met her there, armed, red-faced and furious. The space outside the door, in the hallway, was moving, seething. Ted and I hacked our way out into the hallway. It was a goddamned ambush, dozens, maybe hundreds, all of them fumbling up the stairwell toward us. I leaned over the banister, Ted protecting me. At the bottom of the stairs I could see the maintenance room door wide open and more and more undead pouring inside.

"*Fucking bastard, fucking goddamned bastard.*" I pushed past Ted and back into the apartment. Janette was crumpled on the floor, curled up, sobbing. Matt and Phil appeared with their golf clubs and Dapper barked and barked, dancing back and forth behind Ted.

"Janette," I said, going to the window. "Janette! Fucking get up! Get up and get the wine down."

"The wine?" she stammered.

"JUST FUCKING DO WHAT I TELL YOU!"

Janette scrambled to her feet behind me and I could hear the clink of bottles as she laid them out on the countertop. There were only three, but that should be enough. Out on the street I could see Zack getting away, carrying our things, our food. It was slow going and there might just be a way . . .

"Bring him the ax, Janette. Ted!" I shouted, going to the wine bottles. "Can you hold them off at the door?"

"Yeah, but whatever you're doing, hurry it up!"

I could barely hear him over the baseball bat and then the chopping of the ax. Phil and Matt stood behind him, whacking at anything that got too close.

"Janette, I need you to focus, okay? Get these open and pour out as much as you can. Down the sink, get it?"

She nodded frantically, her eyes leaking tears as she took the corkscrew I'd forced into her trembling hands. I slammed open the doors beneath the sink and shoved Formula 409 and Drano and sponges out of the way until I found it hiding in the back: a little silver nugget with a bright-red top. From the linen closet, I grabbed an old fitted sheet. Thankfully we'd kept the lighters in an easy to reach place, and Janette had emptied out most of the first bottle. I grabbed it and shook hard, watching the good pinot noir drip down the drain. Janette went to open more as I tore a long strip of fabric off the sheet. I tore off two more and pulled off the red top on the turpentine. I heard Janette gag from the smell as the bottle was filled halfway, and then the next, and then the last.

"Allison! Come on! Fuck!"

"I'm almost done!" I shouted back, meaning it. I shoved the cloth strips inside and jammed the corks back down onto the bottles.

I ran back to the bedroom and packed up the laptop, nearly dropping it as I shoved it into the carrier and swung it up diagonally across my shoulders. Ted was grunting with effort as I arrived back in the living room, his swings growing more and more erratic.

"Okay, we need to clear a path to the fire escape. I've got our retreat covered."

Ted handed me back my ax and together we mowed down a path. It wasn't very clear, and more than once I felt my heart fly up into my throat as a hand grabbed my sleeve or shoe. Ted went first with Matt and Phil, Janette sandwiched in the middle carrying my bottles. Matt got one hand on Dapper's collar, pulling the mutt along. I heard the window open and the clang-clang of their feet on the metal grates of the fire escape. My hands were locked so tightly around the ax I could feel my knuckles creaking with rage. If I didn't hold it tight, it'd slip right out of my grasp from the sweat. I put the lighter in my mouth, and it was hard to breathe and swing, but I managed. The apartment was filling up and the noise was astounding—screeching and groaning, a whole buffet's worth of hungry, angry, desperate undead shoving themselves through the door. They were tearing at each other just trying to get to us.

"Okay! We're out!"

I took the lighter out of my mouth. "Get down the ladder. Go! Go!"

I ducked into the kitchen and out onto the fire escape, keeping the window open. The apartment was filled to capacity now and there were bodies wriggling into the kitchen, mouths hanging open, tongues missing altogether or hanging by a thread of muscle. I'd never made a Molotov cocktail before but I'd seen it on TV and that would just have to be good enough. I lit the first wick and, having no idea how long to wait, tossed it right away. This was both a good and bad decision.

The cocktail exploded somewhere in the living room and the blast was unbelievable. It reached through the kitchen, the heat of it slamming through the window and into my chest. I almost went ass over head off the balcony, but I managed to stumble back up to my feet, my back screaming in pain. There was warmth on my face where the blast licked my skin. I skidded down the ladder and beckoned the others away. I jogged backward a few paces before lighting the second one and hurling it at the window. Fire and body parts shot into the air, cascading over our heads and the retaining wall. We were out behind the store now and the building was beginning to burn.

I remember Dapper whining as he sat at my feet.

"Right," I said, turning to face the others. I knew I looked crazy because they were gaping at me like I'd completely lost my mind. "Ted, you're coming with me. The rest of you head for the university. We'll meet you there."

"But . . . where are you going? You have to come with us," Janette said, still clutching the third bottle to her chest.

"Ted and I have some unfinished business to look after," I told them. I shook Matt's hand and then Phil's. "You'll be fine, I know you will. It's not far. Take care of that bottle, Janette. Use it if you have to. Take Dapper with you, okay?"

Janette nodded, but I could see the look in her eyes. She was thinking: ten blocks, *ten blocks*, that may as well be in Sri Lanka. Trembling, she dragged Dapper away. He didn't want to go with them but I knew it was safer. I knew I wasn't in my right mind right then.

Ted and I circled around the retaining wall, giving the building a wide birth. The crackle of fire reached the street level. The entire top floor of the apartments was ablaze, the smoke and flames twinkling in the windows. The street was almost empty, littered here and there with debris, scorch marks and brown, faded bloodstains.

Sure, Zack had a good head start on us but he was slow, weighed down, and we knew what direction he was headed. He wouldn't come back to the apartments and he wouldn't go near the university. There was no catharsis, no time to mourn Holly or to worry about the others. Ted and I were light on our feet, armed, and pushed forward by something terrible, something consuming. And both of us were burning for a fight. We were out now and there was no stopping us. Zack was out there, yeah, but so was my mom and now was my chance to find her once and for all.

COMMENTS

> **Isaac says:**
> *October 6, 2009 at 11:21 pm*
> Allison I know you're pissed but be careful. Don't get reckless or we'll never hear from you again.
>
>> **Brooklyn Girl says:**
>> *October 6, 2009 at 11:56 pm*
>> Isaac is right. You're grieving, you're afraid but you have to keep your head screwed on tight. Tell Ted I know his pain. We sent one of our own to his maker and it was the best choice I've made in a while. Keep yourself safe, Allison, and post again soon.

October 7, 2009—Things Fall Apart, Pt. II

We headed east pursuing Zack, jogging down the right lane of Langdon.

"What do you think he's got? Ten minutes? Fifteen minutes on us?" Ted asked.

"Ten," I replied. "I'd put it at ten."

He had just ten minutes, but ten minutes could make all the difference. If he was smart he wouldn't slow down even with the precautions he put in place. I hoped that he underestimated us, that he slowed down to a walk as soon as the apartments were out of sight. They were still burning behind us, the black smoke thickening the atmosphere.

"So what's the plan if we *do* catch him?" Ted whispered. We were trying to keep a low profile, which meant soft voices and soft feet. There weren't many Groaners about, just a few lost Floaters drifting around in the alleys. As we headed away from the city center the roads got a little clearer, less cluttered with cars and Vespas and bicycles.

"I don't give a shit about the food, Ted. I just want to teach this asshole a lesson. But safety first, okay? We don't know if he managed to get a weapon. Play it like we want the food back, that it's all we're interested in."

"You really think he'll believe that?"

"No, but it might be enough to get him to come in close—close enough."

We were about to dodge around a charred SUV when I saw it. It was pearly brown, wedged near the blackened tire, dusted with soot. Ted stumbled to a stop when he saw me go over to the tire and kneel. I picked it up, the leather purse cool and smooth in my hands.

It was my mother's.

"There's no way," Ted said, reading my face. "She wouldn't get this far off Main Street."

"Maybe not. But if they were chased . . ."

There was nothing around the SUV or the purse or the tire, just scarred road and ash. I kept expecting to find blood or some sign of my mom but it was just the purse, abandoned, seemingly without a fight. I could see that Ted was impatient, waiting, but I had to know. Inside the purse her wallet was missing. There was a hairbrush, a pack of gum, a few coins and a blue Post-it note stuck to the bottom lining. I took it out carefully, recognizing her handwriting at once.

Aunt Tammy

Fort Morgan

<u>Liberty Village</u>

Liberty Village was underlined twice and the handwriting was sloppy, rushed. The word Tammy was smudged and runny.

"What does that even mean?" Ted asked, peering over my shoulder.

"Aunt Tammy lives in Fort Morgan. No idea what Liberty Village is," I replied, trying hard to hold back the cold knot in my throat. If I breathed, if I swallowed too hard, I'd cry. I stood, holding the purse and the note. "She must have heard from Tammy. Maybe that's where they're headed."

"I thought they were going to the apartments."

"So did I," I said, frowning. "But maybe they wanted to take us to Fort Morgan. Maybe that's where she's going now. Jesus, they got so close. Just a few blocks more and . . ."

"Allison . . ."

"I know," I said, looking up. Ted was half-poised to run, his arms flexed, trembling. I put the Post-it in my pocket and shouldered the purse. There was no sign of my mom or her companions, no indication of what direction they'd gone. I had to make the call. Ted would never do it for me.

"Zack first," I told him. "Then the campus. They might have gone there if they were ambushed."

"You sure?"

"Yes, I'm sure. Let's go."

We glanced down each alley, making sure he hadn't dodged off the main road. The buildings were so dilapidated, so hollow that it was unlikely he'd stop here. If he did, we'd have spotted him through the broken, empty windows. Ted and I sped up again, unwilling to tire.

When we made it about eleven blocks from the apartments, we reached a dead end, literally. Right in front of us was a cemetery, a quiet little plot with maybe sixty or so tombstones. In silence we slowed to a stop, standing just in front of the low, wrought-iron fence. It would be easy to jump, but neither of us made a move.

"It's not like *Night of the Living Dead*, they're not going to jump out of the graves," I told him, but there was no confidence there, no authority. Ted nodded and looped a leg over the fence, dropping down on the other side.

"Allison," he murmured, but he didn't need to. I'd seen it too. In the distance, across the field of speckled headstones and weepy, low-hanging trees: a flash of brown, of yellow. It was Zack, his afghan and the boxes. He paused beneath a tree, bent double, catching his breath probably. Lucky for us, running with your arms full of twenty-pound boxes is exhausting work.

I lifted a finger to my lips and we slid across the graveyard together, soundless shadows whispering across the spongy ground. The ax felt heavier in my grasp, as if it were asking me to take a moment and consider my actions. I was wary of every twig, every crisp leaf, afraid that one snapping branch and Zack would be off and running. The tree he slumped against was probably ten yards off, so Ted and I slunk around to the left, trying to keep the trunk of the tree between us and Zack. The problem with an ax is that it's a short-range weapon; you have to get in close, real close. Suddenly I was wishing I hadn't given Janette that last cocktail. I couldn't think of anything more satisfying than watching Zack go up in a crackling blaze of flames.

And of course I nearly botched it, stepping on a wayward twig just a few feet from the tree. Zack's head snapped up and around. The boxes dropped out of his hands as soon as he saw us and he was off, sprinting across the northern edge of the graveyard. All sense of stealth abandoned, Ted and I pursued, chewing up the ground, closing the gap until Ted, springing forward, managed to trip him up. His legs tangled and he fell, tumbling forward, making a few rotations on the ground before trying to get up and keep running. But it was too late. We had him.

Ted stopped him with a preliminary whack to the ribs. Zack crumpled on the ground at our feet, panting and holding his hands up in defense. He stared up at us, his eyes wild with terror. He could see things more clearly now, he could see who we were and what we were prepared to do.

"Please!" he cried, crab-walking away from us. Ted cracked him fast and hard on the knee to slow him down. "God! Just! I'll do whatever you want, take the food! Take it! Jesus—I'm sorry, okay? I'm so sorry."

"No you're not. Not yet."

His right foot came away at the ankle. It only took one sweep of the ax. There was so much blood, more than I expected, and it rushed out in jerking sprays, pumped hard by his racing heart. He could hardly shout but he started in on gibberish, stringing nonsense together as he tried to flail out of our reach. We let him go a few feet, watching him squirm away like a centipede missing its tail.

"Turns out you're a star, Zack . . . or Jack—which is it? We heard all about you on the radio, about how you stole from the university, from a *relief effort*," I said, catching up to him. There was nothing more for him to do, nowhere to go. "What the fuck is wrong with you? We're all in this together, you *motherfucker*." I punctuated that last word with his other foot. I could see he was about to pass out so I put the ax down. Ted tapped his cheek with the end of the bat.

"We're going to leave you now, Zack. I do hope you remember my face when they come for you."

Ted and I turned to go, silent, bound by a deep, profound loathing for what we'd just done. But as hard as I try, there's no regret to be found. I can still hear him muttering "Please, please" over and over again as he lay in the tall, dead grass.

We didn't make it ten feet before we realized our serious mistake. I was beginning to understand what made these things tick, and fresh blood certainly does seem to have the same effect as a church bell. They'd been called, summoned, driven out of hiding by the scent of Zack's suffering. It made the bombardment in the apartment look like a trip out for ice cream.

They came surging toward us from every surrounding block. There was no cover, no way out, just a solid sea of these things lurching toward us. I knew that even if we managed to cut through the first few lines we didn't have the coverage to make it safely through to the street.

Behind us, Zack was dying, really dying, becoming one of

them. He wouldn't get far without feet, but it didn't make me feel any better about our predicament. The graveyard suddenly smelled like a graveyard should, wet and sandy and sweet with too much decay. Ted and I stood back to back, waiting, letting them come. It began to rain; the clouds opened up and let loose.

I briefly thought about climbing a tree, waiting there for help, but I knew it was easier to face them this way than to sit up in a tree like an idiot, waiting for a rescue party that doesn't exist. I looked at my mom's purse and hugged it close to my chest.

"It's been real, Ted," I said. "I promise, if you go first I'll finish you off."

"Thank you. It's been a pleasure, Allie."

I felt calm, secure in the knowledge that at least I might go down swinging, struggling. I wouldn't starve to death in a break room or get scurvy and waste away in a university gymnasium, I would die on my feet and with Ted. And maybe my mother was already gone. Maybe I had found the last clue to her existence. I felt like I could breathe again, like I could see the end and it really wasn't so bad. But I did wish for my mom, to see her one last time.

Just as I was starting to get real comfortable with the idea of dying, just as the groaning and scraping had reached its peak, I heard an earsplitting racket from the street. Gunfire, tons of it, spray after spray of bullets. I covered my ears, deafened. The heads and bodies surrounding us exploded, turned to liquid ash by the unbelievable firepower going off in every direction. Through the haze of vaporized goo and tissue I could see a big black form, a truck, and hanging out the back a figure. The truck smashed through the nearest line of Groaners, splattering them across our shoes. It was a truck all right, a gutted Land Rover with a cargo net for a ceiling. I couldn't imagine what kind of mental case drove this thing, but I found out soon enough when the man hanging off the back jumped down to us. He fired off a few rounds into the Groaners creeping up behind Ted and me. I was too stunned to move, awed by the miraculous arrival of these two angels.

"They okay?" the driver shouted, jumping out.

"Seems so," the other said, yanking off his mask. They were both dressed in black fatigues and flak jackets. Soldiers, maybe. The nearer one had a blue and red patch on his right sleeve with a crown and a bird. He had flaming red hair and a ginger beard and pale, pale blue eyes. He looked at both of us, his brow furrowed.

"May I ask what you two kittens are doing out here?"

I opened my mouth to grunt out an answer, but from behind us came a terrified scream. It was Zack, still alive, pulling himself toward us, scooting along on his elbows. The red-haired man took one look at the ax in my hand and Zack's missing feet and grabbed me by the wrist. It felt like my arm was going to come right out of its socket as he pushed me toward the truck.

"Fucking hell . . . It's like that, is it?" he asked. He had an accent, British, but it was weak. The driver leveled his rifle at Ted and nodded toward the car.

"Sir? Sir! This isn't what it looks like," I told him, struggling for air. My arm was killing me, twisted and pulsing, shot through with pain.

"Yeah, I've heard that one before," he said, laughing humorlessly as he tossed Ted and me into the back. "Gone a bit mad, have you? I'd love to shoot you right now and leave you with that poor bastard, but I think I'd rather toss you in lockup and let you think about it for a few days."

"No! You don't understand, sir. He stole from us! Those boxes, go look, I swear, he took all our food!" I shouted, struggling against his iron grip. Ted tried to say the same but the man cuffed him across the face. "Don't hit him! What is wrong with you? We're on your side! Jesus Christ, let us go! We're not criminals. Why aren't you listening to me? Listen to me, you fucking idiot!"

He raised his hand and I shut my mouth, settling back against the hard steel of the truck. The vehicle jerked to life, the boxes left on the ground, jumbled and opened like a few abandoned toy chests. Zack watched the truck roll away, his hand reaching after us.

They blindfolded us and our hands were secured. It didn't feel like handcuffs; zip ties maybe. We were more or less tossed out of the truck and onto pavement, then yanked around until we could stand. They marched us up a steep hill, no stairs, gun firmly planted between my shoulder blades. They took my laptop and our weapons and all I could think about was getting that ax back, and persuading this jerkoff that I wasn't a maniac. I suppose persuading him with an ax might have proven just the opposite, but I was too angry and confused to care.

A door swung open. I could tell from the sound of the hinges and the riotous noise inside just where we were: the gymnasium. It's that sound, the way the words bounce around off the high ceilings and wood floors, the way sneakers squeak and squeal on the shiny surface. The soldiers' boots clapped rhythmically as they pushed us through the gymnasium. We went through another set of doors, into a cool, damp hallway, and then down two short flights of stairs. It felt like a basement, moldy-smelling and claustrophobic.

They took our blindfolds off and left us in the dark in separate rooms. I was tossed into a little office with a window. The red-haired soldier left my hands bound. He smelled like fireworks and scotch. The table in the corner had a heavy layer of dust and a few blank spaces, voids where a computer monitor and keyboard might have been. Everything smelled perpetually wet, ruined, like it was once flooded and never completely dried out. It was probably a coach's office, but they certainly made it feel like a cell.

They didn't bring food. I couldn't sleep. I didn't know if there was any getting out of this one.

Today

Someone comes to check on me bright and early, before I can really remember where I am or what I'm supposed to be doing. They had taken my weapon and my mom's purse, but they didn't take the Post-it note. I maneuver it out of my pocket as best I can and run my fingers over the writing. She wouldn't give up, I just know she wouldn't.

For the last hour or two I've been passing in and out of a dream state, so exhausted and scared that I'm not at rest, but my brain has stopped actively trying to think of a way out. When the key goes into the lock and I hear the click, I'm expecting to see the red-haired soldier again with his funny beard and wide, sideways grin. But it isn't him. It's someone totally different.

"Hello there."

I quickly palm the Post-it and stare up at him, my knees tucked tightly to my chest. The zip tie around my wrists is making them ache like hell and I can feel the skin getting raw and blistered. The pain is momentary because I know this person, somehow I know him. He doesn't seem threatening. Intimidating maybe, but not threatening. Even carrying a big fuck-off assault rifle he doesn't come off as particularly aggressive. It might just be how small the room is, but he seems to take up all of it. He's dressed in black fatigues too, but the front buttons look like they've been done up hastily. I glance at his shoulder, and the crown and bird patch are there too.

"I'm Collin, Collin Crane." After a pause he adds, "I know you can speak. Finn says you've got a barb on the end of that tongue. Don't be foolish," he says, crouching down. "I'm not here to hurt you."

That's when it hits me.

"It was the age of wisdom, it was the age of foolishness. . . ."

"It's you."

"I beg your pardon?"

"The Voice, it's you! The man on the radio! Holy shit, I can't believe it! *It's you.*"

Crouched down to my level, I can see his face clearly now. He's older than the other soldiers, probably in his early fifties, with dark, close-cropped waves graying about the temples and a pair of bright, formidable hazel green eyes. I can't help but wonder what his hair would look like if it were a bit longer, freer. There's a deep dent in his chin and his eyebrows are dark and very straight. His eyes smile at the corners, creased with age and experience. His eyes smile just like the way his lips are smiling at me now.

"You've heard me on the radio, have you?" he asks, puffing out a laugh.

"'He is five-eight, blond, green eyes, about one hundred and seventy pounds,'" I repeat. "Zack . . . Jack . . . whoever he was. That's him, that's why I'm here. I tried to explain it to your men but they wouldn't listen." I can feel my mouth running away with me, the words tumbling out too fast. He puts up a hand, cocking his head to the side.

"I know about that."

"You do? That's great, I—wait, you know? Then why am I still in here?"

"I wanted to see you for myself," he says. His voice is wilder in person, but still very much striking, an opal finished off with sandpaper. He has an accent too, like the red-haired soldier, but thicker. "That bastard had been the scourge of our supplies for weeks now. We were hours away from offering a reward when you and your friend turned up."

"How did you know to come for us?" I ask, making sure my poor, aching wrists are in full view.

"A dog, actually."

"A dog—Dapper? So they made it, then. Thank Christ." Relief is sudden and glorious, quenching, and the knot in my stomach relaxes a little. But the man's face is tensed, fraught with craggy lines.

"They? No, there was just the one, the dog. We thought maybe he was rabid. He bit my nephew. You met him I think, my nephew. At any rate, we figured stranger things have happened; maybe the dog is agitated for a reason. I sent them out on patrol and that's when they found you. What happened to your dog? His tail was singed. It's almost half gone."

"No. No, no, god*damn it*, Janette."

I can picture it so easily and that hurts.

"Were you expecting someone?" he asks gently. This is when he pulls a gleaming bowie knife out of his belt and flicks the blade across my zip ties. I rub at my raw wrists, alternately wincing and sighing. I try to hide the Post-it but he's caught a glimpse. He tries to take it and I jerk my hands away.

"My friends . . . My friends were supposed to come."

"From what direction?" he asks, suddenly all business.

"East, directly, um, probably down Dayton."

He stands up, backing a few steps away. That's more than enough. He doesn't have to tell me that Dayton is dangerous or swarmed or whatever. I'm sure what he has to say next will sting so I prepare for it, which is something I've simply learned to do, like tying my shoes or making a sandwich.

"Dayton . . . No, I'm very sorry, Dayton isn't passable. There are so many cars. . . . The police tried to set up a barricade but that only made it worse."

Janette must have panicked and thrown the cocktail. Poor Dapper.

"Am I in trouble?" I ask, staring down at the floor. It helps to concentrate on the pits in the cement, on the grooves worn into the concrete by a chair or desk. What if I run into their families? What if I have to be the messenger?

"No, no, nothing like that," he says, laughing again. It's a big, full, boisterous laugh that fills up the little room, testing its boundaries. "I'll have a word with my nephew. I apologize on his behalf. He can get a bit . . . well, overzealous."

"I noticed."

"Sorry about the wrists," he says, offering a hand. I take it, pulling myself up, finding that I'm starving and weak. He sees me wobbling, listing to the right. "We'll get you some food and a place to rest."

"And Ted? My friend?"

"He can come too. And what should I call you?"

"Allison. My name is Allison."

I stop at the door. My feet are leaden and aching and I can feel every tug and pull of the tendons in my ankles and wrists. I just want to drop down right there and sleep for days. Collin waits for me, watching me fixedly from his great height. For some reason I can't meet his eyes. I don't want to, I don't want him to see how full of anger and disappointment I am. This is not a good introduction. This is not who I am.

"Have you . . . Has anyone with the name Hewitt showed up? Lynn Hewitt? She would be about my height, in her fifties, pretty?"

"I don't think so," he says. "But I don't know everyone who passes through here. Is she your mother?"

"Yes." I can barely hear my own voice, something is drowning it out. My throat is so tight it's a chore just squeezing down enough air to breathe. My knees tremble but I stay on my feet, keeping my head down, my eyes away from Collin.

"It's not guilt," he murmurs, and I can hear the soft rhythm in his voice, the same sound that would float out of the radio speakers like a childhood ghost.

"What?"

"It's not guilt, what you're feeling right now. It's shock."

"Oh."

"There's an important difference: shock wears off eventually. Guilt, I'm afraid, does not."

"And you would know this because . . . ?"

"Let's call it personal experience, shall we?"

But I'm not smiling, I'm not giving him the reaction he wants. His face, which has the same quixotic, expressive quality as the surface of a shiny buckle, settles quickly into a sympathetic frown. "You killed a man," he says. "That tears the soul. But it's just a tear, Allison, and tears can mend."

"Stick to reading the classics, please. I can take care of myself."

"I see Finn was right about your winning charm," he replies, but there's a bounce, a hint of laughter to his voice. "But I'm sorry to tell you that you won't frighten me. I've taught know-it-alls and geniuses and idiots your age for many years. Nothing surprises this old man."

"You're a professor?" I ask, inching toward the door.

"*Was* a professor, yes, of astronomy."

"A professor of astronomy with shitloads of guns?"

"We all have our hobbies."

Ted is with me now. They've given us hot food and chamomile tea and stale cookies. And they gave me back my laptop. Ted's glasses are even worse now, one lens almost falling out altogether, but he's otherwise unharmed. It's good to have my friend back, to see his bright eyes flashing beneath his mop of black fringe. There's a village of tents in the arena and Collin managed to track one down for us. Collin estimates there are maybe one hundred and fifty people in the gymnasium with more arriving every day. Dapper couldn't be happier; he doesn't seem to miss the other half of his tail and I appreciate his unfailing enthusiasm. He smells a bit like charcoal and chemicals, but we've been given the go-ahead to bathe him tomorrow. The generators here produce so much power that they've managed to hook up a few hand-pump showers and water heaters.

Ted is almost asleep. His chemistry recitations have degraded into incoherent mumbling. I want to sleep, I want badly to rest and to forget, but every time I close my eyes I see Janette. I see Phil. I see Matt and even Zack. I don't want to regret or hate, I want to be the person I was before all of this started: Allison Hewitt, Graduate Student, Student of Literature, Faulkner Enthusiast, Field Hockey Player, Daughter, Normal Person.

Those titles don't exist anymore. Collin is no longer a professor, Ted is no longer a biochemist and I'm just a survivor. I don't even know who Zack was, what he loved to do, what he was in his former life. He told me that he was a cook, that he ran track, that he liked to golf and that he was applying for an internship at an environmental issues magazine. Any of those things could be true and any of those things could be false.

Collin says I shouldn't regret what I did. He says it will only hurt for a few days, a few weeks. I think he's wrong. I think it will hurt forever. I think the sting will endure past all tolerance or understanding and it will follow me until I either learn to be someone else or I die.

And worst of all, my mother isn't here. I searched but I didn't need to: I can feel it. She's out there somewhere in the world, struggling to survive and I'm here, safe, helpless to protect her.

COMMENTS

Isaac says:

October 7, 2009 at 3:55 pm

I'm glad you're alive. If your mom is out there you'll find her or she'll find you. Food is getting low here, morale too. I'm not sure how much longer we can hold out. Going it alone sounds good right now but I know that's just pride talking. Don't give up, Allison, you're carrying all of us with you.

Brooklyn Girl says:

October 7, 2009 at 5:25 pm

This is the last time you'll hear from me but I wanted to say good luck and so long. You'll do just fine, Allison, I know it. This morning our block caught fire and it's only getting worse. We have to leave. I have no idea where we'll go but there's no choice. It's time to move on.

amanda says:

October 7, 2009 at 6:23 pm

please . . . i can't wait.

i know that i don't have much longer before the cold consumes me or they do. yet i've come to rely on your group to keep me company; i was trapped here alone and have found your blog as the only contact i've had with 'real' people. i will mourn holly along with you . . . as long as i'm able to . . . but please keep writing.

i can't wait.

October 8, 2009—Letters to a Young Poet

Amanda:

Seeing as how we're technically now part of a relief effort (whatever that means), Ted and I have decided to embark on a project of sorts. We have begun collecting haiku from the survivors here in order to bring you a little hope, a little sunshine. Also, many of the people I've met here are intrigued by the blog. They think I'm a bit mad, but I don't mind.

We cannot get out
but the arena is huge
and they have showers.

—Ted

Chemistry is hard
but it's extra hard if you're
dumb like Allison.

—Ted

Ted smells like an ass,
but really, that's nothing new.
Thank God for showers.

—Allison

Um, I don't get it,
why are you writing poems
for the Internet?
—Collin (Ghost Written by Allison)

I'm learning to shoot;
the guns are loud and heavy.
C says: Deal with it.
—Allison

What is a haiku?
I'm just a big stupid mutt;
Oh look! A pork bone.
—Take a Wild Fucking Guess—he's
licking his butt right now . . .

- -

COMMENTS

Carlene says:

October 8, 2009 at 2:33 pm

Surviving here in Alaska. It's good to know there are still conscious, living people out there in the world . . . Keep telling your story. Keep reminding us there is hope to regain our planet. Keep reminding us that you are alive.

Allison says:

October 8, 2009 at 4:43 pm

You couldn't catch some salmon and ship them down here, could you? I guess the trucks aren't running and I don't know what we could trade. Books maybe, or goodwill? On second thought, keep the salmon for yourself; I'm sure you need it too.

amanda says:

October 8, 2009 at 5:07 pm

thanks for the poems! they made my day a little better ◁

October 9, 2009—Haunted

"Another day in paradise," Ted says, up bright and early and way before I feel even the slightest inclination to open my eyes. "You want me to go grab us some breakfast?"

"You go. I'm not hungry yet."

"Okay, but when I get back you better be here. No chasing after your mom or ditching me for Liberty Village. There's frozen waffles here, Allison. Waffles. Think about that."

Ironically, everyone here calls it The Village. Sure it's okay, but it's not *Liberty* Village, which is, I've come to believe, the place to be.

The tents range from the very small to the extravagant, family-sized monstrosities that look capable of concealing a small circus. They have amenities here that I couldn't even imagine finding at the apartment. Lake water, pump showers, water heaters, bandages and antiseptic wash, Q-tips, coolers, ice packs and tampons—life is made significantly easier by things like these. You don't realize until you've gone without Q-tips and tampons how instrumental they are to your comfort and sanity. Just knowing that I can wake up and clean my ears is a relief.

The Village is mainly separated into two areas: the Black Earth Wives and Everyone Else.

It didn't take long for Ted and me to notice this split. The Wives tend to broadcast their general *differentness*. They don't do it with alternative music or tattoos. They do it with their religion. Ted and I aren't really sure what denomination they are, but it's the very, very strict kind. Every morning at nine, like clockwork, a sign-up clipboard gets passed around from tent to tent. The purpose of the clipboard is to solicit names for the prayer hour. The Black Earth Wives gather in a ring at the center of their tents and hold hands and pray, spending a moment on every single name on the list, praying for their souls or for their safe passage.

They've reached out to our side of The Village, mainly in the form of childcare. There are a handful of single mothers and fathers here, people who lost their husbands or wives, boyfriends or partners in the chaos and who have been left to raise a child or children on their own. It's amazing to watch, the slow progression of the Wives as they infiltrate our half of the arena, oozing through the gaps in the tents. They search out the women and men who sit dazed, their eyes glazed over with a general mistrust of the world.

Collin took me around today, introducing me to the families he knows the best, telling them that I helped get rid of "that bloody vermin." He's simultaneously deferential and authoritative; no mean feat, but one that seems to instantly and pleasantly ingratiate him no matter the audience. The introductions feel good at first but then it gets tired, played out. I'm not a hero and it feels peculiar to be lauded for a swift and cruel act of revenge. So I force a smile for each new face and shake their hands and listen to their stories. They thank me for getting rid of Zack and I bow my head shyly and try not to think of his agonized face and his raw, bloody stumps lying in the dead grass.

We visit the Wives last. I ask why there are so many of them, where they came from, and why they are alone. I can't help but think that if my mother were here, she would stay far, far away from these women.

"I'm starting to think all of this started somewhere outside the city, that the suburbs went first and that's why the city was overrun so quickly," Collin says. He doesn't go anywhere without a gun, but no one here seems to mind; they look to him as their undisputed leader and protector. Today it's a Glock tucked into the back of his fatigues. Collin greets everyone by name.

"Black Earth got hit hard," says Collin. "One house at a time, the residents realized they had to do something. There were a lot of families there, a lot of children. They decided to round up all the kids in one van and get them out while the dads, avid hunters, went out to hold off the onslaught. It didn't work. They were out-numbered too badly and the husbands went down 'fighting like angels of the Lord,' as the wives will tell you."

"And the van?" I ask, knowing its fate already.

"They came across it when they left, heading toward the city. It was overturned in a ditch. Empty."

It didn't surprise me, the way their story unfolded. This is the land of hunting, of fishing and farms and Harley-Davidson. I never felt close to that part of our state but I can't help but feel for them, for the way they tried like hell to defend themselves. We cross the thin, empty strip of floor that separates the Wives from everyone else. There are plenty of people here that seem to ignore or outright dislike the Wives. They sense, rightly, that the Wives are proud of who and what they are and may be a bit insane, taken to the ex-treme end of charity by the horrible losses they have suffered. I hear that some children are cautioned to stay away from that side of the arena and some tents have purposely been set up as far away from the Wives as possible.

It's a lot like *West Side Story* but without all the dancing.

Their tents are all gathered in a ring, the entrances facing the middle. You might expect to see a big bonfire there, but instead they've put up a cross made out of two-by-fours and duct tape. There is a strange kind of symmetry to it, their low hobbit holes all circled up like a brigade of wagons with a big, foreboding cross watching over them all. They emerge from the tents one by one, as if summoned by an invisible gong.

And they're hollow, completely empty, and trying so hard to be full again.

The Wives are bustling today, excited. A new family has arrived, the Stocktons. They're not from Black Earth but that doesn't matter; any and all families are warmly welcomed and invited to live among the Wives. The Wives are, across the board, turned down. But the Stocktons seem promising, or that's the rumor. I don't remember meeting them.

"They're at the med tent," Collin murmurs. "The father suffered a few minor abrasions, maybe a sprained ankle. You should meet them later. I'll introduce you."

But first I need to meet the Wives. It's a daunting experience, a bit like parachuting into the middle of a Stepford Wives convention and being bombarded with questions and pats on the back. Collin (who they primly refer to as Mr. Crane), of course, tells them about my harrowing deed, the vanquishing of the evil Zack. Of all the villagers, they are the most impressed, the most thankful and awed. They stare at me as if I've just come to hand them the blood of Christ, their mouths forming wide Os of shock. It's their reactions that frighten me the most.

"Bless you, bless you, God bless you for seeing to that . . . rat."

"God be with you—He must be. He must be."

On and on it goes. I try to be humble, to look like the martyred hero they expect. But it doesn't feel authentic. Collin notices my discomfort and steers me away from the group, bringing me over to one Wife sitting apart. She's perched on an empty plastic crate, her hands tucked demurely into her lap. She's wearing a gingham skirt and a loose blue sweater with daisies embroidered around the collar. Her permed red hair is matted and greasy. When she looks up at us I see that the front of her sweater is stained down the front with a broad brush stroke of blood.

"Marianne? This is Allison."

She doesn't extend her hand or really even show that she's seen me. Her eyes go straight through my body, through my veins and bones and I can feel the steely chill. At first I think we're done, that Collin is going to drag me away from this phantom, this ghost, but her eyes crackle to life suddenly and her chapped lips drop open.

"My son," she says in a whimper, breathing hard as though she's just noticed that he's gone missing. "My son . . . My son ate my baby girl. My son ate my baby girl!"

She repeats it again and again, her voice rising until she's screaming at me at the top of her lungs.

"MY SON ATE MY BABY GIRL!"

This is when Collin drags me away, shooting a look at the other Wives who hurry over to take care of Marianne. They enfold her in a tangle of arms, rocking her, clucking softly at her like a brood of giant mother hens, their foreheads all bowed to touch her face. Marianne disappears behind them, silenced, lost in the sea of their sudden and overwhelming care.

"Holy shit," I mutter, shaking my head to try and stop the painful ringing in my ears. Collin nods.

"Marianne is . . . Well, she's lost, I think. There are a few people like that here, but she's the worst. I asked Susan about her once. She told me Marianne's house was hit first, that she watched her son . . . Well, you heard her."

I did. It's hard to get that sound out of my head and when I blink I see her terror-stricken eyes. They look like Holly's—vacant, swept under.

Collin takes me out of the arena and down a long, narrow

corridor. We go outside into a fine October mist. It's certainly brisk out here, but there are plenty of extra clothes now, and the Wives have been busy sewing blankets and turning university jerseys into thick, patchy sweaters. They're not very warm but they do a decent job against the wind. As soon as we walk outside I hear gunfire. I'm getting used to that, to hearing shots every time I step into the open air.

The pale sun behind the clouds with its teasing hint of warmth has made the mist rise up on the horizon. Everything is gray beyond the close border of the arena yard. You can just make out a hint of tennis courts and a sidewalk, and a few yards in front of that a parked truck with a man standing guard behind it. There's ash in the air and the strange, briny smell of warmth seeping out of the ground. It rained last night but now the earth is almost dry.

Luckily, the nearest gunfire is just practice. Collin and his red-headed nephew, Finn, have set up a firing range out here. They've decided to take Ted and me and turn us into soldiers. But Ted is still inside at the med tent. He seems far more interested in learning how to suture wounds and set bones than to come with me to target practice.

"Where did they all come from?" I ask, nodding toward the gun Collin is now aiming at a far-off stack of wooden crates. He seems different with the gun primed and ready to fire. He's more distant, pulled behind a kind of sobering veil. His face is still gently creased, his eyes are still bright, but the feeling he exudes is chilling. There are so many weapons, so many supplies, that I can't help asking. It seems like something that should be left unsaid; it doesn't matter where the guns came from, it only matters that there are people here who know how to use them.

"The police. They're not trained for stuff like this. Maybe in New York or Chicago they would have experience with rioters and gang violence, but here they just weren't prepared. There's a difference between keeping a cool head under pressure and being intelligent under pressure." Collin must be immune to the sound of gunfire because he barely flinches as he pulls the trigger and the round explodes out of the barrel. I, however, am not used to this sound and it's deafening and scary every single time.

"They wanted to get citizens into the arena, to keep a safe, solid perimeter and have a central location for survivors to go to. That was a good step, a good idea. But then they set up that damn barricade right out front, right down the main artery. I'm sure they were thinking that a wall would keep the undead out. They were right, sort of, but it also kept citizens out. I don't know if you can guess, but when you have panicking citizens with a barricade on one side and undead on the other . . . Well, now you have a problem because you have three times as many undead as you did before. That barricade is coming down and your perimeter has gone to hell."

"So the police, they left? They just left those people there to die?"

"No," he says, lowering the gun. "They died too."

"So the flak jackets and the truck and the guns—those belonged to the cops?" I ask.

Collin nods, reloading the gun slowly so I can watch and then handing it to me. He seems to have returned to his former self, the man with the ready teacher's smile and prodding eyes. The gun is warm from his grip.

"Finn served in the Royal Air Force, and so did I. It was a family tradition. I kept my uniforms around for, oh I don't know, something like sentiment, a reminder of being a young man. The uniforms are just for peace of mind, for show. If you have a bunch of frightened people, desperate for help, nothing creates a little order like uniforms and assault rifles. Once you have order you can organize raids on the corner markets, on the libraries and the pharmacies and the ambulances, and once you have supplies you have happy people."

"You did all that by yourself?"

"Finn helped."

"Right. But you did it by yourself?"

"Of course," he says, tapping my elbow. He's impatient. He thinks I'll make a good soldier if I can just learn to shoot without tensing up every time I squeeze the trigger. I can't help it. I know that sound is coming, the explosion. "You don't think in situations like this, Allison, you act. I think you know that already."

"But you're just so . . . so calm. How do you do that? How do you not just completely lose it?"

"Hold on," he says, firmly pushing on my arms until the gun is pointed at the ground in front of us. "Did you lose someone? More than one person?"

"My mother," I stammer, caught off guard. "I don't . . . I don't know where she is. We were supposed to meet up but she never showed."

"I see. I lost my wife. I don't know where she is either, but I can guess. I'm not invincible, Allison. I'm just doing the best I can. And really, that's all I'm asking of you."

Target practice goes badly. I can't focus and I can't stop thinking about my mom. I shouldn't have told Collin about her, I should have just kept my mouth shut.

Ted doesn't come back to the tent until very late. He's been taking care of the Stocktons. He really likes them, especially their two young sons. Dapper is my only company as I wait up for Ted, and even the dog seems uninterested in my sulky mood. When Ted gets back he falls asleep right away, exhausted by a hard day's work. I want him to stay up. I want to talk and joke, to tell him that I'm useless with a gun, and hear him laugh when I say that Collin thinks I'm a complete sissy. These days Ted's unruly hair has all but colonized the surface of his glasses and he's reduced to constantly pushing it out of his face just to see where he's going. When he flops down on his sleeping bag his dark hair fans out around his head like a handful of daggers.

Collin has asked if I want to have a drink. Finn will be there because Collin wants his nephew to apologize. I'm sure he wants us all to get on. I remember that's the phrase he uses, "Get on." I politely tell him no, that I'm not interested, that I'm very tired.

Now I wish I had accepted the invitation because I'm sitting here reading what all of you have said. You're alive. A few of you are doing more than surviving, and I can easily imagine your disdain for someone like me, someone who can do nothing but sit around and wallow and stare at my sleeping roommate like a creepy shut-in. I shouldn't be alone like this. I should be having a whiskey with Collin and his nephew, I should be letting myself live.

But then again, every time I think of Collin, of his voice and how I looked to it on the radio for guidance and peace, I automatically think of Zack. After that catastrophic misstep, how can I trust my judgment? How can I trust myself?

Tomorrow, Collin wants me to meet the Stocktons. They're a very nice family, he says. A real, whole family.

I miss you, Mom. If you're reading this: I miss you.

- -

COMMENTS

Rev. Brown says:

October 9, 2009 at 6:45 pm

We survivors know your soul, Allison. I read aloud from what you write in the Kingdom House here in Atlanta. And it was my Jamal, all of nine, who offered me both solutions to your moral problem.

Allison, you can't know if what you did was a sin. You know you had righteous cause and you sought virtuous justice. Your manner may have lept towards malice—your soul may have blackened with a stain of mere, cruel vengeance—but God does not command that we forgive our enemies. Jesus Christ our Lord has demanded we treat others as we would be treated ourselves. And I know, just as I feel His spirit stir in your words, that His word would move you. If you stole a collective's food, you'd demand your own hands be taken, just as our forebears demanded of thieves.

It's all The Lord's work.

Logan says:

October 9, 2009 at 7:09 pm

Took a while to find it, working internet. I'm using SNet, is that what you're using too? Such a thing I used to take for granted, but you know the saying. See, where I'm at here in Colorado, we had warning. A few sparse broadcasts before They came. Most of us just meandered on with the daily routines, but some of us . . . Some of us knew that it wouldn't stop before it got to us.

We, myself and a few others from the area where I work, took the two weeks of warning, and prepared. At least I thought we did. In retrospect there wasn't much we really could have done to truly prepare for what was coming. A few of us even got arrested by the police for stealing before The Infected even showed up in . . . person. Not sure what happened to them, but lets take a look outside the window shall we? It's not too terribly hard to guess. I guess the military taught me things I never really realized. Survival is not a right, but more something earned. Survival of the Fittest indeed.

God or not, keep up the good fight. There ARE others and

we WILL "fix" this, even if that means putting a 9mm bullet or the blade of a sword or axe in between the eyes of every last one of Them.

Matthew H says:
October 9, 2009 at 7:36 pm
Dear Allison,
Your words give us so much hope. Just knowing that there are others who have made it is so very encouraging. I'm very sorry to hear about your friends who have passed. We have each lost loved ones here as well.

We found this yesterday via Blackberry (we have a charger(!), a working outlet just outside(!!), and the satellite Internet still works for now—I wonder for how long?). There are four of us staying in a storefront church on the north side of Las Vegas. You write of the "disdain" that we must have for you. Allison, nothing could be further from the truth. You have brought us into a network of the living—that gives hope, not resentment. Please continue to keep us posted. We'll stay in touch. We are so very grateful that so many of you are alive.

In peace,

Matthew, Caroline, Jamie, Gideon

October 10, 2009—A Room With a View

"You kill zomblies too?"

"Yes, Evan," I say, patting the little golden boy on his head. "Just like your mom and dad."

Right away I can see why Ted admires the Stocktons. Corie and Ned make up a tall, attractive couple with the kind of vigorous likeability that seems to transcend the mire of depression and shock in the Village. Their two sons are extremely charming. Not in the disturbing, doped-up-on-Ritalin sort of way. They have energy and they're talkative, but you can tell within a few seconds of knowing them that they've had a swell childhood full of climbed trees and captured dragonflies. Mikey, the older son, is ten and has the intense, dusky look of his olive-skinned, dark-haired mother. He's more reserved than his younger brother and informs me in a discrete, adult whisper that his little brother is still "just a baby." Evan is four, a scrapper, with the all-American J. Crew looks of his dad. Evan is still learning to talk. He travels only by shoulders, straddling his dad's neck, perched up there like a guru on a mountaintop. Evan wins me over right away when the first words out of his mouth are:

"I don't like the zomblies much. Dad says they're bad. You kill zomblies too?"

It would be easy to underestimate Corie and Ned, and it's tempting to write them off as a youngish yuppy couple who are prim and self-possessed on the outside while they hide a turbulent, hateful marriage. But they seem cool, legitimately cool, the kind of people you meet and think later on: I'd like to be like them someday. Corie's the sort of woman you always dream of outclassing at a high school reunion. Then you get there, smug, educated, successful, only to discover that Corie is now a Pilates instructor and has only become more humble and sweet and that she's aged gracefully—in fact, she's more beautiful now in her thirties than she ever was as a teenager. And you might want to hate her, but then you see her now, in a confusing, shattered world where it's easy to become numb and depressed and she's still laughing for her kids, still a rock-solid mom.

Ned and I don't hit it off immediately, but then, in a side conversation with Collin and me, he turns into someone I really, really want to know better. He and Corie lived in a suburb not far from Black Earth. When the undead arrived their neighborhood splintered. No one banded together, no one stayed to fight. One neighbor discovered that fire is a powerful weapon against the undead, but it also has a tendency to get out of control. Within an hour their entire cul-de-sac was in flames.

"I didn't say, 'We're staying, this is our house and we're staying no matter what.' Screw that. I knew we had to go. There wasn't going to be anything left. I knew it. I could feel the house coming down around us and Evan was just screaming. They were coming up the yard, up the drive, everywhere. So I said: honey, make sure the boys are with you, get them up. We're getting out of here. I didn't know where we would go. It didn't matter."

(Not that exciting, I know, but this next bit is when I just about nominated him for Village president.)

"And so I lit the PT Cruiser on fire and pushed it down the driveway."

Collin and I share a glance at this, both of us realizing then and there that Ned is going to fit in just fine around here. He and Collin then discover that they're both ex-military. Ned was an engineer for the U.S. Army in his twenties. This is enough to make them long-lost brothers and they're soon pounding each other on the back like real compadres. It's my freshman year of undergrad all over again, when even the most general, tenuous connection helped you befriend strangers. You're lonely and unsure and scared, so any shared interest at all is enough to forge a lifelong bond—"You like peas? No way! *I* like peas. Wanna get drunk?"

That's Ned and Collin—two camouflaged peas in a pod. Maybe they should be the new Hollianted—Nollin? Cod? Christ. Never mind.

I have a feeling this means I'll see a lot less of Collin and a lot more of Corie and the kids. So after listening to Evan's spirited, broken recount of their journey to the arena, I join Collin and Ned for target practice. Ned hasn't shot a gun in years, but the way he picks it back up again tells you he's a natural. Right away he picks a soda can off of a distant fence and then a baseball tossed into the air. He makes me look like a blind old porch-sitter taking pot-shots at squirrels. It's hard not to be impressed, hard not to be swept up by Ned's tornadolike vortex of affability and well, *cool*.

Sadly, I've barely seen Ted at all today. He's become so busy with the nurses and patients at the med tent that I'm beginning to wonder if he's actively avoiding me. I hope that's not it. I miss having him around.

In happier news, Dapper is thrilled that Evan and Mikey have entered his life. The two boys are enamored of the mutt and I think it's safe to say that the feeling is mutual. And yet with all of this, all this new stuff, I worry a little about Corie. It's not that she's fragile, the opposite really, but I know she'll have a harder time fitting in. The Black Earth Wives have already begun to swarm, cunningly asking for her advice on motherly things when clearly no advice is needed. They're trying to lure her into their twisted little Tupperware club and I'm afraid it might happen. Collin thinks they're harmless, that it's good they try to keep themselves busy instead of letting loss rule their lives.

Subtle, Collin. Reeeal subtle.

I've been thinking about the nature of potential, about how all of us maybe have the potential to be what Zack was. I know there is a kind of ugliness inside of me—a violence that I never knew existed, that I never had occasion to encourage until I focused all that ugliness on Zack. I try to push that part of me down but then I remember how often it's saved me and saved Ted. I think that ugliness is in Ted too. He might be a disheveled, good-hearted boy scout on the outside, but inside . . . inside I think he might be like me. Cold. It hurts to think that I might steal and kill, or that if I'm bitten, infected, I too will become one of those horrible things. All of these potential outcomes are locked away inside of me but now, one by one, they're beginning to emerge. I wish I had the key. I wish I knew the combination to the lock. I'd close it up forever.

Collin asks me again if I want to join him and Finn for a drink and this time I accept. I thought maybe he wouldn't ask me again, but it cheers me up considerably to find that he hasn't written me off completely. It's pleasant. So pleasant, in fact, that there's almost nothing to say about it. Finn is even more fiery and blasphemous when he's drunk, a whirlwind of curse words and bawdy stories and ginger hair. And Collin? He seems to be one of those people that are simply immune to alcohol. He might have gotten a little rosier, but he stays, as always, a bit of a mystery—reserved and tucked away from us, hiding behind his serenely handsome face. It's something he's very good at, I think, presenting the illusion of openness while really concealing most of his personality. I don't think he has anything to hide. He just prefers to sit behind a shroud of secrecy, silently and comfortably apart.

When Finn has passed out with his flaming red head on the table, Collin takes me to the radio booth. I see now where his broadcasts came from. He's been using the glass box over the arena, the booth where the newscasters would call the games. It's a bird's-eye view of the Village, and for a moment or two we sit together quietly and watch the darkened camp restlessly sleeping. Every once in a while a flashlight will bounce around the ceiling of a tent, lighting up the colored nylon like a glowworm in a green glass jar.

There's a stack of books on the floor by a cushy swivel chair. I pour over the titles, entranced just by the simple act of holding them in my hands. Holding a book is a simple thing, *was* a simple thing, and now it holds a kind of thrilling magic I never noticed before. Collin tells me the survivors were able to pool the books they had saved and ones they had rescued from the library.

"Should I read one?" Collin asks, sitting in the swivel chair.

"Now? It's so late."

"Didn't you listen late at night? Isn't that how you found us?" he asks. He's right, of course, and I nod, chuckling, tickled by the thought of how excited I was about a voice, just a voice.

"What's so amusing?" he asks.

"It's silly. . . . No . . . It's gross."

"What is it?"

"Are you sure you want to know?"

"Yes. Absolutely," he says, helping me sort through the books. He pauses over *Wise Children*.

"I listened to you one night and Zack was there next to me. I thought I was going to . . . I don't know, fall for him or something. God. Can you imagine? Can you even imagine being that idiotic?"

"I can, actually."

I wait for him to say more but that's it, that's all he's willing to share.

"Still," I say, "that's not so bad. At least you didn't marry a kleptomaniac like Zack."

"That I know of." He nods toward the neat stack of books in my hands and I take the seat across from him. I can't decide. There are too many good ones.

"Which one will it be?"

Collin whistles "Let's Go Fly a Kite" from *Mary Poppins* while I try to decide; it's something he does when he's idle, waiting. I'm a little drunk, so I pick Durrell's *Justine*. Collin briefly questions the choice with a raised eyebrow and then takes the book from me anyway. It's a book for the voice, for the ears.

"I'm not even going to ask who rescued this one," I murmur, settling back into the chair like a Persian cat angling for a nice, long nap.

"It was me, if you must know."

"Hedonist."

"Mountebank."

"Oh!" I cry, feeling the booze. "Good one!"

"May I begin, or would you like to flirt a while longer?"

"Sorry," I say, startled. "Please start."

I see then that there's a ripped page taped to the space above the switchboard. Collin turns a few knobs and clears his throat, scooting the chair closer to the microphone. He begins to speak, slowly and deliberately in that great, rusted old voice of his. He reads from the page.

"I don't know how many of you are listening, or how many of you are still trying desperately to survive, but I want you to know this: all hope is not lost. You have somewhere to go, somewhere to seek. It's late and you feel afraid, hopeless, but don't despair." He pauses here in the familiar spiel and looks over at me, smiling faintly. "Why, just a few days ago a woman came to us. She was very nearly killed trying to get here but she made it. She heard us, she persevered, and I'm very grateful that she arrived in one piece. Her name is Allison. And so to honor Allison and her courage, I've chosen to read from a book of her choosing this evening. So dear listeners, close your eyes, let the worry drain away and listen, and please do remember: if you don't like this book, it wasn't my choice."

I scowl and raise my fist and threaten him silently as he chuckles at my indignation. Then he clears his throat again and takes a brief moment to scan the open book in front of him. The room around is so dark, so soft and silent that I can almost hear the deep thunder of his heart. And then, at last, he begins to read.

After only a moment I begin to feel sleepy. I'm drunk on Collin's "retirement" whiskey, a fancy bottle he had been saving for many years, a bottle he was hoping to open after his retirement from teaching. That day would have been many years off still, but he was sick and tired of waiting and so he decided to share it with Finn and me. It's probably the most expensive liquor I've ever had, and while it burned on the way down it was a good, satisfying ache, like the first radiant sunburn of summer. I feel warm and ancient and I start to realize that Collin is watching me over the flimsy lip of the book.

Somehow the radio didn't quite convey the loveliness of his reading voice. It distorted it, as if all the death and ugliness hanging between us in space had corroded the quality of his voice until it was a thin imitation. Even then, even with Zack next to me, it had been beautiful; but now, seeing him, being in the same room as the text and the man and the voice, it's incandescent.

Potential.

There are times when our potential grows weary of trembling in shadow and comes suddenly, violently, to the fore. Like a song forced through our pores, or water crashing over a broken dam, that potential arrives, determined, demanding our attention.

Maybe there are other things in that locked vault—maybe there's more than just violence and deception and coldness. Maybe there is radiance, love, a kind of longing that singes you inside.

I return to my tent giddy, aflame, "Let's Go Fly a Kite" stuck stubbornly in my head.

COMMENTS

Rev. Brown says:
October 10, 2009 at 11:21 pm
God Jehovah makes known our potential through His only Son:
"However, we have this treasure in earthen vessels, that the power beyond what is normal may be God's and not that out of ourselves. We are pressed in every way, but not cramped beyond movement; we are perplexed, but not absolutely with no way out; we are persecuted, but not left in the lurch; we are thrown down, but not destroyed. Always we endure everywhere in our body the death-dealing treatment given to Jesus, that the life of Jesus may also be made manifest in our body. For we who live are ever being brought face to face with death for Jesus' sake, that the life of Jesus may also be made manifest in our mortal flesh. Consequently death is at work in us, but life in YOU."
II Corinthians 4:7–12

Andrew N says:
October 10, 2009 at 11:45 pm
Allison,
I wish you, Ted, and The Village all the best. Finding your words and the stories of fellow readers gives me hope that not all is lost and that humanity will survive.

After cashing out my stocks at the Dot-Com I was at, I decided to sail around the world. I took my boat out of Newport Beach, California and headed north to Alaska as my first destination. I'm working my way down the pacific coast stopping wherever I can to get fresh supplies. Fresh water is running low. At least I have solar panels to help me out with the electricity. Satellite internet is spotty; I lost the sat-phone in Salem after being chased by Groaners. I haven't found any other sailors in CB radio range. I keep trying every hour.

Any other sailors out there, I should hit San Francisco Bay in a few days time. I have enough supplies to last till then; then I'll need to worry about fresh water.
Good luck to everyone out there.

> **Elizabeth says:**
> *October 11, 2009 at 12:31 am*
> Sailor here, checking in! At the outset, we managed to make it to a sailboat that my boyfriend's father owns in Newport Beach, CA (hello Andrew!). There are three of us. Me, my boyfriend, and his dad. We tried to get my boyfriend's mom to come with us, to try to run ahead of the undead masses, but she was always a homebody and took off to "save" her Alzheimer's ridden mother. We waited for as long as we could at the dock, but she never showed.
>
> We keep hoping to see someone, anyone, on the seas or alive at the ports, but it looks like even Avalon (on an island) didn't escape the undead. Maybe a passenger ship transported the undead? Who knows. Maybe we'll find survivors on the other islands, trapped at campsites. It's still so risky here to go on land, there are still so many undead waiting for our inattention. I just hope that they can die of

hunger. Maybe if they can't get more of us, it'll end. Keep posting, Allison. There are other survivors here, maybe more than we think.

Allison says:

October 11, 2009 at 9:23 am

The water sounds like a good choice. You don't know what it means to me that you all take the time to write, to say that you are finding a way through. Evan and Mikey are enamored of the idea of going to sea. They want to become pirates, "Scrooge of the Zomblies," as Evan will say, and then Mikey corrects: "Scourge of the Zombies, dodo head." They're so young, but already they're turning into fighters.

October 13, 2009—Microterrors

They just keep coming, more and more of them, arriving alone or in clumps, dazed and staring as they're brought inside. It's hard not to look at their faces; you see something incredible there, a fleeting look of disbelief as they step inside from the cold. It's hard to find a minute to get away and write. Collin and Finn insist that every single newcomer is checked for bites, for scratches, for any signs of carrying the danger in here. So far everyone has checked out fine. I can't imagine having to turn anyone away, to tell them no, I'm sorry, you're not allowed to be safe.

But Ted thinks that's what has to happen now. He's taken the day off today. He's been sitting in our tent all afternoon scribbling calculations down in a notebook, his shaggy hair hanging down over his spectacles and nose, making grunting noises of frustration, and erasing furiously before beginning again. It's difficult to find the old Ted in the new. I know why he's become this way—he needed a distraction, an activity to throw himself into. Holly, her life, her death, is still terribly near for him. The detailed work of helping people, of suturing wounds and taking down symptoms has saved him in a way, saved him from a long, lonely road traveled in total misery.

I know he didn't want to tell me, but he's so obviously nervous about something. And so I had to ask. Now I wish I hadn't.

"It could be anything. We don't have the equipment to find out where it's come from or whether it's just an isolated case. . . ."

"What are you talking about?" I ask. Outside the tent I can hear Evan and Mikey chasing Dapper. Their laughter pierces through the incoherent bustling of the villagers. I scoot closer to Ted, trying to catch a glance at his notebook. He pulls the pages toward his body, hiding them.

"It was just William, that janitor, and we thought it might just be because he's old. But now there's someone else, and I'm sure tomorrow it will be another case and then another," he says, his black brows meeting at the perfect center of his forehead. He shakes his moppy head around, sighing deeply through clenched teeth. He shoves his glasses up the bridge of his nose; I'm worried the damn frames will simply evaporate from all the poking and abuse. "The vomiting, the diarrhea . . . I think it might be giardia, something in the water. That would explain it."

"The *water*? There's something wrong with our water?"

"Think about it," he says. "The sanitation is getting worse. The more people we pack in here the easier it is for something contagious to spread. And if just one person, just one, gets in and they're infected, really infected . . ."

"That's impossible," I snap. "I've been helping them check. We won't let anyone slip by."

"What if it's an animal? What if you can't stop them?" he asks. He looks at me then, his dark eyes wide and glossy. I know what he's thinking: it only took a rodent to kill Holly.

"It won't happen, Ted. What happened to Holly . . . it was . . . it wasn't our fault. It was a fluke. There's no one here like Zack. No one would put us in danger," I say, touching his knee, trying to remind him that we're friends, that he has a friend. He doesn't flinch, but I can see his expression icing over.

"It wasn't Zack," he says after a long pause. Someone has tried to mend his glasses; there is medical tape wound around both edges. I can see the electrical tape underneath from previous patch jobs.

"What? Of course it was. Who else would've left the window open like that?"

"Me. I did."

I pull my hand away from him and I feel his eyes sweeping my face. I had always just assumed Zack had opened that window, that he had hoped for something bad to happen. But I suppose it could've just been an accident, a careless mistake. I reach for Ted's hand and he lets me take it. We sit in silence for a moment, not out of reverence, but because I can't think of a damn thing to say.

"Are you okay?" I finally ask.

"Yes," he says. "I'd be a lot better if you would just move on."

"Me? What are you talking about?" This conversation isn't supposed to be about me. I don't want him to sneak out of this, to turn his back on confronting what I'm sure is an unmanageable burden. He smiles down at his notebook, avoiding my eyes.

"Zack. It wasn't your fault. We can trust the people here, Allison. You said so yourself."

"I know that."

"No, I don't think you do, because if you did, your damn boyfriend wouldn't come and ask me for permission to see you."

"He—my—*what*?"

"Collin stopped me last night on the way back to the tent," Ted says, still avoiding my eyes. It's a good thing he is, otherwise I'd burn them right out of their sockets. "He asked if you were . . . you know, okay."

"Oh my God."

"Yeah. I told him you were fine, just a little shook up from the thing with Zack and that you were worried about your mom. Torn about staying or something. I, uh . . . I hope that was the right thing to say?"

"Of course it was. I mean . . . Shit . . . It's true, isn't it?"

"Stop holding back, Allison," Ted murmurs, shutting his note-book and shrugging away from me. He gets to his feet and stops before leaving. "Forget Zack and stick close to Collin. There might come a time when this place isn't safe and when that time comes I want him on our side. I like him."

I watch him leave, my mouth flapping like a flag in the wind. "Did it ever occur to you that I don't *like* him that way!?" I shout after him, but he's gone.

"Like who?"

An unruly blond head pops into the tent. It's Evan, his pale eyes dancing. He looks and acts so much like his father it's almost like talking to a miniature adult. I can imagine this is exactly how Ned looked as a boy: all gristle and fight and bouncy curls.

"None of your beeswax, Evan, that's who," I say, grabbing him around the middle as I leave the tent. He squeals, flailing as I tip him upside down and spin, turning him into an airplane. Mikey, too mature for such shenanigans, watches with his hand resting on Dapper's head, his disapproving grimace firmly in place. I let Evan land and he twirls a little, his balance shot. Then he col-lapses in a fit of giggles, prey for Dapper to lick and sniff.

"Where's your dad?" I ask, anxious to be out of sight. If I don't keep my mind busy I'll start thinking about Collin. I should be more upset, but it really doesn't surprise me at this point. Ted is right, I have been holding out.

"He's in the basement. Mom says you guys found a gym," Mikey replies.

"Thanks. Go easy on Dapper."

I keep a low profile, sticking to the far side of the arena, as far away from the line check for incoming survivors as possible. Collin is over there, his height placing his dark head above most of the others. He's there, probably wondering why I'm being so distant, but that's a conversation that can wait.

On the way I see Corie sitting in a circle with the Wives, her hands tangled in the thick, shiny curtain of her hair. The Wives are sewing, or knitting, or quilting or whatever it is they do all day. Corie looks strange, too pretty and spry to be sitting in their group. Her head is slightly bowed, her dark hair an unbroken sheet tumbling to one side. She doesn't see me. She doesn't see me looking at her sad, faraway eyes.

As I search for Ned I catch myself whistling "Let's Go Fly a Kite." I stop myself, disappointed that my subconscious is determined to undermine me. I find Ned down in the bowels of the arena. We're not allowed to hook up the treadmills to the generators. Collin has been bold enough to make an exception for me and I get to use generator time to charge my laptop. But *sh-hhh*, that's just between us.

Treadmills aside, there are benches and weights and plenty of ways to get in shape. Ned is teaching me to lift weights. It feels good to put energy toward something tangible, something I can see and feel in the tension of my muscles. I'm woefully out of shape and Ned is merciless, putting me through the army training he experienced years ago. He's an avid squash player and rowed crew for his university. It's embarrassing to discover that a thirtysomething dad is in better shape than me, but I try to use that constructively, as motivation.

When I arrive, Ned is in the middle of a set of push-ups and cries out like he's been stabbed when he finishes and rolls onto his side. Ned is a bit shorter than Collin, with big swimmer's legs and a chin as square and sharp as an ironing board. His brassy brown hair is starting to thin above his high forehead. He has a weekend, mow-the-lawn tan and a tightly composed face of pointed, masculine features, except for his rather pretty and unusual lips. I've seen prettier L.L.Bean models, but not many. I throw him a towel and he manages to catch it before it hits his face.

"Thanks," he says, dabbing at his forehead and neck. "Done upstairs?"

"If I have to smell one more rank armpit or inspect another funky-ass foot I'm going to give up on life."

"Ha ha!" he says, laughing just like that, in short, breathy spurts. His eyes dance as he sits up, groaning like a creaky old corpse. "Shouldn't it be colder in here? I'm dying."

"It's not cold anywhere," I say, sitting down on a bench. The ceiling is low in here and everything echoes despite the thickly padded floor. The machines and equipment are brand-new and well-maintained, funded, no doubt, by very generous donors to the university. "There are so many people here now; it's like the god-damn rain forest up there."

"Yeah, but rain forests are supposed to be that way—you know, muggy because they're jungles, not because of too many freaking—sorry—fucking bodies," he says, grimacing just like his son. "What's the matter?"

"Hm?"

"You just . . . I don't know. Your face sorta fell when I said that."

"Oh," I say, scratching idly at my shoulder. I'm not sure I can play this one off or concoct a suitable lie. "Ted's being an ass, freaking me out, that's all."

"Yeah?"

"He says we're getting too cramped and that it's dangerous. He thinks maybe the water might be contaminated."

"We've been boiling everything on a hot plate," Ned says, resting his elbows on his knees. His legs are covered in dense, curly brown hairs.

"Yeah, so have we, but not everyone is that careful."

"Well, we could expand to other parts of the building, or other buildings altogether. There are plenty of options," he says. "But you're not convinced?"

"What if someone gets in? One of *them*."

"But we're checking everyone."

"I know that, Ned, but still . . . It's just . . . it's not foolproof, ya know?"

"Listen," he says, getting to his feet, his long legs unfolding. "You have to stop thinking like that. I've been to some pretty low states of mind in the past few weeks, and you just can't allow yourself to get that way. You're stronger than this. I know you are."

"Right. You've known me all of, what, three days?"

"That doesn't matter. You can tell, you just have to. There's no time for bullshitting around anymore. You just have to look at someone and decide: I can trust you or I can't," he says, coming to sit next to me on the bench. His sleeves are soaking wet and he smells faintly of salt and baby powder. I feel like a child next to him.

"Yeah? I'm not really so good at making those snap decisions."

"Well I am, idiot, and I say this: you have to stop looking at the dark side. There are positives here. We have food, we have a roof over our heads and weapons and we have us, okay? You and me. We're not people who give up. We're fighters. I can train you. We can train together, and if the day comes when we have to fight here, right upstairs, we'll do it and we'll be okay."

"Why do you put up with me?" I ask, laughing. "I'm a shithead. I promise I'll do better."

"Good," he says, getting to his feet. "Just boil that darn water and leave no funky toenail unturned."

"Darn?"

"Sorry, Dadism," he says. "Corie weaned me off of swearing. She caught Mikey dropping an F-bomb during soccer practice and that was that."

We work out. We train. It feels good to train, to feel like a soldier, like I'm working toward something. I know tomorrow my body is going to hate me for this and that every single joint and muscle will cry out in agony and frustration, but I won't stop. Tonight I'll talk to Collin and I won't hold back. I'll stop turning him away, I'll stop feeling so fucking . . . *congested.*

Before the workout is through I'm puking in a garbage can, my wrists shaking as I try to get back up on my wobbling legs. I look like total hell and I feel like I'm about to pass out on Ned's shoulder at any second, but it's good. It feels good.

I won't let Ted get to me. I don't care if he's worried—there are people here doing their very best to make sure we're safe and I'm one of them. If I have to check and double-check every motherfucker coming through the doors I will, and if I have to go around and boil everyone's water for them, I will. This place is a good place, too good to give up.

COMMENTS

Andrew N says:

October 13, 2009 at 5:20 pm

It's Andrew again and just checking in. I sailed past the San Francisco Bay area and things don't look good. I can't find a place to dock without getting overrun. Anyone have any tips?

I'm running low on food, and I'm contemplating fishing. I know it should be a last resort as I have no idea if the fish are infected either. I've figured out how to distill salt water into regular water though; so that should help me for a few days.

Elizabeth says:

October 13, 2009 at 5:56 pm

The fish haven't harmed us yet so I think you can feel safe using them for food. Just inspect them carefully before you dig in. We've been killing them and then waiting a moment to see if they reanimate. So far they've been safe to eat.

Dave in the Midwest says:

October 13, 2009 at 7:03 pm

Does anyone have any knowledge about what this is from? Please help. Resources limited . . . anybody found any antibiotics or anything that can reverse it? Please . . . my son . . . I have to save him.

Allison says:

October 13, 2009 at 9:22 pm

I'm afraid you'll have to leave your son to his fate. It isn't pleasant, Dave, but that's the reality of the situation.

October 14, 2009—The Good Soldier

"Does Corie seem weird to you? Distant?"

"Who?" Ted asks, his face shoved into a bowl of steaming Ramen noodles. His glasses fog as he roots around in the noodles with his plastic fork.

"Jesus, Ted, *Corie,* you know? Ned's wife Corie?"

"Hm, I haven't noticed anything."

"Forget it." Ted continues eating, ignoring me. He's out of the loop anyway.

"I'm late," he says, slurping up the last of his Ramen. "Should've been at the med tent ages ago."

"I'm worried about Corie," I say, holding the tent flap aside and peering out at the arena as it wakes. "Do you think I should say something to Ned?"

"Say whatever you want," Ted says. "I've gotta go."

I think—no—I *know* Corie's fallen in with the wrong crowd. She's quickly gone the way of the dodo. I use dodo in the sense that she is simply no longer around. When Evan needs her she's impossible to track down. He scraped his elbow yesterday playing with Dapper and Mikey and it took me almost forty-five minutes to locate his mother. It turns out she was up on the roof, sitting up there in a semicircle praying with the Black Earth Wives.

In a way, I saw this coming. Maybe it's my fault. I feel like I've completely commandeered her husband. Ted and I have been monopolizing his time, encouraging him to put us through back-breaking workouts until we're crawling on all fours, panting like wanderers dragging ourselves across the desert.

I thought Corie would shape up into a leader around here, but I was wrong. I was hoping to find strength in her. After all, she managed to get two little boys across a wilderness of burning wreckage and flesh-eating monsters. She deserves, at the very least, my respect. But I haven't found that leader I was hoping for and I've watched her drift away, inching out of my reach until her allegiance shifted completely.

The clipboard is no longer taken from tent to tent in the morning. The Black Earth Wives are contracting, drawing their considerable numbers up and inward, curling up like a dead crab on its back. Between spending time in the gym with Ned and Ted (ha, that rhymes!) and check-in duty, I haven't been able to keep tabs on the Wives. These days, they're suspiciously hard to find.

But this afternoon I had to find Corie. Mikey and Evan wanted her to teach them about geometry, but Corie wasn't in their family tent and she wasn't in shouting distance. I was given the thankless task of tracking her down while Evan and Mikey ate string cheese and threw a ratty old tennis ball for Dapper. I'm not even sure he's my dog anymore. I think he's officially defected.

At last I find her. She and the rest of the Wives are being herded back inside by a very distressed-looking Finn. He's grimacing as he tries to gently shove a particularly rotund old woman back inside the building, his face turning the same garish shade of red as his hair. They've tried to go out the northeast exit to the parking lot. There's a perimeter set up there and a few people standing watch, but it's by no means safe.

"You can pray in the gym with everyone else," Finn grunts, slamming the door shut behind him. He physically plants himself in the way, making sure they can see the beefy assault rifle locked across his chest.

"But the damned! We must pray for them! To them!"

"What a bloody nightmare."

"Corie!" I shout, wading into the sea of floral cardigans and Clinique "Happy"–scented tennis bracelets. I grab her by the elbow and extract her from the angry mass of housewives. They stay to pout at Finn and his black mood. It's not hard to pull Corie away; her elbow fits neatly in my palm. "Evan and Mikey were hoping you could do a geometry lesson."

We slowly make our way down the dark, low corridor. There's muted gunfire from outside and the buzzing of soft voices at our backs. I know the Wives are watching us, glaring at me as I take Corie away from them. Corie trembles a little and then draws herself up. I can see the mother, the warrior, creeping back into her face. She's so terribly gaunt now, it's a miracle any hopeful light can radiate through her sallow skin.

"I should teach them," she says obtusely, nodding to herself. Her black hair settles in a ripple down her back. "Are they very lonely?"

"No, no, I don't think so. Dapper is good company," I say, smiling for her. "They're all worn out by the end of the afternoon." She knows all of this and I'm not sure why I have to remind her. Something is up. It's all too obvious that hanging around with the Wives has sapped her.

"Is everything okay?" I ask.

"Oh? Yes, everything is fine," she says. We stand in the doorway just before the opening to the arena. The empty pipes over our heads sing in the chill of the hall. If we go much farther we'll run into the stream of survivors being brought in from the cold.

"It's just . . . You haven't spent much time with the boys lately, or Ned."

"Hmph," she says, tossing her hair. "Oh. *Right*."

"I . . . Sorry? Didn't mean to touch on a sore spot."

"No it's okay. I just . . . Forget it, it's not important, not anymore."

I jerk her a little back down the corridor, making sure she can't escape. It feels awkward to be doing this to a woman older than I am, a woman who should be vigorous and fearsome. I want so badly for her to wake up, to shake off the fog she's fallen into. It dawns on me that she hasn't been making friends at all but hiding.

"Is something going on with you and Ned?"

"No."

"Corie . . . Come *on*."

"We . . . We were . . ." She glances around, her dark blue eyes darting over my shoulders.

With a shrug she bites down a little on her lower lip. She's so beautiful, it's difficult not to cave and comfort her. I can imagine her as a young girl running in the sunshine, her arrow-straight black hair flying in every direction. She must have been stunning, a heartbreaker. "Things between us . . . We were going to try a separation. I wanted to divorce him but he convinced me to go for a separation first."

This is incomprehensible to me. I'm not some huge proponent of marriage necessarily—my mom got along well enough after my dad died and never felt like remarrying—but I can't for the life of me see the point in divorcing someone like Ned. I want desperately to take Corie's side, but it's hard to sympathize when Ned is still energetic and engaged and Corie is looking more and more like an extra from a Tim Burton film. Her skin is ashy around her lips and eyes and I can't help but wonder if she's getting enough to eat.

"Ned seems like a great guy. I'm sure it was just a bumpy patch. All couples go through that."

"He *is* a great guy, that's why we're still together. I don't know. . . . I feel like such a coward, but I can't stop thinking about the separation. It's hard to believe I almost left him. . . . And then, well everything just went to hell and I couldn't leave him, not then, not like that. I don't know why I can't stop thinking about it, Allison."

It starts to make a disastrous sort of sense—the distancing herself, the religion, the malnutrition. I'm sure a divorce, especially now, would be more than enough to test anyone's faith.

"Hey, hey, it's okay. We all go through tough shit and, ya know, people change their minds. They can do that, Corie, and there's nothing wrong with it. No one has to know, no one. And look, there will be time later to think about all this, about marriages and futures and all that stuff. But right now I think we should all just focus on hunkering down, making this place livable and safe, okay?"

"Okay," she says in a very small voice. I let go of her elbow after rubbing it a bit. It doesn't seem right to let her go without a small gesture of solace. She brushes past me with her eyes red and puffy and her fingertips worrying along the edge of her chin. If she just trusts, if she just looks at Evan and Mikey, if she sees what she has, how lucky she is. And then I hear a snippet of *Mary Poppins* music and . . .

"Everything all right here?"

I turn around to find an enormous bandolier of ammunition staring me in the face. When I tip my chin up I find a pair of startling hazel eyes above the bullets. It's Collin and he's smiling apologetically. *Wonderful.* I do not like when large men make this face. It is entirely too charming.

"Collin!" It comes out in a squeal even louder than the shade of scarlet my cheeks are turning. "Everything is fine, just having a chat with Corie."

"Is she all right?"

"I think so," I mumble. "Yeah . . . Getting there."

"I see."

It's getting awkward; I can tell he's about to give up on this conversation, I can feel his shoulders hitching up as he prepares to leave. I can't have him asking Ted permission to see me. I need to be a grown-up.

"Can we go somewhere?" I ask. "To . . . to talk?"

"Now?"

"Sure."

"Not now, I'm afraid," he says, looking crestfallen. He's shaved his hair down short and he's developed a habit of running his free hand over it as he thinks. It's a bit like watching a hopeful dreamer rub the belly of a lamp, and I wonder if ribbons of blue smoke will coil out of his nose. But there's no genie, just a snort of frustration. "Later? Could we do this later?"

"Yeah."

"Come by after nine."

I do, all the while carrying around a queasy knot of tension. I can't stop worrying about Corie. I can almost feel the *Emma* compulsion, the forceful desire to make sure she and Ned stick together, to scheme and plot and make them dance a dainty dance of courtship. But that's a fantasy. There's no room for that kind of frolicking, no room for risk. They have to stand by each other, if not for Evan and Mikey then for our general survival.

As planned, I leave my laptop to charge at one of the generators and go to Collin's tent at nine. I feel like a crook, tiptoeing through the deadened air, the cold just beginning to creep back in over the sleeping, sweaty bodies sprawled out in tents and sleeping bags. I can almost feel a hundred pairs of watchful, suspicious eyes on me as I navigate the labyrinth of tents.

His tent, not surprisingly, is black and lit up with the gently muted glow of an old-fashioned lantern. When I climb inside I can smell the slowly melting beeswax rising in thin, black stripes from the flame. The floor of the tent is a mess of pillows and old blankets and an open sleeping bag. It's not a very big tent so I sit close to him, cross-legged and growing extremely warm from the lantern.

"Thanks for coming," he says, his voice just above a whisper.

"It's no problem," I reply.

It was a bit of a dilemma getting dressed for this. It's not a date so there's no use looking nice, but I didn't want to show up in pajamas. I settled on a long-sleeve thermal T and my usual pair of jeans. Collin is out of his fatigues and it's rather nice to see him in a soft button-down open over a T-shirt.

"It's a bit cramped in here," he says, laughing quietly. "I didn't think it right to take one of the big tents just for myself."

"Don't worry," I tell him. "It's a big upgrade from snoring and dog, I promise."

"I think I owe you an apology," he says, grinning in a way that makes his dimples stream down his face toward his jawline.

"I was just about to say the same thing."

"Really? What on earth are you sorry about?"

"I should've come to see you sooner. To talk."

"About what exactly?" he asks and the dimples vanish into his frown.

"I just . . . I've been distracted lately, and sad, I guess. I keep expecting my mom to show up, but she hasn't so then I get to thinking that maybe I should leave and go look for her." Deep breath.

"Is that everything?"

"And I should have told you that you make me a little nervous," I say, feeling my throat grow dry and lumpy. "It's nothing you did, not anything bad. I just thought maybe I should, ya know, not try to move in on you."

It sounds even worse than it looks. My words are so jumbled up and ridiculous that I cringe even as they fall out of my mouth. I'm a goddamn adult and I can't even say what I mean to say, which is obvious, because Collin looks befuddled. I scrunch up my face, preparing for the big one, one end of the knot that's been living in my gut for days now. "It's your wife. It weirds me out. It weirds me out that you lost her. It just seems wrong and too soon . . . and weird."

"You mentioned the weird bit."

"Sorry."

"A few times, actually."

"Yeah."

"Allison," he says, and it's not a voice coming through a radio but a voice right there next to me, close and warm and skimming across my forearms. He puts a big, heavy hand on my knee and I can feel his palms sweating even through my jeans. "Is that all?"

"*Is that all?*"

"I don't want you to worry about her or about me, okay? I'm older than you are, Allison, I've seen a lot more than you have. I can safely say that there is nothing in my life that even begins to compare to this monumentally fucked-up situation. I can question it, I can hate it, I can rage against it all I like, but the fact remains: this is who we are now. I don't need to tell you that every day here is fleeting, every moment a gift. I shouldn't have to prove to you that I'm capable of making up my own mind. Do you understand what I'm saying?"

"Yes."

"What am I saying?" he asks, fixing his hazel eyes on me in the semidarkness. His face doesn't look so unreadable now, as if he's stripped away part of the armor that held him at a distance.

"You're saying I should stop being such an idiot, that I should stop overthinking every shit, piss and breath I take from now on."

"Right."

"So . . . It's not weird?" I ask, noticing then that his knee is touching mine. I've almost forgotten that we're surrounded, hemmed in on every side by people just like us—survivors, humans.

"It's not weird," he says.

"It's not weird."

I don't return to the other tent for hours. It's nice to think that I have two tents now, that I can have two homes. I think maybe I'm a bit of a nomad now. I think perhaps we all are.

- -

COMMENTS

> **Dave in the Midwest says:**
>
> *October 14, 2009 at 10:01 pm*
>
> Please . . . does ANYONE have any information on reversing this? My son was infected and I've . . . well . . . he's safe. He can't hurt anyone else but I know he's suffering. He's just so delusional and angry; he never says a word just deep growls when I come close to him. But I'm sure this isn't permanent. It just can't be. Can someone please offer any advice??? I'm posting this anywhere I can find help.
>
>> **Logan says:**
>>
>> *October 14, 2009 at 10:27 pm*
>>
>> You have to let go. Don't think. Don't fret. Just get rid of him.
>>
>>> **Isaac says:**
>>>
>>> *October 14, 2009 at 11:53 pm*
>>>
>>> He's not your son anymore. It's time to let him go.

October 16, 2009—Invisible Monsters

"Have you boiled that? Did you double-check the expiration date?"

It's become a script, the magic words I mutter over every cup of water we distribute and every package of soup we give away. Mostly my questions are met with grunts or sighs.

"I know you're hungry, but if it's expired you can't eat it."

"My kid is starving!" they say, clutching the Ramen or beets, hanging on desperately.

"I know that but it's not safe. Young kids are especially susceptible. They can get sick and die. You have to take precautions, you have to boil *everything*."

More and more survivors are becoming ill. I don't know if Ted was right, if it's coming from the water or from something else. Maybe some of the food has gone rancid or there's a flu going around, and we're all in a panic trying to track down the source, the cause.

I feel now as our ancestors must have felt at the beginning, that water is the greatest of treasures, the mother nurturing the cradle of life. Water, the most valuable possession on our planet, the thing that sustains us, fuels us, and helps us grow—it is now under suspicion. I feel fine, most of us do, but those who are ill wail and wail all day long, singing their suffering to the rest of us, making us feel guilty for having our health.

How could I leave this place? And yet, how can we stay? I look at Evan and Mikey, boys who have barely begun to understand the world—are we endangering them just by spending another day in this crowded, surging, bulging refugee camp? The survivors arrive in a constant stream, not always a strong current, sometimes only a trickle, but constant nonetheless. They are straining our resources—no, the resources are for them too—but soon the supplies will be spread so thin that no one will have much of anything.

Maybe this is the excuse I needed all along. I've waited too long to go after my mother. I shouldn't have waited at all.

I boil my water twice, sometimes three times before drinking it, and after every sip I begin to feel sick, not from illness but from fear.

Poisoned. Poisoned from the inside out . . . I will not let that be my fate, not after so many days of hard-won survival. I will devise a plan, a solution, no matter how many hours of sleep I must lose, or meals I must skip. This is our fortress, our safe haven and a threat is a threat whether it comes from outside or within.

It's time to go. Maybe I should pry Collin away from this place, or knock him over the head and just drag him out. Then we could look after ourselves. We could go it alone and I could find my mom. It's useless to speculate but I can't help . . . I can't help but wonder.

- -

COMMENTS

Dave in the Midwest says:

October 16, 2009 at 7:08 pm

With provisions gone, there isn't a lot left for me. My son . . . my poor son . . . I never thought he would survive this long after becoming infected. I realize now that I won't live to see him saved. I can only hope that someone else will save my boy.

Once I realized what I needed to do, it became very easy to finalize my plans. As I mentioned, there isn't anything left anymore. No more food. No more water. Just the persistent angry moaning of my son and the gnawing knowledge of my failures grinding at my brain. There aren't many people that will truly understand what I have to do, but I have to give my son every chance to live long enough for someone to find a cure. Maybe if he's the strongest of the infected. Maybe if he can live the longest he will have a chance to be cured. Since I am lost, I can only hope my gift to him will give him that chance.

Please. Find a cure. Find a way to save my son. Don't let my sacrifice be an empty one. I do not hesitate anymore. I will release my son and let him draw strength from my body. Thank you all for fighting on.

Allison says:

October 16, 2009 at 8:22 pm

Dave, I sometimes think you're braver than all of us. I beg you to reconsider: Don't prolong your son's pain. Either let him go or finish him off. You have to remember that he's not living right now, he's dying over and over again every day. The choice is yours but please, think about it.

Isaac says:

October 16, 2009 at 9:10 pm

Allison is right. You have to stop thinking about yourself. Think about him. Do the right thing and end it.

October 19, 2009—The Awakening

"Let's just go, today, right now!"

"I can't go, you know that. I have a responsibility to these people, Allison."

I feel like we have this conversation every morning. Collin won't budge but sometimes it's as if I can see him imagining an escape, the two of us together on the road, and his face softens. Then we'll hear someone calling for him and the look will disappear.

"I'm really good at road trips," I say, sweetening the pot with an arm around his waist. "You're not even a little interested?"

"You know it's tempting and you know that I can't."

I see now that my hopes of escape, of happiness, were foolish.

Everything that we have done, all of the scrimping, struggling and railing has been nothing at all, just flailing, beating our heads against a solid iron wall. No matter what we do, what we try, something will undermine our efforts. So we redouble, we swear up and down that we will do whatever it takes, whatever we possibly can until we're too exhausted to go on. Maybe we should just stop prolonging the inevitable loss. Maybe we should fling the doors open and let our fate come marching in.

We've tried to switch people over to rainwater but now the rain won't come. Thick, silent clouds hang over us, teasingly holding over our heads what we need most of all. Sleep is out of the question, since the arena is now filled with coughing and groaning every hour of every day. The sick get sicker, the strong—which are few— get stronger, and we watch our once-peaceful, hopeful village turn into a refugee camp plagued with failing health and dying spirits. We are all too busy just keeping things from falling apart that no one has the time or energy to send out broadcasts; our one reliable entertainment is gone, replaced by constant toil. There are no spare tents anymore, so people sleep on the floor, on top of sleep- ing bags or piles of moth-eaten blankets. Our food supply is stretched to its absolute limit and many of us eat less than we should so that the very ill can regain some strength.

And on top of all that, the Black Earth Wives have begun to challenge Collin's leadership. They insist he's driving the camp into the ground, imposing too many rules, keeping people from food that is rightly theirs, letting in riffraff instead of guarding the villagers. All of the calm debate in the world won't drown out their cries for new leadership, a new regime. He tries to keep or- der in the only way he knows how: keeping us safe, fortifying the perimeter, listening to problems and mediating and keeping the Black Earth Wives as quiet as possible. It's not persecution, it's just good management.

The ire of the Wives seems to extend to me simply by my being associated with Collin. They know, of course, that he and I have become very close and I'm sure they know that I sleep almost ex- clusively in his tent each night. I don't know what to tell them, how to react. On the one hand I realize they have a right to be upset that the arena has overreached its capacity, but I also think they should offer a workable solution instead of complaining and spreading gossip.

I've suggested to Collin, more than once, that we pack up and leave. "If they want to take over so badly then let them," I said. "Let them find out what an exhausting, thankless job it is."

But he won't give up on us, even now as everything seems to go wrong.

Today Ned and I had the unenviable task of resolving the sanitation problem. With all the vomiting and diarrhea, the toilets are in no way usable. With Finn standing watch, Ned and I dragged Port-o-Potties over from the tennis courts, lining them up just outside the arena. Keeping them outside is more dangerous but we decided it was better than having the smell and germs inside. Ned's brutal workout sessions must be paying off; dragging the johns over wasn't difficult in the least. Ned's tan is fading. Too much time indoors, living under artificial lights, living in the gloom.

Since our chat, Corie has been doggedly avoiding me. She suspects, I think, that I'm so firmly on Ned's side there's no point in even trying to win me over. She's wrong, though. I'd be more than willing to listen to her side of the story if she were prepared to give it. But she's chosen her side, and even though she doesn't rage against Collin as viciously as the other Wives, I can see in her slumped posture, her vacant eyes, that she's allied herself with them completely. I don't even know why she does it; I think maybe the presence of so many women acts like a shield. In their tight circle she can hide from all of us, especially from Ned.

And all the while Ned is fearfully silent. He refuses to talk about her involvement with the Wives, but I often catch him staring at his wife. I wonder if they've argued or if she's given him some sign that their life together is over.

Dragging Port-o-Potties around was just the beginning of my day. Ned and I assisted Ted with some of the sickest patients. They seem to have some kind of terrible influenza or stomach infection. They can't keep food down and when they do, it seems to cause them a lot of pain. After that, I worked with Evan and Mikey on their Halloween costumes.

Halloween is Mikey's favorite holiday and the boys insisted that we begin constructing their costumes early. Apparently, Ned began a legacy of constructing elaborate outfits for his boys; last year Mikey was a Transformer and the eyes of the mask actually lit up. I didn't have the heart to tell them that there wouldn't be much candy, that no one else would bother getting dressed up. I'm hoping I can come up with a costume to at least keep the fantasy of normalcy going for a minute or two.

Mikey wants to be Zorro, so we're making him a cape and mask out of an old tarp and some basketball jerseys we found in the basement. Dapper will be playing his trusty steed. Evan couldn't decide between a pirate and Wall-E, and was heartbroken at the idea that he would have to choose. Despite his older brother's mocking, we decided to combine the two and make him Pirate Wall-E. His costume will mainly be made of cardboard boxes, soda cans, rubber plumbing tubes and a bit of jersey—for the eye patch, of course.

It's no light-up Transformer, but it will have to do.

After helping the boys with phase one of costume construction, I put in a bit of time at the door checking in new arrivals. The people that come now are the worst we've ever seen, so starved and terrified that they can only mumble incoherently as we ask them to step behind a curtain and remove their clothing. Spending so much time with Evan and Mikey has shed light on a rather alarming trend: there are almost no very young or very old people. Everyone here seems to be between the ages of eighteen and sixty. Evan and Mikey are two of only a handful of young children, and I can only picture six or seven elderly folks that are still around. It makes me afraid that there will be no generation to follow us, no one educated enough to face our problems with fresh, new ideas.

What will become of us?

I hadn't eaten since the morning so Collin and I took a break from line duty and ate together in his tent. Even there, comforted by his presence and the privacy of the tent, the outside world persists, invades. The sounds of coughing, hacking, wheezing follows you everywhere, reminding you that there are people all around you in agony. After sharing a can of soup and some granola bars, we went outside to shoot targets.

In the brisk, October chill he told me about how much he missed teaching, how he missed his classes and grading assignments. He even missed dealing with the most insufferable members of the faculty.

"I would trade everything for just one last day as a teacher," he says, reloading a clip for me. "A day where I knew I had to savor it, had to pay attention to every detail."

I'm expecting that faraway look to come into his eyes but it never does. He seems relaxed around me now, his lined face resembling something peaceful. And then he's quiet before adding, "But then again, I might never have met you. Life would have gone on as it always did—placid, complicated in the human way we like to complicate things. We might never even have met. Strange, isn't it? I can't imagine life without you."

"That's not strange," I tell him. "That's totally awesome."

There's no point in using targets anymore for practice. Instead, Collin takes me to the edge of the fence and I shoot at the Floaters wandering in the mist. I'm getting better at hitting moving targets, but Ned's and Collin's proficiency puts me to shame. I take the ear off of one Groaner who's gotten the brilliant idea of charging the fence.

"Ah, darling," Collin says with that positively slaying accent of his, "I could watch you shoot zombies all day."

Collin puts his arm around me, hugging me to his side. Through the flak jacket I can feel his warmth. "You're getting better," he adds. "Much. You're getting—dare I say it? Artistic even? Soon I'll have to train you on the assault rifles."

"You're sweet," I say, blushing. "Sweet, but wrong."

"It'll come with time," he says. "Once you learn to stop seeing them as people and see them for what they really are."

"Sorry. An ax feels more humane somehow. At least that way I can put them at peace and look them in the eye when I do it."

"Don't apologize for that," he says, kissing the top of my head.

I can't remember how long we stood in silence, just watching the shadows skulking around outside the perimeter of our defenses. "Do you think," I begin quietly, "someone is to blame for all of this?"

"What do you mean?"

"Do you think maybe there's a scientist somewhere who knows he did this, engineered this? What else could it be? I mean, if it's not an experiment or a weapon, what could make this happen?" I gesture to the world outside, the world beyond our little team of two. It's too cold out for a long philosophical discussion, but my extremities can bear another minute or two.

"If this was 1982 I'd blame the Russians," he says. He's fixing to say more, and considers his next comment with his hazel eyes trained on my face. They burn through me. "Whoever's responsible," he says at last, "they're probably already dead."

I nod. "I don't think I want to know."

"Seriously?"

"Seriously. I'm not sure I could keep fighting so hard if I knew any one person was responsible. It's too much evil to fathom."

Collin kisses my head again and smiles a little sadly. It's impossible to tell, but judging from the strange glint in his eyes, in that moment I think I rose in his estimation. "Come on, your ears are going to freeze right off. Let's go in."

It sounds clichéd, but this is, in all honesty, the happiest moment I've had in many, many wretched days. Everything seems to be moving toward peace. And this is the day that I feel closest to him, when it really does stop feeling weird, when it starts to seem normal, natural even and so damn *nice*. And this is the day when I feel certain that even if the Wives have their way and our village tears apart at the seams, I'll have something worth saving, something tangible to grasp. And this is the day when Ted makes a bit of headway and thinks maybe there's a way to cure the ill, a way to keep us going for a bit longer.

And this is the day when—without warning, like a twenty-ton semitruck blazing through a red light—yet another group of survivors arrive, and with them, limping, hungry but undeniably alive, is Collin's wife, Lydia.

- -

COMMENTS

Elizabeth says:

October 19, 2009 at 4:46 pm

Things are almost sleepy on the ocean. Occasionally we raid a port; Avalon has proved itself to be an asset due to its general low population numbers, and therefore low number of the undead. At one point we sailed north to the Vandenberg Airforce Base, and it looked completely deserted. Camp Pendelton in San Diego had some activity, but in all honesty it looks safer on the boat.

We've made contact with a few survivors who were out on

the more remote islands camping, as well as some scientists who were doing studies.

I'd suggest moving on, Allison. Take those who want to live, who want to fight to do so, and leave. Good luck, stay alive, and let's hope that things are happening elsewhere in our favor (like the good folks at NOAA suggest).

Amy says:
October 19, 2009 at 5:02 pm
Allison! She's back? How did she make it there?

> **Allison says:**
> *October 19, 2009 at 5:46 pm*
> VooDoo? The Great and Terrible Power of Irony? Whatever it is, I wish it a thousand fiery deaths.

j. witt says:
October 19, 2009 at 8:08 pm
omg Allison I'm so sorry. what happened?

October 20, 2009—Hours of Idleness

"Ted?" Nobody answers. "Ted? Is anyone there? Dapper?"

The earth is scorched and blood-swollen, just like my bare feet; the ground is littered with discarded weapons, shields and shattered remnants of armor, footsteps sunken deep into the damp, pebbly sand, footsteps that falter, leading nowhere. A veil of smoke shifts a few feet to the north, urged along by a tepid wind. Behind the smoke is a distant wall, pitted and pocked with the ferocity of a thousand hurled boulders, scarred as if gods had descended to personally practice their discus throws here, on this beach, against this nation.

"Hello?"

[Author's note: What follows is the absolutely true account of what can happen when, in the midst of crappy boy trouble, one very misguided individual chooses to mix hard liquor and ill-gotten prescription muscle relaxants. This behavior is not to be advised—unless of course communion with long-dead Grecian kings is something the reader considers a desired outcome.]

It's staggeringly hot and my eyes are crunchy and tired, dry like they've been cured by the smoke of a campfire. Ted and Dapper are nowhere to be found. There's a strange sound rising, thundering drums and the cymbal-crash explosion of waves slamming against rocks. It's a shore and there's sand beneath me, sticking to my hands and face and digging into my knees. A great sea tosses at my back and an ancient wall crumbles ahead. Frankly, I've had nicer dreams.

And if this is a dream my will should count for something. But as hard as I try, I can't wish the black sand away. No amount of mental power swaps the ash and flame for a couple of swaying palm trees and a lime margarita on the rocks.

A steep hill rises to my left, jagged and covered with low bushes that cling to the sharp outcroppings of rock, holding on with their roots for dear life. The rocks climb toward a high plateau and the sheer drop facing the sea is dusted with a flaky crust of salt. There's a smell beneath the ashen smoke, a whiff of sea salt like a hint of perfume clinging to a dead woman's wrist. A few clumsy steps later and I trip over the uneven terrain, flailing and cursing before landing in the sand. I stand up and the ugly pain in my head peaks. My brain whistles, rattling like a teakettle about to explode.

"Where *am* I?"

"Troy, tiny future human. What's left of it."

A long shadow accompanies the booming voice and when I turn, there's a man behind me, a circular shield obscuring half of his bulk, a sharp sword clenched in his other hand.

"As in *Trojan Horse*? That Troy?" I can barely hear my voice. There's a noise building up ahead near the broken wall, a wild thrashing that's quickly, alarmingly building to a crescendo. I don't know where to look but I keep my eyes firmly on the soldier, on the tall, crested bronze helmet and the hazel eyes that peer back at me.

"I went back in time?"

"I would not assume so," he says. "It is not uncommon for a warrior in doubt to be visited by a guide of sorts. I myself have communed with the goddess Athena and she, in her unfathomable wisdom, continues to watch over me."

"Athena? That's hard-core."

"It is what?"

But I don't have a chance to answer, not now. The wall of smoke breaks suddenly and a trickle of soldiers rushes out toward us, racing down the sloping bank just in front of the wall. By contrast, these fellows are almost familiar, comforting—the bony knuckles, the ragged faces and panting groans: undead, dozens of them, armored and breaking away to shamble toward us. Their bronze helmets bob on what's left of their heads, their cuirasses dangling at awkward angles, ill-fitting on the decomposing chests and shoulders. As they draw closer, the soldier at my side shoves something into my hand. It almost has the same heft as an ax but it's a sword, long and razor sharp.

"And are those Trojan zombies?" I ask, strategically taking a step back. He can take the first few. He looks capable enough.

"They would appear to be, yes," he says, raising his shield just a little.

"Am I drunk?"

For a quick second he looks harder at me, squinting past the bronze nosepiece of his helmet. "Probably."

He takes a fast, exacting swing at the first undead soldier, taking its head clean off. Like a butcher performing his daily chores, like a man practiced and not possessed, he dismantles soldier after soldier, mowing down the line with lightning-fast precision.

"You're fast for an old dude."

"Forty-five!" he roars, going in for another decapitation. "And fit as an ox."

"It's all that olive oil, I bet. And lugging that shield around all day. Coming up fast on your left."

He whirls, cutting the oncoming zombie cleanly in half at the waist, performing a quick spin to slam his shield into the one trailing immediately behind. "Thank you, small human. Some assistance, if you would!"

"Anytime," I say, swinging the sword experimentally. It's heavier than my ax, but the blade and handle have a nice balance. There are only a few stragglers left, but I'm out of breath as they fall, crumbling onto the stained dunes. The soldier takes a few steps forward and lowers his shield. It's quiet for the moment, but the restless smoke cloud up ahead tells me it's not quite over. I look at his footsteps in the sand next to mine.

"Jesus, you are huge."

My bare foot takes up about a quarter of the mark left by his sandal. I fit my foot into the impression, like a kid slipping her baby toes into her father's loafers.

"Or perhaps, strange future human," he says, laughing with the bass bravado of thunder, "you are very small."

"I know I'm going to regret asking this, but who are you?" The desire to see his face and to recognize him brings me a few steps closer. His heavy cape was once the color of fresh cream but now it's ragged and torn, the designs along the edges obscured by a gritty mixture of blood and sand. The soldier reaches up, plucking the heavy bronze helmet from his head. When he turns I feel a pang of recognition, in the same perplexing way a rabbit senses danger or a newborn senses its mother. The man's face is long, weathered and deeply scarred, with a patrician nose that looks as if it's been broken and reset many times. His solemn hazel green eyes are surrounded by dark, feathery lashes.

"Odysseus," he says gently, looking at me as if it's glaringly obvious. "King of Ithaca."

The desire to simultaneously wither, die and crap my pants is compelling, but so is the desire to maintain a fleeting iota of dignity. I'm hallucinating, badly, and either my high school health teacher said something about not mixing prescription meds and alcohol or those Lorazepam were past their expiration date. It beats moaning about Lydia, I guess.

"So you're my totem, then?"

"Guide."

"Right, that. So do you have some advice for me now or how does this work? Do I need to spill some lamb's blood?" I ask, hesitating in his shadow. He moves aside, giving me a clear view of the Trojan wall and the ash cloud and what I suspect is another wave of undead waiting in the veil of smoke.

"We fight," he says. And as if on cue, more armored undead emerge, tumbling over the dunes as they amble toward us. "We fight until you are too exhausted to think."

"That can't be right."

But they're on us, groaning and screeching their nerve-jarring, wailing song. Odysseus bellows with laughter, jamming his helmet back onto his head. He slows down, letting me take on more of the undead, purposely sidestepping them to make sure I'm up to bat. I quickly learn that I'm hopeless with the heavy sword so I take up a shield too, hoping to deflect the onslaught of clawing hands. The horde in front of us is growing and now they're arriving in a constant stream. Their shrieks drown out the crashing of the waves behind us.

"Where is everybody?" I shout over the hacking and groaning.

"Gone," he says. "All gone. They've gone back to their homes, to their wives and families and kingdoms."

"But not you?"

"No, not me. Not yet."

For a moment it's tempting to fill him in on the impending ten-year gauntlet he'll be running soon. But then I catch a glimpse of his sword, flashing with godlike celerity and accuracy, and wisely reconsider. And I suspect he knows. I suspect maybe that's why he's lingering here on this deserted beach, doling out life lessons to a drug-addled, heartbroken bookstore clerk from the future.

This is when I discover that he's right. It *is* exhausting and my mind is blank. I'm failing, floundering and he saves me more than once, leaping to intercept a zombie that I've neglected to see. The armor makes them difficult to dismember, but I'm learning to find the weakness, to aim carefully for the vulnerable necks.

When the last of the horde is laid out on the ground I'm out of breath, sweating in torrents that gather at my temples and collarbone. Odysseus pats me on the back and it takes all of my strength to keep from sprawling forward into the sand.

"Ease up, man," I say, standing up and panting for breath. "That fist of yours is like a goddamn bulldozer."

"Explain this to me," he says, turning to face me, ripping off his helmet again. "This dozer of bulls."

"It's not important," I say, waving him off, watching sweat fling from my fingers to his cuirass. "Sorry. It's so hot. Can we just get on with the guidance thing?"

"You should be honored," he says gruffly. "To fight at my side, to fight in the blood and footsteps of Greece's finest warriors—this, fragile human, is to live!"

"Yeah, La'chaim."

"Very well, I can see you are sapped of strength," he says. For a moment he looks away. When he turns back I can't help but gasp, staggering away from him as shock, like a cattle prod to the chest, steals all thought of rebuttal or speech. His face is transforming, the nose and mouth sloughing off like a papery mask. And now it's Collin staring down at me, a bronze helmet tucked under his elbow, a sword gripped in his bloody hand. The eyes. The eyes are still the same.

"You're leaving me, aren't you?" he asks.

"What? No! I mean, I might have to, I don't know," I mumble, trying to look away. Is being stumped by your own subconscious a sign of latent schizophrenia? "I just don't know if I can stay here, not with your wife—it's . . . humiliating. I want you to myself. I'm selfish. I can't help it."

"Do you think you're ready to leave? Do you know what's out there?" he asks, gesturing to the battlefield, the dunes, and the pile of broken, undead bodies. "Where will you go?"

"My mom," I reply. "I need to find her. I've waited here too long. I waited so I could stay with you. But now . . ."

"Now you want to leave me."

"No, goddamn it, no I don't," I say, stabbing the sand with my sword, "but the things you said, that you couldn't imagine life without me, that's all worthless now. Seeing you with her . . . I can't deal with it. It's just too much—people are dying, the world is unraveling, my mom is missing and now *this*. I don't want to leave you, I want you to leave Lydia. You can't expect me to stick around and watch you two together."

"I see," he says, nodding gravely. "There was love between us, yes?"

"Of course there was."

"And now it's gone?"

"Not for my part," I whisper. "But my part doesn't matter now. I can't have her looking at me like I'm some kind of cockroach. I won't be a burden."

When he looks at me again it's bracing, the kind of frank reassessment that never feels good. It's like a test and, as he gazes at me and his lips twitch downward, I know I've failed.

"I don't have to tell you to be careful, and if you think this is an escape, then by all means, go."

The sand seems to shift beneath my feet and I struggle to stay upright. My head is pounding or it's the waves or thousands of urgent feet heading our way. The smoke is everything now, smearing out the wall, the sky, the ground and him, taking him away.

"When you start a journey," he says, "and you cannot know the obstacles, the only way to persevere, to stay alive, is to have a home."

I can no longer see my hands or my toes. The gathering gray and black mass is overtaking us, choking the air. Before it wipes him out completely I see his face, his sad, forgiving smile as he looks at me, looking as if it's the very last time.

"Do you have a home, Allison?" he asks. "Do you have a home?"

- -

COMMENTS

Isaac says:

October 20, 2009 at 11:26 pm

I . . . Wow. What is there . . . I mean . . . What can I say to that?

> **Allison says:**
>
> *October 20, 2009 at 11:50 pm*
>
> How about: Go easy on the crazy pills?

> > **Isaac says:**
> >
> > *October 20, 2009 at 11:59 pm*
> >
> > Yeah. That just about covers it.

Isaac says:

October 22, 2009 at 2:09 pm

Allison? Any news? Please tell me you're not hanging with ancient Grecian warriors again. Don't mess around with those pills.

steveinchicago says:

October 22, 2009 at 5:29 pm

getting worried over here. you okay, allison?

Norway says:

October 25, 2009 at 9:47 am

No word for days. : (The radio silence is killing me. Did something happen to you?

> **steveinchicago says:**
>
> *October 26, 2009 at 6:14 am*
>
> RIP.

October 26, 2009—Possession, Pt. I

"Ugh. Not good. Head not good."

"Yeah, on second thought I don't think those pills were the best idea."

Ted's blurry face stares back at me the morning after my little time-traveling adventure in ancient Greece. Seeing a friend doesn't help, not at all, and the coffee he shoves into my hand helps only marginally more.

"Thanks, Ted," I mumble, a searing white light flashing across my eyes. "You are officially the worst drug dealer in the history of bad drug dealers."

"Are you okay? You were saying some trippy shit."

"Not important," I tell him, sticking my nose deep into the Styrofoam cup. "Never will you speak of this. Coffee now all that matters. No food, not yet. There is . . . another Skywalker."

That morning—once the hangover dissipates—I discover a new feeling, a feeling I soon realize I have to get used to: the bleakness of an inmate confined to a prison.

And I have to apologize to you all for the long gap in updates. I didn't mean to make you worry. I promise there was a good reason. Well, not a "good" reason per se, but a reason all the same. I'll try to describe the events of the last week with clarity and detail but some information is lost forever, lost to memory, and it has nothing to do with expired meds.

As you can imagine, the arrival of Collin's wife threw a bit of a wrench into my plans for a normal life. Whatever sickness had been ravaging our survivors only worsened with the arrival of Lydia and her companions. They're a ragtag bunch with no real connection to each other—a lawyer, a gardener, an accountant— just a shared goal of surviving long enough to reach the campus and the arena. They too heard the radio broadcast and supposed the worst when the transmissions stopped coming. Without Lydia and her dogged persistence, they might never have arrived at all.

Lydia's a tall, voluptuous Amazon of a woman with arrow-straight silvery hair and a free, artistic face. The first thing that came to mind when I saw her was "too much"—too much hair, too much woman, too much ice, like a curvy snowwoman with a thin, straight mouth and a shiny sheet of thick hair.

I tried not to form a negative opinion of her, I really did, I tried to remain objective, but objectivity in this case is pretty much impossible. She either intuited something had happened between Collin and me, or she just plain doesn't like me. Have I mentioned the Sith can use the Force too?

Our first interaction was awkward and strained and, happily, took place far away from Collin. Lydia singled me out among the individuals in charge. She found me arguing with a handful of Black Earth Wives as they tried, again, to protest Collin's leadership.

"Hello," she said, dragging her hand across her face to clear the hair from her eyes. She is, I think, close to Collin's age. She has a dramatic way of speaking, giving each of her words equal and melodic weight, putting on an unintelligible, watery accent from God knows where.

"Hey," I replied, hoping I sounded as distracted as I felt.

"You must be Allison."

"Yeah, that's me, sorry, a bit busy here."

This didn't seem to matter to her, as she continued standing a few feet away, regarding me with cold, veiled eyes, both hands on her curvy hips. She had her head cocked to the side as she inspected me from top to toe. Ned came over to help and, without a word, stepped in to try and bargain with the Wives. They were demanding more food, more clothing, more, more, more. He had a way of persuading them to stay quiet for a day or so, and they were almost unanimously charmed by his easygoing personality and looks, but they seemed to outright mistrust me.

"Is that Ned?" Lydia asked as I backed away. I thought it best to leave Ned to this one, and there were plenty of cans to open over at the food tables. One of the Wives held up a makeshift cross and Ned gently lowered her wrist to get the Popsicle sticks out of his face.

"Yeah. He's a huge help around here and a good friend."

"Hm. He looked taller from a distance."

"Yes, well, he's not exactly the Colossus of Rhodes, but I'm sure from your lofty height everyone else looks positively Lilliputian." Yuck. Not my best. I didn't expect Lydia to respond, but life is full of unpleasant surprises.

"Never cared for Swift, really."

"Well if he rises from the grave too I'll be sure to let him know."

The conversation ended there. I can't bring myself to look at her face and I can't bring myself to face Collin. It doesn't seem fair to demand he choose or even defend the situation. No one is really to blame. As usual, Ted is nowhere to be found. He has a way of disappearing at the worst moments, the moments when I need him the most. Ned is a sympathetic ear. He is determined to stay on my side and for that bias I am deeply, sincerely grateful. His sympathy, however, is part of what got us into a bit of trouble, and by bit of trouble I of course mean a shithole so deep it may as well have led to the center of the earth. Verne would be proud.

The Black Earth Wives have come to a decision: they want to leave. Now.

Word from Collin reaches us that they should be allowed to go. After all, this isn't a fascist state, they can leave if they want to. It's their funeral. Ned insists that I stay with him while the initial shock of Lydia's arrival is still fresh and terrible and turning me into a ghoul with a hair-trigger temper and a propensity for bizarre hallucinations. He can see what the others can't: my stability, unfortunately, has been somewhat wrapped up in my bond with Collin and now I will need to find another outlet. Experimenting with drugs only goes so far, I know that.

Accordingly, we spend two hours in the gym and it's brutal but it's a distraction that I desperately need. Then Ned and I take Dapper to the cordoned-off part of the parking lot where the vehicles are kept. The Black Earth Wives are being given one of the long vans that seats six to eight people. It's a generous gift, one I don't think they deserve.

"What is *wrong* with me? I've turned into a total hag," I say, checking the trunk for any unwanted stragglers. We've been assigned to clean out the van and make sure it's in good working order. There are worse tasks, like shoveling zombie body parts into a pit or sharing a cup of tea and a frosty silence with Lydia.

"Just stay the heck away from her. It's all you can do."

"You're right. I can't be trusted."

Ned laughs, his electric blue eyes flashing as he sweeps an

eye-watering pile of dust out of the van. I let his Dadism go by un-noticed. "If it's any consolation, I don't like her much."

"She thinks you're short," I tell him encouragingly.

"And I think she's a rotten bitch."

"BFF, Ned. BFF."

Dapper jumps onto one of the seats, claiming it for his own. I can't imagine there will be anywhere peaceful to write so I sit on the seat beside him and take my laptop out of its backpack. Ned slows the cleaning down to a crawl so if anyone comes to check on us it looks like we're still busy. We are both notoriously good at avoiding med tent duty. Ted's God complex is soothed by the back-breaking work but Ned and I prefer target practice or the gym. It's cold out in the parking lot and my fingers start to go a little numb as I type. Dapper tries to dart his tongue along my wrist as I write.

This is where it starts to get fuzzy. I remember Ned standing outside the van, his head bent as he checked beneath the front passenger seat and I remember hearing footsteps outside on the pavement. There were a few whispers and then a flash of pale brown as something hard and heavy hit the back of my head.

My memory is wobbly but I'll do my best to recall what happened. I wake up and the back of my head feels soft and wet. I'm in the dark, an echoing, clammy dark. Everything is a little damp and freezing. It feels like the basement of the arena but it smells differ-ent, more metallic and dusty. I touch the back of my head and my fingers come back sticky and damp; a lick of my fingertips tells me the crown of my head is bleeding but it's tacky and starting to heal. Groaning, I sit up and squint into the thick darkness.

"Hello?" I croak. "Anyone? Not this shit again. Fuck me. *Odys-seus?*"

There's no answer, just my voice coming back to me from a few different directions. This time, if I'm lucky, there won't be any epic battles raging or Greek heroes milling about. There's a faint perfume lingering above my head, a few feet off the ground. It smells a bit like lavender soap, with the tangy dryness of potpourri. Shivering, I crawl around on the floor trying to find the parameters of the room. It's small, probably ten feet by ten feet, with two walls made of coarse chains that smell strongly of rust. The other walls are bumpy, cold cement. There's no light to adjust to, but I can make out a kind of window way up above me. It's covered with cardboard, shutting out the daylight or starlight. I have no idea what time it is, no recollection of the time between sitting in the van and waking up on the floor. There's a bucket in one corner and I can only presume that's supposed to be my toilet.

What worries me the most is that I'm alone, that neither Ned nor Dapper seem to be near.

I wait for what must be hours, curled up against the wall with only questions to keep me company. I feel almost nothing because I know that whatever happens now is probably out of my hands. There is no surge of power, no moment of great anger because I can't imagine having much more taken away from me. There is only one option: to wait.

At last, with my stomach growling and rumbling every twenty seconds or so, I hear footsteps. A flashlight appears, the thin, yellow beam bouncing along the concrete. I see now that I'm probably in a basement, that this was at one time a kind of storage facility. The flashlight illuminates a pile of deflated soccer balls and basketballs in a far corner and the remains of a miniature hockey net. The light flashes in my eyes and it makes my already tender head explode with pain. I shield my eyes and then squint through the piercing brightness to see who has come for me. She's very tall, wide, with broad, manly shoulders and a limp mop of curly hair that clings to her head like a greasy helmet. Her mouth is small and puckered and there's a drawn tightness around her eyes. She's at least as tall as Ned, maybe six feet.

"Where am I?" I ask, finding that my voice has only gotten more hoarse.

"You eat now," she grunts, kneeling with great effort to slide a shallow plate beneath the crack in the chain door. There's a big, nasty padlock around the door handle. "In a few hours I come back."

"Wait, please," I say, scrambling forward on all fours. "Can you just tell me who you are? *Who are you?*"

"Not important," she says, her English heavily accented with German or maybe a Swedish accent, a recent import from the mother country. "I come back soon for you."

Well, she's a filthy liar because she doesn't come back for hours. In the meantime I eat what she's brought. It's a meager, watery portion of oatmeal and it tastes stale, and I can imagine it languishing in the back of a cobwebbed pantry for decades. Still, I eat it, hoping that it isn't laced with something. I try to think of a way to keep time, but without any sun on the floor it's impossible to really get a feel for time passing.

In the meantime I fantasize about busting through the wall Superman-style, flying through the air with my eagle-eyed vision, scouring the land for my mom. Then I'd swoop down, take her to a fortress on a mountaintop and eat butterscotch pudding cups with her until we died from it.

When I hear another sound it's in the room next to mine. The flashlight comes again and the same woman, but instead of opening my door or coming to see me she opens the room next to mine and pushes someone inside. There's a scrabbling of shoes on the cement and a crash as the door is shut and a padlock looped around the handle.

"Don't struggle. You were given a chance."

This time it isn't the jailer speaking but someone else, a low feminine voice I vaguely recognize. The flashlight is firmly on the floor, and I can't see her face.

"Bite me."

My heart squirms into my throat. Thank *God*. It's Ned.

He spits on the ground and I hear a gasp from the woman and a strained chuckle from the big German chick with keys. "May the Lord have mercy on you, Edward. Though I don't think he will."

They leave, the flashlight bouncing away until they turn a corner and disappear.

"Ned? Is that you?"

"Jesus, Allison, you're alive!" he says. It's alarming that he sounds so surprised by this fact. I can hear him shuffle over to our shared wall. I crawl over in that direction, running my hands across the chains until I feel his fingertips.

"Where are we?" I ask, so thankful for company that I can feel tears welling in my eyes.

"I think it's a preschool or something. The walls upstairs are all pink and yellow and green."

"And Dapper?"

"I didn't see him," Ned says, his frown coming through in his voice. "I can't believe you're alive. God, Allison, it's horrible. These are terrible people. I don't know what will happen to us."

"Slow down—*who* is terrible?"

"The Wives, the Black Earth Wives, that's where we are, it's who . . . God*darnit*. They took the van, they must have, and they took us too."

"But that doesn't make any sense. Why would they take us? Why risk it?" I ask. I can feel his hands trembling, shaking the chain wall and making it tinkle gently like a wind chime.

"It's me. They want—*wanted*—me."

"*You?*"

"Thanks a lot."

"That wasn't a comment on your general fuckability, Ned, I meant, what for?"

"They've lost it, Allison, all of them. They're crazy. . . ."

"But if they want you, why are you down here with me?"

"I wouldn't . . . I wouldn't do what they asked. It's like a cult or something, something bad. I don't know what the fuck is going on," he says, his voice breaking in the middle of the sentence. Something is wrong, really wrong, and the wall shakes harder. "They tried to . . . They tried to make me have sex with them."

"Jesus."

"Exactly, Allison. They think it's the end of days, Armageddon. They want to repopulate the earth, but only with *true believers*. They kept calling me Adam. And Corie . . . She was standing right there, just right there, and she didn't do anything, didn't try to stop them. It's so *efffed* . . . And now . . . now I think they'll probably just kill us."

"Kill *us*? What the hell did I ever do?"

"We're sinners. And I . . . I couldn't . . . They have my boys. They have Evan and Mikey."

"Jesus, Ned," I say, feeling my skin try to disappear. The stale oatmeal is threatening to come back up, and fast. "You should've . . . You should just do what they say. Don't worry about me. Just get your kids to safety. I mean it, that's like a direct order."

"Don't be an idiot," he says. "I wouldn't let my boys see me like that. They won't be hurt, at least. . . . Well, I don't know, but they're just children."

"So what now?" I ask, squeezing his fingers.

"They'll look for their Adam or whatever, I guess and we . . . Well, we aren't needed. They kept talking about sacrifice, sacrificing the unworthy. They're rebuilding the world, I suppose, re-building it the way they want."

Anything is better. Swimming in a tank of hungry sharks would be better. Even being locked in a closet with Collin and his wife for the rest of eternity would be better than this. Evan and Mikey are up there with a bunch of crazies, probably scared to death and wondering where their dad is. And who knows what they're being told or shown. . . .

"We'll get out of here," I say, squeezing his hand again. "We have to. It's not over, not until we're dead. We've come too far to die here. I'm not letting a bunch of ape-shit housewives take me down, not after coming so far."

There's no hope but I search for it anyway, trying to dig deep, almost forgetting that I'm not dealing with mindless undead any-more. I want to forget. I want to forget everything, to find a numb space where there's no thinking, no feeling. But something won't let me, something tells me I have to push again, something tells me I'm not allowed to be defeated. I want my dog back. I want my freedom, and most of all, I want a home. I want my mommy.

COMMENTS

steveinchicago says:
October 26, 2009 at 5:27 pm
yes! you're back. sorry for that rip business. anyway, i know the feeling, allison. i want my mommy too. stay away from the prescription meds from now on. they dull the senses.

> **Isaac says:**
> *October 26, 2009 at 6:01 pm*
> Glad to see you're, well, alive. I think we all want our mommies. Now hurry up and tell us the rest, woman!

Elizabeth says:

October 26, 2009 at 8:46 pm

I think this is the last time I'll be checking in. It's getting harder
and harder to find a connection. We're stockpiling fish just in
case the plague ruins the ocean's ecosystem. We've got racks
and racks of dried fish. I would kill for a burrito but I should feel
lucky for our food supply, any food supply. The ocean has been
our savior and I'm thankful every single day for our safety. I
know you can't get here, Allison, but I wish you could. If you
ever make it to the coast, you've got friends on the waves.

October 27, 2009—Possession, Pt. II

I approached the problem in steps.

The first step was to get my laptop back, to go for little victories and see just what I could get out of our jailer. The next time she came to give us food I was waiting at the door.

"Can I have my laptop?" I ask, using my most polite voice. She laughs, shaking her head, shoving the plate underneath the door so hard that most of the oatmeal spilled out. "Please?"

"No."

The next time she came I tried the same thing. "Can I have my laptop? I just want something to do. I'm going crazy down here."

"You will call for help," she says, shining the flashlight right in my eyes. "Too much funny business."

"No," I say, shaking my head emphatically. "If there's no Internet, no connection, then I can't call for help. Look, I promise, I just want something to keep me busy. No funny business."

"No."

"But . . ." *Fuck, what will get her to go for it . . .* "But I just need to work out some thoughts, ya know? I've been doing some thinking and . . . Well, maybe you guys are right, you know? About this whole end-of-the-world thing."

"We are *right*?"

"Yeah! Yes! I just want to think some things over and . . . writing out my feelings . . . It really helps, helps me sort out my thoughts. No funny business, I promise."

"No funny business?" she repeats, intrigued.

"None."

She comes back an hour later with my backpack. Before opening the padlock she searches through it, taking out anything she thinks might be "funny"—a USB drive, a pocketknife, a hairpin, a CD. I wait on the other side of the room from her to make her feel more at ease and she carefully unlocks the padlock, drops the bag in and slams the door.

"No funny business!" she shouts, rattling the door menacingly.

"Deal. No funny business."

There's no outlet and probably no electricity anyway so I'm forced to use the battery conservatively. I only open the laptop to shine it around and check out the cell and to write bits and pieces so I will be able to remember things later. I know now that there might be a way out. Our jailer isn't terribly bright and that makes me giddy with hope. I shine the screen at Ned's cell. He's sitting close to the chains and squints back at me, his blue eyes shining in the glow of the computer. There's a deep cut over his eye and a bruise along his cheekbone.

"Phase one complete," I say, grinning. My head is still killing me and the headaches are pretty much nonstop, but this is something to be proud of.

"I can't believe you," Ned says, shaking his head. "You're going to be seriously fucked when they figure out you haven't had a change of heart. They'll bash your head in with your own laptop."

"This conversion thing might not be so bad. I mean, what exactly would a change of heart entail? Fucking you?"

"Ha. Ha."

"Maybe they'll find someone dead sexy for their Adam. You never know. . . ."

"You've lost it."

"Don't be so judgmental, Ned. We all grieve in different ways. Some of us try to go on living, looking for the good in the bad, relying on the silver lining, and others go fucking bat-shit insane and start an end-of-days cult. Each to their own and all that. Who are you to say they're wrong?"

"I think your one small victory has gone to your head," he says, stretching out on the floor.

"Not at all. I mean, what have we learned today? Helga is an imbecile, gullible as all get-out, and willing to bargain with us. I'd say that's one giant leap for mankind."

"Yes, and unless you're freaking MacGyver, that laptop isn't going to break us out."

"Baby steps, Ned, baby steps."

"You know if you do manage to get us out of here, I'll personally bump off Lydia for you," he says, laughing and then choking on it when he doesn't get a response. There's an unsettling kind of icy blackness that settles in your stomach when you're reminded of a deep unpleasantness.

"Sorry," he says.

"It's fine," I say, too impatiently.

"We can talk about it. I'm a good listener."

"We could talk about you and Corie too."

More silence. Ouch.

"That's . . . She's part of all this, Allison. At this point I'm just hoping there's enough of the old Corie left to keep my kids safe." His voice falters on the last word. "Anything more would be miraculous. And anyway I need a distraction from . . . all that. So you talk."

"There's nothing to say."

Silence. Gradually I hear a soft dripping a few feet away, the *plip-plop* of a dank puddle forming, the birth of a mold colony. Then, out of the clammy darkness, comes a low whistling, tentative at first and then more confident. The tune is relentless, going 'round and 'round and the words come effortlessly, cruelly, to mind . . .

Let's go fly a kite
Up to the highest height!

"Stop that!" I snap, throwing a handy chunk of broken cement at the bars. Ned's breathy laughter skitters across the damp floor. He's quiet for a moment and then: "Can I just . . . Can I say something?" he asks. I hear the rasp of his jeans on the floor as he gets closer to the chain wall separating us. I can't think of an answer so he goes on. "There's a wall between us so I'm just going to go ahead and be honest. Lydia's just a convenient excuse. You were frightened of caring about Collin too much all along."

"She's not an excuse, *Edward*," I say. "They're married, you know, bound in holy matrimony and all that?"

"Sure, but that doesn't change the fact that you're terrified of losing him."

"Of course I'm afraid. If you hadn't noticed, the world is kind of falling to pieces. People die all the time. That's a little scary. Well, that and he married a complete idiot."

"How on earth could a man resist an attitude like that?"

"Shut up."

He's lucky that chain wall is there. I'd probably have my hands around his chino-loving neck if it wasn't.

"You're not even going to put up a fight? Demonstrate a little fire? A little commitment?"

"I can't commit to a married man. That's like ... I don't know. . . . Trying to eat a hamburger on a hot-dog bun."

"*What?*"

"Just ... forget it, I'm hungry," I mutter. "What I mean is, there's nothing to commit to if the man is already committed. . . . Or something. There's nothing to be afraid of anymore because he's not mine, he never was."

"Committed? His wife is missing for a few freaking weeks and he falls for you? You don't think that's a sign of, oh I don't know, inner-marital turmoil? That doesn't scream imminent and inevitable divorce?"

"Feel free to jump off that high married-guy horse at any point here."

"There's no horse, Allison, not anymore. My wife is ... somewhere else. . . . Someone else," he says, his voice weaving into the thinness of the air. "And maybe that's the point. People change. Maybe he and Lydia were already on the rocks. You might have found out for sure if you had bothered to talk to him about it."

"No, no way! You can't say put up a fight, demonstrate some fire, and then admit that you've given up on Corie—you just can't!"

"Do you love him?"

"Drop it."

"*Do you?*"

"Yes."

"Then stop being such a goddamn fucking pussy."

"Wow," I say, colliding into the cement wall at my back. Forget the wall, the chains, the space. I can feel that hit right in the gut. "You're really getting over your Dadisms, that's for sure."

"Am I right?" he asks.

"Sure, yes. You're right."

"Then get back to work and get us out of here."

COMMENTS

Isaac says:

October 27, 2009 at 1:34 pm

Way to keep us in suspense for a whole day. Is there a part 3?
There had better be.

> **steveinchicago says:**
>
> *October 27, 2009 at 2:06 pm*
>
> she likes to torture us, isaac. speaking of, how does it feel to
> be locked up with dr. phil? and don't tell me we have to wait
> another day to find out more!

October 28, 2009—Possession, Pt. III

Baby steps are no longer adequate.

Ned and I have a new friend. Her name is Renny and she is living in my cell now. We are cellmates. She's a spitfire—loud, opinionated and destined to share in our gruesome fate (I'm not totally convinced they want to kill us, but Ned insists). Renny had the piss-poor luck of wandering into the Black Earth Wives' compound. I call it a compound because I like to think of them as supervillains in some kind of horrible, low-budget horror film. I keep telling Ned we need to cut off the head of the snake but, biblical allusions aside, he is not amused. When Renny refused to partake in their "prayer service" she was tossed down here with the rest of the garbage. She is an invaluable resource.

"Fucking bitches."

Those are her first words to me and they hint at a deep and meaningful friendship to come. She has a smooth, dark complexion, high forehead and sharp cheekbones. Her nails are chipped but were once painted fluorescent orange and yellow. Her reddish-black hair is a mess of tight corkscrews that stick out in every single direction, held back by a wide headband. I pat the space next to me and she comes to have a seat.

"What did you see up there?" I ask.

"Other than some crazy bitches? They asked me to pray with them, fine, whatever, I'll pray if you're gonna give me a sandwich.

They took me to the boiler room and they had cranked up the heat to like a million degrees and made me kneel with them to 'purify' me. All right, weird, but whatever. Then it got weird, seriously fucking weird, ya know? They told me I had to fuck some guy and carry his child and continue the legacy of Adam and a bunch of loony shit like that. No thanks, I don't care if that sandwich is two feet tall, I'm not doing that."

"He not your type?"

"Nu-uh."

"Religious?"

"Male."

Renny shares Ned's opinion that getting my laptop back is nothing to celebrate. They lack imagination. We pass the time trading stories. Renny worked in advertising, right in downtown Madison. She was on her lunch break when the undead arrived and she tried to leave, joined by a few coworkers. Over the coming days they would get separated and she would wander from house to house, scavenging and using whatever she found to defend herself. She confirms Ned's story that we're being held in the basement of a preschool. "Daisies and all that shit on the walls. Something just plain wrong about it."

Two days pass. Renny is good company, but Ned is growing more and more distant. I know he's worried about his kids, about what might be happening to them. No one has come to talk to me about my possible conversion and I think maybe they know I'm a lost cause. But after two days something happens, something that demands action. They come for Renny.

I haven't known her long but I know she's a friend worth hanging on to. She has a fighter's soul, a glint in her eye that can't be worn down no matter what the circumstance, but they take her. They take her kicking and screaming. It takes three women to yank her out of the cell, one to keep a gun pointed at me and two to handle Renny and her sharp jabs. "You fucking cunts, I will fucking ruin you, just try me, just try and fight me fair!"

She has an imaginative, salty mouth. I can't let them take someone like her.

"This is it," I tell Ned as Renny's voice fades, the last of the echoes reaching us in a quiet, vibrating murmur. "Our time is up."

"Allison," he says, but he stops there.

"You know, Ned," I say, "of all the ways to kill yourself I really think self-immolation is the way to go."

"Allison."

"No, seriously. I mean, to me it really says: Hey man, I'm dying . . . *with feeling.*"

"I know you don't want them to take you but even if you did want to kill yourself there's no way to do it in here," he says, and sighs in the darkness.

"You're just not thinking outside the box."

"I guess you could always hang yourself with the computer cord. It's useless anyway."

Ned. Ned you goddamn bloody genius.

"That's it."

"What? What's it? No, don't even think about it."

"I don't mean *me*, idiot," I say. "But I promised you we'd get out of here and help your kids and that's what we're going to do."

"What do you mean? With your computer cord? I'm lost."

"What were you training me for? What were all those hours in the gym about if not this? I'm getting us out of here one way or a-fucking-nother."

Ned is huffing and puffing, trying to talk me down. I'm grateful for his concern but Renny is in danger now too, and I have a feeling that every moment we waste lessens her chance for survival. And besides, I'm sick of this place, bored to tears, about ready to rip my hair out just for the fun of it. There are only so many games of "I Spy" I can play, especially in the dark.

Ned quiets down after a while, probably convinced that I've let the idea go. But I haven't, not one bit. Helga comes an hour later to bring us food and I'm ready for her, sitting close to the door with my laptop opened. I train my eyes intently on the screen, typing away, muttering and giggling to myself. She sees this and stops just before shoving the plate underneath the door.

"What is that? What are you doing?" she asks, drenching me in the flashlight's beam. I don't respond, giggling even more as I pretend to type. She rattles the door, shouting at me.

"You! I told you! No funny business!" she screams, pounding on the door. Next door I can hear Ned shuffling over to the wall. "What are you doing?"

"Funny business."

A growl starts deep in her throat and builds until she's floundering for her keys, muttering to herself and at me, cursing me, threatening me. She finally finds the right key and unlocks the padlock, flinging the door open. I scoot back a few feet, shielding the screen from her. I need her to come in close, real close, or it won't work. She follows, taking the bait, and tries to see the screen. I keep giggling like a maniac and it only makes her madder. For a religious whacko she certainly does have a startling command of inappropriate and colorful language.

She's right on me now, so first things first. I check for a gun but don't see one, not in her pocket or tucked into her waistband. She's a solid linebacker of a woman so they must not have armed her. This is going to be worse, much worse than I thought. When she's bent over to look at the screen I spring into action, snatching the power cord from behind my back and throwing it around her neck. She straightens up in surprise, staggering backward a few steps. But I'm ready for her, I have been for the last hour, and I jump to my feet, faster, more agile. I grab the other end of the cord and pull, hard, tightening the plastic around her neck.

I hear Ned's hands hit the wall, his fingers tightening around the chains.

The laptop is open, the screen pointed at us, the pale, stark light falling on our struggle. Helga has almost a foot on me and when she bends over it lifts me right off my feet. My grip is good and strong and I tighten it again, the cord meeting the hard knot of her throat. This looks so much easier in the movies. She decides she won't throw me off her back that way, so she slams herself backward against the concrete wall.

This is an unfortunate and unexpected turn of events.

My spine shudders as she tries to crush me against the wall, sandwiching me between her sweaty back and the concrete. But I won't let go and I realize now that who lives and who dies depends on which of us can stick to our guns.

"Allison! Allison, no!"

I can hear Ned screaming wildly, shaking the chains of the wall. His voice is starting to fade, though, as I feel my lungs giving way from Helga grinding me against the wall. My vision is getting bad, blurry, and it's becoming impossible to breathe. But I imagine my mom, the Post-it note and her face, her voice urging me on, telling me not to quit.

My hands are slipping on the hard plastic cord but it's not from my sweat. There's something slippery on the cord, and seeping in around my fingers. I can't let go, can't let my grip go for even a second. I pull harder, the last breath in my lungs coming out in one long scream as I feel my fingernails digging deep into my palms. Helga is making this terrible noise, gargling and grunting and flailing back against me. She's covered in sweat and I can feel the front of my shirt getting soaking wet. It hurts and hurts, my chest aching like I've just gone round after round in a boxing ring. My heart and lungs are going to explode any minute, and if I can't get one more gasp of air, just one, I'll be dead. Ned's voice is rising higher and higher and the chains are rattling and rattling . . .

If only the cord weren't so damn slippery, if only I could breathe, if only my eyes would hold on for one more second . . .

Then it all goes slack and dark and I'm pitching forward. I don't know if I'm dead or alive, if Helga has won or finally given up. I hit the floor hard, my elbow screaming with a hundred pinpricks as it hits the concrete. Maybe my arm is broken, maybe I've finally run out of air . . .

When I wake up my arm is aching and my head feels like it's been split open again. I can hear someone crying softly, sobbing.

"Ugh."

"God!" Ned practically screams. "Fuck! Goddamn it, you're alive! Damn it, Allison, don't fucking . . . God . . . I thought you were dead."

"How long was I out?"

"Two minutes maybe."

I slowly sit up, maneuvering the laptop until I can see what's all over my hands. It's blood, tons of it. Helga is on the floor a few inches away, facedown with the computer cord still looped around her neck. I roll her over with my foot and see that the plastic had started to chew into her skin. I wipe my hands off on her sweaty shirt and take a moment to steady myself. My chest still aches but air is getting to my lungs and my pulse is starting to regulate itself.

"I can't believe it."

"No shit," I say, getting shakily to my feet. We need to get going fast before someone comes to check on Helga. I pack up the laptop and wipe the cord off on her jeans. I take the keys and let myself out and then unlock Ned's padlock. His bright blue eyes meet me at the door. My hands won't stop shaking.

Ned picks me up and we hug for a long minute, relieved, terrified, his whole big body trembling like mine.

"Let's go get your kids," I whisper and together we skulk away into the shadows, Helga's flashlight in one hand and the ring of heavy keys in the other.

- -

COMMENTS

Isaac says:

October 28, 2009 at 11:07 am

Yes! I knew there had to be more.

> **Allison says:**
>
> *October 28, 2009 at 11:45 am*
>
> Sorry for the delay. Takes a while to type all that shit up.
>
> > **Isaac says:**
> >
> > *October 28, 2009 at 12:09 pm*
> >
> > Well then type more . . . and faster!

Andrew N says:

October 28, 2009 at 12:17 pm

No more word from Elizabeth? The ocean seemed feasible but now we're going to port, maybe for good. I'm afraid of the cold but more afraid of starving on a boat. If we're lucky we can avoid the crazies hiding out in the woods and the hordes swarming the cities. I wish I could promise to stay in touch, Allison but I think we're going off the map. When I think of you I'll imagine you've found your mom, that you two are safe and sound.

Allison says:

October 28, 2009 at 1:52 pm

Andrew, I'm glad to hear you're still going. Be careful, especially with those crazies. Seriously, they're no good. I was hoping you and Elizabeth could meet up but at least you're not stranded. Check in if you can, maybe we'll catch up when things quiet down.

October 28, 2009—The Fires of Heaven

"Tell me it's going to be okay."

"It's going to be okay."

"Now tell me we're going to get our asses out of here alive."

"Allison, I'm getting your ass out of here alive," Ned replies. It sounds like a promise.

"Ned?" I ask.

"Yeah?"

"I know you might never meet her, but promise you won't tell my mom I did that, okay?"

"You got it."

From the moment we leave our prisons behind I can feel him closing in on me, staying close, hovering over me like I'm still in danger of dropping dead. He senses, as I do, a disturbance in the Force. This is a bad place, a very bad place, and we're only now going to discover the thick of it.

We have the flashlight but I'm afraid to use it. I know we don't have long. Soon someone will realize that Helga hasn't returned. Her blood is still caked beneath my fingertips, ground into the cracks on my palms. We move as quietly as we can through the murky darkness of the basement. Without an ax or a gun I feel naked, but the only baseball bats we find are covered in foam and nothing can be fashioned into a respectable weapon.

I trip over a step and find the stairwell leading up and out of the basement. There's a door at the top of the stairs faintly glowing from a crack of light. At the bottom of the door I see the shape of feet moving slowly back and forth, back and forth. We take a moment, huddling just on the other side of the door. If she's facing away we might have a chance to get the upper hand, but if she's watching the door then chances are we're screwed.

Holding my breath, I slowly reach out and nudge the door open. By some miracle, the hinges are silent and the door opens a few inches. She's facing the other direction, a soda can dangling from her left hand and a pistol tucked into the back of her high-waisted jeans. I recognize the pistol; it's the kind we've been using for target practice at the arena. It makes me wonder how long they've been planning this exodus, how long they've been stealing supplies and scheming. At what point did they decide that just holding prayer circles wasn't enough? On what day did they decide to abandon faith and brotherly love for zealotry?

I yank the pistol out of her waistband. She gives a startled, helpless little yelp but when she spins and finds the pistol aimed at her face she gets quiet real quick. I can't even imagine what I must look like to her: my hair matted with sweat and blood, a laptop bag strapped across my chest, my hands and face streaked with the last gasping life of another human being. I can already feel the deep, aching bruises forming on my back and chest. I'm more or less sure that one of my ribs is cracked, because the pain there is constant, radiating upward toward my throat in red-hot waves.

"Where's my dog?" I ask. She opens and closes her mouth a few times. She's wearing a silver chain around her neck with a cross and a few little people made out of pewter. There are three little people charms, one for each child maybe. I take the pistol and grasp it by the cold barrel and let it fly. The grip hits her right across the cheekbone.

God I've always wanted to do that.

She flinches but Ned is silent and still at my side. I can feel his focus, his attention directed entirely at her, at our objective.

"I'll ask you one more time," I whisper, pulling the slide back on the gun, just to illustrate a point really. *"Where's my dog?"*

"H-he's in the cafeteria at the end of the hall."

"You sure about that?"

"Yes, one hundred percent."

"And his kids?" I ask, nodding toward Ned. Her gray eyes slowly shift toward him and a tremor starts in her chin as if suddenly afraid. I raise the gun barrel, making sure it's level with her nose. "Answer me or I'm sure you'll regret it. One hundred percent sure."

"D-down the hall, east wing," she says, pointing to our right.

"What's your name?" I ask.

"Molly, Molly Albertson."

"I'm sorry about this, Molly." I hit her again, much harder this time, and she crumples against the wall. Ned lets out a long, deep breath and I do too. I didn't realize I had been holding it in. He puts a hand on my shoulder and I find that my whole body is one stinging loop of tension.

"You any good with that thing?" he asks.

"No," I reply. "Not really. Give me a good solid ax any day of the week."

"Then give me that, you big baby."

Ned takes the pistol, and just from the way his fingers wrap around the grip I know it's best that he has it. He checks the magazine and frowns.

"Full clip," he says. "I doubt she even knew how to fire it."

"We can boo-hoo about that later. Kids first, dog second, conscience a distant third."

It's eerie, this place that should be a sanctuary, this graveyard of a building that should be filled with laughter and learning. It's a relief that the halls aren't crawling with more people like Molly, but at the same time I can't help but wonder where everyone is. The feeling of wrong, pure, bone-chilling wrong returns, and I clench my fists to keep a shudder from rocking through my spine. We crouch as we slink along the walls. Why do we crouch? If they see us they see us, but for some reason this makes me feel stealthier. We pass classrooms, open doors, closed doors, and each room is painted in a different color theme—red, blue, green, indigo, daisies, roses, clouds. But everywhere there's evidence of struggle, of death. There should never be blood on the floor of a preschool, but here it's on the walls, the floor, the ceiling, sprayed in every direction as if Jackson Pollock had a massive, day-long seizure. Interior design by Ed Gein.

I let Ned go first since he's got the gun. Every time we pass a classroom I experience a sickening jolt of fear, expecting anything and everything to burst out from behind the toppled desks and piles of miniature chairs. But no one comes for us. There's nothing in the hall to focus on, but far ahead, at the end of the hall, I can hear a bizarre sound like a drum.

"Kumbaya Hour at the loony bin," Ned mutters, shaking his head. We've almost gotten to the end of this corridor and so we begin checking every room carefully, searching for any small sign of Mikey and Evan. I want badly to believe that they're fine but the empty halls and the strange, pulsing drums farther on are giving me an inescapable feeling of dread.

"You okay?" Ned asks.

"Me? Yeah, fine. Why?"

"You're just . . . breathing awfully heavy, that's all."

"Sorry. Lungs hurt."

"You are one lucky son of a bitch."

"*Daughter.*"

"My point stands. . . ."

We reach a fork, with two hallways going in opposite directions. It smells like something is burning, not the pleasant woodsmoke you smell outside in the fall, but bitter, acrid, like burning plastic or singed hair. It's coming from down one of the halls and a pair of big, steel doors that look like they lead to a cafeteria or gymnasium. The distant, echoing beat and the emptiness of the hall is making me nervous and panicky, and I can't help but glance in every direction as we try silently to decide which way to go.

"Look, let's just go that way. If we get to the doors and there's no sign of your kids then we can turn back," I say. Ned is sweating, a dark ring forming around the collar of his T-shirt, his brassy hair wet at the temples.

I don't know what it is about preschools but they're bizarre, especially when you can feel the weird unrest of angry souls flickering around you. Why are little kids so scary? They're just children. Maybe it's our expectation that they'll be innocent and pure. Corrupt that expectation and adults squirm like they've sat on a pile of snakes. There are no devil children here, but there's the indelible presence of eyes, many eyes pressing and watching.

We keep checking doors, our movements becoming quicker, sloppier as we become desperate to find Evan and Mikey. I can feel Ned getting more and more nervous, and I know he's wondering if Molly fed us a bunch of BS. The smoke and the smell are nauseating, the air thickening with a dark, ashy fog. We check room after empty room, coat closets and maintenance lockers and then finally, at last, we find Evan and Mikey in a teachers' lounge just a few feet away from the big steel doors that are shut, the smell and the smoke belching out from the cracks along the floor and ceiling.

"Daddy!"

It's a heavenly sound, so simple but filled with enough relief and excitement to make your heart spin. The boys give me a hug after they wrestle out of their father's arms. Ned's face is wet and he turns away to wipe the tears off his cheeks. The boys are a little dirty and scraped up, but otherwise healthy. It appears Corie has at least kept part of her wits about her.

"Are you two okay?" I ask.

"Mommy said we had to stay here," Mikey informs us. He says it with so much guilt, so much doubt, that Ned nearly turns away again.

"It's okay, we're going to get you guys out of here," I tell them, ruffling Evan's fluffy hair. "Your dad gave us permission."

"But Mom will be so mad," Evan protests, both arms locked around his father's knees.

"True. But not nearly as mad as *I'm* going to be."

It was bound to happen eventually.

I recognize her at once. It's like Hitler or Genghis Khan or Emperor Palpatine—you take one look at them and know they're the one in charge. She was one of the outspoken ones, one of the women determined to oust Collin in favor of a new regime. I think her name is Sadie or Sally, I can't remember, I just know I've seen her cold, calculating eyes before and her bedraggled perm. She's not much taller than I am and thin, with an unpleasant hollowness in her cheeks where there was once jolly plumpness. I can see Corie standing behind her, lingering in the doorway. The tragedy of her life, of her mistake, is written plainly on her sad, pretty face.

Sadie/Sally has a sawed-off shotgun, undoubtedly another gem stolen from Collin. It's pointed directly at little Evan.

I think of Collin, of Ted, of Dapper, of how close we came to getting out and finding a way back to them.

"Put the gun down," she says, staring at Ned. He looks to me and then at his children, blue eyes ablaze with something like desperation. I don't want him to drop it but I know deep down that he has to, that he will.

Ned slowly kneels, placing the gun on the floor, and then stands back up with his palms open and flat. Sadie or Sally smiles and begins to back out. She motions for us to follow, the gun still pointed at Evan. I know she's probably not all that strong, but I'm weak, I know it. I can still feel Helga's shoulder blades crushing my lungs. If I just had a little more strength . . .

"Easy now, easy," she says.

When we get out into the hallway the steel doors are open and a dense cloud of black ash hits me right in the face. I can't help but cough; the stench is overwhelming. Sadie or Sally flicks the gun at us and Ned and I walk into the room, which I see now is the old cafeteria. The long, gray tables have been pushed to the side. The seats, attached to the lunch tables, are alternating blue and pale green. Gradually, figures stamp themselves into the scenery, blooming out of the wall of smoke. They're too distant to recognize, but they form a sort of wall, their backs to us.

My eyes follow the rolling of the smoke to the back part of the cafeteria where they've fashioned a makeshift fire pit. A few tables are on their sides, forming the walls of the pit where old desks and cabinets are piled and burning. My vision begins to adjust and I see Renny standing near the wall of Wives, a gun aimed between her shoulders.

"Bring her here!"

Corie drags Evan and Mikey away, ignoring their protests, turning them away from us. That's not a good sign.

Renny joins us, her lips a firm line of disgust.

"What'd you all do?" she asks me, smirking.

"Long story."

"Shut up," Sadie or Sally says, waving the shotgun around like it's a scepter. It doesn't take a trained eye to see that she doesn't know what she's doing with the gun, but fortunately for her the blast radius on that thing means a blind monkey could take you down. At this range, there's no hope for us.

Renny, Ned and I shoulder up together. Sadie or Sally paces in front of us, the gun clutched tightly in her knobby hands. She looks trigger happy, ready to explode. The heat is incredible, rolling off of the fire pit in thick, clotted waves. I can't pin down exactly what the smell is, but it's definitely not barbecue. The drumming is coming from in front of the line of Wives, where a few women sit cross-legged, beating on the bottoms of buckets. Nearby there are a handful of women dancing, throwing their hands in the air and jumping as if in religious ecstasy. There are, strangely enough, no men to be found, not even a bound and coerced one.

"Change of plans?" I ask, noting the distinct lack of an Adam.

"He was . . . uncooperative."

"Good boy," Ned whispers.

"I take it he's the charming odor we're experiencing now? *L'air de Infidel*?"

"He is indeed," she replies, smacking the barrel of the shotgun gleefully with her palm. "A warning to you all, a hint of what's to come if you don't repent and kneel to us now. And you," she hisses, rounding on Ned, "will rethink your position."

He laughs, bitterly, his lips quirking to the side. "You crazy broads just don't get it, do you?"

She raises the butt of the gun, apparently to strike him, so I jump in to spare him the inconvenience. "Look, bitch, just toss us on the bonfire already before it dies down. And throw some kerosene on that shit because it's going to take more than a pansy-ass flicker like that to shut us up."

"You fools, you . . . you unworthy, irredeemable *sinners*!" Sadie or Sally says, sighing and rolling her eyes. "You don't know what you're passing up. You could remake the world with us, reform this imperfect, immoral world and create a place of wonder, a paradise. God has given us a chance. He has seen our greed, our lust, our corrupt hearts and He has sent a scourge to destroy the disbelievers. It is a test, a divine test, a test to seek out those who would be Warriors of God and the protectors of His new and holy children."

"Answer's still no, bitch," Renny says, crossing her arms across her chest.

"Isn't this cozy? Now I know just how Han felt before being pushed into the Sarlacc Pit," I say. "So, you know, check that one off the To Do Before I Die list."

"I think the smell is actually worse here," Ned adds. For all his bluster he's still sweating; I can feel his hard shoulder getting damp as it rests against mine. But then again, he could just be perspiring from the inferno up ahead. Behind us, I can hear Evan throwing a tantrum and Corie trying to shush him.

"Could I get a dash of garlic powder before the main event?" I ask, hoping that Sadie or Sally will get distracted and get close to us or get frazzled enough to drop the gun. It just takes one distraction, one well-aimed dart . . .

"Oh," she says, laughing, her bosoms shaking beneath her stained Tommy Hilfiger sweater. "Oh you aren't going in the fire. No, that death is too quick, too easy for filth such as you. The time has come. Let the damned eat the damned. Let them free!"

Now, I half expected a herd of angry mothers to come storming out to tar and feather us, but I have to admit, Sadie or Sally surprised me, truly, genuinely shocked the hell out of me. There's twisted, and then there's just goddamn fucked.

"Jesus."

I can barely hear Ned above the ramming of my own heart. From a side door there's a sound, a lurching like enormous metal gears grinding together in protest. I squint through the smoke and see a lunch table being dragged forward, letting the doors it was barring swing open. And swing open they do, letting in a tremendous flood of zombies. There are Groaners all right, but they're so weak, so starved for flesh that they look like little more than skeletons with bits of skin and entrails sticking to their frames. They immediately head toward us, limping across the linoleum, grunting and shrieking, their bony feet making awful scraping noises on the floor. I see that there are a few people sitting near the doors, their hands bound. They must be like us, nonbelievers, sinners. Ned goes completely still, his shoulders clenching so tightly that I can actually feel his muscles contract into one solid knot of fear. I have no idea how Sadie or Sally plans to swing this and save herself, but she's got that gun trained on us and a look on her face like she's just cracked a home run out of the park.

Then I see that the Wives have been busy making a little fence, like a gate used for herding pigs or cattle, so the undead are headed just for us, for Ned, Renny and me.

"Fuck," Renny whispers. "Fucking shit."

They're quick with the tables and now I can see that there are more Wives congregating at our side, hemming us in with the tables. They're making a corral, a corral winding around and leading us back toward the fire. A few of the undead have toppled over the barrier and into the bonfire, roaring as their scalps ignite. I know I should be thinking, coming up with some way out of this, but my mind is racing uselessly, the wheels in my brain spin in the mud. And all I can focus on is Ned and his reeky armpits and the eyes of the prisoners being torn apart, their white, staring eyes and ravaged bodies. The undead aren't slowing down, they just roll over whatever is in their path, consuming, tearing, surging forward. I try to shrug away. I don't want to watch, but all there is to see are the Wives building their corral of doom and us shuffling away as slowly as we can to avoid provoking Sadie or Sally.

I just keep staring at this one woman, this woman with a blank face and mean, twisted hands and the way she holds the table like it's her sworn duty. And I can smell Ned and hear Renny swearing under her breath and see this stupid woman with her ugly, stupid flannel shirt and it makes me think of Matt. Of all people, at the moment of my death, I didn't think it would be Matt, the assistant manager, the nerd with his conspiracy theories and his flannel shirts and his maddening death glares.

Matt.

And it hits me. So simple, so stupidly simple . . .

"You!" I shout, pointing at Sadie or Sally. "Tell me, are those the damned?"

"Yes, the damned, of *course* they are. The damned!" she screams.

"And if you were to be one of them, would you then be damned too?"

"You can't save yourself, girl. Judgment is now."

"Really? Well, good job. You win at the judgment game, I guess."

"Win? This is the wrath of God Himself, not a game!"

I stumble a few feet toward her, hoping and hoping for one last chance. It's a long shot, but anything is worth a try with bonfire looming and a flood of undead monsters bearing down on you and your friends.

"You've killed us all," I say, throwing up my hands. I point at the edge of the bonfire where a few undead are still smoldering. "The ash."

"What? *What* ash?"

"*Their* ash, you moron. The damned. Don't you know even the first fucking thing about . . . about anything? Just breathing it in, getting their tissue in your lungs is enough. You haven't just damned us, you've damned yourself."

It takes a moment, but the idea dawns on her and her face, her once-smiling face, falls.

"I don't believe you," she says, raising an eyebrow. The gun is leveled at my face and I can feel the sweat falling down my temples in fat, splashing beads. Ned is close, so close . . .

"Ouch!" he shouts. To be fair, I *did* stomp on his foot. But then he smartens up, catches my meaning, and stays doubled over. Then he begins to moan, clutching his head, covering his ears and then lurching forward, spitting up on the floor. He's not half bad at it. Renny joins in, bless her, and clutches her throat, her eyes rolling back, showing the whites as she grunts and spasms.

"Look!" I bellow, letting the fear shake my limbs. "Look what you've done!"

"No!" she screams, her eyes wild as she gapes at Ned, who has gone so far as to scratch at his own pretty face, writhing on the floor. I make a mental note to alert the Academy. I smell an Oscar, or maybe that's just the stink of burning zombies. "It can't be! It can't! Oh Jesus, oh Lord, how could you abandon me, *how*?"

She's begun to cry, to sob, and I know that now is my chance if ever there was one.

"No," I say, taking a step toward her. "You abandoned Him."

The shotgun is in my hands and it feels good. All the lessons, all the target practices come flooding back in one racing, heated rush of adrenaline. My fingers know what to do, they know how to cradle the weapon, how to aim and squeeze the trigger and brace for the recoil. It kicks like a goddamned stallion on steroids, but I stay steady. My chest is so sore and achy that it's tempting to drop the gun. The noise is amazing, like a rocketship firing directly out of my ear.

Her face is gone, most of it anyway, but the look of surprise and horror stays on what's left of it.

Ned is lightning fast, smart, and takes the gun out of my hands and begins to fire, not randomly, but carefully, taking out the closest undead and then firing warning shots at any Wives that get too close. Their aim is terrible and the smoke is so thick that they can't get a decent shot off anyway. There's no longer an L.L.Bean poster boy standing next to me, he's a soldier. Renny and I vault over the tables and run for Evan and Mikey, sweeping them into our arms without a thought. The doors are already open and we run into the hall, gasping for cleaner air. I turn, looking for Ned and see that he's trying to drag Corie away from the undead, away from the gunfire and the smoke. But she won't go; she's dug her heels into the floor. I see it in her face, in her posture.

She's made her decision.

A lot of the rest is fuzzy, a blur. I know we ran, I know we could hear the undead on our heels, chasing us, following us through the halls. I know the pure rush of relief carried me through, keeping me from collapsing from exhaustion and pain. And I know Renny took the laptop bag for me, wore it and kept it safe, unburdening me as we ran through the school. We found Dapper in an art classroom on the other side of the building, hungry, scared, but ready with a wagging tail for us.

And I know that when we got outside we went immediately to the stolen van. I remember lying down on the backseat, Dapper licking my hands and face, Mikey and Evan sitting in silent shock in the seats nearby. And finally, I remember the sound, the cry of anguish as Ned rounded the corner that would take us home, to the arena, to Collin and Ted and Finn. It made me sit up, that sound, it made me forget the pain for a moment.

We looked together, no one saying a word. We looked at the campus, at the arena, in flames.

COMMENTS

Isaac says:

October 28, 2009 at 7:23 pm

It's good to finally hear the whole story. And I know the feeling,
Allison, that "what now?" feeling. We had to torch our barn last
night. A whole herd of Groaners showed up. I think the cold is
making them desperate. We cornered them in the barn and
there was no other way . . . We burned it. It feels like a loss.
There was food in there, a lot of it and now everything is just a
little bit harder. So you're not alone, you're not the only person
asking: "What now?"

> **steveinchicago says:**
>
> *October 28, 2009 at 7:55 pm*
>
> that's rough. you make it out and the arena is gone? you
> okay otherwise?

> **Allison says:**
>
> *October 28, 2009 at 8:04 pm*
>
> Hey thanks you guys. It is rough but what isn't? We'll
> manage. We're going to regroup and come up with a way
> to go forward. If nothing else now's a good time to check
> out Colorado.

October 29, 2009—Into the Wild

I update now when I can, where I can, in the little moments between the long stretches of panic and fear. I apologize if I worried some of you; without the arena, without generators, without a steady connection to the outside world, my resources become more and more limited and I update as soon as we come across a weak wireless signal, a momentary flickering.

But once again this becomes more than just a rundown of events, a laundry list of troubles and thoughts; it becomes a way for me to work out what exactly I need to do. It was not an easy decision and in a way I know for certain that I'm being selfish. But this is what I need. This is what must happen in order to guarantee my sanity and, just maybe, my safety.

This decision came after the shock of discovering our home, our HQ, had been destroyed. We didn't even bother trying to get close. It was clear from a distance that surviving the inferno and seething mass of undead was extremely unlikely. And so we turned around, went back, drove aimlessly until a vehicle approached, rumbling out of the smoke and ash that has become our everyday atmosphere. This is no longer a city, but one giant oven churning out black plumes of smoke and the smell of decay.

They came at us and for a moment I didn't believe my eyes. I recognized the vehicle and I remembered with perfect clarity the first time I saw that truck. I was so relieved to see it again, a gutted truck and a uniformed driver behind the wheel. And Collin. We rendezvoused in a park, or what was once a park, a big open space to keep an eye on any encroaching undead. The lake is nearby. I can smell the faintly fishy, sandy scent of the water. There's a pavilion in the distance and a charming bridge with white railings. The park feels familiar, but most of the street signs are gone, mowed down by cars or mangled by falling traffic lights.

Even there, in the park among grass and trees and little brightly painted benches, the stench of death and suffering persists. All of us tumbled out of the van and I, without thinking, ran straight to Collin.

It didn't enter my mind that, technically, I had lost the right to care for him. He hugged me, hard, and picked me up off the ground. Maybe he forgot too.

The truck emptied out: Ted, Finn and, yes, Lydia too.

It's not that I hoped she wouldn't survive the blaze in the arena, I just had stopped thinking of her altogether. After Ned reminded me that I had a responsibility to Collin to stop acting like a complete baby, I sort of stopped remembering Lydia existed, which was, admittedly, a mistake. To find her there, her spine rigid, her cool eyes distant and staring, it filled me with sudden anger. Sudden and stupid anger. She survived too, as I did, and she has every right to demand respect for that. No one's knack for survival is better or more impressive, but that doesn't mean I was happy to see her.

"You have no idea," Ned was saying, shaking Ted by the shoulders, jostling the poor kid's glasses. "You have no idea, man, how glad I am to see you guys again."

"Let me guess," Ted replied. "The Wives?"

"With a vengeance," I answered, pulling Renny toward them by her bicep. "This is Renny. She's good people."

A quick round of introductions and we were moving on, planning, scheming, thanks to Collin and his laser-guided ability to coolly assess sticky situations. It turns out the Wives that stayed behind at the arena caused just enough trouble, just enough confusion to distract the people keeping watch on the entrance. Unsurprisingly, this allowed one, just one, infected person to slip by. That was all it took. The violence, the death rippled through the arena before Collin and Finn could find the infected person and quarantine them. The Black Earth Wives panicked, tried to set the undead on fire and ended up torching the entire arena and everyone inside, which—sadly enough—was actually the best thing that could happen. Collin and Finn did their best to keep the fire and the undead contained, but some, they admit, probably escaped.

And while they're explaining this to us, telling their story after we tell ours, I can't help but stare up at the trees around us. Everything is scary now, anything could be a source of trouble, of injury or death. But there are just a few birds up there, scattered among the bare branches, their feathers ruffled up around their heads to keep out the cold. I wonder if maybe they forgot to migrate, if all hell breaking loose on the human side of things meant they just plain forgot. Maybe the ecosystem is fucked forever. Maybe these birds will be the last of their species, letting the hours pass by, letting humanity tear itself apart under their quiet watch. I think of being an undergrad, of Biology 101 . . .

Yet, second only to habitat loss, the introduction of nonnative or "exotic" species is a major threat to biodiversity. These species are often invasive creatures that adversely affect the habitats they enter ecologically, environmentally, or economically . . .

"Something up there?" Ned whispers, leaning over. Finn is going on about the gun, about how many they lost, how many had to be left behind.

"G-God?" I stammer. "Is that you?"

"Ha. Ha. What do you see?"

"A robin maybe, maybe two or three," I say. "I can't tell."

"American robin. The state bird," he replies. He's weary, it shows in his bloodshot eyes. I can hear it in his voice too. I can still smell the smoke from the fires in the preschool cafeteria and the underlying bitterness of burnt human hair and flesh. He needs a bath, badly.

"Yeah?" I ask.

"Yup," he replies, then nods discretely toward Lydia. "Do I need to worry or are you gonna be okay?"

"What? Oh, you mean the state bitch? Yeah, I'll manage."

"Allison."

"I'm over it."

"I hope not," he says.

"We managed to save a few tents," Collin says. I begin to pay attention, knowing that the birds have a better chance of making it through this than we do. They'll manage. "We should find a safe place for tonight and then think about where we want to go."

I hang back with Renny, Ned and his kids while Collin and Finn take the truck to scout for a good place to pitch the tents. Everyone is slumped, exhausted, and I have a feeling we won't be going far, not tonight. Evan and Mikey are quiet, too quiet for little kids. I can tell they're wandering through a fog, lost without their mother but transfixed by the terror they only just escaped from. Ted comes to stand by me, leaving Lydia alone, dangling there like some aloof and much-feared CEO facing down a boardroom of strangers. Ted takes my hand and squeezes it, flipping his dark hair out of his face and away from his glasses as he takes a good long look at me. I can see him noting the blood on my clothes, on my hands and in my nails.

He pulls me into a hug and I wince.

"You get hurt?" he asks in a low tone. His dark smudges of eyebrows knit over the top of his glasses.

"I'll be okay, just a scuffle," I reply.

"A real bloody scuffle?"

"You could say that."

"Hey, you don't have to talk about it. Not if you don't want to," Ted murmurs. I can tell he's hurt by my silence. He kicks at the dirt with the toe of his Chuck Taylor.

"I'll tell you later," I tell him gently. "I just don't want to think about it right now."

It's freezing out and we huddle together. With a little grimace of satisfaction I note that Lydia is cold too but no one invites her to join us. It's official. I'm a monster. Still, when you're already freezing it's not exactly appealing to invite the ice queen over to huddle. I'd rather sleep in a graveyard.

As we stand together shivering, I can't escape the feeling that I've been to this park before. It makes me wonder if I'm near my house, if my mom is close by, holding out in our basement with a crowbar and some canned food.

Collin and Finn return in ten minutes, cutting the engine with a big, dramatic swivel of the truck. They hop out, Finn's red head bobbing behind Collin's dark one, and gesture in the direction of the hill behind us. It's not terribly steep but it's clearer at the top. An October fog is beginning to roll in, carrying with it a mist that digs down right into your bones. I can't wait to lie down, to rest, to cuddle up with Dapper and catch whatever sleep I can. No one questions Collin and Finn's decision. It seems like a sound judgment call and none of us have the energy to argue. My ribs are killing me and I can feel the fatigue dripping down into my legs, my knees, my toenails.

We pile into the van and Ned drives us up the hill. Renny plays

Rock, Paper, Scissors with the boys and, after a minute or two, they seem to be returning to their old selves. From over their shoulders I give Renny a thumbs-up.

We leave behind the fog but it follows, creeping up the hill inexorably, swallowing up the trees and happy-colored benches. It obliterates any sign of the road, of the way we came.

There are three tents and I push aside my pain long enough to help get them set up. Lydia, Collin and Finn take one, Ned and his kids take another and Ted, Renny and I take the third. They're not huge but the three of us manage to arrange ourselves comfortably. It's snug and Dapper doesn't help the situation, but we're all glad for an avid foot warmer, even if he does smell a bit like corn chips.

Just as Dapper begins to snore gently, something hard taps against my knee. Sitting up, I see a smooth, bright handle resting against my leg. Ted smiles crookedly at me, his blush hidden by the chilly darkness. It's hidden, sure, but I know it's there.

"What's this?" I ask, leaning to grab it with an ache shooting through my side.

"Just an old friend. I thought you might like to have it."

It's my ax, a bit singed, but otherwise whole.

"Ted . . . I . . . But you didn't know I would—"

"Of course I knew," he says, chuckling. "I knew it'd take more than a few cranky housewives to take you out. Besides, nothing's gonna keep you from finding your mom, right?"

"I'm flattered."

"It's nothing."

"No, really, it means a lot."

He lays back down, still smiling, and I turn onto my side but it hurts. Everything hurts. I finally settle on my back, punching the sweatshirt I have for a pillow into a little square. I shove it under my neck for support but it's useless. Sleep doesn't come, doesn't even whisper at me from afar. I wait a while, wait until I'm certain Ted and Renny are asleep.

C-six, H-six benzene, A-G-two-O silver oxide, C-U-Fe-S-two copper iron sulfide . . .

When I get up and stumble over the dog, Ted mumbles in his sleep. "I just have to pee," I whisper and he goes quiet again.

Outside it's freezing and I take the sweater-pillow and pull it on. Autumn is slipping away from us and now it's cold in earnest. It was bound to happen and I can't help but feel even more helpless against the constant march of danger that comes toward us, inch by terrible inch. If we aren't ripped apart by monsters or murdered by our own kind then we'll die of the cold, or of hunger, or of some disease that will steal our strength, our lives and, in the end, our dignity.

No wonder I can't fucking sleep.

I walk to the topmost point of the hill, the point where it begins to slope back down toward, what? A pool? Some fences? The fog has let itself out and now it's just a sparkling, silvery mist below us. The moon is bright and the sky is almost clear, just a few smudgy clouds gliding across the stars. There are the very last remnants of crickets and it seems amazing they haven't died off yet. How can their little cricket bodies go on? How can they stand the cold?

The hill spreads itself out at my feet, the grass shining and wet and glittering with hundreds of tiny ice crystals. We'll wake up under a frost with our breaths painting milky shadows across the tent walls . . . But sleep . . . I don't know if I can manage it. Even if my chest stopped aching, even if my body felt fine, I don't think my thoughts would allow me to rest.

There are footsteps behind me, soft sounds coming across the crunchy grass. I know it's not one of the undead. Their footsteps are never even, there's always a limp or a drag or a stutter to the step. I know, in fact, exactly who it is, but I don't want to turn around to face him. The warmth of his presence is preceded by a few whistled bars of a *Mary Poppins* tune. A song about kites never sounded so doleful.

"Can't sleep?" he asks, gently.

"Too crowded in the tent," I say.

"I know you're upset. You don't have to lie to me," Collin says, standing very close. The same familiar scent, and an unfamiliar, unwelcome jolt of desire. "Just because . . . things are different, it doesn't mean you have to lie."

"Okay."

"You're hurt. I saw when we were putting up the tents. You could've just rested, you know."

"I know."

"Is it bad?"

"I don't know," I say honestly. I wish he would leave. I wish he would take his warmth and his concern and his goddamn accent somewhere else. Somewhere far away. Somewhere not so tempting. "Probably just a cracked rib or something."

"You and Ned were a bit vague about the particulars. I had a feeling it was intentional. You don't have to elaborate if you don't—"

"I killed someone," I say.

"The guard, yes. He mentioned you . . . sort of . . . knocking her out."

"I didn't *knock her out*, Collin. I strangled her with my computer cord. I strangled her and then . . . then her blood was all over my hands. She was suffocating me, crushing me against the wall. It was her or me, her or me. And it was almost me."

"Christ. Maybe I didn't want to know that."

"I killed Zack. I killed . . . others. I feel hideous."

"You're not, I promise. I can't take my eyes off you."

"Sure you can," I say. "You've got your wife back. Everything is good again."

"You know I don't think that," he says, laughing bitterly. "I don't know what to say because I'm afraid I'll just . . . I'm afraid you'll think I'm a very bad person. But I don't know what you think, do I?"

"Let's keep it that way," I tell him. "Let's just . . . I don't know. . . . Let's just keep some distance. It'd make things easier on me."

Collin's quiet then but he won't go away. I should tell him I'm afraid, that I really do want to be with him, but the chance that he'll refuse me, rebuff me . . .

He looks distant, his face resolving itself into a death mask, pale and aloof, the unexpectedly attractive and unmovable gaze of a pharaoh staring out from his painted coffin. We stand together in the stark, shattering cold, neither of us wanting to break, to bend, to talk. *This is why I want to leave,* I say to him in my mind, *because I can't be around you; I can't be around you and not want you to myself.*

I hear his breath catch and I think maybe he's spotted a wandering Groaner. But then I see it, at the bottom of the hill, bright and strange and completely out of place. It's so unexpected that for a moment I don't believe that it's really there. Maybe it's an illusion, a shared hallucination, just a vision in the mist.

A black and white horse, a zebra, blinks up at us from the base of the hill.

"God," he says. "It's so beautiful."

And then I remember where we are, the paths, the benches, the mangled street signs and why the park looked familiar. It's Henry Vilas Park. My mom took me here twice when I was a little kid, and just next door, butting right up against the park with its jungle gyms and picnic tables and pretty benches is the Henry Vilas Park Zoo.

As it trots to the base of the hill, the zebra seems to sense us up on the hill watching it. It stops, turning a complete circle, its hooves muffled on the cold, hard ground, and then stares at us. The long, striped nose is lowered and then tipped to the side as it regards us, the black eyes closing and opening with that disturbing, equine sensitivity. *I know,* it seems to say. *I'm lost too.*

I wonder how many of the animals have survived, if there are tigers and elephants and giraffes waiting in the mist too. The thought doesn't last for long. Collin takes my hand and holds it, not pressing, just cradling.

"Do you hate me?" he whispers.

"No. No, it isn't your fault."

Maybe it's the cold. Maybe it's the chill mist hovering at the bottom of the hill. Or maybe it's the beast watching us, the stranger, the thing that doesn't belong, the thing so far away from its home and so totally out of place. Whatever it is, we're kissing and the pain in my chest is there again but this time it's different and it's not my ribs.

I must be exhausted because my reaction time is terrible. There are voices, angry, shouting voices, but I'm not going anywhere, as if I've suddenly been submerged in a murky pool of water. The voices are muted, contorted, but I don't want to let go . . . Not now . . . Not this minute . . . His lips have stunned me.

"What the hell is *wrong* with you?"

It's Lydia. She's screaming and waving her arms and pushing me. I don't hit back. I want to hit back. I look down the hill and watch the zebra disappear back into the mist, startled back into hiding, startled into reality.

"Calm down, Lydia. Just calm down."

They're fighting, sighing, rolling their eyes at each other. I stand off to the side and watch, alarmed by how fed up I feel, how detached and sad I've become. It isn't the right moment for a revelation like that but it doesn't matter. I turn away, let them continue the argument. Lydia says something like "Come back here, don't you dare walk away from me." But I go back to the tent and quietly take a piece of paper out of my laptop bag. I take a pen and, squinting into the darkness, draw a line down the center and, at the top, write: PROS & CONS.

A few minutes later it looks something like this:

PROS

I like Ted.
I like Ned.
I like Evan and Mikey.
I like Renny.
I love Collin.
Collin and Finn have weapons and knowledge.
Strength in numbers
Vehicles

CONS

Lydia.
More mouths to feed
More people, more noise
Lydia.
Bickering and dissent
Attachment
Pandering
Lydia.
My mom is out there.

I didn't even need to make the list. Just thinking about it all, just writing this has convinced me that I know what I want to do. It isn't an easy decision and I know it won't be a popular one, but it's my life, my survival and I'm determined to be proactive even in the face of so many . . . complications.

Tomorrow I'll tell the others. I'll stand in front of them, take a deep breath and say: I've decided to go it alone. Thank you for your help, thank you for being my friends but it's time for me to go. My mother is out there somewhere, and I'm going to find her or die trying. I've waited too long as it is. Don't look for a post-card, there won't be one.

Then I'll take Dapper, my laptop bag and my ax and I'll find my mom's house and make sure she isn't there. I'll forget about Collin. I'll find my mother because I owe it to her. I'll find her because it's time.

But for now I need to rest, friends, and so do all of you. Stay safe, stay alert and stay in touch. I'll write again soon when I've reached another safe place, another stop on the way forward.

COMMENTS

steveinchicago says:
October 29, 2009 at 3:06 pm
I had your optimism for so long, and I don't mean in comparison, your optimistic and usually cheerful demeanor regarding the circumstances we've been put in were a beacon of inspiration. Still not knowing why we keep up this charade of normalcy could have only ever lasted so long and now we here see what can happen from being too generous and welcoming in the face of extinction. I hate to say it but I feel so bad that there were people like you and collin . . . people like me . . . that

were generous and helpful in the time when we shouldn't have
been. Maybe I was lucky, maybe we were lucky to have not
been brave enough to try to find a bigger shelter and some
more permanent holdout.

Allison, don't leave them . . . they need you as much as you
want them.

Norway says:

October 29, 2009 at 4:21 pm

Good luck! I'm not sure I agree with your decision, but if you
can find the coast, and a boat, we have a nice, warm, dry,
spacious and Lydia-free cave over here on the other side of the
Atlantic. Same goes for anyone else in the neighbourhood. We
have a radio signal, scouts say it transmits fine to the coast.

Allison says:

October 29, 2009 at 4:46 pm

That's very tempting! You're the third survivor to suggest
a boat but I'm not much of a sailor. We're also tragically
landlocked here. Maybe your post will attract some help; the
people around here seem to know the score.

October 30, 2009—Housekeeping

Maybe I'm selfish or reckless or both, but honestly? I can live with that.

Ted and Renny are fast asleep when I get up. Dapper is too, but he doesn't protest much when I nudge him to get out of the tent. It's early, only a few hours after going back to bed, and I haven't slept much at all. We sleep in our clothes, in our shoes, in our coats. I don't have much to take with me and it doesn't seem right to take their food or their supplies so I just take my ax and my laptop bag and a few granola bars. There will be places to ransack, to pilfer, I tell myself, and they won't suffer much without me, not when they have Captain Commando and Ned I-Can-Hit-A-Splintered-Toothpick-At-Thirty-Yards Stockton. I'm injured, and a lousy shot anyway.

I stretch and do a few careful jumping jacks on the crunchy, frosty ground. I'm getting used to the feeling of being cold all the time and of living with that little twisted pit of hunger in my stomach. I've taken on the life of just about every Dickens character I can think of. Dapper sits and scratches his ear, unperturbed by my morning calisthenics and unaware that soon, very soon, he won't get to steal food out of Evan's little hand or clean Ted's palms after he's eaten a bag of cheese puffs.

I try not to think about those things. I try to forget that in a matter of minutes, as soon as I dip down below the hill and make it behind a building or two, there will be no more Ted, no more Collin and no more ankle biters. I can't let Ted know I'm leaving. He knows about Liberty Village and he'll try to follow. I can't let that happen. It's sad, sure, but sadness and hunger are hard to tease apart this early in the morning. The grass is stiff and loud as I take a deep breath and set off down the hill. I think, judging by the sunrise, I'm heading vaguely east. There are no zebras in the mist this morning, no lions or giraffes, and no humans to stop me.

Before I make for Colorado I've got to be sure, certain, that my mom has left for good. It doesn't feel right to get on the road without first checking my house. She could still be there waiting for me.

I lost my mother's purse long ago, gone in the fires at the arena, but it doesn't matter. I know that Post-it by heart and I'll never forget it.

There's a *zip-crack* in the distance, Finn's sniper rifle. I know it's him because he's in love with that gun and Collin generally uses an assault rifle that sounds more like *rat-ki-tat*. Finn must have switched guard duty with Collin sometime in the night. I pick up the pace, trotting down the hill and toward a cluster of trees at the base of the hill. If Finn mistakes me for one of the undead then my little adventure will be very short-lived. I make it to the trees, my heart pounding, my lungs practically breaking with the soreness of my ribs. I keep hoping that there's nothing really wrong with me, that the sprain or break will heal on its own, that I'm not quietly, secretly bleeding to death of some horrible internal injury.

Dapper stays close, his nose more or less glued to the back of my knee as I slow down and head toward the street. It's real now. I've put distance between me and the camp and going back would mean an extra awkward conversation with the group. I won't go back, I won't.

I don't know if they'll guess where I've gone, but it doesn't matter; no one knows how to get there. I cross what must be Wingra Street and turn south toward Erin Street. For now I'll just have to guess, because most of the distinguishing features of the neighborhood have been destroyed by fire. The buildings and brownstones are nothing but charred, hollowed-out skeletons with the broken windows empty, staring down at the forlorn street, standing watch over the fallen mailboxes and stopped cars.

The roads are quiet until I get to Orchard, where a group of Groaners move up the right lane toward me. There's three of them and they've got that disjointed, desperate speed that tells me they're starving. Luckily it also means they're weak and clumsy and too distracted by their own driving hunger to be much of a threat. And it doesn't bother me. Not anymore. I can't even imagine what a psychologist would have to say about that. I can look at a decomposing human, a person reduced to meat, to flesh and bone and their raw, brittle parts and feel only the faintest pang of revulsion.

Luckily, whatever part of Dapper is German shepherd makes him a natural at commands. I've taught him sit and stay and he does, his tail twitching with excitement and frustration as I take the ax to the three Groaners. He wants to help, to defend me, but if he so much as licks one of them I'll be short a good dog and a loyal companion.

I'm out of breath after that, the ax hanging limply in my right hand. Without sleep, without enough food, I'm not much use against the undead. It hurts to pull a full breath into my lungs and the pain has made my arms weak. I make a promise to treat myself better, to eat more and exercise and regain the strength that I've lost. There's no room for mistakes now, no one to pick up the slack for me if I stumble or hesitate.

Taking a rest, I kneel down and carefully clean the ax on one of the Groaner's torn Windbreakers. I'm worried Dapper will try to lick it and get himself sick.

It takes us another thirty minutes to get to Lowell and every time we encounter one of the wandering undead it gets harder and harder to swing the ax. Maybe this was a mistake. Maybe I should have waited until I was stronger, healed, before striking out on my own. Who will keep watch while I sleep? Dapper? Suddenly, martyrdom seems significantly less glamorous and a lot more like a slow, creeping death.

It's quiet on Lowell Street, which is simultaneously encouraging and a little alarming. There's not a normal human being to be found, no wandering dogs, nothing to indicate that life remains. I'm not used to seeing the neighborhood like this—still, silent, filled up with wind and the eerie sense that time passes here with no one to mark its movement. I had seen it like this a few times before; whenever the St. Patrick's Day Parade or Easter Hat Parade rolled around, the houses would empty out early in the morning and no one would return until lunchtime. But at least then there was the promise of return, the feeling that soon the neighbors would walk up the drive, tired or sunburned, but pleasantly so.

Like every other neighborhood we've slogged through, there are signs of a hasty retreat: front doors hang open, windows have been smashed and never replaced, SUVs and sedans clutter up the yards where escapes failed or the driver simply abandoned the car. The grass has grown long, tickling the top fenders of the SUVs, growing up and out as if to swallow the cars or turn them into ancient, tattered monuments to What Once Was.

The Hewitt residence is more than halfway down the block on the right side. It's not a big house but I've always loved it. It's just big enough to feel spacious and cozy enough to feel personal and loved and lived-in, like an oversized pair of knobby old house slippers. There are no Groaners here and no Floaters, just the sound of morning moving forward and a few birds greeting the sun as it winks at the city and then moves behind a bank of clouds. It's an old brick two-story house with a sharply slanted roof and a porch with white, wooden railings. We always had plans to make it a screened-in porch to keep the mosquitoes out during the summer. We talked about getting the *New Yorker* and some mint juleps and reading aloud to each other on the muggy July nights when there was nothing to do but sit and bask in the wet, dizzy heat.

There's a flag still hanging outside our house, a big white flag with a green peace sign. My mom was always a serious hippie and I could never convince her to get rid of that stupid flag. It seems vulgar now, swinging there, blaring a message of peace that means nothing at all anymore.

The car is gone, the garage door shut. I tell myself this is a good sign. I look for all kinds of signs, clues, hints that will tell me where she is, if she's come back here or not. And like all signs, like all palm-readers and self-styled mystics, I'm grasping in the dark. But it's an earnest grasping and I can't seem to stop. The mailbox is empty and most of the windows are still okay. When I get onto the porch there are brown stains on the wood floor but that doesn't necessarily mean something bad happened. It could be anything. Anything.

I have to kick the door down. That makes me smile. What a tender touch, Mom, locking the door when Armageddon is coming for you. Inside it stinks, but it's a human kind of stink, a stench I recognize by now. There's food somewhere that's spoiled and the dirty dishes in the sink have begun a new and exciting mold colony. Tiny untold worlds have sprung up all over the house—cobwebs, mold, a trail of leaves leading to a broken window. But there's no sign of my mother, just a sense that things were left in a hurry.

"Mom?" I call, being careful not to be too loud, to draw too much attention. "Mom, you there? It's Allison."

There's a line of shoes against the wall of the mudroom but her gardening work boots are missing. Our matching flip-flops are there, reminding me again of the way we relished summer, the way we made it our own and squeezed every last warm, lazy day out of it.

Now there's the smell of rotten milk and it doesn't matter that the refrigerator door is closed because the decay, the rot, is everywhere. The spiders have made good use of the kitchen, constructing webs in every corner, stringing their houses from faucet to knob, from cookbook to fruit bowl. There are two black, caved-in apples in that bowl and a folded card next to it.

Remember us again next year! The Landry Family Apple Orchard

The card is trimmed in gold and red and a fragile little ribbon wound through a puncture at the top. I pick up the card, wipe the thin film of dust off of it, and tuck it into my back pocket. Dapper is busy sniffing every possible source of food and I keep a sharp eye on him, concerned that he'll think a decidedly rotten piece of fruit is edible. His doggy curiosity does not include a matured sense of taste.

I explore the living room, the breakfast nook, the back porch. The upstairs is empty too, but my mother's closet is still open, a trail of socks and underwear leading to the bed. There's an impression on the mattress, a little square dent where maybe a suitcase sat. She got out, I think, she really did try to get to the apartments. I touch the mattress, forcing back a sickening wave of disappointment, she left and she never made it to the bookstore or the arena. There's a third and worse possibility: that she arrived at the arena after the Black Earth Wives kidnapped Ned and me. She could've been caught in the chaos, in the blaze.

And still I don't know why I want her to be here in the house. If she stayed she would be dead. Leaving, of course, was her only option.

I take some soap, shampoo, toothpaste and floss and go into my old bedroom. The windows are grimy and covered with the wispy patterns of cobwebs. I pack up some spare clothes in an old My Little Pony rucksack, the only thing in my closet with decent capacity. My grown-up things are at my apartment, but that's too close to the thick of things, to whatever managed to survive the arena blaze. The clothes I choose will probably be on the snug side since they're from high school, but it's better than nothing. I try to find things of value to bring with me, things that might be worth trading for food or medicine. I find a box of old condoms underneath the mattress in my room; they're past the expiration date but I know from the arena that they're just as valuable as cigarettes. There's a pack of those under my mattress too, stale and crappy, but maybe worth a can of green beans.

Before leaving, I go back downstairs and check near the phone. The phone is off the cradle, lying on a cluttered desk where my mom kept the mail and bills. It's an antique, something from my grandmother's attic and it still smells like sour books after all these years. The answering machine is there, but without electricity it's useless. There is, however, a Post-it note near the machine, folded and faded but stuck in a prominent position. I pick it up, carefully smoothing down the edges.

Minny—
    I hope you're safe. Aunt Tammy called and she said they're setting up a camp in Fort Morgan. Take 39 down to 88, then

to 80. Just follow 80 until you hit 76. It's a long way and I don't know if we'll make it. I'm leaving with the Andersons from next door. We're going to find Allison first.

And then at the bottom, underlined:

See you soon in Liberty Village!

Fort Morgan. Fort Morgan, Colorado. I've been there a few times to see Aunt Tammy and her family. They're good people—outdoorsy types, hunters, fishers, kayakers. But that's many states away, many hundreds and hundreds of miles away from here. She's left the note for her cousin Minny, a woman I'd met a few times at family barbecues and holidays. I bet Mom never expected me to get my hands on it. So they were definitely headed to Colorado after picking me up.

My mom's on the road with my neighbors, then. She didn't make it to the apartments and she didn't make it to the arena but that's not proof that she's dead. There's the purse of course, but that could mean anything, anything at all. What made them go without me?

I go back upstairs, feeling a strange heaviness in my hands, and go into my mother's bedroom. She's left her perfume behind. I always loved the way she smelled, and that she never ever changed the perfume she wore. The scent has breathed into everything in that room and Anna Sui's name might be on the bottle, but it's my mom's scent. I take the perfume bottle and hold it up to the light. Through the purple glass I can see there's just a quarter of an inch left in the bottle. I shove it into my backpack and turn to go.

But there's a sound downstairs, footsteps on the porch. There's a stumble and a crack and my ax is up and ready to swing. I whisper to Dapper, who begrudgingly sits behind me, staring up at me with those wounded brown eyes. "I know you want to help, boy, but it's for your own good."

The footsteps come up the stairs, scraping across the wood, elbows or arms bumping against the wall. I can feel a little burst of energy come to me, a caffeine and adrenaline tenacity—the will to defend what's mine. They won't come in my house, my *mother's* house. They won't get me, not here and not now.

See you soon in Liberty Village!

I move a few steps closer to the open door. I need to get the drop on them because I have no idea how many they are. It could be just one but it sounds more like two or three. Tiptoeing, I command my heart to slow down, to give me a rest so I can concentrate, but the adrenaline is coming too fast and making my hands shake.

There's a peek of skin at the door, a hand maybe, and I wind up and let out a barbaric scream as I aim the blade at neck level.

Whud!

"Gah—I—*Jesus!*"

"Fuck!"

"Oh Jesus, Jesus *Christ*, Allison!"

It's Ted and, thank Christ, his neck is still attached. The ax is buried two inches in the door frame and Ted is on the floor, his hands over his head. Renny stands in the doorway, clutching her chest with fright.

"Ted! Fuck! I could've fucking killed you!" I scream, jumping back and nearly tripping over Dapper.

"You could've fucking *beheaded* me," Ted corrects, his shriek just about reaching the same panicked pitch.

Too overcome with excitement to stay sitting, the dog runs to Ted, licking his face and hands. If my heart was pounding before then it's jackhammering a hole through my chest now. Ted looks at me from the ground, thunderclouds gathering in his eyes.

"Oh," I say, straightening up as my pulse finally starts to regulate. Ted gets to his feet, busted glasses and rakish hair askew, placating Dapper with head scratches. "Funny meeting you here," I say.

"We followed you," says Ted.

"Yeah, I can see that."

"My idea," Renny boasts, yanking the ax out of the door frame. "He said you'd be mad but I didn't expect this." She nods toward the mangled wood.

"I thought you were . . . Whatever. What are you doing here?" I ask, taking the ax back from her. A little shower of splinters falls on Dapper's head.

"We asked Ned to come too. I think he wanted to, but Evan and Mikey could use a change of pace, you know, some time to rest," Ted replies.

"That doesn't answer my question," I say, shaking my head.

"You can't make it on your own. It's . . . it's a stupid idea, Allison, and I think you know that," he says.

"And I wasn't going to let you pawn me off on a bunch of strangers," Renny adds, glaring at me.

"But you know Ned," I tell her. "And the kids."

"No, I don't. I don't even know *you* but I'd rather be stuck with you all. Less chance of getting shot."

"Collin and Finn know what they're doing," I say.

"Yeah? Then why'd *you* leave?"

"Oh I don't know," I say breezily. "Things were getting a little exhausting ever since my life turned into a fucking Mariah Carey song."

"Lydia's just . . . She's just one person, you know? We could've figured it out. But I guess that doesn't matter now. Not really, because we're coming with you," Ted says, peering at me from the long black fringe over his eyes. "There's no point in arguing because we'll just follow you and I *know* where you're thinking of going."

"Ted . . ."

"No, listen to me, please. I know I'm wrong sometimes but not always and I think you and me . . . We owe it to each other. We've been together from the start of this mess and we've managed to stay alive. That means something, doesn't it? Doesn't that matter to you?"

"Sure it matters, but . . . I don't know . . . I just thought it was time for a change," I say, avoiding his eyes. "It's nothing against you, or you, Renny. I thought maybe it'd be better somehow."

"Well, it's not," Renny says, throwing up her hands. "It's a dumb-ass idea and you could've gotten yourself killed. Here." She hands me a gun, a narrow little pistol. "Ned said to take this. He gave all of us a few things. He said to wish you luck and to give you this." And here she takes my hand and shakes it, hard, like one professional to another.

"Fuck," I say, feeling like she socked me in the stomach instead. I want to see Ned again and I want to see his kids. But more than that, I want my mom. This is the cost.

"Wanted to double-check?" Ted asks. Of course. He was there. He saw the purse and the note and coming here instead of heading straight for Colorado must have looked suspicious.

"I found this," I say, handing them the Post-it in my pocket. I'm glad they have something to look at so I can quickly dab my eyes with the backs of my fingers. I don't say to them "I'm so glad you're here" or "I could really use the help" but I'm thinking it. The relief of having them there—of having them inadvertently correct my enormous blunder—makes me feel like a weepy baby.

"Liberty Village? What the fuck kind of joke is that?" Renny asks, chuckling.

"It's not a *joke*," I say, snatching the Post-it out of her hands. "This is where my mom went and it's where I'm going too. This is the second time she's mentioned it. I found a note in her purse a while ago. It's the place, I know it. It's where *we're* going, if you two insist on following me."

"Liberty Village it is then," Ted chirps. "Watch out . . . Uh . . . Where is that again?"

"Colorado."

"Oh. Right! Watch out, Colorado, here we come!"

"Stirring," I say, tucking the pistol into the back of my waistband. "Come on, let's get downstairs and see if there are any canned rations left."

"My Little Pony, eh?" Renny asks, patting the big pink insignia on my backpack.

"Yeah. You know how I roll."

COMMENTS

Norway says:
October 28, 2009 at 5:07 pm
I'm so glad that you are still alright.
Scared me half to death when you said you were going by yourself!
Keep strong Allison and please; keep safe.

steveinchicago says:
October 30, 2009 at 5:24 pm
you're lucky to have such good friends. it's obvious you should stick together. strength in numbers, allison, don't forget that.

Allison says:

October 30, 2009 at 6:03 pm

Yeah, yeah you were right, Steve. I guess I'm stuck with these jokers forever.

October 31, 2009 (Halloween)— The Demon-Haunted World

"That's close!"

"It's not close."

"Did you *hear* that one? That was definitely close," Ted says, covering his head as if we're stuck in an earthquake and not driving on the interstate. But I can sympathize; the rumbling is making me nervous too. There are bombs falling on Iowa City tonight.

We reach the city limits in good time. It's amazing how fast one can go when there are no speed traps, no cops, no traffic at all except for the occasional detour. In some places the highway is backed up for miles, empty cars standing in neat rows with dead drivers or no drivers at all. It's strange to see this go on for miles, hundreds of cars all waiting patiently for some unspoken signal. Every time we come upon one of these blocks I'm convinced the cars will start moving or someone will hail us for help but it never happens. There's just the bleak feeling that whatever battle was to take place there happened long ago.

To be honest, I'm not sure if there are actual bombs falling, but it sure sounds like it. The noise is deafening on certain stretches of road and there are flickers of orange light in the distance, gunfire, the muted roar of far-off engines. The thunder of war ripples across Iowa City on Halloween Night and there's not a trick-or-treater in sight, not one friendly house with the lights on, nobody home.

The old Chevy Cavalier we managed to steal has what we need to keep us going on the road but not much more. There are few amenities; the heat sputters, beginning in fits and starts, warming the car for a few minutes before dying down to a fan that blows neither hot nor cold. I can't complain—with the three of us and our body heat we manage to keep it at a decent temperature. It's not really the time to be picky anyway; finding a car that a) worked and b) had keys and gas was a misadventure convoluted enough to make Odysseus point and laugh. I think we must have tried three dozen cars before we discovered the Cavalier parked up on the curb in front of an Ethiopian restaurant. The keys were on the ground outside the open driver's side door. We take turns driving but Ted never wants to sit in the passenger seat; there's a mysterious stain on the slate gray upholstery. I try not to think about the mauling that may or may not have taken place directly beneath my ass.

Dapper curls up in the backseat with Ted, his furry chin resting on Ted's thigh. He doesn't care when it comes to cuddling—no human is safe from the laser-guided mutt love.

The road to Iowa City down Route 88 is spent in long stretches of silence followed by short bursts of conversation. Renny drives like there's a demon on our backs and maybe there is. I like when she's behind the wheel—she's aggressive without being stupid. At one point, near Davenport, she mows down a line of straggling Floaters that have wandered into the road, nailing them right at knee level. Watching them spin up into the air, arms and lungs akimbo as they somersault into the ditch is nothing short of breathtaking.

"Your restraint is admirable," I tell her, a little stunned.

"If you wanna make it to Colorado before Christmas I suggest you let me drive the way I like to drive."

"I take it this is a newly acquired habit? Or were you creaming pedestrians in your former life too?"

"Pedestrians? You're fucking crazy. Those things aren't *pedestrians*. Pedestrians have a destination in mind, they have *brains*. Were those motherfuckers skipping across the crosswalk, heading to the drugstore for Tylenol?"

"I'll keep score," Ted says, chuckling from the backseat. He takes off his bent glasses and breathes on the lenses, inspecting them before rubbing the fog off on his shirt. "Ten points each."

Renny looks at me but I keep quiet. I've killed my share of them, but it seems a little inhuman to treat them like bowling pins. Having the car, being inside of it, makes me feel strangely normal again and all those pesky things like morality come slithering back from whatever rock they were hiding under. They look so vulnerable out there, the undead, wobbling on their mangled legs, stumbling toward us as if they had a chance. I don't know why I care but I do, and I close my eyes every time Renny tries to hit another one.

Things get boring for a while after Davenport so we start trading stories about Halloween.

"Evan and Mikey were so excited. I hope Ned managed to make them costumes," I say.

"Out of what?" Ted asks. "Grass and Scotch tape?"

"I don't know, dickhead, use your imagination. I'm going to make Dapper a moose costume at the next pee break," I say, reaching back to ruffle the dog's ears. He rouses long enough to lick my hand and then Ted's pants. "Would you like that, boy? You're a great big moose, aren't you?"

"I went as a TV one year," Renny says. "I put on a leotard and my dad cut a hole in a box and stuck some rabbit ears on top. We got fancy with it in my house. Oh and once, once we had the interns at the office trick-or-treat to the other firms in the building. We made them get all dressed up like rabbits and pumpkins and ghosts and sent them around to get candy for us. 'Do we have to?' one asked, God he was a whiny bitch, and I said, 'If you wanna keep your job you do.' So we sent them out, but no one had candy, they had no idea trick-or-treaters were coming so the interns came back with Red Bulls and cough drops and Altoids!"

Renny was in advertising. There are a lot more stories like that from her and most, if not all of them, involve terrorizing the sad, gullible interns. "Tough love" she calls it, something they all had to do too when they were young and stupid and desperate to enter the professional world.

"My mom slaved over this mermaid costume for me," I tell her, resting my heels on the dashboard. "She wasn't much of a seamstress but she made it work and I remember I was heartbroken because that was the year there was a fluke snowstorm right before Halloween. Waddling around in that fin in two feet of snow was . . . Well, I looked stupid as hell. I remember she and her friend had to lift me up the stairs to the neighbors' houses to get candy. Why the fuck do they do that?"

"Who?" Ted asks, taking off his glasses to mess with the tape wound around the edges. It doesn't matter what he does, the glasses are beyond salvaging.

"Parents. It's . . . the fact that she lifted me up every single one of those stairs, and just because I had chosen the dumbest possible costume. . . . A fin . . . Christ. And of course it was ruined by the end of the night, absolutely soaked through from the snow. She was so cheerful, so happy for me when I got home and showed her all the candy I had gotten. I bet she was exhausted too but she never showed it, not to me."

"This why we're doing this? Driving to Colorado because you feel guilty for ruining your mermaid costume?" Renny asks, smirking. I know she's prodding me so I shrug it off.

"Maybe. Maybe that's exactly why."

"Boring!" Ted shouts from the backseat. "Next!"

"Fine, how's this: last year, I accidentally ordered a book about the sex trade for the store's Halloween display. The word *trick*, you know, has two very different meanings," I say. Ted cracks up, pounding his fist against my headrest to show his approval. ". . . One of which is not appropriate reading material for a nine-year-old in a Princess Jasmine costume. We figured it out, thank God, before any customers saw it."

"Ted?" Renny asks, steering us around an overturned semi. The back of the truck is entirely made up of wire cages, all of which are either open, ruined or bloody. A thick trail of feathers is still pasted to the road.

"What?"

"Your turn," Renny says.

"We don't really have Halloween in China," he replies, drumming his fingers on the door. "There's Teng Chieh, I guess, and the Feast of the Hungry Ghosts."

"You shitting me?" Renny asks.

"No I am not shitting you, Renny. I don't see what's so unbelievable about that. Sure, I didn't have the privilege of getting dressed up in a box with rabbit ears to humiliate myself in the street, but it wasn't so bad."

"Ass."

"Although . . ." he says, pushing the black hair off of his forehead. "Heh, one time I did set my grandfather's photograph on fire during Teng Chieh. It was an accident but man, my mom was *pissed*. I mean, come on, lanterns fucking *everywhere*. . . . It's bound to happen."

"You sound real remorseful there, Ted," I say. "Your mom must be so proud."

"Or dead. Probably . . ."

"Well," Renny says, sighing, "that tears it."

We're quiet again until Iowa City. I can't help but think of what Ted said about his mom. I know that it's a defense, being so cavalier about her death, but it's worse somehow than if he were crying over it. Maybe he's come to accept it, maybe he knows he'll never see his family again. To lose a family, an entire family, and Holly too . . . There must be something in him, something welling up, waiting to escape, but he won't let us see it. I think maybe he's not the only one who's lost everything. Renny and I have no guarantee that any of our family or friends have made it. Sure, I have the note from my mom, I know where she was headed, but part of me feels it's impossible, just *impossible* to see her again.

I open my laptop from time to time, looking for a pocket of wireless connection, some way to reach the outside, but there's nothing. The last flicker of a connection was just before we got on the road and that was my last chance, my last opportunity to reach you all.

We reach Iowa City at dusk. It's a war zone, worse than the barricade outside the arena, worse than any of the empty, burning towns we've driven through. Renny guides us onto 80 and we watch the city go by on our left, the buildings smoldering, glowing like red eyes in the veiled twilight. Ted rolls down the window an inch or two and we can hear the crackling of burning buildings and then the gunfire; Dapper gets up, sniffing the air.

"They must be trying to hold off a lot of them," Ted murmurs, his nose pressed against the glass.

Then in front of us, stretched across the highway from railing to railing, is a solid wall of stalled cars. There's no end in sight to the blockage, no way forward, too many cars, semis, motorcycles all piled up together like a giant had gotten carried away at playtime, and in a tantrum, flung his toys everywhere. So we turn back and look for an exit ramp. We get off 80 looking for a frontage road, some route to bypass the clogged highway and exit into a little commercial valley with fast-food places and hardware stores.

There are lights at the bottom of the exit ramp, but not traffic lights; lamps glowing brightly in a parking lot across the street. It's a big grocery store or department store, but it's hard to make it out in the dusk. Renny slows down and we see that the road is blocked in on almost every side with lines of cars.

"That doesn't look like a pileup," I breathe. "That looks intentional."

I get that pain in my stomach, that uneasiness and I'm trapped in that preschool all over again, feeling the dread ooze up into my throat. We ease across the blocked-in intersection to a parking lot. There's movement there, figures, shadows. It's Halloween. I should be helping Evan and Mikey get into their costumes, putting the finishing touches on Pirate Wall-E, but instead I'm sitting here in a cold car, wringing my hands as an enormous man with a beard steps up to the window.

Renny slowly rolls it down, just a little, because we can see the gun straps draped over each of his shoulders. He's got some kind of rough insignia embroidered onto his coat pocket and the smell of pipe tobacco wafts into the sedan as he pokes his nose right up to the glass.

"Stop, citizen, stop!" he says. The cry is taken up by a few other men, all of them circling the car. I say men, but it's hard to tell who or what they are. I can see the glow of cigarettes, the little red cherries pulsing as they inhale and exhale.

"You're gonna have to get out of the car, young lady," he says, prodding the glass with the barrel of his rifle. It squeaks as the metal scrapes across the frosty glass. "I'm only gonna ask one time. The rest of you, you get out too."

Renny looks at me. The parking lot is clear up ahead, but we might have to hit a few "pedestrians" in order to make a break for it. I nod almost imperceptibly and she begins to roll up the window. "You can kiss my ass, cowboy," she says. The man grabs the rifle with both hands, trying to ram the end of it against the window to break the glass. Dapper erupts, barking and growling, his tail beating out a quick tattoo against the backseat.

"Nigger bitch!" he screams. Renny stomps on the gas, the sedan leaps forward, clipping one of the other men. The window is up and I don't hear much of his shout. Then I can see the night lighting up in the side mirror and the familiar *rat-ti-clack* of gunfire. The back window shatters, imploding after we've gone only a few yards.

"Get down!" I scream. But it's too late, I can hear Ted moaning in the backseat, swearing and huffing and puffing.

"Oh God, where are you hit?" I shout, keeping my head low as I unbuckle my seat belt and crawl into the back. The gunfire is relentless, peppering the back of the car, getting gradually softer and softer as we outrun them.

"Where am I going?" Renny shouts, the sedan careening wildly through the parking lot.

"Fucking anywhere, just get us out of here!"

I roll Ted onto his back and see that his shoulder is rapidly turning black, his sweatshirt soaking up the blood from his wound. I push Dapper away, who yelps, trying to nose his way beneath my arm. "Shit," I mutter. "Shit, shit, Renny, he's hit!"

"Hold on!"

I grab Ted around the shoulders and hold him tightly to me. The Cavalier hits a steep curb and rocks from side to side, the trunk flying open from the impact. Ted is shaking and wailing with pain into my neck and I can feel the wetness of his blood on my hands as I try to keep him still. I'm not qualified to handle this. Anything I know about treating a wound comes from bad TV and I know that's only going to get us so far. I pull off my sweatshirt and ball it up, shoving it into Ted's shoulder.

"Guh, fuck, what are you doing?" he pants.

"I'm . . . putting pressure on the wound! I'm putting pressure on the wound, okay?"

"Okay."

Renny is driving like a maniac, swerving and laying on the gas and I'm worried the next speed bump will send Ted, Dapper and me flying through the air like a trio of drunk astronauts. Ted seems to have calmed down—that, or he's about to pass out.

"I think we're okay," she says, out of breath. There certainly are fewer bumps now. Still holding onto the sweatshirt, I pop my head up and glance out the window; we're passing beneath I-80, the enormous concrete beams on either side of us as we speed across the grass. I hold tight to Ted as Renny crashes through a chain-link fence and then drives up a shallow embankment. Through the hazy darkness I can make out a group of low buildings across the road in front of us. We've looped around, leaving the shopping center behind only to come upon another parking lot with some kind of mall.

"Renny," I say, watching a cluster of lights bouncing toward us—a few are flashlight beams, a few are honest to God fire. "Renny, someone's coming."

She turns around in the driver's seat and together we watch the flames getting closer and closer to the car. I roll down the window slowly and pull the pistol out of my waistband, aiming it at the closest flashlight. The torches are waving back and forth as if they're trying to hail a plane.

"You had best be coming in peace," I shout, tapping the butt of the gun on the edge of the glass. Dapper squishes his nose against the bottom of the glass, watching the strangers approach.

"Friends," one of them says, a stout woman with curly brown hair, "don't shoot, don't shoot. We heard the gunfire, are you all right?"

"No," I say, keeping the gun aimed at her face. "One of us is wounded."

"You have nothing to fear from us," she says, holding up her palms. The flashlight beam bounces off into the dark. "I take it you ran into the Territorials."

"The who what?"

"The Territorials. They're the militia around these parts," she says, lowering her hands. "Look, I can tell you all about it, just please, lower your gun. We won't hurt you."

"Do it, Allison," Renny says, cutting the engine.

"No, no," the woman says. "Start up the car. Follow us back to camp."

I put the gun away and Renny steers us around to the right, slowly following behind the group. They lead us about one hundred yards away to a cluster of makeshift tents set up between a concrete girder and a shabby, bullet-riddled brick building. It looks like some kind of maintenance shed, but there are other buildings a little ways off—a gutted gas station and what might have been a Starbucks. Fires have ruined most of the distinguishing features, leaving the buildings charred and faceless.

"Should we get out?" I ask. Renny looks at me and her eyes almost glow as she stares at Ted curled up on the floor.

"Maybe they can help," she says, shrugging. "And we can't just keep driving, not when he's like that."

"Then we agree. We stay here until Ted can manage, and then we keep going?"

"Yeah, but why are you asking me?"

"Because, if this is a colossal fuckup, I don't want to be the only one responsible for it."

"I don't think we have much of a choice," Renny says, shrugging again. "He's in bad shape."

Renny gets out and comes around to help me with Ted. His eyelashes flutter on his cheeks as we carefully maneuver him out of the sedan. A low, pained groan streams from his lips, but he seems to have passed into unconsciousness. Dapper trots beside us, trying to lick Ted's face, presumably to comfort him.

"Bring him over here," the brunette woman says, lighting our way with her flashlight. There are two others with her, a tall man with a stained Stetson and a slim, lanky woman with a big mane of black hair. The cowboy disappears into the shadows for a second and then returns, wiping off a serious-looking hatchet on his jeans. "Sorry," he mumbles. "The damn things just don't quit."

They keep the path lit up as Renny and I shoulder Ted along, trying to bump his shoulder as little as possible. I can see the stain has crawled down his shoulder and onto his elbow. I can't think about it, I can't think about the possibility of Ted bleeding out as we stand there watching, helpless.

The tents are crude, but sturdy enough. The woman, however, directs us into the maintenance shed where a pale, buzzing yellow light still works. I can't help but stare in awe at the lightbulb. Maybe I'll get a chance to charge up the laptop again.

"Emergency power," she says, whispering it like a prayer. "We just hope it holds on."

She and the other two disappear and return with a sleeping bag and some pillows and a trash bag. They lay out the bed for Ted and cover part of it with the plastic to keep him from soiling the sleeping bag. He grunts and trembles as we put him down, his face breaking out into a hard sweat.

"Thanks," I say, extending my hand to the brunette. She shakes it, not even flinching at the fact that there's blood all over my fingers.

"Nanette," she says, nodding her head. Her nose is very narrow, a little crooked, and most of her features are pinched but still friendly. She's wearing a stained plaid shirt with heavy-duty coveralls on top.

"Allison," I reply. "And this is Renny, the dog is Dapper, and that poor bastard is Ted."

Nanette introduces the others, who are Dobbs (with the hat) and Maria (with the black hair).

"I'm sorry you had to run into those fiends," Nannette says with a grimace. "They're just . . . Oh they're just *unspeakable*, unspeakable people. The way they bully us, the way they just take— just take what they want, whatever they want! Despicable!"

Nanette speaks the way a dachshund must think, rapid-fire and with incredible nervous energy, her thoughts tripping and tumbling over each other as she speeds toward her point.

"Slow down," I say, glancing nervously at Ted, who seems to be worsening in front of our eyes. "Who are those people?"

"The Territorials," Dobbs says. "They think it's their job to hold down the fort until the government gets here. But they don't get it. The government ain't coming. No one is coming. They just wanted what was ours."

"Which was?" Renny asks.

"The Walmart," he replies. "We had a pretty good thing going there—defensible, lots of supplies, guns and food and all that. Then the Territorials showed up and damn near killed us all. They said it belonged to them, that it was their duty to . . . to *appropriate* it. That's what they said. Appropriate, my ass. They're thieves—dirty, lying thieves."

"That must be what we drove through," Renny says.

"It's a fortress now and they've got more guns than they know what to do with."

"That sucks," I say. "And I'm really sorry but . . . Look, we just need to get Ted patched up. Do any of you know a doctor? Do you have like a first aid kit or something? There were plenty of tents out there—anyone a nurse? Anything?"

"Well," Dobbs says, shifting his eyes to the side, "we had a doctor."

"Had?"

Fuck.

"Julian. That's my . . . That's his name. When those militia boys cleared us out they had their guns, sure, but they had explosives too, handmade shit, and Julian fell behind. They either blew him clear to hell or he's stuck in there. I don't think they'd kill 'im, no, the son of a bitch is too valuable."

Nanette puts a hand on his shoulder, looking for all the world like her beloved dog just got steamrolled by a cement truck. Dobbs shakes her off, hiding his eyes with the brim of his hat.

"So then you don't have a doctor and there's nothing we can do?" Renny asks.

Dobbs and Nanette share a look, a very bad look. Even Dapper has the instinct to shrink back against my shins.

"Well . . ."

"No," I say. "No way. You're fucking crazy if you think we're going in there to get him."

"You have a gun," Maria says, pointing.

"Your point being . . . ? Didn't you say they're armed to the teeth? This pistol will do fuck-all when they're shooting at us with rifles."

"Maria knows that place inside and out. She could show you the way in," Nanette suggests.

"No. Absolutely not."

On the floor, Ted has begun to wake up, shaking from side to side, groaning. I can't recall the details. I won't.

"Allison," Renny says, touching my elbow, "can I talk to you for a minute? Alone?"

We go outside, standing in the harsh, ugly glow of the emergency light. Dapper sits next to me, and out of habit I rest my hand on the top of his head. I can see Renny's mouth trembling as she looks past me, out at the highway. "We've got two choices. We can either leave Ted here and go on our way, or we can try and get this doctor."

"No, three. Three choices, Renny. We could forget the doctor and try and do it ourselves."

"Surgery? I—*Us*?"

"I'm not leaving him here, Ren. I can't. He's been with me since the beginning. He doesn't deserve that."

"Did you *see* his fucking shoulder? It's a mess!"

"I'm not a good shot, Renny. If Ned was here, or Collin . . . Look, it's pointless to speculate. But I know that busting in there guns blazing is just about the worst idea in the world."

Biting down on her lower lip, Renny glances over her shoulder, lowering her voice as she turns back to me. "Dobbs looks capable. It might not be so bad. Maybe there's a back way in."

"Yeah I'm sure he's Jesse fucking James or whatever, but three of us won't cut it, you know that."

"Then what about just one of us," she says, meeting my eyes with a stare that, God help me, makes my spine freeze. "If that person doesn't make it out then the other one will do what they can for Ted."

I really should give it more thought, mull it over for an hour or so, but there's no time to waste, not now, not with Ted moving closer and closer to that light at the end of the tunnel.

"Best of three?"

Scissor beats Paper—Fuck!

Rock beats Scissors—Huzzah!

Paper beats Rock—Double fuck.

"Happy trails," Renny says, smirking. "I'll take good care of Dapper."

"Don't look so smug. At least I won't have to be elbow deep in Ted's scapula."

Renny hugs me and we stay like that for a minute, letting the relief come and then the despair. We both sense the moment when another second might trigger tears and we pull apart.

"If I were into pussy, you'd be my first choice, baby," I say.

"You should be so lucky," she says, punching my shoulder.

"There's a file on my computer, a document. It should be 103109 on the desktop. Just walk around outside for a bit tonight, maybe toward the Walmart, and see if you can find a signal and upload it. You'll see the program, it's minimized. There will be a place to upload the—"

"I'm not a total moron, you know. I *have* used a computer before."

"Good. Thanks. Now get Maria out here. Tell her we're leaving now. She doesn't have to go inside, just as far as the door."

I watch Renny go back inside. Immediately, Dapper begins licking my hand, sensing, as he always does, that something is the matter. I don't know how he does that, how all dogs manage to inherit that talent, to know exactly when things have turned from bad to worse. I scratch him behind the ears, kneeling down to his level to let him lick at my face a few times. He whines at me. He's hungry. We all are.

"Be good, boy," I say, touching my cold nose to his. "And take care of Ted. He'll need some cheering up when he comes to. And say hi to my mom when you see her. I think she'll like you just fine."

COMMENTS

Isaac says:

October 31, 2009 at 6:12 pm

Allison, I really don't think this is a good idea, not a good idea at all. Halloween? Sounds like bad luck to me.

steveinchicago says:

October 31, 2009 at 7:04 pm

jesus, possession parts 1–3 all over again. come back out. don't make me lose sleep again, allison.

Norway says:

October 31, 2009 at 7:27 pm

Cave! Cave! Run, don't walk, to the nearest boat and get your ass over here. I don't have a good feeling about this, Allison.

> **Isaac says:**
>
> *October 31, 2009 at 8:34 pm*
>
> Too late, I think. She's already gone.

November 1, 2009—Survival of the Sickest

"Careful," I say in a whisper, putting a hand on Maria's shoulder. "We can't use the gun. Not yet."

With only one gun between the two of us and stealth being the prime objective, Maria and I are forced to take out the undead by hand. She's pretty handy with a hatchet and I've still got my ax, so we manage well enough. In the dark, without the aid of even a flashlight, it's hard to see them coming. They tend to blend in with the dark, fading into the shadows and then coming at you with little to no warning. The slight crunch to the grass saves my ass more than once.

Maria shows me the back way through a low hedge of bastard plants that try to rip the flesh right off my bones, and under a few scrawny trees. There are dozens of semitrucks out back, slumbering giants still plugged into the store, ready to unload sporting goods or ladies underwear or cantaloupes. Whatever was stored inside is probably long gone by now, bartered or used by the Territorials. Maria and I take it slow, crouching behind shrubs and scrawny, barren trees. It's not very good cover, but in the dark it's enough to cloak us for a minute or two.

All the while I can't stop thinking about what a goddamn ridiculous plan this is. Then again, there's another persistent thought that trails just behind that one. Having a doctor around, *saving* a doctor, might potentially make our lives much easier.

Maria points out a patrol who pass just a few feet in front of us, their cigarettes leaking thin, silvery snakes that mingle with the short puffs of their breaths. They're close enough for me to smell the cheap tobacco. They laugh and chitchat, passing out of view behind one of the semitrucks. Maria takes me by the hand and together we pad across the little river of gravel between us and the store.

"Here's the door," she says. "It shouldn't lock. We busted it when we escaped the first time. Take this."

She shoves a crinkled piece of paper into my hands.

"What's this?"

"A map. It's not very good, but it should give you an idea of how the hallways go. It's not a maze in there or anything but it might help."

"Thank you," I say, squinting down at the hieroglyphic mess of squiggles and squares. "Good luck getting back."

"Ha," she says, patting me on the shoulder. "Same to you."

I don't wait for her to leave and carefully pluck open the back door. I'm worried the patrol will be back soon and I'm not ready to waste another second. It's a suicide mission anyway so I suppose I might as well get it over with quickly. I crouch along the wall, moving through the icy, dark hall, keeping my hand on the wall for balance. Maria's map is more or less incomprehensible. Dead Sea Scrolls are more legible. It indicates, I think, that this back door is the employee entrance and—judging by the amount of cigarette butts scattered across the floor—the favored place for smoke breaks. The hall has three offshoots, two of which have doors and one of which is a connected corridor. There is a vague indication of where I should go, a suggestion of little red tic marks on the map, and I remember Dobbs mentioning a blast so I go forward, keeping my eyes peeled for signs of an explosion.

Voices come and go, echoing down the halls, bursting out of

vents high up above me. It's miserable. There's no reliable way to tell whether the guards are just around the corner or down at the end of another hall. It's like walking in a winding, hollow pipeline where everything echoes and clangs. I pass what looks like a break room. It's empty except for a few tables and vending machines with the glass smashed in. Everything, every color and tile, is sterile and cold, and the idea of living there long-term makes my skin crawl. That's not to say the arena was anything glamorous, but at least it had plenty of colorful tents. Maybe it's just the circumstances, maybe it's really not so bad and only seems this dismal because I'm sneaking around like some ludicrous, low-rent ninja, clutching a scribbled map with a vain, dim hope.

"You'll eat it, you faggot, and you'll like it."

I stop, feeling my blood turn to ice water. A door slams close by, too close, and a lighter *flick-flick-flicks* but doesn't catch flame. I hold my breath, all too aware that if he lights up the hall he'll see me flattened against the wall.

"Not again. Damn thing," he says, shoving the lighter and the unlit cigarette back into his pocket. This is the first and only time in my life I've felt such a deep and profound kinship with the intrepid, Dumpster-diving scavengers of the night, our masked friend the raccoon. The guard's shadow falls over my head and then ripples, passing over me and away. I find myself just a foot or two in front of the last door at the end of the hall. It's one of the doors marked on the map. The guard disappears down the adjacent corridor, muttering to himself about the faulty lighter as he goes. I know he can't actually *hear* my heart hammering against my rib cage, but it seems like any person with a pair of working ears *should*.

I let a moment pass, just in case the guard decides to come back, but there's nothing, just the far-off clatter of footsteps and voices. I breathe out all at once, letting the air shudder out of my lungs. Even so, I don't feel much relief. I kiss the map and stick it into my pocket alongside the apple orchard card and my mom's Post-it.

The door's lock is busted, hanging off by one mangled screw. They've hammered two brackets on either side of the door, a wooden plank sitting across the brackets. I lift the two-by-four off the brackets and open the door, bringing the plank with me—

Shink!

A tin plate smashes into the wall near my head, some kind of grainy, gray substance raining down on me.

"I told you I'd rather die than eat that poison!"

"It's not poison," I say, licking a bit of the porridge off my fingers. "Runny, kinda gross, but not poison."

"Who are you? You're not the jailer."

"The jailer is long gone," I say. "I'm Allison and your friend Nanette sent me."

"Ah. A rescue! And a woman . . . The plot thickens."

I lean the board against the wall and take a few steps into the room. It's a storage room, the walls lined with half-empty shelves, an emergency light buzzing overhead, filling the room with a cold, yellow glow. After a cursory glance I spot a basketball, a rusted canister and a pack of cotton Ts. There's a man sitting against the far wall, his legs sprawled out in front of him, his right arm in a makeshift sling.

"*You're* Julian?" I ask.

"Yes, Julian Clarke. *Doctor* Julian Clarke."

"You don't look much like a doctor."

"Having second thoughts?"

"Very funny," I say, rolling my eyes. "Can we skip ahead a bit, we need to get out of here before your friend gets back."

"I hope you're stronger than you look, sweetheart," he says, nodding toward his legs. "We'll be on our merry way if you can carry all two hundred pounds of me."

That's when I notice the dark stain on his rumpled khakis, a big bloodstain right on the inner thigh above his knee. Yes. Perfect. A doctor who looks more like a *Survivor: Iowa* participant than a surgeon, who can't walk and can't use his right arm. I make a mental note to crucify Nanette—*slowly*—if we ever make it out of here.

"Then I guess you're stuck here forever," I say, shrugging and turning back to the door.

"That's the spirit."

"Well what do you want me to do? If you can't walk then I really don't have much use for you."

"Feeling's mutual, honey."

"Okay, one: stop with the bullshit pet names. Two: either throw out a suggestion or get prepared to have your ass dragged out of here."

"Your eyes as sharp as your mouth?" he asks, still reclining against the shelves. If obnoxiously smug had a poster child, Dr. Clarke would be candidate #1. He looks a bit like Dobbs if Dobbs had spent most of his life in air-conditioned offices and expensive medical schools instead of on the open range. He has a high forehead with a scraggly head of brown hair like the tufts of a lion's mane, a flashy smile and a big Grecian-vase nose.

"My eyes are just fine, thanks very much," I say. "What did you have in mind?" His eyebrows jump.

"Practical answer or primal deep freeze?"

"Practical, please."

"See that?" he asks, nodding toward the rusted can on the shelf.

"Yeah."

"Go poke around behind it. I think I saw some brown bottles when they tossed me in here."

The rusted can is an old gasoline receptacle, but behind it, just as Julian said, are a few dark brown plastic bottles. Rubbing alcohol, hydrogen peroxide, Vaseline . . . I report as much.

"Grab those T-shirts, the rubbing alcohol and hydrogen peroxide," he says. I reach to grab them and hesitate. "Ugh, Jesus, *please. Please*, oh mistress mine, would you bring them here?"

"Sure, no problem."

This is about when a horrible, gross feeling begins in my stomach because I'm beginning to guess his intentions. I'm almost flattered at the idea that, after only a minute or two of meeting, he trusts me this much. Then again, what choice does either of us have? If I can just imagine my mother, imagine a healthy, happy Ted and all of us bouncing along the road to Colorado . . .

"Have a seat," he says, patting the floor with his uninjured hand.

"What happened to you?" I ask.

"Arm or leg?"

"Well, both?"

"Arm is a long story, best left for later when we have more time. Leg happened in the explosion. Like an idiot I was trying to grab some things on the way out of here and it didn't work out so great. As you can see, my leg is now the proud owner of about three inches of steel."

"Can I ask what you were trying to grab? Do I want to know?"

"Two words, babe: Pinot Grigio."

"Oh for fuck's sake."

"What? I'd rather lick an elephant's ass than spend the rest of this hell sober. After an hour or two around my brother it's either get a little soused or fucking fratricide."

"I knew you looked familiar."

"We can chitchat later. Let's stay focused, shall we?" he asks. I scoot closer to him on the concrete floor, lining up the bottles and the package of shirts next to his leg. "Good. Now reach into my pocket."

"Yeah. Sure. Nice try."

"Look, baby, if I wanted you to grab my junk I'd just fucking ask. No, I want you to get my knife."

"They didn't pat you down?"

"Yes, a bunch of gunslinging Iowa country boys are really going to jump at the chance to feel me up. They figure that whatever I'm packing is smaller than what they're packing, and they're right. What am I going to do? Stab them to death with a pocket-knife? They've got shotguns."

"You'd be surprised what you can do with everyday objects," I say, smiling to myself.

"I'll ask later. Get the knife. There should be a lighter in there too."

Inside his left pocket is a small Swiss Army knife, just big enough to have a few of the basic tools. It's a nice one, engraved with his name. There's a lighter too, a sleek silver Zippo. It's at this point that the bad feeling in my stomach really starts to have fun, making my insides squish and squirm with discomfort. I'm not great around blood and I have this feeling that—

"Surgery 101: don't do anything I don't fucking tell you to. Got it?"

"Whoa, whoa, *surgery*? I'm cutting that thing out of you?"

"Unless of course you'd rather use your teeth. Yes, you're cutting it out of me. Is that a problem?"

"I'm just . . ."

"Afraid?"

"*No*. I'm just not great with . . . you know . . . blood and veins and gore and stuff."

"Sweetie, if you lasted this long then you must have seen some bad shit, am I right?"

"Sure."

"And judging from that sinister smile a second ago you've killed a person or two. Still right?"

"I . . . Yes. Still right."

"So you can use a weapon *against* someone but you can't use a weapon to help me? Besides, since you're here and not Maria or my brother I figure you need my help. They said the magic word 'doctor' and you risked your life to get me—it's that or you're going for sainthood. So what happened? Someone on the outside get hurt, someone you care about?"

"Okay, put like that," I say, swallowing hard, "there's just . . . more pressure with this. And anyway, how have you not *died*?"

"If I pull on the damn thing and don't have a way of staunching the blood flow then I'll bleed out. To death. Time is running out as it is, I probably would've attempted it on my own if you hadn't shown up. It's . . . You know, it's complicated, all right?"

"Fine," I say.

"If I could use my damn arm it wouldn't be such a problem, but as it is . . ."

"Right, right. I get it. So how do we start?"

Julian straightens his injured leg out, crooking the other one beneath him. I move closer, slowly, feeling my stomach lurch and do a quick audition for Cirque du Soleil. Somehow this is so much worse than bashing the undead in the head with an ax. One wrong move, one slip, one hesitation and I could kill an innocent man with my incompetence.

No pressure.

"You're sweating," he says. "Good, that's step one, anyway."

"I'm about to cut your leg open. Some manners, please."

"First things first," he says. "We're, uh, going to need some more supplies."

"What?"

"Don't panic. We can probably just use stuff in here."

"Like what?" I ask, glancing around at the spare shelves. Julian also looks around with me, scanning the miscellaneous items scattered here and there.

"It's not going to be *pretty* but—"

"Will it work?" I ask.

"Probably."

"That's good enough," I say, shrugging and getting to my feet. It's his leg. "What do we need?"

"Grab that camping hot plate and . . . That, there. Is that an iron? Get it."

I collect the large, clumsy hot plate and the iron, bringing them back to Julian and the other supplies. It feels like we've been thrust back into the Middle Ages. I can almost imagine an arrow shaft sticking out of his leg. I unbox the iron and grill, wary of Julian's intentions.

"You'll have to get a flame going. Is there a fuel canister?"

I glance in the box and pull out a round canister the size of a sweet potato, and other than that there's nothing in the box but a few loose parts.

"That's it, that's the fuel. There's a hookup there, shouldn't be hard to figure out," Julian explains and then points to the back of the hot plate. I'm sick of being ordered around, but part of me is curious just to see where he's going with this.

"Is it going in? Nice, that should work. All right, get a flame going, hot, as hot as you can manage. Put the iron on it and just let it sit."

As I kneel next to him again, the plan begins to take gruesome shape in my mind.

"Right then, no time like the present. Let's get to it. Cut off the pant leg a few inches above the wound. You'll need space. I know the light in here is shit so get close if you have to."

The hot plate hisses away, the flame turning bluish as it heats the iron. I can smell the fuel burning, the bitter and sweet tang that reminds me of barbecuing in the summer. I do as he says, feeling like an idiot as he gives me the step by step, enunciating clearly as if I were a toddler. It doesn't matter. I can put up with his attitude if it means he makes it out of here and Ted gets aid. And then I remember . . .

"Fuck," I say, leaning back hard on my heels. I'm supposed to be *avoiding* doing surgery this way.

"What is it? Oh God, did you kill me already?"

"No . . . your . . . *your arm*. Son of a bitch, how did I not think of this before?"

"We'll cross that bridge when we get to it. Who knows, if this goes well maybe I can talk you through helping your friend, right?"

"I hate you."

"Now sterilize the blade," he says, smiling and going on. "Use the biggest knife on the tool. Give it a good burn on every side. Get one of those Ts out and rip off a few strips. Rinse your hands in the hydrogen peroxide, wipe them off on a T and then get some of that on the blade too. Good. Good. Dry off the blade and we're ready to rock."

"Jesus."

"Take a deep breath, Allison," he says, turning serious for a moment. Hearing my name, hearing him use a consoling tone of voice, helps. Not a lot, but enough to make me think I can handle this. When I look up at him his smile is gone. He's not bad-looking once he eases off on the asshole grins. And the seriousness, the quiet pleading in his eyes that makes me steady my hands and turn back to his legs. It doesn't matter if he can help Ted. Julian deserves to live too, even if he is a complete mongoloid.

"Take one of the strips and tie it tightly around my thigh a few inches above the metal. Damn it! Christ! Not *that* tight."

"*Sorry!* Sorry, is that better?" This is already hard. Harder than he made it sound, anyway.

"Yes, that's fine. You just need to slow the blood flow," he says, wiping the back of his forehead with his left hand. He's sweating too, the droplets collecting in his stubble. "Think of the shrapnel like a compass, okay? I'll give you directions that way, so north is toward my belt, south toward my feet. Got it?"

"I can't believe we're doing this."

"*Got it?*"

"Yes. Got it. Jesus, your legs are hairy. I can't see a damn thing."

"You're going to insert the tip of the knife just to the east of the metal, touching it, okay? Then you'll make a small incision, not too deep, and pull the knife east. East not south, never south, okay?"

"Sure," I say, my voice trembling as I lift the knife. I'm waiting, waiting, hoping I won't actually have to go through with it.

"Don't worry, Allison, you're doing fine."

The knife goes in and it's easy . . . Well, easy*ish*, less resistant than I expected. I hold my breath, forcing my hand to stay steady. I do as he says, dragging the knife an inch or two. The blood comes to the surface at once, outlining the path of the blade. It makes my hand start to shake so I pull it away.

"That's normal. That's supposed to happen," he says gently. "You're doing great. Now you've got some wiggle room so grab the metal. Don't yank, just pull in one smooth motion. Draw a line with your eyes from the end of the metal out and away and follow that line. Smooth, just pull, don't struggle against it, just let the path decide itself."

I pull firmly but slowly, taking great care to try and feel how the metal is lodged in his leg, what the shape of it is. He's lucky because it's almost completely straight, not bent or curved, just dented here and there. It's not so bad except for the blood bubbling

up around the metal and the bright sheen of red coating the shrapnel itself. That's when I start to smell it, the strong, coppery odor
of human blood and my stomach starts to go again.

"It's okay, it's okay, you're doing fine, you're doing great," he
says, reading the pallor of my face. My lungs are starting to ache
from holding my breath for so long but it helps to keep me steady.
I can't stop now, I have to just keep pulling, carefully, slowly, but
with purpose. The metal seems to go on forever but then it comes
free, the pointed end dripping a little as it comes away in my
hand.

"You did it," he says and we both breathe out at the same time.

"Fuck," I say, dropping the shrapnel on one of the Ts. "Piece of
cake."

"That was just step one, sweetie. Now comes the real fun."

Julian nods toward the iron, his blue-green eyes dancing with
mischief.

"Are you sure?" I ask.

"Yes, because I'm bleeding now so there's no going back. Pick it
up, Allison. You know what to do."

I can feel the heat of the iron even around the handle. The flat
bottom is smoking, red-hot. I go fast, with a quick, hard strike
before the doubts can start to form.

Julian claps a hand over his mouth but I still hear "Gaaagh-
haagggghwhyamInotdrunk!"

Julian's muffled squeal quickly dies down to a long, drawn-out
hiss. If he keeps that up the guards will be joining us for his recovery. I pull the iron away and the flesh is sealed and bright red,
the wound closed, cauterized. His leg smokes, and the smell of his
burnt leg hair stamps out the stink of the fuel. There's a distinc-
tive pointed shape to the closed wound, like a Star Trek insignia,
but with a few decorative dots.

Julian's eyes are watering but there's a smile through the cascade of tears.

"You did it! You fucking did it," he says, grabbing my shoulder and shaking. I put the hot iron aside, noticing the transfer of his skin. It looks like rubbery wax molded across the top of the iron.

"So," I begin, sitting back and wiping at the sweat on my face and neck, "can you walk?"

"Patience!" he says, chuckling. "Can I have a second or two? You *did* just burn the living hell out of my thigh."

"Yeah," I say. "Heh, look at that, it's still smoking."

"Something tells me you liked doing that a little too much."

He lets go of my shoulder and leans back with a great heaving sigh. We sit in silence for a moment but I can't rest, can't stop thinking about Ted and his shoulder. What if he's already dead?

"All right, let's go," Julian says, staring at me.

"Hmm?"

"Your friend, let's go help him."

"And how do you know it's a him?" I ask. I get to my feet and extend a hand. It takes a moment or two of wrestling to get Julian up on his feet. He inhales sharply through his teeth, bouncing a little on his left foot as he feels the pain of the surgery. With his left hand he steadies himself, using my shoulder for balance. He's tall, which wasn't easy to tell when he was sprawled out on the floor.

"Honey, I know," he says, "because I have eyes and because you walked your crazy ass in here to get me, a doctor."

"It's not like that, he's just a good friend."

"Well well well then . . . My day just gets better and better."

"Just . . . No. Gross," I say, shaking my head. "We're leaving."

"Lead the way, baby."

COMMENTS

Isaac says:

November 1, 2009 at 12:03 am

You're updating, which means you made it out. That's a relief. And leg surgery? Well I can't say I'm surprised, but I'm sure as hell impressed!

November 2, 2009—The Comfort of Strangers

I have seen inside Ted.

"A toast!"

I turn, startled out of my thoughts. It's Julian and he's brought a bottle, hobbling up to me, the pain flickering in his face, in the tension of his body, but not in his voice. I've offered to keep the first watch, and maybe all the watches, since I can't fathom resting until I know Ted is safely out of danger. Renny is with him and has promised to let me know as soon as he's awake.

She was kind enough to let me know there's a glimmer of wireless about twenty yards southeast of the camp.

"A toast?" I ask, turning to face Julian. "To what?" He joins me on the low concrete retaining wall at the north end of the encampment. He still smells of the hydrogen peroxide, of the rubbing alcohol, and I do too.

"To you, of course," he says. "Or to us! Or—no—to something better: to potential! God knows you've got it." He takes a big swig from the bottle and as he raises it to his lips I see the Johnnie Walker label wink in and out of view.

"Where the hell did you find that?" I ask, enthusiastically taking the slender bottle from him. I absolutely need a drink.

"Stole it from Sam," he says. "Fuck, sorry, I mean Dobbs." He scoffs, taking the whiskey back from me. His faces scrunches up as he swallows and his lips smack together with supreme satisfaction.

I have to admit, I feel the same. I haven't had booze this good since . . . Since sharing a drink with Collin.

Fuck.

"Won't he be pissed?"

"Sure, but I'm his big brother. That's what I'm for!"

The biceps tendon adheres the biceps muscle to the shoulder and stabilizes the joint. Four separate muscles originate on the scapula and pass out and around the shoulder where the tendons unite together to make up the rotator cuff . . .

"Hello? Allison?" he says, snapping his fingers in front of my face. "Jesus. I didn't know. . . . I guess I'm so used to it, to surgery. Never shakes me up anymore."

"I thought I was going to kill him. I think I held onto the same breath the whole time." I can't stop looking at my hands, at the blood still wedged in the cracks. Ted's blood.

"Heads up."

I follow Julian's hand and see the decomposing Groaner shuffling toward us. He's all but trumpeted his arrival, letting out one long depressed grunt. It's as if he already knows we're armed and ready. I pull the pistol out of my back waistband and drop him with three shots to the head. I might have done better but my hands won't stop shaking.

"Nice," Julian says, beaming at me. The man has no levels, there is only one. Big, white teeth glaring at you like the broadside of Moby Dick's ass. Tail. Fin. Whatever. "I can see we're in good hands."

My hands are starting to steady and they look beautiful almost, perched on the tops of my thighs like two weary doves resting after a long flight. I can still see the muscles parting under the knife, the tissue, the *blood . . .*

"Thank you," I murmur.

"For what? You did it all, sweetheart."

"Stop calling me that. And no, I didn't do it all. I couldn't have done that without you, not in a million years. So . . . thank you."

"You're welcome," he says, handing me the bottle.

"And thank you," I continue, "for being nice."

"I *could* be a lot nicer."

I toss him a sideways glance to see if he's kidding. He isn't. And so, "Forget it," I say, shaking my head.

"Roll those eyes any harder and you'll be picking your corneas up out of the dirt."

"Do you ever stop? I mean . . . ever?"

"Nope."

The whiskey is a good, burning mouthful of honeyed smoke. I can feel the clear path it marks down my throat, warming as it goes. We sit in silence for a moment, the colorless, gray world stretched out in front of us, riddled with pain, riddled with danger. I wonder how many are coming toward us right now, how many are hobbling on broken legs, torn limbs, and all to get to us. What must their pain be? I hope they don't suffer. I hope their existence is numb.

"If it's not Ted, then who is it?"

Julian pries the bottle out of my hand and pauses with it halfway to his lips, waiting for my answer. For a total gimp he sure doesn't seem too hindered, in the physical sense anyway.

"Oh Jesus, I can't just turn you down because—shock and horror—I don't find you attractive? I know that, being a doctor, you're probably used to chicks throwing themselves at you or whatever but that's not for me."

"Okeydoke," Julian says, shrugging his shoulder and nodding toward the field in front of us. Another Groaner limps toward us and I take aim. "But who is he?"

"He's just . . . a guy. A married guy. A dumb married guy that I'll never see again. Satisfied?"

"Not really," he says, sipping the whiskey. "But it's a start. I take it that against all fucking odds the wife's still in the picture?"

"Yup." The gun fires, hitting the Groaner square in the forehead.

"Ah-haaa. And you don't much care for her?"

"Nope."

"You tell him that?"

"Aren't you a fucking doctor? Where the hell is your bedside manner? What kind of doctor are you anyway? No, wait, let me guess—OB/GYN?"

"You'd like that, wouldn't you? I already offered to show you my bedside manner and, if memory serves—and it does—you turned me down." He stops, hesitating for a moment before taking another swig of whiskey. Then, squinting away from me and into the distance he says, "I was a pediatrician."

"Wow. Kids?"

"Kids."

"That's gotta be tough."

"It is." His voice is already deep and low, but it drops another register before he says, "But when things go right it's just exactly where you wanna be."

"See, that's nice. That's a nice change for you. I like you better when you're being, you know, not a dick."

For a moment I'm sure he's going to retort, but he's quiet, rubbing the edge of his jaw thoughtfully. The light is so strange here, so purely dark and yet glittering with stars. Without the lights of Iowa City to bleach out the moon and stars the glow from the sky is hypnotizing. I think about pointing this out but keep it to myself. Julian has changed his pants, abandoning the one-legged trouser look for a scuffed pair of dark khaki dungarees. He dresses like an Australian cattle herder, a roughneck, and yet it's not quite a stretch to imagine him in a doctor's coat.

"So," he says after the long silence, "does Married Guy actually know that you're torn up about this?"

"None of your business, really."

"You got somewhere pressing to be? No? Didn't think so."

"You're a man," I say, humoring him. He hands me the whiskey bottle. "Would *you* know?"

"Phew, that's loaded. But," he says, gesturing with a little bow and a hand pointed to his chest, "if it were *me*, maybe I'd want someone to just smack me over the head and say, 'Hey moron, your wife's a bloodsucking harpy.'"

"That's not my job. That's not even my place. . . ." I should stop there, but the whiskey is starting to work and when that happens I feel like talking. And I have to admit that, unfortunately, talking helps. "A friend of mine used to say that, you know, if you like a guy who has a girlfriend then it's fair game to tell him so. If he likes you better than her then there you go; if not, then at least you tried. But with married people it's not fair to even plant that seed, you know? It's just . . . destructive."

"Maybe that's what he needs," Julian says brightly. "A little destruction."

"No. The landscape is different now. He should hold onto her, she's part of his other life, his normal life. And relationships . . . It's all new. Friendships are made so fast that you can't dwell, no, you have to just move on. How many people have I met recently that I liked, really liked, and then lost? How many people have tricked me? Lied to me? I need to keep focused, keep focused on just staying alive and getting to my mom. It's not worth it to dwell, not when our expiration dates are so—"

"Unpredictable?"

"Exactly."

"You know, there's a Latin phrase for this."

"No there isn't."

"Yes there is," he insists.

I'm getting drunk. That is the only explanation for why I'm even indulging in this conversation. It's like I can see the path in front of me, see exactly where the edge of the cliff is and when I'll tumble over it but somehow, *somehow*, my feet just keep on moving. You and me, Johnnie Walker, you and me are quits.

"Fuck. Fine. Let's have it then," I say, throwing up my hands.

"*Carpe connubium.*"

"You'd almost be charming if you weren't a complete manchild."

"Trouble, one o'clock," he says, suddenly serious. There are two of them, quieter than the others. The smell drifts all the way over to us from their rotting bodies. You can never forget that smell. I take care of them, checking the clip to make sure I'm okay on bullets. I'm running low. I need to conserve.

"Is this just about sex? I get it, Julian. You're horny. There isn't exactly a romantic vibe going around."

"No," Julian says, and for once the white whale smile is gone. He goes on, rambling, saying things like, "This is about you rescuing my ass from that redneck hellhole. It's about you saying 'Not me, never, I'm bad with blood' and then performing a fucking *medieval* surgery on my leg. It's about you, cool and collected under pressure, saving your friend's life. And it's about you and me having a drink while you shoot zombies in the head. I mean, you're kinda *scary*, but no one's perfect."

"I think it's time we said good night."

"It's early yet."

"You should get some rest. You've had a big day," I say, making sure he has the whiskey. I can't be left alone with it. "I can take the watch from here."

"Allison . . ."

"*Good night*, Julian."

I should follow my own advice and ask for someone to cover the watch. But there's nothing appealing about sleeping on the hard ground under a torn tarp, or in a car stained with blood. It's not insomnia, just my preference for being awake to face the demons. In sleep they have more power; in sleep there's no way to turn away from what's coming for you.

Half an hour later Renny comes looking for me. Ted is sound asleep and, she thinks, out of danger. It takes her all of two seconds to smell the whiskey on my breath.

"Caveman getting you drunk?" she asks. She's wide awake for this time of night, her dark eyes gleaming like ancient jewels. "Bold move."

"I'm not interested."

"No? You sure? Man is in the middle of surgery and he still can't keep his eyes off you."

"What are you saying?" I ask, wishing that I hadn't been so hasty about letting that whiskey go.

"I *would* say he's smitten, but I'm gonna go ahead and keep my mouth shut. I'm just looking out for you. He's hungry for it, is all I'm saying."

"I know that, Renny. Seriously. I know. He's not exactly the king of subtlety."

"I wouldn't ordinarily advocate running away from a potential lay, that's not my style, but I feel—as your friend—that I have an obligation to point out that Julian is, in all likelihood, a slime-ball," she says. "And I don't give a *fuck* if he's a doctor or an astronaut or whatever. I think you should steer clear."

"You're right," I say, permitting myself a smile. "And coincidentally I'm writing the inspirational poster in my head right now. 'Abstinence: Hey, motherfuckers, don't knock it till you try it.'

Times New Roman. All caps. And it'll be right below a big ol' picture of an industrial-grade chastity belt."

"Don't you mean a big, sloppy red heart?" Renny asks. She isn't moved by my stony look. "Don't be shy. You can't fool me when it comes to this shit."

"Apparently *nobody's* fooled. So okay, Miss Marple, it's got nothing to do with the boneage. Happy?"

"Absolutely. I barely got to meet your friend Collin," she says, giving me a sidelong glance, "but, to borrow a phrase, he seems like good people. His wife on the other hand . . ."

"Ha. You don't have to tell me twice."

Our laughter dies down and we're left standing in the cold, consuming night. I don't want to look at her but there's something in her face, something open and totally new that tells me I can trust her. It makes me wonder if she had siblings, younger siblings, people who looked up to her and depended on her for that wide-open, welcoming look. I could curl up in that look.

"Something you wanna tell me?" she asks.

"I just . . . I guess I feel stupid hanging onto *sentiment*. I know logically that I should just renounce this whole monogamy thing. There are new needs, you know? New parameters. We might be an endangered species. But something won't let me move on. I keep telling myself I just need more time, that it will get easier, that I'll stop thinking about him . . . but I won't. I know that now." There's something nice about this, something warm and calm in Renny's eyes that lets me know she's been down this road before.

"You're right," she says. "You won't stop, but that doesn't mean it won't get easier."

"Was she pretty?"

"Like a shiny new tube of lipstick." It's pure, liquid dark out, but I can hear the smile in her voice.

"You ever think maybe . . . I mean, what if we end up being, like, the last people on earth?" I say. "Would you . . . you know . . . have a kid?"

She readjusts her stance in the dark, resting one leg on the retaining wall I've been leaning against. She laughs quietly, letting out a long breath like the exhalation of a pensive drag on a cigarette. "My mom asked me that when I came out."

"You're shitting me."

"No, she actually asked me. Thanksgiving table, no less. She had balls, that woman, brass balls, but she forgot she was my mama, that I inherited those balls from her too. So I said, 'No, Mother, no I would not; not now, not ever, not at the end of the world or the motherfucking beginning of it. I would not, could not on a boat, I would not could not, so fuck. You.'"

"I bet that went over well."

"She didn't talk to me for a month after that," Renny says, chuckling. "But now? Fuck it, I'd probably do it, I mean if it was getting real dire. I told my mom no because I knew why she was asking me. She wanted me to admit that deep down inside I was still a good little Christian straight girl. But I'm not and she needed to understand that."

"Don't do it," I tell her. "Even if you're the last woman on earth."

"You serious?"

"Absolutely. I mean, what's the point? If this is what you're giving a child," I say, gesturing to the soggy field littered with oozing corpses. "If this is what they have to look forward to, you're better off just sticking to who you are, to what you believe. It's more valuable, I think, in the end."

It's one of those bad nights, an uncomfortable, lonely night and I wish I hadn't let that whiskey get away. I wish I could hear a bit of *Mary Poppins* whistled in the dark.

COMMENTS

C in C says:

November 2, 2009 at 7:09 pm

The privilege and the heartache of marriage is the picture it presents to the outside world. If a star explodes there's a little more violence in the universe but there's a little more beauty too, right? There's more to say but I can't think what, and so instead I'll let someone smarter, someone wiser than I say what I mean to say: "There were times when he could not read the face he had studied so long and when this lonely girl was a greater mystery to him than any woman of the world with a ring of satellites to help her." Perhaps a goodbye is in order. I think instead I'll simply say: See you later.

Allison says:

November 2, 2009 at 8:03 pm

That sounds ominous, C. My battery's low and I have to go beg Nanette to use their back-up generator so I'll keep this short. Don't give up. I know I sound grouchy, but don't give up, never stop fighting.

Isaac says:

November 2, 2009 at 8:58 pm

Allison knows a thing or two about hopelessness. Listen to her and to me, don't give up man. Fight the good fight.

November 4, 2009—In Dubious Battle

"Renny."

"Uhmf, hm?"

"Renny!"

"What *is* it?"

"Get up. Get up quickly and quietly. We've got company."

It's early, the pink fringes of dawn just beginning to cluster around the distant tree line. My mind, I can say with certainty, is hazy. Julian is waiting outside the tent when I step out and he's alternately rubbing his bicep to stay warm and flinching from the pain of upsetting his injured arm. There are dark bags beneath his blue-green eyes. His face is pale, bloodless. There aren't many extra supplies at the encampment so we've had to make due with sweatshirts and jeans to keep us warm and little else.

"I know I shouldn't take it personally, but it's a little disconcerting that they didn't notice I was gone until *an entire day later*," he says. He flinches again as his left hand bumps the sling.

"Stop doing that," I say. "You look ridiculous. And keep it down."

"It's freezing."

"It's a hell of a lot colder in the grave."

Maria woke us up just moments ago, reporting back from her watch that she had seen movement over at the Territorials camp, headlights, the rumble of engines gunning to life. She wasn't sure what it all meant but I had a pretty good idea. I suspected they might retaliate after we stole Julian back, but part of me hoped they would just ignore it. They didn't seem to be too attached to him, considering they were prepared to let him bleed to death in a closet.

Renny emerges from the tent, her springy hair held back by a thick black headband. There are bags under her eyes but she's already wide awake, determined. Dapper trots out of the tent and sits with his muzzle resting against my knee. Renny hands me my ax; lately we've been sharing it. "What do we do about Ted?"

"I think we should move him into the car," I say, adjusting the shoulder strap of my laptop bag.

"But the car is shot to shit."

"Just for safekeeping," I reply. "Until we have a clear getaway. If he's lying down in the back they won't be able to see him. They'll check the tents first if anything."

"Julian, go help the others pack up. Renny and I can move Ted to the car." I go to him, pull him a few feet away from Renny and take a tight hold on his healthy arm. "Can I ask you a very personal question?"

"Of course," he says. "Jesus, Allison, you can ask me anything."

"Do you know what a Molotov cocktail is and could you please make some?"

"I . . . Roughly . . . I guess?"

"Good, great!" I shout. "Get to it."

Before Julian can answer, Renny and I duck into the tent. Ted is there, his sweatshirt bulging at the shoulder where the heavy bandages are wrapped. He's pale and sweating, but alive. We carefully move him into a sitting position and then lift, taking care not to put a strain on his shoulder. It's slow going. The natural place to lift someone up is their shoulder joint, but instead I have to sort of grab him around the middle and heave upward. In the middle of this, he begins to wake up.

"Mmf?" he asks, his head lolling against Renny's shoulder.

"We're just moving you to a safer spot," I tell him, smoothing back the damp hair on his forehead, adjusting his skewed glasses. It's easier with him awake, since he can at least use his legs to help us along. He's still dozing as we sandwich him between us and guide him away from the tents. We head for the sedan parked on the edge of the camp. There's a fine, chilly mist clinging to the ground and the yellow grass crunches from the frost as we hobble along together in stride. Every once in a while Ted grunts with discomfort and we adjust to put less pressure on his injury.

There's still a trickle of blood on the ground marking the path we took getting Ted out of the car. The backseat is a complete mess, littered with glass and stained with Ted's blood on the seats and the floor. At least the shattered windows have allowed it to air out a bit. Renny stands staring at it all with the door open, her mouth twisted into a scowl of revulsion.

"It's just for a little while and he's sleeping anyway."

She nods, reaching in to sweep the glass off the seat and onto the floor. Together, we slowly help Ted into the backseat, prodding him this way and that until he's lying down with his knees curled beneath him. He grumbles incoherently, scrunching up his nose as he squirms around trying to get comfortable.

"For the record, I don't think we should mention this to him when he wakes up," Renny says.

"Yeah. Agreed."

When we reach the tents, Maria, Nanette and Dobbs are busy loading up their supplies into his pickup. Julian is nowhere to be found. A plan has begun to form in my mind, and I'm hoping we have a chance of getting most of these people to safety. The Territorials have guns and vehicles, it's true, but they'll rely on those things, perhaps too much.

"Maria!" I call, jogging up to them. "Could I talk to you for a minute?"

She and I peel off from the group. It looks like they've almost managed to pack up most of the makeshift tents and supplies. They didn't have much to begin with, and it's obvious that this was never meant to be a permanent solution. "I know this is going to sound like a weird question, but can you think of any place nearby that might be . . . well . . . infested? Somewhere there might be a lot of undead, maybe a store or a warehouse or something?"

"I . . . Well . . . I'm not really sure," she says, giving me a suspicious look. "But I suppose you might try the movie theater. The police sealed it off that first night and I haven't seen anything or anyone come out of there. So unless someone tried to get in—"

"Perfect. Where is it?"

"Just there," she says, pointing west toward the Walmart. "It's on the other side down the frontage road, maybe half a mile away."

"Thank you. Tell the others to hurry."

"Could . . . could I ask why?"

"Why what?" I ask.

"Why would you want to know that? Where the infested are?"

"Oh. That's where we're headed."

Maria watches me walk away, her mouth hanging open a little. After a moment she turns and goes back to the others, wringing her hands and glancing over her shoulder at me every second or two. I feel, oddly enough, close to Collin for a second. I know I'm channeling him from a distance, mimicking his cool, collected demeanor. I only wish there was time to miss him.

It's probably not the best plan I've ever had, but a healthy dose of chaos might be just what we need to unbalance the Territorials and swing things in our favor. Between the undead, my pistol and the Molotov cocktails, we might have just enough confusion.

Renny finds me before I can track down Julian. She's out of breath, bending over to rest her palms on her knees as she pants. "Allison, they're . . . they're coming. We're out of time."

I follow her back to Dobbs and his truck. The pickup is heavily weighed down, the flatbed filled to overflowing with wood, tarps, buckets and odds and ends. There are a few tools in the very bottom and what looks like a lunch box and a workman's kit. Probably useless. Dobbs, Nanette and Maria stand around in a semicircle as I pull down the back of the truck and open up the workman's kit. Dapper tries to jump into the flatbed but I shove him out of the way.

"What are you doing? We have to go!" Nanette is screaming, shaking me by the shoulders. Renny pulls her off and tries to calm her down, but Nanette bats her away.

"You don't get it! They'll kill us!"

"Just calm down," I mutter, raking through the three-inch-deep mess of screws, nails, scraps of sandpaper and empty glass jars. It doesn't seem to matter that it's cold. I can feel the sweat gathering at my temples. I grab a handful of screws and shove them at Renny. "When Julian gets back, tell him to toss a few of these in the cocktails."

"In the *what*?"

"Just . . . You'll see when he gets here."

They're all staring at me, waiting, waiting for me to save them. *Ha, ha, Julian*, I want to scream, see what happens when no one is tough? When no one takes the lead? They're paralyzed, frozen into inaction by what they think is an insurmountable danger. But it's not too late, not insurmountable, not yet . . .

"Back!"

It's Julian. His good arm is full of bottles sloshing gasoline down his sleeve as he limps at top speed toward us. He's cheerful as can be as he gently bends to line up the jars and bottles on the tailgate. Other people have gathered at the truck, people staying in the camp that I never had a chance to meet. There's a husband and wife with a little Hispanic girl wedged between them, and there are two teenage boys. I don't know their names and I've only seen glimpses of them as they went from tent to tent. "One, two, three, four, five . . . six!" Julian says, stepping back from his work, glancing around at us as if to say "Didn't I do just great?"

"Here," Renny says. "Allison said to add these."

I hear the screws dropping into the gasoline as I finally, finally come across something useful.

"Anyone have a pair of gloves?" I call, my fingers dusting off the top of a big, plastic bottle. I tip it up to face me and the faded label is almost completely gone but I can just make out the small, black print.

NAOH

I think of Ted reciting chemical compounds as he goes to sleep, that sad, boyish whisper in the dark. I think of Ted curled up in the back of a chewed-up sedan, lying on his own crusted bloodstains and I know without a doubt that this is the way forward. This little bottle is the key.

"There should be a pair of work gloves in the kit," Dobbs says, shouldering his way through the others. "There," he says, pointing at a floppy pair of men's work gloves. They're heavy duty and leather, but way too big for my hands.

"Too big," I say. "Anyone else?"

I pull out the plastic bottle and set it aside. The lunch box reeks of moldy apples and rotting cheese but I brave the smell long enough to yank out a used plastic lunch bag. There's a tug on the back of my sweatshirt and I look down to see the little girl holding a pair of fleecy black gloves up to my nose. I pull them on and, while they're a bit snug, they fit okay. There are black cats and candy corns embroidered onto the backs.

"Are you sure?" I ask.

"Yes. My sister doesn't need them anymore." She scuttles back to the man and woman, ducking behind them at once. They don't look like her biological parents, but it doesn't matter. She goes back to them, both hands hooking behind their knees.

"What do you need us to do?" Dobbs asks, taking off his Stetson and throwing it into the back of the truck.

"Get everyone together and—"

The gunfire starts, quietly at first, but building fast as the Territorials get closer. They're spraying a barrage of bullets at the camp. We huddle in close together, taking shelter behind the pickup and its towering cargo. The little girl puts both hands over her eyes.

"That way!" I point, trying to talk over the noise. "Go as fast as you can, take cover as you go."

"But our things!" Nanette protests, gesturing toward the pickup truck.

"You can get them later, right now you need to get as far away from here as you can."

Dobbs takes Maria by the hand and crouches, leading the group away from the truck, using it as a barrier. The front of the truck starts to take a heavy beating from the bullets. Julian and Renny kneel down beside me.

"Light those up," I shout, "and throw them all."

The three of us take turns with Julian's Zippo, lighting the ends of the wicks (remnants of Julian's one-legged pants) before hurling the wine bottles, bean jars and, yes, Johnnie Walker over the truck. "Try to fan them out in a line!" I shout, but I'm not sure they can hear me over the sound of igniting fire and booming rifles. Julian reeks of gasoline and I make him stay back as we light up the second to last cocktail and fling it over our heads. Crouching low, I peek around the edge of the flatbed in time to see one of the Territorial's Humvees explode, the cocktail hitting it square on the hood. I hear a sharp hiss as the pickup truck's front tires are shot out.

"Go with the others," I say to Renny, grabbing her by the forearm. "And take Dapper."

"I'm not going anywhere," she says. "What about Ted?"

"They won't find him, he's not even in their line of sight. Please, go. I can handle this."

Renny takes one look at the fuzzy black gloves, the ax and the pistol and rolls her eyes before grabbing Dapper by the collar. "If you get your ass killed I'm burying you in those."

"Fair enough."

We shake hands and she goes. Julian is staring at me with his serious face, challenging me to send him away.

"I'm not going to ask you to leave, if that's what you're waiting for," I tell him.

"Well I won't go—Oh! Oh."

"There's one cocktail left and I might need you to cover my retreat. Just in case things go wrong."

I pull off my laptop bag and shove it under his good arm. "Hold onto that. Don't let anything happen to it. And this too." I check the clip and then hand him the pistol. Two shots left—not many, but maybe enough. I grab my ax and nod toward the plastic bottle on the tailgate.

"Put on the work gloves and fill that sandwich baggy about halfway with powder," I say.

Julian picks up the bottle and glances at the label, his eyes growing wide. "Lye? What the fuck are you gonna do with this?"

"Just sit tight. I know what I'm doing." This is not, strictly speaking, the truth but there must be something trustworthy about my face at that moment, because Julian sits back, crouching against the tailgate. "I'll be right back, okay?"

"What?" he hisses, trying to grab my wrist. I tiptoe out of his reach. "No you won't! Allison, come—Allison!"

"I'm coming out!" I scream, trying to top the sound of burning metal and gunfire. The shots slow down and then stop. "Don't shoot! I'm coming out!"

"Hold your fire!"

I carefully step out from behind the pickup, holding my hands in the air as a sign of surrender. I'm not absolutely positive they won't gun me down anyway, but something tells me they want to say their piece. A little spray of dirt goes up at my feet, accompanied by the *fut-fut-fut* of a rifle.

"I said hold your goddamn fire!"

I take a big gasping swallow, forcing myself to keep going. In front of me, there are three cars lined up with the burning Humvee several yards away from the others. If only it had been a little closer the explosion might have caused a domino effect. The interior of the Humvee is still burning, the black smoke churning into the air above the other cars. I say cars, but they're more like modified Jeeps. The tops are gone and they've been painted matte black. There's an insignia painted on each hood, the design clumsily transferred by hand and already beginning to fleck and fade.

"Don't shoot!" I shout again and my voice cracks. "I'm not armed."

"Citizen! Drop the ax!"

The man calling to me is standing up, his head poking up above the roll cage of the Jeep. He's got an enormous, bushy black beard and very red lips. There's a floppy canvas hat with a camouflage print on his head and a semiautomatic aimed right at me. I take a few more steps forward and then slowly, slowly crouch down and drop the ax into the dirt.

"You killed two of my guys," Black Beard shouts, running the back of his hand under his nose. I can feel the pressure of their weapons, the heat of eight or nine guns aimed at me. Aimed to kill.

"You fired first," I call back. I don't even know if these are bad men, but I suspect they are. They would have gunned us down, killed people they might have instead had as allies. I look at their faces, at their intense, angry eyes and wonder, who is the enemy?

"Where's the doctor?"

"We have him," I say and shout back over my shoulder, "Julian! Wave at the nice men!"

A hand pokes out from behind the tailgate, Julian's hand. It wiggles back and forth like a puppy tail.

"Look, *citizen*," I say, close enough now that I don't need to shout, "we can do this like civilized human beings. There are innocent people here—if you let them go then I'll give you the doctor. I think it's a fair trade. Those people had nothing to do with it. I'm the one who rescued him."

"Like civilized people, eh?" Black Beard says, chuckling. There's a thin trickle of snot caught in his mustache. I can't stop staring at it. "I think it's a little late for that. We want what's ours. Our *val-ya-buls*."

The wind shifts, pouring the black smoke over the Humvee's hood and right into my eyes. Lovely.

"Like I said, no one else needs to get hurt," I say slowly, taking the opportunity to get a little closer. I scan the Jeeps: two men in the first car, three (including Black Beard) in the middle one and two in the third. Now I know. Now I know . . . If only there were more bullets. "I'll get him for you, okay? Just . . . don't shoot anybody. I'll get your valuables."

"You best," Black Beard says, grinning again with a shark's mouth. "You best."

I walk backward, never letting my eyes leave the Territorials.

I can't imagine this is all of them. There must be more at the Walmart, but it doesn't matter. They've played their hand and now it's time for me to lay down my cards too.

When I reach the pickup truck, Julian is ready with an ice-cold, petulant glare.

"Shhh," I whisper, kneeling down next to him. "Calm down. I'm not actually handing you over."

"Then what was all that about?" he hisses, shoving his face close to mine.

"I needed to see how many. We're going to have to get creative. Just stay here and for fuck's sake, don't throw any of those things while I'm out there. When you hear a commotion, see if you can take out one of the cars. After that, you go with the others in the opposite direction. Opposite direction, got it?"

"We don't have anything to fight with, they'll flatten us."

"No they won't. Just trust me, you'll see. Do you have the bag?"

He hands me the plastic bag and I maneuver around until my right side is close to him. "Hold my pocket open."

"Yeah. Sure," he says, smiling sadly. "Nice try."

"Look, baby, if I wanted you to grab my crotch I'd just fucking ask."

Julian pulls open my jean pocket and holds it, his fingers still encased in the work glove. His hand is trembling badly. The wind is strong now, whipping at our clothes and hair but the powder is safe, undisturbed.

"It's okay," I tell him. "It's okay."

With a deep breath I take the baggy and set it into my pocket, making sure the opening is facing up. It's difficult to do with the clumsy fleece gloves, but there's no time to make mistakes, or to hesitate.

"There," I say, and Julian lets go of my pocket. I take the gun from the tailgate and tuck it into the back of my waistband, tugging down my sweatshirt until I'm sure it's concealed.

I look at Julian, at the forlorn little smile that still puts dimples in his cheeks. I can't tell if he's going to cry or punch me. There's something different about him, something vulnerable. I can almost see what he might have been like as a kid, as an infant. And I feel that way too—innocent and scared and on the cusp of doing something I abhor.

"I have to go," I say. "Please get out of here. Please keep my friends safe."

"I'll see you again."

"Yeah," I tell him. "You will."

I leap out from behind the pickup and walk toward the Jeeps, fast, picking up speed, striding as quickly as I can without running. I pass the ax and let it lie. They see it on my face. I know they see it. The passenger in Black Beard's car shifts, squinting at me through the windshield. It feels like walking across a border, entering into a new land with new rules.

"Hey, hey, *hey*!" Black Beard shouts, scrambling to get a good aim on me. "Not so fast."

"Calm down. Jesus. He won't come," I say, stone-faced. I'm at the driver's side of Black Beard's Jeep and he's dropped down to see me face-to-face. "If he won't come then I'll just bring you to him. It's only fair."

"You're cold," Black Beard says, appraising me with new admiration. He puts up a hand and the rest of the men seem to relax. "You're damn cold."

"He's a one-armed doctor. What the fuck am I supposed to do with a one-armed doctor anyway?"

This is what we do in the name of survival. This is who we are now.

"Do you like Captain America?" I ask conversationally as Black

Beard gets out of the Jeep. I hold the door for him and move, just a little, so that I'm between him and the car. "I imagine you do."

"What the hell are you going on about, bitch?"

"I'm not a big fan myself, but I remember this one scene in a Spider-Man comic—I'll never forget it. He said, 'When the mob and the press and the whole world tell you to move, your job is to plant yourself like a tree beside the river of truth, and tell the whole world: no—"

Bang—bang!

"—*you* move.'"

No more bullets, time for the big finish. I dip my hand into the baggy, digging in and grabbing as much powder as I can before flinging it at Black Beard. It hits him in the face, the eyes, crackling like a bag of Pop Rocks, the flesh bubbling and rupturing. I kick him too, right in the stomach. It's a heartwarming Steven Seagal moment. The other men are scrambling to get a shot off without hitting their fearless leader, who is screaming and clutching his melting face.

It's too late.

I'm in the Jeep, shoving it into reverse and slamming on the gas. The radio blasts to life, which certainly doesn't help the fact that I already feel like my heart is going to explode. I kill the radio as the Jeep speeds directly backward. I jam on the brakes and turn it ninety degrees, heading the other way. I'm sure they all experience a moment of panic, a moment where they wonder whether to pursue the refugees or me. They choose me.

Three people dead so ten others can live—eleven if I somehow manage to make it out alive.

The gunfire follows, hitting the frame of the Jeep, singing like xylophone mallets against the metal. I hear the Molotov cocktail hit but Julian misses, and the two cars stay on me, not far enough behind. I pull the baggy of lye out of my pocket and toss it out the window; I throw the gloves out too. Now I just need to find that movie theater.

"Just there. It's on the other side down the frontage road, maybe half a mile away."

Where is the fucking thing? I careen around a corner, taking it hard to avoid a stalled minivan in the road. The dead Territorial in the passenger seat bounces against the window, a single bead of blood dripping down from my bullet hole in his forehead, his skull slamming into the glass. The semitrucks are on my left and I glimpse the door where I sneaked in to get Julian. I check the rearview mirror; one of the cars is lagging behind, one of the back tires sagging. Julian's cocktail must have sent a screw or two into that tire and now they can barely keep up with their comrades.

The Walmart seems to go on forever, the road curving tightly around the back of it. It's a divided road, a concrete strip down the middle with trees and shrubs planted at two-foot intervals. Through the bare trees I see the edge of the Walmart and then a stretch of road and an intersection. There are cars strewn across the road haphazardly, like a deck of cards dropped and scattered on the floor. My chest is aching but I don't know if it's from my cracked rib or my heartbeat. There's nothing left to do but carry on, go forward, bring these violent Neanderthals to their knees.

A bright marquee shoots up behind a strip mall. The sign is navy blue and yellow, announcing some movie that looks more like a fill-in-the-blank SAT question than an advertisement. Most of the letters are missing, too many to even make a guess at what movie it might have been. I try to step harder on the gas, but I'm already pushing it into the floor. That's when I hear it, the groaning and swearing in the backseat.

I really need to work on my aim.

He sits up and comes for me as we make the movie theater parking lot. The lot is full, as if everyone has come out for an exciting new blockbuster. I get the feeling Maria is right; acres of cars out here means hundreds of people—undead people—in there.

The Territorial in the back grabs for the steering wheel with one hand and for his gun with the other. I duck my head, staying low as we fly down the open lane leading toward the theater. At this speed, we'll hit the doors in about a minute. There's the sound of automatic guns nailing the Jeep from behind and a sickening jolt as one of our back tires is hit. When he can't reach the steering wheel he goes for my neck, his fingers slipping on my throat, wet with his own blood. As much as I struggle, he keeps scratching at me, clawing. We have to make it, we have to keep going . . .

I elbow the guy, aiming for his face but hitting his shoulder instead. The gun goes off, and judging from the close little zip, less than an inch from my head. The theater looms up ahead, the marquee disappearing as we pass beneath the embellished over-hang. There's no time to stop this guy, no time to fight back. I snap my seat belt into place and watch the doors coming straight at us, watch the Jeep on our tail get closer and closer.

I keep my eyes glued to the odometer and watch the needle climb.

45 mph . . . 50 mph . . . 55 mph . . .

The impact sends me rocking forward, the air bag deploying against my cheeks as the doors to the theater implode against the Jeep. The Jeep seems to jump upward, the back tires lifting a few feet off the ground before slamming back down onto the concrete. It hurts, but I'm alert enough on impact to look up and see the Territorial sail out of the backseat like a missile, smashing through the windshield and into the lobby. Glass rains down on the hood, piling up against the shattered windshield. It's hard to move, and it feels like I've had a deep tissue massage with a base-ball bat, but I wriggle out of the seatbelt and—after snatching the gun off the dead Territorial beside me—fall hard against the door, tumbling out into the darkened lobby.

The groaning, the outright desperate moaning, sounds more like a bacchanalian orgy than a horde of hungry undead. It's as if they come from the very walls, shuffling up the corridors, oozing out from every open door and archway. The smell is downright spellbinding.

There are already so many of them. They've been locked up in here for weeks now and whoever hasn't been devoured has been turned into an emaciated shell of a human being with dead, staring eyes and a slavering, open mouth. The guard is probably dead or dying, but they descend on him at once, covering him like a swarm of hungry flies.

I stay close against the Jeep just as the other car slams into the doors, spinning out and coming to a stop against the concession counter. We've made enough noise now to alert the rest of the theatergoers, so I limp away from the Jeep, ducking beneath a mangled door. I glance over my shoulder to see the other Territorials being pulled from the wrecked car. It almost seems right, grotesquely poetic in a way, feeding monsters with monsters.

There is an unforeseen complication, of course, the fact that I'm now without a vehicle and the other car will catch up eventually. I stray to the left side of the parking lot, ducking behind abandoned cars to keep out of sight. The undead in the theater make quick work of the Territorials and soon come streaming out of the lobby, one unbroken chain of starving, desperate zombies heading right for me.

I can outpace them for a while, but my chest is starting to hurt in earnest and I must have sprained my ankle because it feels twisted, full of pins and needles. The gun in my waistband is down to two bullets, not nearly enough to stem the onslaught of undead just ten yards or so behind me. But I know that this has been enough, that Renny, and Ted, and Julian and the others will have time to get away. I know that even if I don't make it back to the camp, the others now have a fighting chance.

The third Jeep finally makes the scene, rolling into the parking lot, slowing down as they presumably take note of the carnage in the lobby and the remarkably orderly line of undead beelining for yours truly.

They start to shoot at the undead, drawing their attention, which takes a little pressure off of me, but doesn't do much about the closest zombies that follow doggedly, determined, unhindered by human exhaustion or pain. *Breathe,* I command, *breathe deeply.*

My ankle is slowing me down, giving me a bad limp, and I've only made it halfway across the parking lot. How long can I keep this up? How long before I trip or collapse or run into more rednecks with guns looking for their friends?

Up ahead I can see the frontage road and the divider filled with decorative trees. I'll be out in the open there and an easy target but I'm not sure where else to go. I make the road, huffing and puffing like a marathon runner, dragging my ankle, biting down on my lip to keep a lid on the string of expletives I'm dying to scream. There's a glimmer of silvery gray up ahead and a sound like a dying engine trying like hell to stay alive.

I shield my eyes to stare at it and watch it approach but I don't dare slow down. I can hear the undead, they're close, so close . . . I take the pistol and fire but the clip clicks back at me, empty.

The car horn sounds, making me jump, and I look up in time to see Renny come screeching by, creaming the undead following me. She's all business, shouting something at the man in the passenger seat. The door opens with a *ding-ding-ding* and Julian pulls me inside, grabbing me around the middle with his good arm and shutting the door before I can even catch my breath and look around. Renny stomps her foot on the gas pedal and we leave the movie theater behind.

I can hardly hear anything over the sound of my own labored breathing and the sedan's puttering engine. This is when I notice that not only does my ankle feel like it's about to fall off, but my face is wet and it's not from crying.

"Jesus, look at you," Julian says. I try to sit up, try to crawl off of his lap, but Ted is still lying down in the back, Dapper is on the floor next to him, and there's nowhere for me to go. Ted looks so peaceful back there. Quiet. Sedate. Julian takes his sleeve and wipes at my face. It stings.

"I drove the Jeep into the movie theater," I say.

Julian pulls something out of my hairline. It feels like a red-hot needle sliding out of my scalp. "Fucking *ouch*! What the *fuck*?" A sharply-tapered piece of bloody glass comes away in his hands.

"Can you breathe?" he asks, frowning at me.

"Sorta," I mutter, struggling again. "Can I sit up?"

"Yeah, but take it easy."

Julian was right. (Under no circumstance am I to be quoted on that.) I need a break from all this.

Julian shifts to the side, making a small space for me to wedge into. He pulls down the visor and flips open the mirror so I can see my reflection. There are nicks all over my face and a drip of blood falling down my forehead where he took out the glass shard. Wrapping around my neck is a distinctly warlike handprint in blood. I look down and find glass trapped in my sweatshirt pocket and in the cuffs of my sleeves. Glass everywhere, cuts everywhere. Blood everywhere . . .

Dapper sticks his head into the front of the car and licks at my cut-up hand. He noses my palm, letting me know he's glad to have me back.

"And the others?" I ask, trying to straighten out my ankle.

"They . . . won't be joining us. They want to stay," Julian mutters.

"What? *Stay*? Stay where?"

"They're going to my brother's farm, north a ways. They were only staying behind because of me and now that I'm okay . . . Renny told them about Liberty Village, and we offered to find them a car, but they want to stay."

"Your job is to plant yourself like a tree beside the river of truth, and tell the whole world: no, you move."

"I wish I could've thanked them," I say. "I wish I could've known them better."

"About that," Renny says. Her eyes stay on the road. She's merged us onto County Road 6, ignoring the posted signs that ask her to please go 45 mph. We're driving parallel to the highway on our left. "I had a few of them write out how they got here—you know, the way you do on your thingie."

"Blog?"

"Yeah, blog," she says. "They're not typed up or anything, but I put them in your laptop bag."

"When did—"

"Yesterday," Renny says. "I thought it might be good, you know. I thought Ted might like to know them."

"You going for your Junior Anthropologist badge?" I ask. Renny raises her fist to punch my shoulder and then stops, remembering that I currently have the structural integrity of days-old sashimi.

"We need to stop and get something to clean her up," Julian says, squishing himself against the passenger door to make more room for me. "Some of those cuts are nasty."

"Let's get back on the highway first. I want to put a little distance between us and the good ol' boys. We'll need to get food anyway," Renny replies.

As if to prove her point, my stomach lets loose a growl that would give a Doberman pinscher a run for its Alpo.

"Hungry," I say, frowning.

"We'll stop soon," Renny says. "I promise."

"I can't believe you used that Johnnie Walker bottle."

"Desperate times, honey. Desperate times," Julian murmurs, staring out the window.

I glance back between the seat and watch the city falling away behind us. The smoke rises from Iowa City, from Coralville, from every small stop in between. Somewhere Dobbs is leading survivors to his farm and I don't know if that's a new beginning or a kind of end. I can't decide if we did any good at all. Is this what we can expect—to leave a place in ashes, to leave our footprint in fire?

COMMENTS

Isaac says:

November 4, 2009 at 1:23 pm

Thank goodness for small miracles. Close one, eh? Glad you made it out. We've knocked over every store in a fifteen mile radius and I think soon we'll need to find a new area. If we can push north before the first really bad snow we might be able to make a more permanent home. It's only fair, right? You're getting Liberty Village and we need something too.

Allison says:

November 4, 2009 at 2:04 pm

Well hey, if Canada sucks you could always try Colorado!

November 5, 2009—On the Road

"Now that we know there's life beyond the grave—"

"A *kind* of life."

"Right, a *kind* of life, does that make anyone else a little more interested in this whole heaven-and-hell thing?"

Julian and I have been asked to keep watch outside the Kum & Go on 235. Des Moines is a ghost town, an eerily silent counterpart to Iowa City's chaos. Renny is inside, filling a few grocery bags with chips and drinks. It's already been raided but we've learned to search the storage rooms of these places, break down the locked doors that hide a few crates of water, soda or juice. In these places one can almost re-create the panic. Renny has asked us to stay outside for this exact reason. Julian and I got a little too into playing *CSI: Des Moines* at the last gas station.

Judging by the trail of blood to the employee break room, the brunt of the attack took place here.

What else do you see, Greg?

Well, Grissom, there are finger marks on the door, like someone tried to crawl their way in. It must be locked. I'll get that broken tooth fragment over to Trace, that might be corn chips stuck in the crown.

Oh Greg, you're so delightfully edgy and fashion-forward. You truly are the lovable Padawan of this diverse and emotionally crippled crack team of scientists! Also you will never be given a love interest because no one would date someone with hair like that.

Thanks, Griss! You're such a tough but ultimately well-meaning papa bear in my life.

You're welcome, Greg. Now stop talking and take a swab of that urine puddle.

Yeah. You can see why we were given guard duty this time.

"I'm not curious about heaven," I tell him. "I'm not curious about anything right now except food. Let me eat something and I'll get back to you."

Julian makes me sit down on the curb (and by make I of course mean nagged me to do it until I relented) so he could administer first aid. The first Kum & Go was out of Band-Aids and antibiotic cream. It was, however, fully stocked with gross puns for Julian. Thankfully the childlike joy of counting Kum & Gos wore off about forty-five minutes ago and now Julian has returned to fussing over my health. Sure, the cuts sting and my ankle feels like an elephant herd River Danced all over it, but it could be worse. I could be Ted.

"Are we ever going to change his bandages?" I ask. My gaze wanders to the sedan where Ted is still asleep. We haven't changed his dressings since the surgery.

"Sure. I can do it if you're afraid to look," Julian replies.

The sun is out, taking the edge off the stiff November wind. Julian looks warm enough; he grabbed a hideous Windbreaker at the last gas station. It's no surprise that it was left behind in the raids. It's puke-green and there's a little howling wolf embroidered on the left side. The parking lot is small and treeless and it whistles like the Great Plains. Weeds stick out at awkward angles from the cracks in the macadam. They're brown and short, as if they couldn't wait to get out from under the parking lot and then thought better of it when the cold moved in. I can almost imagine the entire place covered in weeds, taken over, reclaimed for the Earth. Part of me wouldn't be surprised to see a stegosaurus or herd of buffalo wander in from off the interstate.

"Why do you think I'm afraid all the time? Do I need to swallow a goddamn flaming sword to get you past this or what? *Ouch!* Fuck, Jules."

"Stay still," he says. "I don't think you're afraid generally speaking. But I *do* think you don't like to be confronted with Ted's mortality."

"You're the one getting all philosophical. I take it back, I don't need food. I'll answer your question now. No, the presence of a third choice—undeath—does not convince me that heaven and hell are real. If anything, it makes me sure they aren't."

"And if they do exist?" he asks.

"They don't."

"Come on, indulge me."

"And if they do, I hope heaven is a road trip. I hope it's you and me and Renny and Ted with nothing but time on our hands. I hope it's, I don't know, crossing an immeasurable distance with your closest friends."

Julian pulls his hand and the cotton swab away from my face. With the sun overhead I can see my face reflected in his bright blue-green eyes. His dimples emerge, hugging his sudden smile. He makes a little sound of confusion or maybe pleasure in his throat and then puts the cotton ball on my forehead. It feels cool for a moment and then begins to sting.

"I don't need to think about hell," I conclude. "I already know what it's like."

Renny comes out of the gas station with her arms full. She drops the bags on the curb beside us. "Trip one. There's so much shit in the back room, we'll be set for the rest of the trip."

"Cool, take your time," I say.

Renny goes back inside, humming to herself as she goes.

"You look tired," he says.

"Yeah I'm not sleeping the best. I've never been good at sleeping in cars."

"We could raid a house or two," he suggests. "Look for some night-night pills."

"No," I say quickly, thinking of the arena and the vodka and a big scary King of Ithaca telling me to follow my heart home. I shudder.

"Something the matter?"

"I've sworn off medication," I say. "The last time I took anything stronger than a Tylenol I ended up hallucinating that I was on the beach at Troy and Odysseus was my spirit guide. Dude is hard-core."

He guffaws and then, realizing I'm serious, adds, "Well, that's a pretty good spirit guide. Mine would probably be a moose."

"Or Diana Ross."

Renny returns, another load of full bags in her arms. I get up off the curb and take one to lighten her load. She nods toward the bag I've just taken from her.

"Look inside, there's a surprise."

I pull the lip of the bag forward and spot a hint of gray metal.

"A new ax!" I say, beaming. Best news I've had all day.

"Found it in the back. I can't fucking believe how many stores still keep these things around. I mean, it's gotta be a fucking safety hazard," she says.

"Thanks for this," I tell her. I test the heft of the ax. It's heavier than my first and the head could use a sharpening. Alas, you never forget your first. "I felt naked without one."

"Hey!"

In unison, all three of us turn toward the sedan. A mop of messy black hair and a pair of dazed brown eyes stare back at us, his busted glasses cocked to the side. "Thank Christ. I thought you had abandoned me in a parking lot."

"How could you think that?" I shout. I run over to the car and find Ted sitting up in the back, still pale but alert and smiling. "We would never abandon Dapper."

"Smart-ass."

"Glad to have you back," I say, pretending to punch his good shoulder. Renny and Julian catch up, a bottle of water out and uncapped for Ted.

"Welcome back," Renny says. "This is Julian, he's a doctor."

"So you're the one I should be thanking?" Ted asks, squinting up at Julian.

"Yes and no," Julian replies, pulling a hand through his shaggy hair. "It was a collaborative effort. How are you feeling?"

"Sore . . . and groggy, but I can move my hand so that's good, right?"

"We've got road trip munchies thanks to Renny," I say. "And Julian is going to change your bandages before we head out."

"Any beef jerky in there for me?" Ted asks. Renny is already loading the grocery bags into the backseat next to Ted.

"All you can eat," Renny replies. "I hope you like teriyaki. Couldn't find any black pepper."

"You win some, you lose some," he says.

It's good to see him smiling, to see him drinking and scarfing down jerky. He lets Dapper take a bite and then eats from the same piece. Yup. Our Ted is back.

"There's something happening," I say, clutching my chest. "I think . . . Yes . . . My frozen heart is melting a little. We were so worried about you, Teddy."

"*I* was worried about me," he says. "I had some seriously trippy dreams—giants and big-ass bugs and mermaids and shit."

"I bet they'd be even better if we could find some morphine," Julian says.

"Now then I'd have to kiss you," Ted says.

"I'd pay to see that," Renny adds, patting Julian on the back. He shrinks away, pulling a face.

"I think we'd all rather see you and Allison go at it," Julian replies. "And by all, I actually mean Ted and myself."

"Unlikely," I say, frowning. "Renny is way out of my league."

"Amen," Renny says. "Shall we?"

While Ted has his bandages checked, Renny lays down a few plastic bags on the backseat to cover up the crunchy bloodstains. I take the opportunity to grab my laptop and wander around the parking lot, keeping a close eye on the little stepped wireless meter. It's a miracle I'm still finding any kind of signal and it makes me wonder where it's coming from. There are either scattered bastions of civilization functioning or I managed to buy the one magical laptop in the store.

In the far corner of the lot there's a blip, one tiny green bar and I crouch down on the cement to upload an entry. WOULD YOU LIKE TO CONNECT TO SNET? Yes, indeed, I certainly would. Just that one blinking green bar of connection gives me hope. It reminds me that one sliver of civilization endures, somewhere, maybe even close by.

Through the thin line of trees at the edge of the lot I can see a figure, a shuffling of ragged feet.

I close the laptop and take up the ax. It's second nature now, it's how a mother must feel when she holds her newborn, it's how a missionary feels when they take up the banner, the cross, the cause. There's a crackle as the tree branches part and a glimmer like hunger or hope in the lurker's eyes. It doesn't matter what's there, I raise the ax, wind up and swing.

When the Groaner's head is on the ground at my feet I see that it's a middle-aged woman with her throat torn out and both ears missing. It looks like she had a perm and she's dressed in a flowery nightgown. She was someone's mother, someone's lover and now she's missing her mind and her head. That's not my mother, I think to myself, that's not my mother's fate. We're getting so close to our destination now and I know I'll see her when we get there, Liberty Village, looming like Disneyland on the horizon, a place where all your dreams come true. I can't help it. I feel like a kid—the excitement, the anticipation is growing stronger every minute.

COMMENTS

Isaac says:

November 5, 2009 at 4:37 pm

The area's getting too dangerous so we're moving on. I just wanted to say goodbye and good luck. You've kept our spirits up and now that you're nearly home I think it's time for me to move on too. We're going to try moving north, maybe to Canada. If we find somewhere safe and good I'll pass on a message but it sounds like you're home free, Allison. All the best and happy trails.

Allison says:

November 5, 2009 at 5:01 pm

Cheers, Isaac. I'm actually sorta . . . choked up. I feel like I'm losing a friend. Not *losing*, but, you know. I hope you find your way safely to Canada. It's been a strange, horrible ride but I think you made it a little easier for me, for all of us. Don't forget to keep your eyes peeled for ambulances and grocery stores.

November 7, 2009—Gates of Fire

"This is the song that doesn't end; yes it goes on and on my friend . . ."

"Oh it ends," Renny says, gripping the wheel like a trucker blazing through the last hour of a speed high. "It ends with your skull rolling down the interstate and my tire making chicken paillard out of your large intestine."

"Come on, you guys," I say, rubbing Renny's shoulder. "We're almost there. After that you never have to step foot in this car again."

A lot of weird things become normal when you're constantly in fear for your life. So it follows that when you experience an emotion that, once upon a time, came easily and freely you tend to notice. Which is why, when we see the sign that previously read: FORT MORGAN 45 and it's been scratched off and repainted to say: LIBERTY VILLAGE 45, I can't help but feel an overwhelming rush of ecstatic, endorphin-flooding glee. This is joy, and relief, and the feeling that at last, at long last, a pure-hearted wish has come true.

"Forty-five," Ted repeats, making a song out of it. "Motherfucking forty-five miles, miles, miles!"

Renny and I have switched back and forth, trading places so the other one can sleep. Renny won't let Julian drive because she doesn't trust him, claiming that only people with the use of both hands can drive the car. He doesn't seem to mind and has slept most of the ride to Colorado. All of us are tired and, in the safety of the car, are allowed to nap and nap and nap. It's a good feeling, even if I'm dying for a shower and an actual meal.

We're all awake after that Liberty Village sign, not speaking but sitting in excited, apprehensive silence. I know that for my part I can hardly believe it's true. I keep thinking that if I blink, if I fall asleep again then the city itself will vanish, an apparition. The view is beginning to change. The rolling hills of the Midwestern plains giving way to the mountainous disunity of Colorado, an unpredictable scenery that possesses its own strange harmony of form and color. There are so many greens and grays, so many new textures to appreciate. And there's a kind of shared feeling in the Chevy, a buzz in the air. It takes me a while (too long) to put my finger on it but then, with a jolt, I know it.

Hope.

It's been a miserable time. A sweaty, dysfunctional car ride with plenty of complaints and body odor and grumpy silences but now . . . but now . . . now the future has ignited our good sides.

"The first thing I'm going to do is change my fucking underwear," Julian says, breaking the tense silence.

"I hope you didn't mean to say that aloud," Renny mumbles.

"Lighten up, Renny," I say. And then: "The first thing I'm going to do is find my mom and hug her until she begs for mercy."

"I'm going to find a bed and *sleep* in it," Ted says. "Sleep the shit out of it."

"I'm going to get *laid*," Renny cries, honking the horn.

"Amen," shouts Julian, and Ted expresses his enthusiastic agreement. I don't quite know what to say. Any enthusiasm I might feel on that score is dampened by the knowledge that I'm not ready to let go of Collin, not yet. I'll have my mom and she'll be the best possible distraction. Even so, I can feel that nagging emptiness inside, the anxiety that says: you're marked, marked by something you might never resolve. You miss him.

I look around the car. Goddamn. They're laughing, *laughing together*, giggling like a bunch of feel-good idiots at the end of a *Brady Bunch* episode. It's fantastic and I can't help but join in.

"What's that?" Julian asks. He's pointing at something out ahead, maybe seven or eight miles down the interstate.

Life, so they say, is never as simple as it seems.

Renny slows down and gradually it dawns on us. It's a barricade, and in front of that barricade is a mile-deep horde of undead. They're trying, like us, to get to Liberty Village. Such a heavy concentration of living, breathing human beings must have attracted them like flies to shit. The barricade looks like some kind of bridge, as if both sides had been detonated and dropped into the road to stem the tide of undead. Along the top edge of the barricade there's a barrier of flame, a flickering wall of fire and smoke.

"There must be hundreds of them," Renny whispers.

"How the hell do they expect us to get through?" Ted asks.

"Maybe they don't," I say. "Fuck."

"There must be a way around," Julian says.

"And if there isn't?" I ask.

"Yes, let's get this far and then give up without even trying!"

"Shut *up*!" Renny says. "Both of you."

She stops the car about two miles from the barricade, close enough to hear the roaring of the crowd. We stare at the milling flood of slavering undead blocking our path. I reach into my pocket and take out the Post-it note.

See you soon in Liberty Village!

When I was six my mom insisted I learn how to swim. I was never very good at it and that stayed with me for the rest of my life. But she wanted me to try, to know how to do it, just in case.

I remember paddling like hell across the pool, gasping, swallowing mouthfuls of chlorinated water as I did my best to mimic a breaststroke. She was there at the end of the pool, bending over and clapping at the surface of the water, cheering me. "You're so close!" she'd say, and every time my head popped above water I'd hear it: "You're close!"

At that age nothing was better than the feeling of making it across that pool, of pressing my fingertips against the opposite wall and seeing my mom look down at me, proud as can be. Would she be proud of me now? Will she be proud?

So close.

There are wet spots on the Post-it, little droplets clouding the ink.

"*Goddamn it.*"

I look up from the Post-it, feeling the pressure of someone watching my face. Julian is staring at me through the crack between the seat and the door. Something passes between us, something transfers. He lets the seat belt go and it zips back into place, swinging a little as it settles against the bracket. I know what he's thinking and my hand shoots out to grab him but the passenger side door opens.

Ding-ding-ding . . . The car is reminding us to please shut the passenger door.

"Julian, no!"

"What the hell does he think he's doing?" Ted shouts.

"I guess that's our cue," Renny says, jamming on the gas.

"No! Are you fucking insane? We can't let him do that!" I scream, scrambling up into the passenger seat.

"He's made his choice," Renny says. "There's a ramp up there, look. He's letting us get through. You want to waste his big sacrifice?"

"Fuck *you*. How dare you—"

"I mean it. Don't waste this chance."

So close.

"Allison! Allison, get back in the fucking car!"

Her voice is getting softer and softer because I'm running. I can ignore my ankle, I can ignore the pain. I'm not letting this happen. There are clouds in the distance, dark clouds split at the edges with glowing cracks of light. It's threatening rain, rain after days of nothing but dry weather.

The bastard is remarkably fast for having a bum leg. I'm out of breath when I catch up. He's been running for the crowd of zombies, veering off to the left, probably in anticipation of leading them that way to let the car get through. When he sees me following he throws up his hand and stumbles to a stop.

"You're not very good at this whole 'plan' thing, are you?" he asks.

"Oh fuck you, Seabiscuit. What the hell was that? You can't martyr yourself. I won't let you."

"Do you want to see your mom again or not?" he shouts. Out of the corner of my eye I can see the crowd of undead has noticed us and a few peel off, shuffling in our direction. The stench is overpowering.

"This isn't about my *mom*. This is about your fucking ego. Don't make this about my mom, okay? Get back in the car with me, we can figure this out."

"Yeah, let's have a powwow and maybe wait for a helicopter or Jesus Christ to drop out of the sky and carry us across on the backs of angels. This will work, Allison, so get out of my way."

He shoves me and I shove right back.

"I hate you so fucking much. I should have left you in that Walmart. I should have let you rot and *die*."

"Allison," he says, lowering his voice. "Allison, come on. . . . You don't mean that."

I take the ax and aim for the nearest Groaner, taking off his head with two overhand swings. There are more coming, and more behind them.

Renny can't seem to make up her mind, driving out of reach of the undead and then circling back around to hover close to us. She's still screaming but I can't hear her over the horrible noise of so many undead.

"You want to die, don't you?" I scream. I feel the first raindrops hit my nose.

"No, I don't. I promise."

"Fine, you want to be a hero? We can arrange that. Let's go. You and me, let's just run headfirst into the crowd and see what happens, see how long we last. Then we'll be remembered, right? And all the bad shit we've done will just disappear. And maybe Ted and Renny will make it, maybe not. Worth a shot though, right?"

"Come here, I didn't—Calm down, okay? It was stupid of me. Calm down!"

I keep going, veering left into the crowd. They're slow. I know they're slow and they won't catch me if I can keep up a good, steady pace. Renny seems to make up her mind, idling over on the right side of the interstate. It's working. Bit by bit the crowd notices fresh meat in arm's reach and the horde starts to thin out on the right side of the road. Julian hovers behind me, ducking when one of the undead gets too close and I have to defend us. There are so many, so many clawing, cloying hands that want me, want my flesh, my blood . . .

"This is it, right? This is what you want? A grand heroic gesture? You *idiot*!"

"Allison, this really isn't the time—Fuck! On your left, your left!"

They're desperate, starving, and way faster than I expected. As a group they have a building inertia they never seem to have on their own. We're forced to jog, then sprint, then jog again when we get too tired. The cabbage fields on either side of the road are withered and black, the unharvested vegetables lying in rows, black, like a field full of rotten brains. The gravel on the shoulder of the road crunches beneath our shoes, Julian limp-running as fast as he can and me screaming at him to keep up, to stay behind me, to stay out of their reach. The rain is falling hard now, spattering across our noses as we head deeper into the crowd. There's no turning back now. The way forward is impossible, but the way back is guaranteed suicide.

I have no idea what we'll do when we actually reach the barrier, but there's no time to think, only time to swing, chop, swing . . .

"This is the *last fucking time* I fucking save your stupid ass."

Part of me—the deliriously reckless part—knows he's right. We might have waited, deliberated, found a way through, but there's a kind of deranged elegance to this plan. It's certainly the ballsiest approach and the simplest if we can actually make it through alive . . . I can just hear Collin now, berating me with those serious eyes, shaking his head at me for being so thoughtless, so hasty, so rash. I don't care. Ted and Renny will probably make it, but us . . . I have no expectation now, just determination, focus, the fierce, controlled swinging of my ax. It's a Zen state, a state full of so much panic and adrenaline that your mind simply empties out, leaving only the goal: maim, decapitate, maim, get through, carve a path.

The odds, it would seem, are against us.

Crawling up the opposite side of the road is the sedan, a little blip of color on the worm-gray horizon. It's tipped heavily to the right as they drive as far on the shoulder as they can, the car leaning dangerously as they almost fall down into the ditch. I keep thinking of all the times we risked our lives for that stupid car, just to get gas, just to siphon enough to go another damn mile.

Reckless, what we do for our friends.

The barricade is getting closer and I can feel the sickening, oppressive heat of so many decomposing bodies pressed in together. A sharp, shriveled hand grabs on to Julian's sling. I don't think, not even for a second. I reach around and unsnap the neck strap. The sling flaps free, Julian yanking his arm out of it as we pick up the pace. I can hear his breathing, the little grunts that make it in between breaths, the indications that every step hurts, every foot kills.

"We're almost there!" I shout. "We're going to make it!"

"Allison, I can't, my leg . . ." he says between breaths. I take hold of his good arm and drag him along. The fallen bridge is near now, tall and looming like a great Trojan bulwark, all darkness and flame, the asphalt showing long, jagged cracks. On the left there's a steep embankment rising up toward the top edge of the bridge. It looks too steep for the clumsy feet of undead and almost too steep for the living, but I can see there are footholds here and there, pieces of metal and concrete lodged into the embankment. It's almost a sheer wall of earth going straight up over our heads, as if the gentle incline of a hill imploded from the dislodged bridge.

"We can climb up," I shout. "We're close!"

The embankment is slick with mud now, the rain sending the topsoil down to pool around our feet, long rivulets trailing down from up above. The fires along the toppled bridge have gone out from the rain, the smoky smell of pitch filling the air around us, nearly overpowering the reek of the undead.

"You first! I'll stay!" I shout, the rain pelting my forehead, dripping into my eyes. I'm not looking forward to scaling this mud wall, but it's the only way up and over.

"No!"

"Just go! I've got the ax!"

I help Julian onto the first foothold, a piece of concrete lodged two feet above the ground. It's hard for him to climb, his broken arm hanging uselessly at his side. He has to pull himself up to the next chunk of cement with one arm. I stay on the ground, flicking the rain and hair out of my eyes, watching the undead close in around us, just a scant few inches of space that I've made from swinging and swinging.

"Allison, you have to climb!"

He's right. If I don't start now there'll be no getting up to the bridge. Now that the fires are out we might be able to get across and meet Renny and Ted. But I think maybe I've waited too long—as soon as I turn my back they'll close the gap.

"Come on! Now!"

If I turn, if I show them my back even for a moment . . .

"Give me the ax!" he shouts, his fingers dangling above my head.

"I can't!"

"Hand it to me! Now! Come on."

I flatten myself against the sliding wall of mud and push the ax handle up toward him. He takes it from me and it feels like losing a limb. My feet find the first foothold and I heave myself up, keeping close to the embankment, trying to keep my arms and legs from flailing. It doesn't help much. I can feel the hands scrabbling against my shoes, my ankles. Above me, Julian is holding on to one piece of broken cement, his injured arm hacking away with the ax, the blade flashing past my shoulder. I can see it hurts him, I can see him grunting through his teeth, pushing through the discomfort and the pain to watch my back.

"Fuck!"

The mud is shifting, moving the cement pieces. The footholds are giving out beneath me, sinking down and down, into the scratching hands of the undead waiting below. I struggle to dig my feet into the embankment, to do something, anything to keep from falling, but the cement foothold drops away completely, tumbling down onto the broken skulls of the zombies clawing at my feet. The mud is pushing at me from above, sliding beneath my elbows and knees and taking me with it.

There's one piece of rebar dangling above my head where Julian's foot is resting. If I grab it then we might both go down, but there's no other choice, I'm slipping, losing my grip . . .

"Grab on!" he shouts.

"It's too high! Fuck! I'm slipping!"

"Grab it!"

The rain pounds into my eyes, brown droplets of mud falling off Julian's shoes onto my face. I can barely see but I can't afford to let go of the sliding concrete to wipe my eyes. Julian is showing me his hand, clenching and opening his fingers in my face.

"Up!" he screams. "Up!"

In the back of my head, pounding like a deranged child on a xylophone, is an old stentorian thump, a pounding like a heartbeat commanding me to reach up. Before I know it, before I can stop it, the *Mary Poppins* song is drilling into my head, crashing around as if someone had taken the lyrics, pulled them apart, studded them with nails and leather and then put the song back together.

Let's go fly a kite
Up to the highest height

It repeats, mercilessly, the rhythm of it getting faster, crazier, until I'm sure my heart will explode with the din of it. Julian is flailing, shouting, I can't hear him, just the song, unhinged and tripping through my brain like a dizzy giant . . .

Screaming, aching, I reach for the bar and pull, shrieking

through my teeth as I wrap my fingers around the bar and hoist myself, refusing to let go, refusing to allow the metal to slip out of my grip. This is it. Last chance. It's up or down, alive or dead and that's when I feel the hard bony hand wrapping around my right ankle . . .

I'm nearly there, the pain, the exhaustion forgotten for the moment as I put every last ounce of strength into raising myself up high enough to reach the next foothold. I feel pressure on my shoulder and look up to see Julian's hand grabbing my shirt, pulling me, his other hand holding onto the ax, digging it into the side of the embankment for purchase like a climber's pick. The zombie's hand detaches at the wrist and I kick the fingers free. There's a second where I'm almost dangling in the air, free, floating, and I watch the faces below, the empty, staring eyes and open mouths. So very many eyes . . .

The rebar holds us both, but I can feel it beginning to give way beneath our weight. Julian flattens himself against the embankment and I climb up, using his back and shoulder to get up and over, onto solid ground. I can see his chest heaving against the wall of mud, his eyelids fluttering with pain. I can't imagine what his broken arm must feel like, his mangled leg.

"Give me your hand, I'll get you up," I say, holding out my hand. "Give me your hand!"

He's fading. That last push to get me up cost him too much. His head rests against the embankment, his body limp, spent. I wave my hand in front of his face. He's big and heavy but it will just take one effort, one monumental outpouring of strength and that, I know, is something I can do, something that's waiting inside of me.

"Come on! Give me your hand!" I scream. He looks up, his eyes blinking rapidly to get the water out of his eyes. He's ready to give up, I can see it. "Give me your fucking hand, Julian!"

Then his hand is in mine, his fingers wrapping around my wrist. I grab his wrist with both hands and lean back, squeezing my shoulder blades until they're touching. But nothing happens. I pull again and again but he's stuck fast. When I look over the edge I see it, the same zombie that had grabbed my leg has now grabbed Julian. Then there's another zombie grabbing him, pulling. There are too many and all of them fighting against me, three and then four and then five hands wrapping around his legs. He's shouting at me to pull harder and I try, I really do, but the rebar is slipping and both of us are going down.

"Allison," he says and then his slick hand is gone, pulled free. He smiles and opens his mouth to say more but he's already falling, sinking backward like a diver, arms wide, dropping into a churning pool. I scramble to get his hand but it's out of reach and I can no longer distinguish his sandy hair and living flesh from the sea of arms and bodies. I watch, helpless, as the undead take him under.

My ax sticks into the embankment where Julian left it. I yank it free, standing. I go. I have to.

There's the rain and the thunder, and the sound of death scream-ing at my feet, insisting that I yield too. Then there's my breathing, deep and relieved and an echo of Julian's laughter, a sound so un-expected, so welcome, that I can't help but laugh too. For a mo-ment it's as if he's there, collapsing next to me on his back, his hand on his chest as he laughs and laughs . . .

But he's not there, he's gone and I'm alone, cold and drenched. The sky is cobalt above me, the clouds spinning across the sky, racing toward some unknowable destination.

I walk along the top of the embankment to the bridge, looking down at the ghouls and their ravenous mouths and gaze at what might have been my fate. There's deep scoring in the ground and what looks like blast marks. I scamper up onto the edge of the bridge where the concrete is three or four feet thick. I walk to the middle, looking back the way I came. There are so many of them. Poor souls. Poor, restless souls . . .

The rain is freezing, so much more noticeable now that we're still, quiet. The way down is a sheer drop, and at the bottom of that drop lies a messy date with the horde of undead and somewhere— truly, peacefully dead I hope—is a friend. The ghouls groan and wheeze, stretched out in a seemingly endless carpet of black and gray. There's a trail of pitch across the bridge where the fires raged but now there's only a suggestion of those flames, the smell of char and smoke, the ghost of fire.

I can see the sedan on the other side of the bridge idling, wait- ing for me. I don't want to go, not yet, but now that the fires are out there will be nothing to keep the undead from getting up the ramp and over to the other side. The horn honks. They're waiting.

A sudden madness grips me and I lean forward over the bridge searching, searching for a sign of my friend. I half expect to see Julian climbing up the sheer face of the bridge, laughing and swearing, but I don't. Of course I don't.

"I could be there with you," I say, standing up again.

Renny is laying on the horn, calling to me. But before I go, I turn back to the edge of the bridge and hold out the ax. I let it drop, tumbling edge over blade, into the seething crowd below.

"Thanks," I say. "Now I have to go. Our friends are waiting."

November 15, 2009—On Liberty

Almost two months ago I was pretty average. Two months ago, if you handed me an ax I would think about splitting logs or maybe hacking down a fallen tree limb. That's not me, not anymore.

It isn't Utopia. I probably don't have to tell you that. It's not paradise, not by a long shot. But I think I can say something now that I could never safely say before: it's my home.

Sure, I thought the bookstore was pretty good and I thought the apartments above that would work too, and I really hoped the arena could be a permanent thing, but this—*this*—is a real home with real buildings, real privacy, real beds and people willing to create a community. I think that's the difference. We're of one mind here, not in some bizzarro hive-mind way, we just want the same things. We want stability, safety, the chance to rebuild something lasting.

There are walls here, tremendously thick walls that might have bothered me once, but I'm used to it. In this life, in this day, a home has walls. We do what we can to keep *them* out and to keep *us* safely in. There's a moat about thirty yards away from the walls. When the moat gets too full we set it on fire. The walls are reinforced with wooden spikes but none of the undead ever manages to make it that far. The village really is more like a fort, a reinforced campground, but there's no discriminating here and all of the living are welcome. If someone manages to make it to the gates then they deserve to come inside. That's the rule.

We keep the barricades primed with fire, we keep our soldiers armed and vigilant and we try to do good things, small, good things that make a difference to someone. It's easier to set a pit of zombies on fire when you know the next morning you'll be teaching Spanish to little kids. The roads are mostly dirt and gravel and the buildings that were burned up are slowly being rebuilt. There's a flag flying above the town center, a white background with a green infinity symbol. It means all are welcome and it means we will go on, go on forever.

We've started a school, the Clarke School. I proposed we call it the Julian Clarke School of Dastardly Snark but that was pretty unanimously shot down. Ted teaches biology and chemistry, Renny gives art classes and I do what I was going to school to do: I teach books.

It's funny, my mom was always the better scholar. When I applied to grad school I had the eerie feeling that everyone knew me and that's because they *did*. Well . . . they knew my mother. They were her colleagues; her admirers more like. She blazed a fucking trail through their dry, exclusive academia Club House and showed them that a woman could read a book and make up bullshit theories as well as they could. I wanted to do that too. I wanted to live in a world where men stuck up their noses at me and I took a hold of those noses and shoved them into my long, preposterously overresearched papers.

I never really got to do that. I never found those people, those snobs that hated me because I was a woman or because I wasn't smart enough, witty enough, crass enough. And maybe they don't exist now. Their place in the world has been snubbed out. What I did find is a bunch of little kids without a school, without books, without teachers.

And she's not here, my mom, not yet. I look for her every day, of course, taking a moment or two out from teaching to go sit on the walls and watch and wait. I'm not giving up hope, not yet, not now when I know that incredible things can happen, that people will surprise you with their will to live.

What I do know about my mom, what I know for sure, is that she would be proud. I don't know if you can think back, way back to when you didn't know *Treasure Island* or *A Tale of Two Cities* or *The Three Musketeers*, but these kids are hearing the stories for the first time. I know it sounds dry but it isn't. Those books weren't in Fort Morgan—Liberty Village—when we got here. The library had been ransacked, destroyed, all but burned to cinders. And so two days ago I helmed a rescue mission of sorts. As far as I'm concerned, Stevenson, Dickens and Dumas were prisoners somewhere and it was my duty to help them. Now they're safe, cherished, right where they belong: in the hands of children who thought their lives were over. You don't know what misery is until you look at a six-year-old and realize that they've experienced greater tragedy in their short life than you will ever live to know.

But they smile. They smile now when we sit together in a circle in the gutted post office and take turns reading aloud. They look to me for guidance, for explanations.

"What does 'sublime' mean?" they ask. "What is 'bespattered'?"

It's not all good. It's not all simple. There are, of course, difficulties. There are, of course, surprises and shocks. I thought that when I left that park I left behind a group of friends that I would never see again. But I was wrong. In fact, not only did Ned, Evan, Mikey, and Collin survive, they beat us here, the crazy bastards.

We didn't run into them until the second day. The first day was, well, pretty much nothing but eating, sleeping and relaxing. They gave us chickens roasted over a fire and we ate like savages, tearing the charred meat off the bone, reveling in the hot juices running down our faces. I think I remember a moment then when Renny smiled and there were bits of char and chicken stuck in her teeth and I felt relieved, as if I had carried the four of us on my back all the way here. It isn't true, of course. We all took our turns shouldering the burden. I didn't tell her about the stuff in her teeth; she looked too contented and free.

Day two brought a whole truckful of surprises. When we finally woke (sometime around noon I think), there were guests waiting outside of our lodge. Lodge is a generous word, I guess, but the right one. The lodges aren't big but they're sturdy, made with the same technique pioneers used to build their frontier homes. Colorado is kind of ridiculous that way, but the fact that they've wholeheartedly embraced adversity with a rousing frontier spirit is remarkable, inspiring. Anyway, when we (Ted, Renny, and I) finally managed to drag our asses out of bed, we found Ned and his kids waiting outside. Evan was wearing his Pirate Wall-E costume, something Ned had helped him with several days after Halloween had come and gone. According to Ned, Evan wouldn't take it off, not until "Allison got to see."

After the shock of seeing them again, and the delight, I had the task of finding Collin. Ned told me of his presence and survival with his usual charm, reminding me with a clandestine wink to be strong and stand up for myself. Ted and Renny stared at him as if he was speaking in gibberish, but I knew exactly what he meant. So I left them to catch up and tell stories. There would be time, after all, to hear all about Evan's Halloween and I wanted to know how they had come to find us here. Ned wouldn't say, of course. He just said: "Ask Collin, it's his fault."

I found Collin helping with the new orphanage, a big building made of rough-hewn timbers in the northeast corner of the town. He was finally out of his black fatigues, wearing a faded gray

T-shirt and jeans, looking darling and shabby and English. His gun lay a safe and close distance away, well-kept and leaning against a wall.

I brought him lemonade.

"Thanks," he said. We walked a ways from the construction. The lemonade was lukewarm. We're still working on how to make ice efficiently. He sipped the drink for a moment, watching me with his dark, serious eyes over the rim of the paper cup.

"I'm glad you made it," Collin said. He wiped at the sweat building at his temples. "I knew you would." There was a smile there I couldn't quite place, a self-satisfaction that made me wonder. . . .

"Shit."

"What?" he asked, and I could see his smile peeking out from behind the edges of the Dixie cup.

"C in C. *You're* C in C."

"Mystery solved," he said, inclining his head as if to an old, respected colleague. "Well done, Holmes."

"That's . . . that's how you knew to come here? You were reading the blog?"

"We stayed with a family in Rockford who were kind enough to let us use their computer," he said. Of course, part of me expected him to withdraw, for that old, familiar remoteness to drag him away from me, but his face remained painfully open, eager even. The other part of me hoped against hope that there was something to fight for. He hadn't changed physically, not at all. There was a new scratch on his cheek and a bit more gray at his temples, but otherwise he stood there, tall and erect, exactly as I remembered. But there was someone new looking at me, someone with an unfamiliar urgency, a voracious curiosity I had never seen before or had somehow managed to forget.

And I felt myself retreating, preparing for the letdown that was surely coming. He would mention her any minute and that would be the beginning of our long and tortured friendship.

"How the hell did you manage to get here?" I asked.

"By truck, by car, anyway we could," he replied, lowering the lemonade cup. He looked down at the cup, fidgeting. "I was sorry to read about your friend."

"Yeah. He would've liked it here." It was the only thing I could think of to say. I felt a lump building in my throat and quickly looked down at my feet. I didn't want to talk about Julian.

"And Lydia?" I asked.

I hadn't seen her yet, not hanging around with Ned and his kids or sulking in the background. Finn, oddly enough, was missing too. At the arena he had been like Collin's redheaded shadow, always pacing somewhere in the background with his gun and his black temper. It was hard, after so many weeks, to expect anything but the worst. I could only imagine what Collin must be thinking of me, of what I said about her, about *him*.

"Good," Collin said, searching my face. "She's good . . . I mean, the last time I saw her, she was doing rather well. As well as one can be, I suppose, considering the times."

"Good," I said, trying and undoubtedly failing to mask my curiosity.

"And you?" he asked. "You're—"

"Good."

"Good!"

"It's good. I mean, it's *nice* to see you," I said, shoving my hands into my back pockets. My cheeks prickled with heat and only grew steadily warmer as I mentally ticked off the number of times I insulted Lydia on the blog and the number of times I said something completely asinine about Collin. And Odysseus—oh Jesus, Odysseus . . . There are sinking feelings and then there are quicksand, clawing for your life, wishing you were dead sinking feelings. I suddenly had a very bad case of the latter.

"So wow, you're here, that's . . . I'm glad. I'm glad we're all here, together," I said, rambling.

"Me too."

"Jesus, Collin! Are you going to tell me or just let me suffer?"

He grinned with almost childlike sweetness and I knew he had been waiting for me to ask, to let the curiosity get the better of me. It was nice to see him out of army fatigues, wearing civilian clothes, looking more like a professor, a teacher, an ordinary man and less like a soldier. At last he drew breath and began to speak, slowly.

"I want to say it's complicated, but I don't think it is," he said, ruffling his hair with the heel of his palm. "She stayed behind in Rockford and Finn as well. It was their decision and I . . . I'm just glad they're happy and safe."

"You mean, they—Finn and Lydia—are together? *Together* together?"

I could feel that breakfast I didn't eat spinning in my stomach.

"Yes, exactly." He chuckled. "She was kind enough to let me know about the . . . Well, her change of heart. I should have seen it coming, really, but as it turned out I was a bit distracted," he said, idly spinning his lemonade cup. His eyes, his smiling eyes, were glowing in the cool, muted sunshine.

"That's . . . crazy. I mean that's unbelievable, Collin. I'm so sorry," I said, knowing that sympathy was my duty, my absolute first duty as a friend. I'd save the happy dance for later, in private.

"No you're not," he said, rightly. "And neither am I."

"But she left you, for a younger man—I mean, *your nephew*."

"Surely her actions are defendable when one considers mine," he said quickly, laughing again. Then his cheeky smile faded to a frown. "Hm. Silly me. I thought you might be pleased."

"Pleased? *Pleased*? I—you—fuck you!"

I could feel my heart, the damned thing, lifting right out of my chest, trying to float out of my throat and up to the clouds. If I could bottle that feeling . . . But I couldn't, it was too much feeling to hold on to. Collin dropped his cup on the hard, frozen ground and rushed to hug me. We held each other and I searched, as I always do, for something important to say. Graciously, Collin saved me the embarrassment.

"Every day was just a version of the one before, a day of trying to forget you. I had to do something. I had to find you," he said, and it's that voice, that beautiful golden voice that came to me over the radio so long ago and guided me, like a ferryman made of light, to a new life. "Maybe it's good I wasn't with you," he said, kissing my face. There were still fresh bandages there from my little Jeep mishap at the movie theater. "You very nearly gave me a heart attack with some of those stunts you pulled."

"And you're not mad?" I asked. "About what I wrote?"

"No, no of course not. A little annoyed maybe," he said, laughing. "But never mad."

There are, as always, disappointments. My mom is still missing, Ted flirted with an early death and a good man died to get me here. But there are joys too. There's winter to look forward to, a season of survival, of hardship and teamwork. Teamwork attempted with a partner, a good partner. I think we'll go looking for *Little House on the Prairie* soon, Collin and I, heading another expedition to restock the library. It should offer some much-needed perspective. We're not that bad off. We're never *that* bad off. And Dapper will get to romp in the snow. Evan and Mikey will get to build snowmen and maybe Collin can teach us to build igloos. Collin and I are hoping to build our own lodge before winter shows up. We probably won't be able to build one fast enough but God knows, we'll try.

And soon the first really dangerous frost will come and maybe that will slow down the undead. Maybe the gunfire at the walls will stop. Maybe when the snowflakes start to gather against the cold glass panes, and we need to boil water to stay alive; maybe then, when the windows are embroidered with icy lace; maybe then we'll know a moment's peace. Spring will follow after that, and maybe my mother will make it here, bringing with her the smile I know so well, the face that isn't my face, the love that is definitely my love. Maybe then a stillness will fall and each of us will look up at the sky and say: it's not so bad, the undead are coming and we might not get out, but for once that's really not so bad.

And maybe I lied. Maybe this *is* Utopia in a way—a tangled, difficult way.

A paradise of infinite possibility.

COMMENTS

Isaac says:

January 2, 2010 at 1:55 pm

Checking in to say we're safe and sound, just rough around the edges. Canada is beautiful and stark this time of year. I won't hope for anymore updates from you guys. It's been months since your last post. I'm going to just keep believing you're doing well and making us proud in Liberty Village.

steveinchicago says:

January 16, 2010 at 3:31 pm

still going. made it christmas and beyond. we're thankful for every day we get and thankful that you made it to where you were going.

> **Norway says:**
>
> *February 2, 2010 at 12:30 pm*
>
> Oslo gone, Drammen gone, undead coming north. It's alright, though, we're ready for them. I thought I had read this thing for the last time and said goodbye forever. I keep checking back. Always. Just in case. I'll probably keep on checking, every few days maybe, staying optimistic until the lights finally go out.

The Witt-Burroughs Press
University of Independence
1640 Johnson Avenue NW
Independence, NY 12404

September 10, 2108

The New University of Northern Colorado
10 South Sherman Street
Liberty Village, CO 80701

Dear Professor Stockton:

Thank you for your continued interest in our press. We owe our long-standing success to devoted individuals such as yourself.

It is with deep regret that I must deny your proposal to have Ms. Hewitt's story included in our forthcoming collection. While I appreciate your interest in the project and admire your dedication to scholarship, I cannot in good faith include this woman in a project designed to laud what is best and most noble about our species. I am, quite frankly, perplexed as to how you ever imagined that such a vulgar, bloodthirsty recount could merit standing among the likes of Shana Lane and Simon Forrest, artists of the highest caliber both morally and spiritually. Dr. Marion Moore will feature prominently in this collection. You will of course recognize Dr. Moore as the brilliant scientific mind responsible for the Z-12 compound, the odorless, colorless chemical that proved harmless to the living and extremely lethal against The Infected. Her work could almost single-handedly be praised as the invention that made widespread containment possible. Despite what her few detractors might say, it was only through Dr. Moore's painstaking research that we were allowed to pinpoint the exact location of the West Virginia facility where the killer virus—for whatever reason—was developed, engineered and ultimately unleashed.

Therefore, Mr. Stockton, I must be candid and say that I am personally offended by your suggestion that Allison Hewitt belongs in our collection. I find her fluid, unidentifiable morality as repugnant and unconscionable as her confessed actions. Murder? Theft? This is the face of the faceless masses, you say? Someone like Dr. Moore saved us from further tragedy. What, exactly, is Ms. Hewitt's great contribution? We here at the Witt-Burroughs Press strive to promote change, to demonstrate that even when faced with the greatest possible adversity, humanity strove forward bravely and righteously, not wallowing in savagery and demeaning the very characteristics that separate us from The Infected. We will not, nor would we ever, include this woman in a work meant to inspire its readers.

We wish you success in all your future endeavors, Professor, and might I also say that I hope you lift your aim a little higher in the pursuit of worthwhile scholarship.

You will of course be receiving a copy of the published collection in the mail—a gift from me and, I hope, an inspiration.

Sincerely,
Dr. George F. Burroughs

Acknowledgments

My humble gratitude goes out to the online readers who made *Allison Hewitt Is Trapped* come alive. Without your support, creativity, and patience, none of this would have been possible. I'm deeply indebted to those of you who contributed your time and energy to the comments section. Thanks also to Wordpress.

Specific thanks to Luis Wu, Isaac, Mel, D.J., bruce (Xunas), Cpt-Crckpot, Brooklyn Girl, Rev. Brown, Bob in Rhode Island, S.W.A.T SGT. jason jeffery, amanda, Carlene, Logan, Matthew H, Andrew N, Elizabeth, Dave in the Midwest, j. witt, steveinchicago, and Norway. I sincerely hope I haven't misrepresented your individual struggles for survival during the Outbreak.

Also deserving of my gratitude are Mom, Pops, Tristan, Nick, Julie, Trevor, and the whole Johnson gang for their support and love. Ari Hurwitz and Valerie Neverman must be acknowledged for encouraging me to write and keep up with the blog; they are true fans in every sense of the word. I'm indebted to Andrea, pen pal extraordinaire, for kicking my ass when I had writer's block. Thanks to the bookstore gang (especially Pete) for putting up with me. I want to also acknowledge Monique Patterson for her insightful suggestions, eagle eyes, and ideas.

Last but absolutely not least, Kate McKean's name just has to appear in this book because she is my hero. Her hard work and belief made a jumbled experiment into something coherent and whole.

Keep reading for a sneak peek at Madeleine Roux's next novel,

SADIE WALKER IS STRANDED

This early in the morning—four o'clock to be exact—Seattle wears an eerie cast of rising purple, like an embarrassed flush, and it's easy to see why. In the chaos, big cities fared the worst. So many people, so many things to destroy and burn—it was unavoidable that the aftermath here would be bleakest. From here, miles away from the waterfront, you can still see the *Golden Princess* cruise liner in the harbor, half sunk, like a miniature city descending gradually to its demise, a white-gold Atlantis. The rumor at the time was that everyone on board the cruise had perished, and not only that, but someone on board was the carrier, the undead transmitter that spread The Outbreak to Seattle.

As I trooped down Boren, the city came slowly to life. Lanterns behind windows sent up low, orange signal fires, and men and women in Wellingtons and fingerless gloves emerged from their homes to tend community gardens.

Looming over the vegetable gardens, hooked to street lamps and windows, are painted wooden signs and graffiti. THEY'RE NOT YOUR FAMILY IF THEY'RE INFECTED, read one. DO THE RIGHT THING: ALERT THE AUTHORITIES, or another, OBSERVE THE CURFEW.

A street pamphlet careened up the street toward me, grabbing at my ankle. I paused and bent to retrieve it. The flyer, as usual, was garish—bright green paper, bold black font like a flyer for a topless bar. Impossible to miss. I read as I walked, perusing the latest news. Most citizens relied on the street pamphlets to deliver their news, and the presses that provided them took an immense amount of pride in their work.

Of course there was always at least one article about the population freaks. They preferred the term Repops or Repopulationists, a kind of religious or social group (some said cult) that feel a divine calling to repopulate the city and—I suppose in their warped minds—the world. The pamphlet was nice enough to refer to them as Repops, but everyone I knew just called them Rabbits, because all they seemed to want to do was shut themselves up in some hidey-hole and screw, screw, screw.

I was still perusing the pamphlet when I reached Pike Place. Not even five in the morning and already the line extended to 1st Avenue. I sidled up close to the stranger in front of me. We might have been a horde of dock workers and clock makers and shoe shiners, a bleak Dickensian postcard of hungry people just trying to eke out a living. But it wasn't 1855. It was 2010 and we weren't recovering from an outbreak of cholera, but from The Outbreak itself.

But since The Outbreak things had stabilized. Stabilized. That's the word the street pamphlets liked to use—"the situation has stabilized."

"Stabilized, my ass."

The man who had gotten in line behind me had read the pamphlet over my shoulder. He had a strong Polish accent. I gave him a wan smile. "Could be better," I said with a shrug, "could be worse."

The first Tuesday of every month, a caravan of trucks snaked into the one gated entrance to the city. They lumbered over to the old Pike Place Fish Market, now strictly a vegetable and food market, and dumped whatever produce they had managed to grow. The lines on Tuesdays started forming at four or five in the morning, winding up and across the cobbled avenue leading down to the market, hundreds, thousands of people huddled together in the pink dawn glow, bags and baskets tucked under their arms.

The crowd was getting louder, rowdy, everyone in line shuffling anxiously, ready to get going and start their day.

"Fucking Rabbits. They haul ass out of Citadel yet?"

I jumped, nearly dropping the street pamphlet. It was Carl, my boyfriend. He wrapped me up in a hug and I was grateful for the warmth. Carl, my boyfriend. Carl my boyfriend who was supposed to be watching Shane. I whirled on him.

"What are you doing here? Where's Shane?"

"Don't sweat it. Shane's with my friends."

"*Which* friends?"

Carl shrugged, his lanky shoulders flying up around his ears like a pair of bony wings. "Dave and Jill," he said. "They're cool. They work over in Queen Gardens."

"I don't care where they work, Carl, I don't know them. You can't just leave Shane with strangers—he's not a Cuisinart!"

Shane is shy, bookish. He doesn't like strangers. He barely tolerates me, his own flesh and blood.

Carl heaves a dramatic sigh, his deep-set brown eyes rolling a complete three-sixty. I fold up the pamphlet and swat him hard on the shoulder with it.

It's hard to stand still knowing that Shane is being watched by strangers. Trust is a commodity these days, and one I'm generally short on. I feel suddenly claustrophobic, short of breath.

"Here," I say, shoving the market bag at Carl. "You stay and get the food. I'll go back to Shane."

"He'll be fine."

"He better be."

The ration papers are in my pocket. They state, in slanted handwriting, that Shane and I, making up a family, are entitled to two bags of mixed vegetables, fruit, and a packet of dried fish. These are in exchange for the beets and cabbages our family garden contributed to the city's food supply.

"Use my papers and yours too," I add. "They'll be more than enough for the month."

Shane and I don't need much and with Carl's rations coming in too, we eat pretty well. I turn to go and Carl grabs me by the forearm.

"I *said* they're my friends. What's the problem?"

"Just get the groceries, okay?"

I didn't feel like arguing with him, not just then, not when poor Shane was probably curled up in the fetal position, convinced that he'd been abandoned again. Shane is my sister's eight-year-old; she and her husband were on a bus when The Outbreak hit downtown. They never made it home and *voilà*, just like winning a twisted game show, I became a mother to a quiet little nerd with sunshine curls and a gap-toothed smile.

Even more people are out and about as I half-run up 1st Avenue. There are dark, burnt-out storefronts on either side of the road and a rundown strip club with greasy windows and sun-bleached posters. The main market still functions as a market, but for basic things now—blankets and clothing and food and a few real gems, like booksellers and wine dealers. The Outbreak hit us in September. By early November, alcohol and books were at a premium.

I turned right, going more steeply uphill, away from the waterfront and toward the apartment. Most things change, but some things never did. The Olympic Mountains loomed over the Citadel, rising out of the fog, silent, stoic watchers that, on a daily basis, managed to remind me that enduring was possible.

My whole body, sensing trouble, sped up. A nasty idea had occurred to me: Carl didn't have friends, Carl had customers. He dealt mainly in knives, self-defense junk, and he had a knack for finding army surplus all over town. Carl kept the knives elsewhere but the only people I'd ever seen him hang around with were in some way tied to his business. I didn't like his business, but it brought in extra food, a lot of it, and you just didn't complain about that sort of thing.

A prickly heat began rising out of the back of my scarf. Fumbling with the keys, I flung open the front door and raced through the sand-colored empty lobby, down the hall and up the back stairs. Our apartment sat right at the top, around a bare two-by-four doorway, close enough to hear the neighbors troop up and down day and night. The door to our apartment was shut, a good sign, but the queasy feeling in my stomach didn't ease. Inside it was dark.

I dropped my portfolio with a thud on the hardwood floor.

"Shane? Shane? It's not a joke. Come out here."

There was a faint tinkling sound, like a distant jingle bell. To the right, the apartment housed a cramped kitchen. Even in the semi-darkness I could see a cupboard door inch open. I grabbed the edge and yanked.

"Shane! Oh God, Shane." I pulled him out of the cupboard, brushing the stray rice off of his little shoulder, and gathered him up in my arms.

"Are they coming back?" he asked in a tiny voice.

"Is who coming back?" I asked. "Carl's friends?"

"They're not friends," he whispered.

"Did they hurt you?" I asked.

"They're not friends," Shane said again.

A flicker of a shadow passed over his face and I heard a quick intake of breath from behind us. But there was no time to react, not with a kid in my arms and my heart rate just starting to slow. Something hard and sharp hit the top of my head. I felt Shane slip and my body tip forward and the ground come for me like a swiftly rising tide. But it wasn't quite enough.

"Hit her again."

It was Carl saying this. Carl speaking, my Carl, telling someone to knock me out. Shane's pale blonde head flashed in front of
me. I turned, stumbling out of the kitchen and pushing past the
blurry stranger who had struck me. A black ink spill was falling
over my eyes, dripping down like a liquid curtain. But I had
enough of my wits to lash out with my arms, reach blindly for my
nephew. He screamed. Shane never screamed—he protested from
time to time quietly in his meek, middle-aged toddler manner,
but never raised his voice above a thoughtful murmur. There was
probably blood on me. Blood would make him scream.

Carl stood in the hallway, his tall, rangy body framed by the
open doorway. I fumbled toward him, batting, my legs failing just
in time to send me pitching forward. Carl and I tumbled out into
the corridor.

"Hit her again. Jesus Christ. Hurry up!"

He slammed into the wall and grunted the air out of his lungs;
my fists balled up and pressed against his chest. I grabbed him by
the collar of his coat and shook and then pulled. But gravity and
my aching head won, and I fell forward again, my weight sending
us both toward the stairwell and the wide open arch of two-by-
fours. Nothing stopped us. The stairs were suddenly there, plum-
meting downward, steeper than I remembered. Carl went down
first, me on top, and I felt every hard crack against his spine as we
toppled and rolled. Everything spun as we finally found the bottom and Carl's neck, encouraged by my weight, crashed into the
baseboard. The last thing I heard was a sound, an unmistakable,
biological crunch as vertebrae met wood.

And then nothing and a deep tugging feeling in my chest, like
I was being dragged down, like I was drowning.